Wenches, Wives & Widows

WENCHES, WIVES & WIDOWS

Sixteen Women of Early Virginia

JoAnn Riley McKey

HERITAGE BOOKS
2007

HERITAGE BOOKS

AN IMPRINT OF HERITAGE BOOKS, INC.

Books, CDs, and more—Worldwide

For our listing of thousands of titles see our website
at
www.HeritageBooks.com

Published 2007 by
HERITAGE BOOKS, INC.
Publishing Division
65 East Main Street
Westminster, Maryland 21157-5026

International Standard Book Number: 978-0-7884-4275-9

This book is for
Hugh and Sophie Riley

Contents

Preface

Isolated on its peninsula between the Atlantic Ocean and Chesapeake Bay, Virginia's Eastern Shore is home to some of the oldest continuous court records in the United States. The earliest existing entries, which bear the date of 7 January 1632/33, were recorded in the books of Accomack County, which was renamed Northampton County nine years later. In 1663, when the county was split in two, the southern part retained the old record books and the name of Northampton while the northern part revived the old name of Accomack and began keeping record books of its own.

In the mid-1990's, I began abstracting the court orders of Accomack County using microfilmed copies of the originals from the Library of Virginia. It did not take me long to realize that many women, as they wove in and out of the records, left hints and clues and even quotes that were begging to be teased out and pieced together into sketches of their lives. Some of the women were prone to bad behavior, others had bad things happen to them, but all of their stories were too good to squander on the few genealogy buffs who might make the effort to dig them up. Besides, some of the incidents are actually more enjoyable if the lady in question does *not* sit on a branch of your family tree.

All of these women lived during the mid to late 1600's, with some of them continuing on into the 1700's. They were young and old, servants and aristocrats, humble and brazen, abused and abusive. Many different circumstances brought them to the attention of the court and its clerk who sometimes scratched out enough facts to fill a chapter. Many other women should have had a chapter's worth, but, for one reason or another, they escaped the court's full notice and left us with only enough for a paragraph.

Ann Toft was one of these, even though she owned a huge plantation and many servants, had a head for business and enjoyed a privileged lifestyle. All the evidence indicates that she was also the mistress of Col. Edmund Scarburgh, the county's most powerful justice. The records cover her business dealings, but barely touch her personal life. Thanks to her well-placed friend, she was effectively shielded from the court and from us.

Other women, usually at the opposite end of the social scale, left records related to a single incident, but little else. A servant named Anne Dupper had been forced to go "in a naked condicon a greate while, & the last Snow that was shee was barefoote and barelegged." Because she wore nothing but a

buckskin hanging around her waist "her nakednes was visible to all
Spectators." It was noted that she had only "a sorry waistcoate full of holes
about her back, noe shift upon her body, nor headclothes upon her head but
an old peece of a hatt." The court ordered immediate relief for Anne and an
investigation into her mistreatment, but their efforts came too late. She died
before help arrived.[1]

 Deborah Edgerly's masters sold her claiming she was healthy except for
a small boil on her arm, but the new master soon discovered otherwise.
Swollen, short of breath and so sick she could barely move, Deborah also
smelled so bad that two other servants complained that they couldn't stand
to work near her; considering the prevailing standards of hygiene in 1667,
Deborah's body odor must have been truly extraordinary. Though she was
still ailing a few years later, Deborah found a less particular friend, and
eventually gave birth to an illegitimate child. A few months later the judges
noted that Deborah was so disabled by childbirth that she was likely to
become a charity case. The justices were concerned about the cost of
supporting Deborah, but they never mentioned costs for the child, which
evidently had not survived. The sheriff took Deborah's lover into custody till
he arranged to pay her expenses, and then Deborah, sick and weak,
disappeared from the records.[2]

 Although Widow Elizabeth Rackliff had her share of this world's goods,
she claimed inexperience in the affairs of the world. She had accepted stolen
pepper, neglected her part in clearing the roadways and failed to arrange for
the inventory of her husband's estate. But Elizabeth had a good heart. She
recognized suffering when she saw it and quietly did her part. In the mid-
1660's she gave food to her neighbor's starving servants and was credited
with keeping at least one of them alive. Almost twenty years later, Elizabeth
came to the rescue of her own daughter Sarie, who, along with her children,
had been deserted by her philandering husband. By this time Elizabeth had
become savvy enough to hire a good attorney. Her will carefully provided for
Sarie while fending off any claims her worthless husband might be able to
make.[3]

 Joan Dawley, a single mother with three half-grown sons, had an affinity
for trouble. Though she complained bitterly about one son's disobedience,
she joined in another son's mischief, and was taken into custody when it was
feared they would burn down a house. Subsequently arrested for swearing,
defamation and disturbing the court, Joane somehow managed to land a job
in the courthouse itself. For 400 pounds of tobacco she agreed to clean the
courthouse for one year and keep a fire going there during the winter. This
connection with the court, however, did not improve her behavior. She got
embroiled in violent disputes and twice was placed in the stocks when her
temper flared, but it was Joane's thievery that brought the court's real wrath
upon her. When she stole four silver buttons and some money, the sheriff

was ordered to give her "29 lashes well lade on upon her bear back." Three months later, when the court ordered another twenty lashes for the theft of two locks and a key, Joane begged to have the second whipping postponed, saying she was "still very sore by cause of ye sd. whiping, soe y^t she is not able to indure it as yet." Though Joane continued to harrass her old enemies, she apparently mellowed a little before she moved away. The two men who had posted a bond for her good behavior came to court in May 1715, and pointed out that for nearly a year Joane had "beheaved her selfe honestly & well."[4]

Before a servant named Ellinor Cowell died in February 1659/60, she bitterly attributed her looming death to her mistress, Katherine Pannwell, who, because she disliked the way Ellinor had placed pigs on the spit, had struck Ellinor in the face while holding a skewer. A fragment of the skewer broke off in Ellinor's cheekbone where it was found by surgeons after Ellinor's death. In their opinion, she died because the piece of skewer "for want of Care by negligence had corrupted ye opticke Nerve of the left Eye; & putrifaction thereby had Issued into the Braine." Katherine Pannwell went to trial, but was acquitted when she received a pardon from the King the following October.[5]

Of course, those who had no kingly connections had to take their punishments. Hannah Snowswell, a servant with an attitude, was sent for water, but replied, "Il'e doe my own busines first." When her mistress struck her for her impudence, Hannah, who must have been a rather husky maid, grabbed her mistress with one arm around her neck and the other around her middle. Frightened, the mistress yelled, "Murder!" Hannah, who claimed she did not intend to hurt her mistress, served an extra year for the assault; for telling tales about her mistress, she received 25 lashes.[6]

That punishment, however, paled beside that meted out to Ann Gray. Marriages among servants were rare, but Ann, had managed to marry Miles Gray while still a servant. Unfortunately Ann soon fell in love with someone else. She and John Hancock repeatedly committed adultery, eventually producing two children and earning a reputation for being "incorrigible fornicators whom no goodness, mercy & admonition can reforme." They, and a similarly guilty couple, received 20 lashes every month for a year.[7]

The following fourteen chapters focus on sixteen girls and women and the experiences that affected their lives. There is no analysis of gender relations or women's role in society, nor is there a scholarly conclusion about women's treatment by the courts. The women in these pages dealt with men, managed plantations and struggled with miscarriages of justice; they lived in colonial Virginia, and in their narratives they speak for themselves.

Flexibility in spelling was the norm for the court clerks who often had to guess at the names of illiterate colonists who neither knew nor cared about how their name should be written. The variation in proper names seen in this volume, along with the spelling of quoted material, reflects the spelling found in the original records.

Until 1752, Britain used the Roman or Julian Calendar. Like their legal counterparts in England, the record keepers of colonial Virginia and Maryland considered the new year to begin on Lady Day, the 25th of March. This meant that December 1670, was followed by January 1670. To avoid confusion in this volume, dates falling between 1 January and 24 March include both years. A date originally written as 17 March 1670, will appear in this volume as 17 March 1670/71.

Chapter One

Mary Burton

Victim of her stepfather

Mary Burton's background is sketchy. In fact, we might never have heard her name if it had not been for the abuse she suffered at the hands of her stepfather and the charges of murder brought against him.

Mary's mother, Sarah, may have been single in 1664, when Mary was born, but it is more likely that Sarah faced widowhood, motherhood and poverty within a brief space of time.[1] In need of food and shelter for herself and her infant daughter, she indentured herself as a servant to Thomas Leatherbury. Unlike many destitute widows, however, Sarah did not agree to the servitude of her child or relinquish any parental rights.[2]

Mary was five years old when her mother's indenture expired in 1669,[3] and though the child never actually became a servant herself, it was a fate she narrowly avoided. She would have served her mother's master till adulthood if it had not been for the help of the court.

When her term of service ended, Sarah's financial situation was still precarious. She would have received the customary corn and clothes when she left the Leatherburys, but that pittance could not sustain Sarah and her growing daughter for long. Probably feeling that she would earn more if she were unencumbered by a small child, Sarah left little Mary on the Leatherbury plantation, the only home the little girl had ever known.

Sometime during the next few years Sarah married Paul Carter, a painter and stainer by trade. Like Sarah, Carter had been married before; he and another wife had been taxed in Northampton County in 1664.[4]

Settled in her new marriage by 1672, Sarah finally felt financially secure enough to retrieve her daughter. When she went to get Mary, however, Thomas Leatherbury refused to release the girl. Now eight years old, Mary was becoming more useful as a servant, and Leatherbury had no intention of letting her go.

So Sarah's husband went to court that April and "petitioned for a Child belonging to his wife in the Custody of Mr. Thomas Letherbury." The court found that Leatherbury was unlawfully keeping the child; they ordered him to deliver the girl to Paul Carter and pay the costs of the suit.[5]

While it seems that Leatherbury did return the girl, he did not let the matter drop; he filed suit against the Carters in May. When the court heard the case in July, Leatherbury demanded to be paid "for Keepinge the said childe three yeare & three moneths after the Expiracon of the mothers tyme by Indenture." If he did not receive such payment, he insisted on having the service of "the child till it was 21 yeares of age."

At first the court found for the Carters, saying they would have to pay nothing, but after "Leatherberryes applyinge himselfe by a Bill in chancery," the court reversed the decision. They ordered the Carters to pay Leatherbury 1200 pounds of tobacco packed in casks or else indenture the child as a servant till she reached adulthood.

Carter was adamantly opposed to paying anything. He angrily asserted that Leatherbury "should have [the child till age 21] rather then hee [Carter] would pay the said Tobacco." Though it appeared that Carter didn't care if the girl came home or not, his wife did care, and Carter requested to appeal the decision to the next General Court.[6]

The county records do not record the higher court's decision, but it must have favored the Carters, who retained custody of Mary. It seems unlikely that someone as opinionated as Paul Carter would have changed his mind and caved in to the demands of his stepdaughter's would-be master.

During the next several years Sarah and her daughter quietly slipped from view and kept a silence typical of colonial females; Paul Carter maintained a more public profile.

He paid taxes, served on the grand jury and dallied over his debts.[7] And when Bacon's Rebellion rocked the colony in 1676, Carter did his part for the Governor. After chafing under the command of Major John West for forty days, Carter spent another six weeks under West "seeking and Killing Beefe for the Countries Service." But Carter's military pay was slow in coming, and in the fall of 1677, he petitioned to be paid.[8]

A few months later Carter purchased 17-year-old John Hancock, who was ordered to serve Carter till adulthood.[9] Carter's financial outlook continued to improve; after acquiring the servant, he was able to fence a field, plant corn in it, and build a new house.

Two years later Carter was accused of deliberately killing a mare that had broken down his fence and destroyed much of his corn field. Carter thought the guilty horse belonged to his old commander, Major West, against whom he was still nursing a grudge, but the real owner was John Parker, who indignantly brought three men to view the dead mare.[10]

These witnesses later came to court and swore "That about the tenth of September last [we] went wth John Parker to Paul Carters and there in the said Carters Cornfeild did see a mare of the said Parkers that was shot in the fore shoulder as we suppose."

Carter noticed the men standing by the dead mare, and when he went out to join them, John Parker asked, "Pawl, have you Killed my mare?"

Carter, who had not intended to trouble Parker, responded with remarkable frankness: "Pawle replied that he had Killed her & was sorry for it, for hee thought hee had Killed Majr. Wests hors."

A little later, according to the men giving the deposition, Carter became even more candid: "Wee went into the hous and there the said Paul shewed us the Gun wherewth hee said he Killed the said Mare & how he held itt." Carter may have been sorry the mare belonged to Parker, but he wasn't sorry he had stopped the horse from destroying his corn, for he "allso sayd if she ware alive again hee would Kill her."

Men who were sent to view the damage determined that Carter had lost three barrels of corn "spoyled by Horses or Mares." They found that the panels in Carter's fence around the cornfield ranged from three feet five inches to five feet in height; the fence was close enough, they said, "but not the Loggs strong enough to Keep out Horses."

Parker sued Carter for killing the horse, and in November 1679, the evidence was presented to a jury. Even though Carter had built a flimsy fence and had admitted to shooting the horse, the gentlemen of the jury found in his favor. "Unruly creatures" in corn fields were a common problem; the jurors probably identified with Carter and his trampled corn.[11]

No one, however, was sympathizing with Carter four months later. His 15-year-old stepdaughter, Mary Burton, had secretly given birth to an infant that died under suspicious circumstances. Paul Carter was the prime suspect–both as the father and the murderer.

On the first of March 1679/80, the entire family was questioned before four justices, one of whom was Paul Carter's detested former officer, John West.

Paul Carter was questioned first:

-Quest–What doe y". Know concerning a Child borne of Mary the Daughter of Sarah the wife of the said Paul:
-Answere–That he doth know that the said Mary had a man child borne of her body and that he & the said Sarah assisted at the birth of the said Childe & that he certainly knoweth not whether it were borne alive or not & that they did endeavour to preserve the life there°f and that it lay betwixt his wife & her Daughter all night and that y⁰ next morning he saw it was dead & he & his Wife buried the said Child but that his Wife carefully washed & dressed it
-Quest: Doe y" know or have you heard who was the father thereof reputed–
-Answere: The said Mary charged one Mr James Tuck therewith.[12]

Paul's wife Sarah incorporated a few more details when she was similarly questioned about the dead child:

-Question: What doe you know concerning a Child borne of Mary y[r] Daughter
-Answere: That about three monthes since being in bed wth her Daughter she perceived her Daughter to be wth Child & charged her therew[th] who was very unwilling to confess but at length charged it upon Mr James Tuck & saith that she assisted at the birth of the said Child & that it was like to dye & did endeavour to preserve it but being dead the next day she & her husband buried it & that it lay all night in bed betwixt her & her daughter & that it was washed & dressed first.[13]

Paul and Sarah Carter's failure to call for help with the child's delivery raised a red flag with the magistrates. Private births, especially illegitimate ones, were against the law. The court depended on the midwife to pressure the agonized mother for the name of the father, and to ensure that even unwanted infants received proper care. If the Carters had complied with the law in this matter–and if Mary had called out the name of James Tuck at the appropriate moment–Paul Carter's crime may never have come to light.[14]

As it was, the suspicions of the justices had not been allayed. They proceeded to interrogate Mary, who was more forthright than either of her elders. (She referred to Paul as her "father-in-law," a 17th century synonym for stepfather.)

The examinacon of Mary Daughter of the said Sarah
Saith–That Mr James Tuck did at first use violence towards her & after she was consenting & that the said Paul her fatherinLaw did doe in like manner & that both of them lay wth her & that she did Keep it from her Mother untill her mother did discover the same in manner as aforesaid & that both her Mother & FatherinLaw assisted her at the birth of the child & that she supposed the Child to be borne alive & that it lay between her mother and herself all night & that in ye morning it was dead & that she thinks her father & Mother buried it & that she thought in her conscience Paul was Father thereto.[15]

Almost as an afterthought, the justices asked Paul and Sarah "whether it was buried in the place where it was then laid it being in a Garden very shallow." The two replied that the baby had originally been buried "in the old house" and later reburied in the garden.[16]

That same day a jury of twelve women, who were sworn in to assist the coroner, ordered that the baby's body be exhumed for the second time so they could examine it. While it is not stated in the records, it was apparently the women's decision to subject the suspects to ordeal by touch. A carryover from medieval times, the method relied on supernatural signs that would supposedly appear when a murderer touched his victim's body.

The women then gave their report to the court:

Wee ye subscrib^rs being sworne to vew ye body of a dead bastard Child Confest by Mary ye daughter of Sarah Carter to be borne of her body wch said Child we caused to be taken out of the ground in the garden where it was very shallow put in. Then we Caused Sarah the wife of Paul Carter & Mother of the said Mary to touch handle & stroake ye Childe in wch time we saw no alteration in the body of ye Childe. Afterwards we Called for Paul Carter to touch ye Sd Child & immediately whi[l]st he was stroaking ye Childe the black & Setled places about the body of the Childe grew fresh & red so that blud was redy to come through ye Skin of the Child. We also observed the Countenance of the sa[i]d Paule Carter to alter into very much paleness. The Childe also appearing to us to be very much neglected in Severall respects as to ye preservacon of such an Infant, & we doe Conclude if ye Child had any violence it was by ye throat wch was very black and Continued so though other places wch were black altered to red & fresh Collered.[17]

Coroner Wm. Custis placed his signature at the bottom of the document as did Mary Hill, Matilda West, Mary Mikell and Amey Parker. The other eight women, Mary Wats, Elizebeth Cutler, Jone Tayler, Margret Jenkins, Mary Anderson, Mary Sipple, Elener Calvert and Ann Fenn made their marks.

The formal language of their report, however, did not convey the drama of the investigation as did the deposition of Madame Matilda West. The 35-year-old wife of Carter's enemy had gathered with the other eleven women at the Carter home, where the ordeal by touch was conducted. Matilda watched the proceedings as Paul Carter was forced to approach the infant. When he reached out and touched the infant's body, Mary Andrews was overwhelmed by a conviction of Paul's guilt. Maybe she was just acting on her long-held suspicions, or maybe she was powerfully moved by the abrupt change in the countenance of Paul, who was standing right beside her. Not one to hold back, Mary suddenly clapped Carter on the back and exclaimed, "Fie, Paul, fie. This is your Child."[18]

With the dead child before him and twelve hostile women surrounding him, he no longer tried to blame James Tuck. A shaken Paul confessed, "I doe not gain say it but it is."

Later, after the ladies of the jury had reached their conclusion, Madam West prepared to leave. As she was coming from the house, she confronted Paul Carter herself, saying, "Were not y^u a wicked Man to ly wth y^r wifes Child?"

He answered, "I was a wicked Man for so doeing, and I must goe to God & not to man for forgiveness."

A little more than two weeks later, on the 16th of March 1679/80, another court was convened and the questioning resumed. The testimonies, though contradictory at times, permit the sordid story to be pieced together.[19]

The pregnancy was not a total surprise to Sarah; she had been aware of her husband's lecherous behavior. One day while trying to catch her mare for a trip to the mill, Sarah came to the "old house & there saw her husband hugg & kiss her Daughter and took up her Daughter's coates up to her Knees." Startled, Sarah indignantly "rebuked him for it & charged him wth debauching her Daughter and Paul her husband Said he did her Daughter no harm & so went away."

For Mary that incident was one among many, Paul Carter "haveing frequently to doe wth her." She recounted how "once in ye old house her Mother found him wth her in his armes wth his hands under her Coates and thinks that her Mother comeing hindred them of any further action." In her next breath Mary amended her previous testimony regarding James Tuck. This time she shifted almost all of the blame to her stepfather by admitting that "James Tuck had once to doe wth her."

According to Sarah, she climbed into bed with Mary one night and discovered that her daughter was more than six months pregnant. Sarah asked some pointed questions, but Mary, perhaps concerned for her own safety, was reluctant to point a finger at her stepfather. Only a few weeks earlier Paul Carter had angrily killed the neighbor's mare. What might he do to Mary? She finally named James Tuck.

Mary claimed that her mother broke the news to Carter about six weeks later. On this point, however, his testimony differed. It is impossible to imagine that Paul could have been oblivious to Mary's condition, but he solemnly swore that up till the time Mary went into labor "he was altogether ignorant that she was with child."

Though Mary claimed the baby arrived in February, her mother said the birth occurred in the early hours of January 13, during a storm. Both Sarah and Paul assisted Mary during the labor and birth, which lasted about two hours. Significantly, they failed to send for a midwife or to ask Mary the name of the child's father while she was in travail. They blamed the weather, but they failed to convince the court, which then wondered if provisions had been made to clothe the baby. After all, if you were planning an infanticide, you weren't likely to assemble a layette. Sarah's testimony was not very satisfactory on this point. She had cut up her own apron to wrap the child and then buried it in the only suit of clothes she had prepared.

Both women said that Paul withdrew from the house shortly after the birth, leaving Sarah, who "cut her blew Apron & put the child in it & a blanket & laid [it] in a Couch & then she herself laid her daughter in the bed." Though Paul claimed it was he that stayed by and assisted Mary to bed, both he and his wife did agree on one thing. Like another woman whose childbirth experience found its way into the court records, Mary did not give birth in bed; she was put there only after the birth was accomplished.

The examiners received three different answers when they asked about the child's physical condition. Paul maintained that he could not tell if the child were born dead or alive. Sarah, who two weeks earlier had claimed she tried to preserve the life of the child, though "it was like to die"–now swore that the baby was born "Dead and never had any signe of life in it."

Contradicting both of them, Mary asserted "That it was borne alive & she heard it give one Shreek & no more at the birth." After her stepfather's departure, Mary saw her mother "bring out Water & Sugar to ye fire Side and offered it to ye Childe & it would not take it." Shortly thereafter, when Sarah laid the child at Mary's breast, Mary detected "That it was a little alive."

For almost two hours the infant lay in the warmth of the bed between his mother and grandmother, but he did not live to see the light of day, and at sunrise Sarah took him away. She carried her grandson to the old house and laid his tiny body in the hole that her husband dug in the dirt floor. When asked "Why did y^u bury ye Child in ye old house & not in ye usuall place that People comonly bury in?" Sarah dodged the obvious answer and replied that "It was her folly so to doe thinking it would be safest there."

In an age when visiting with neighbors was a primary source of entertainment, it was not easy to keep secrets, and the court records specifically noted that the Carters had neighbors nearby. Somebody may have noticed Mary Burton's sudden weight loss. Or someone may have noted the fresh digging in the floor of the old house. When the suspicions came to the attention of the authorities and Paul and Sarah Carter were brought before Col. West and another justice for questioning, they both flatly denied that Mary had been pregnant. Toward the end of February a warrant was served for the search of Mary Burton; midwives would be able to determine if she had recently given birth.[20]

When Paul and Sarah realized an investigation was under way, they discussed their options; he immediately found business elsewhere in the area, and she carried out the plan. She told Mary that she was going to remove the child, dug a new grave in the garden and then reburied the body. Later, when asked why, she excused herself, claiming "she thought it was most convenient for those p[er]sons that were to come to viewe ye body."

With the questioning over, the grand jury immediately got to work. Their job was to determine if the suspects were "so farr Criminall as not by Law to bee further p[ro]ceeded ag[ains]^t in this Court." According to the laws of Virginia, cases as serious as murder could be tried only in Jamestown.[21]

They first considered the presentment of Paul Carter:

> Be it remembred that upon the sixteenth Day of March . . . It is prsented to this Worshipfull Court that Paul Carter of the County aforesaid, painter stainer, not haveing the feare of God before his eyes but being lead and

instigated by the Divell did beget a bastard Child on the body of Mary daughter of Sarah wife of the said Paul: and being further lead & instigated as aforesaid out of meere malice prepensed and forethought did Sometime in the Monthes of January or February last past (as is vehemently suspected) after the birth of the said bastard Child villanously murder and destroy the Said bastard Child and after the Said Murder comitted as aforesd did privily bury the Said bastard Child in an old house thereby to hide and conceale the Same and for the further perpetracon of the Said Crimes as aforesd did Some time after privily take up & remove the body of ye said murdred bastard Child into a Garden place and there allso privily buried the Same, For all wch crimes soe comitted as aforesaid the Said Paul Carter is here prsented to this Worshpll Court that further proceedings may be thereupon had according to ye Lawes in that behalfe provided.[22]

It did not take long for the gentlemen of the jury to reach a decision: "We the Jury vehemently Suspect Paul Carter by circumstance to be guilty of ye Death of the Bastard Child in ye w^{th}in presentment menconed and that he was ye person that dug ye grave in the old house where ye Said Child was first buried as by his confession appeares."[23]

In similar terms Sarah's presentment stated that she "did together wth the said Paul villanously murder & destroy ye sd bastard Child." The jury concluded that she, like her husband, was guilty of the murder; they made special note that it was she who buried the child the second time.[24]

Somewhat more charitable toward Mary, the jury stopped short of murder charges: "Wee ye Jury find according to ye within prsentment that Mary ye daughter of Sarah Wife of Paul Carter had a bastard Child borne of her body alive begotten by Paul Carter and that after ye Death of the said Bastard Child she did conceale that she had a Child."[25]

Since they found a serious crime had been committed, the court ordered that the sheriff immediately take Paul and Sarah Carter into his custody and detain them without bail. They were to be delivered at once to the high sheriff at "James Citty" for further trial before the Governor and his council. Mary also was to appear at the trial, as were six local men, two of the women jurors and written copies of all the evidence.

In Jamestown on the 27th of April 1680, the General Court considered the Carter case. Perhaps more enlightened than their rural cousins, the Governor's councilmen may have questioned the reliability of trial by touch. Unlike the county court, they found no evidence compelling enough to convict Paul and Sarah Carter of murder. But they did not exonerate Paul; they "vehemently Suspected that Paul Carter hath contrary to all good manors & behaviour accompanyed wth Mary ye naturall daughter of Sarah ye wife of him ye sd Paul." They ordered Mary's removal from Carter's home and placed restraints upon him; Paul was not to cohabit or associate with his stepdaughter.[26]

Wasting no time, the county court took Paul into custody until he could post security for his future good behavior and for the performance of the higher court's order. Accordingly, by the middle of May, Mary went to live with Griffin and Bridget Savage.

Unfortunately, conditions there were little better than the situation at home. This time, however, the man of the house caused no trouble. It was his wife. Several months after her stay in the household, Mary was called to give a deposition concerning the activities that occurred during Mr. Savage's absence.[27]

In the habit of entertaining other men, Bridget Savage had been encouraging Mary to do likewise.

Mr. Savage was not at home when Mary had her first memorable encounter with Henry Sadbury. He "came to ye Gate or rayles on hors back where I went to him thinking he had been a stranger there, as he was to me." After making some small talk, "he asked me if I would marry him & appointed me to meet him ye next Satterday after, behinde the house." Clearly, Sadbury's intentions were less than honorable.

Sure enough, the next Saturday after milking was done, Mary saw Sadbury come into the yard. He may have been headed for the back of the house to wait for Mary, but he never made it; he was waylaid by Mrs. Savage, who "Softly desire[d] Hen: Sadbury to come in to ye house." Sadbury, however, "answered as if he might not come there, being forewarned." He did not say who had cautioned him to stay away from Bridget, but he apparently did not take the warning too seriously. Upon Bridget's insistence, he joined her in the house where, according to Mary, they "continued drinking of Cider while I was up with them wch was till very late in ye night when I went to bed."

After Mary retired, Henry and Bridget went to the barn, where, among other things, he must have told Bridget of his interest in the new girl. Beginning the next morning, Mrs. Savage repeatedly set up situations calculated to lure an unwilling Mary into granting favors to Henry Sadbury. Bridget sent Mary to him with messages and tried to coax her to visit him at night. She sent a servant boy for Henry in Mary's name, and when Henry paid a late-night visit she woke Mary, pinching her feet till she agreed to get up.

Either word of goings-on at the Savage place got around, or the court, perhaps already aware of Bridget's reputation, suddenly realized where Carter had placed his stepdaughter. Mary Burton had been with Bridget two and a half months when the court abruptly ordered a constable to take Mary Burton into custody and remove her from the Savage home. He was to convey the girl to the house of Capt. William Custis, whom Mary would have recognized as both the coroner and a justice of the court. She was to remain there as long as Custis or the court saw fit.[28]

A little more than two months later, in October 1680, Mary Burton's life took yet another unexpected turn. Her mother went to court and petitioned for the return of her daughter. Complying with the Governor's order to remove her from home was no longer a concern, "Forasmuch as by sevrl circumstances it may be reasonably prsumed ye sd Paul Carter is drowned in endeavouring to make his escape by water in a Canoe."[29]

This brief reference leads one to wonder about the circumstances of Carter's attempted escape.[30] Had he been imprisoned since the previous May, when he was ordered into custody till finding security for his good behavior and the relocation of his stepdaughter? Or was he arrested when the court discovered he had placed the girl with a lady of questionable character? Or was his attempted escape unrelated to his known offenses?

Whatever the case, with Paul presumed dead, the court set aside the Governor's order and allowed Mary to go home.

That is where she was living when she was summoned to court once more. In January 1680/81, the church wardens called on Mary to answer the nearly year-old charges of fornication. Her mother offered herself as security for the payment of Mary's fine, but the court deemed her offer insufficient; Sarah apparently had less than 500 pounds of tobacco at her disposal.[31]

Mary was given till the next court to find acceptable security. If she failed, she would receive corporal punishment, probably nineteen lashes, perhaps more.[32]

Mary Burton's story does not have a tidy ending. We do not know if her emotional scars were compounded by physical ones, or if she and her mother were forced into new depths of poverty to pay the fine that Paul Carter should have paid.

In a way though, a form of justice really did prevail. Paul Carter paid a high price for his actions, and Mary, back home with her mother, never appeared in court again, which is probably just the way she would have wanted it.

Chapter Two

Mary, Rachel and Eleanor

Servant wenches of John and Rebecca Wallop

Wallops Island, while not actually a household word, does turn up now and again thanks to the NASA Wallops Flight Facility. Both the island and the facility bear the name of the first owner, John Wallop, a surveyor and justice of the peace who lived nearby on the Sea Side of Virginia's Eastern Shore. There, during the late 1600's, he and his wife Rebecca owned thousands of acres.[1] Among the Wallops' many servants were three women, who, by their depositions and misfortunes, afford a rare insight into the food, the work and the quality of life on a colonial plantation.

Mary Storey
The talkative cook

During the summer of 1680, five of Wallops' men servants, with John Dyer as their leader, paid a visit to Captain Custis, one of the court justices, and complained that their master "did cruelly use and punish ye s^d servants by want of food & all other convenient necessaries." When they returned home after registering their grievances, their master gave them further grounds for protest; he whipped Dyer and told him it was for going to complain.

On the third of August, John Wallop, a justice himself, had to leave court while his servants proved their charges to the satisfaction of Wallop's fellow magistrates, who then ordered Wallop to work his servants reasonably and to provide them with adequate food, clothing, and lodging. He was also ordered to pay court costs and to make sure that there was no further cause for complaint. Because John Dyer had convinced the court that he had been unjustly punished, they ordered that his term of service be reduced by one month.[2]

Though the five servants undoubtedly gloated over this success, any victory celebration would have been premature. Their master hired an attorney, and by December had assembled witnesses willing to contradict the testimony of the grumbling servants. Two of those witnesses were Wallop's servant wenches, young women who lived in the servant quarters and had intimate knowledge of the domestic scene on the Wallop plantation.

About 25 years old, the talkative Mary Storey was in charge of preparing food for the other nine servants. She appeared to enjoy the attention she received in court and filled almost three pages of the court record book with minute, repetitious and sometimes contradictory details regarding the diet of everyone she knew, servant and master alike.[3]

Mary described a plantation where corn, at least, was plentiful and readily available to the servants. She told how "her Master Wallop hath a great quantity of Corne lying in an open Tobc [tobacco] house wth out Lock or doore to ye house." Even more accessible were the husked corn and hominy which "stands alwaies in an open tubb in ye servts roome & not under lock." Somewhat more restricted was the ground corn meal, which was carried into their mistress's room till it was sifted. The corn that was "spent off"–which probably meant removed from the cob–was kept in a room with wheat, salt, meat and other things. This room was "allwaies locked at night & ye Key took out of ye doore." But if someone really wanted to raid this storeroom, they would have had little trouble. According to Mary, "in ye daytime ye Key is most times in ye doore."

The Wallop servants "had usually 3 meales a day sumer & winter & enough to eat while they would." To prove her point, Mary, whose work was apparently limited to the home place, recalled that when her "fellow servts worked 4 or 5 daies in ye woods, they had their breakfast in ye morning before they went out & there supper at night, as much as they would eat, & y^t her Mastr in ye day time carried for them bread & Cheese & y^t twice she cut it for them."

One repast stood out in Mary's mind; she described how the ten servants "had a whole leg of beef wth pumpkin & a great loaf of bread for one meal." In spite of this abundance, a teenager named "Tho Worslee told her y^t his belly was not full nor half full altho they left bread wch he migh (sic) have eat if he would."

Mary claimed that left over bread was common, but if they ever did run out of bread or meat, their mistress would provide them with hominy and broth. They never lacked hominy "if they would eat it, for there was homine enough allwaies boiled." If there was no broth, they had milk with their hominy, at least till the cows started going dry.

The servants were given the skim milk, of course; any cream was churned into butter, and though the servants craved and sometimes begged for buttermilk, the Wallops were rather stingy with both the butter and the buttermilk. The servants preferred to eat hominy with "either fatt or butter," but they never had as much as they liked.

Mary Storey also described the diet that precipitated the servants' complaints. She recalled that "They had milk almost untill y^t time they complain'd to Capt. Custis." Even so, for the few meals when milk was lacking, they had plenty of hominy or bread with even a little fat or butter.

On a Sunday morning, two days before matters came to a head, the servants were given milk, and while most of them questioned its freshness, the Wallops seemed to have had no qualms. Mary thought the milk "might have stood in cold wheather 4 or 5 daies." One might question how cold the weather was that summer; clearly some of the servants had their doubts, and those who tasted it, did so gingerly. "This milk some of ye servts said tasted of ye vessell it stood in, & some of the milk was boiled for her mrs [mistress] & Children and turned not, & they eat it, but some of ye servts would not eat of it."

Working on Sunday was prohibited in Virginia during the 1600's, but those restrictions did not apply to cooking, at least not on the Wallop place. Sometime after breakfast one Sunday, the wenches prepared a pot of broth, most likely of the coleworts (loose-leaf cabbage) and beef that Mary mentioned elsewhere in her rambling deposition. It seems that many of the servants took one look at the soup and decided they weren't that hungry; a day and a half later, on Monday evening, there was still a considerable amount left over. Then, tacitly conceding that the broth needed improvement, Mrs. Wallop caused some milk to be added to make it better.

Unfortunately, this tactic did not achieve the desired result, and "ye men servants complain'd it was to thin & would not eat of it." At this point, Mr. Wallop angrily informed the disgruntled servants that they had lost their chance to eat it; he ordered Rachel, Mary's fellow wench, to take the milky broth and "lock it up & keep ye key her self, wch she did." In response, the men servants "all told him they would goe & complaine, & ye next morning betimes [early] before her master was up they were gone."

It seems that at least one of the complainants referred to the quality of the broth served at the Wallop place; in her deposition Mary felt compelled to defend the soup by swearing that no one had ever been forced to "eat broth made onely of Coleworts at their Masters house." Mary said she "never Knew any such made there, but they have eat broth made of beef & Coleworts or Beef & Cabbage wch was ye same y^t there M[aste]r & Mrs [mistress] & Children eat."

Awaking to find his men servants gone, Master Wallop was anxious to be off after them and resorted to the two-day-old milky broth himself. "Mary Store (sic) poured some of it into a Bottle & her Mr carryed it away wth him."

Mrs. Wallop, whose taste was no more discriminating than that of her husband, had the rest of the broth heated for her breakfast. She shared this meal with an Elizabeth Turner, who may have been the servant by that name who was presented in court for fornication a few months later.[4]

Though Mary Storey recounted how her master had taken the broth away, she quickly added that there had been enough hominy. In fact, that was something of an understatement. Immediately after his servants filed their complaint, Mr. Wallop restricted his workers' diet to only salt and hominy for about a week. When they had endured seven days of lye-soaked corn, Mrs. Wallop gave them "milke enough wth their homine evry meale 3 times a day." By killing-time, the Wallops had relaxed restrictions even further and were providing their servants with meat and bread twice a week, and sometimes there was so much meat that some was left over.

Though Wallop initially clamped down on his servants, he was cognizant of the court's concerns and shrewdly moved to make the chief complainer responsible for the servants' food supply. After the August court, Wallop ordered John Dyer to supervise "ye grinding of Corne to see y^t there was enough grinded so that ye servts should not want." Dyer was also commanded to oversee food preparation and to tell Mary and the other wench how much they should boil or bake. To ensure that everyone understood, Wallop "ordered ye servt wenches to boile or back [bake] wt John Dier ordered them & to doe it well or elce she should be Copted [given a blow]."

Boiling corn meal or hominy and baking corn bread should have required only modest cooking skills; nonetheless, Mary experienced some difficulty in meeting her peers' expectations. On one occasion when her cooking displeased the other servants, they actually delivered on their master's promise and struck Mary for her culinary shortcomings. Nor did the problem end there; Mary recalled that "oftentimes after they threatned her."

Even though Wallop had ordered John Dyer to ensure that the servants had sufficient corn, hominy and bread and that none of it be sour or spoiled, Mary claimed that Dyer was negligent in that regard, for "not wth standing her masters order to John Dyer he never looked after any thing, nor ordered her anything to boile or back." In fact, none of the male servants–the ones who claimed to be going hungry–had ever asked her to cook so much as a handful of additional hominy.

Nor did Dyer properly supervise that detested colonial task, the grinding of corn meal. Though a number of commercial water, wind and even horse powered mills were scattered throughout the county, on many plantations the grinding action was still accomplished by the hands of servants rotating one grooved circular stone upon another. Since this was a chore that could be done indoors and in dim light, harsh masters sometimes forced their servants to "work by day and grind by night." [5] Mary had often heard her mistress scold at the servants "for not grinding meal enough & hath often told them yt if they would grinde more corne they might have more bread."

Different references confirm that the servants made more than one official complaint. Mary, in her verbal ramblings, also indicated that Wallop restricted their diet a second time. She said that "after her fellow servts last came from Capt. Custis," their master "ordered them to have enough of homine & salt & bread & no other victualls but w^t can be made of Corne." After that they had meat and bread only on Sundays and a little broth when they requested it. As for buttermilk, "they have often desired buttermilk to eat & her Mrs. often denied them & her Mrs. would not suffer them to eat it except once or twice."[6]

Mistress Wallop and her family could be disagreeable, but there seemed to be no food that disagreed with them. Besides eating the milky broth rejected by the servants, the Wallops consumed two other culinary disasters. Mary recalled that "ye servts found fault wth their bread once but her Mrs took y^t away & her Children & two Coopers eat it." The Wallops refused to waste even a little hominy. "Rachel once boiled homine yt was ye bottom of ye barrell wch when it was boiled looked a little blackish." The servants criticized this hominy, but "it was ye same y^t her mr. & Children did eat of & it tasted well enough but it was blackish."

Rachel Hasted, the other servant wench, besides reporting that the servants were conspiring against their master, further confirmed Mary's story,[7] as did a young man named William Paine, who proved to be an exceptionally close friend of Mary's.

William's testimony was especially damaging to the servants' case; he had heard "Mr. Wallops servants talking amongst themselves y^t they would comitt faults on purpose y^t theire master might beat them soe y^t they might complaine to ye Court of ye said Wallop." Since the servants' last complaint to the court, Paine had often visited Wallop's house while the servants were eating; they had enough meat and so much milk and hominy that they could not eat it all. He also quoted John Broomeley, Wallop's overseer, who said that "Mr. Wallops servants are Rogues, & y^t they had victualls enough & y^t they had meat twice in the week & fared better then he did when he was a servant & that they had good lodging."[8]

After considering such testimony, the court reversed their former position and favorably viewed John Wallop's request to be repaid for the expenses he had incurred because of the false complaints of John Dyer, Thomas Worslee, Thomas Wheeler, Henry Hanscam and William Dixson. Aside from paying an attorney, witnesses and court costs, Wallop claimed he lost forty-seven days' worth of work when the servants went to complain. The court ordered the five servants to serve extra time to satisfy all the charges.[9]

Mary Storey, after her moment of glory in court, went on to seek out other things to talk about; some of her tidbits were even of interest to the authorities. Enjoying an unusual amount of freedom for a servant, in June 1681, Mary was visiting a neighbor's home when Dorothy Watts confided that "Sarah Price carried a bastard child about for Woodman Stockely."

Evidently an admirer of Woodman, Mary bristled and said, "You cannot prove that."

Dorothy shot back that she could.

In light of where her loyalties lay, it seems more than coincidence that Mary happened to be at Dorothy's house a week or so later, when Woodman appeared with a warrant for Dorothy's arrest. Dorothy's vehement reaction enabled Mary to enjoy the spotlight one more time as she informed the court of Dorothy's defiance.[10]

Only a month later the justices again focused on Mary Storey, only this time their attention was less welcome. On 17 August 1681, she appeared before the court and acknowledged committing fornication with William Paine. Mary was placed in custody till posting security for good behavior and the payment of a fine. It is unlikely that she remained incarcerated long, however. Capt. John Wallop presented himself as her security and agreed to pay her fine of 500 pounds of tobacco.[11]

That November Mary petitioned to be discharged from her bond for good behavior. As was the custom, the court ordered a proclamation to be made, but since she had behaved herself, no one objected, and she was released.[12]

About this time two other incidents occurred: John Wallop removed the scheming John Dyer from his plantation, thus stemming the source of complaints about food and mistreatment, and Mary's illegitimate infant died. Dyer's remaining time of service was purchased by Thomas Welbourne, and it was this man, the new master of Mary's old adversary, who issued a warrant for Mary's arrest for the murder of her infant. The circumstances suggest that Welbourne was being manipulated by his vengeful new servant. On 17 June 1682, "Mary Story was bound over to this Court upon Suspicon of murdering her Child by vertue of Mr. Thomas Welburnes warr[an]t."[13]

The court took Mary into custody, where she was to remain without bail till the next court for examination and trial. In the meantime, the court requested John Wallop and Thomas Welbourne to inquire further into the matter and find out the truth. The two gentlemen, however, were unable to find any incriminating evidence, and at court two months later, Mary was discharged with the note that nothing further appeared against her.[14]

After paying court charges, Mary Storey disappeared from the court records. Her term of service probably ended; maybe she moved away, or got married or followed her infant to an early grave. The only records of her humble life portray her simply as a servant, but one day in court she managed to open a window in the fog of time and allowed us a glimpse of her master's indiscriminate taste and of servants eating a leg of beef, pumpkin, cornbread, broth, milk and hominy—lots of hominy.

Rachel Hasted

The Wallops' other wench

A few years younger than her talkative fellow servant, Rachel Hasted (or Hosted or Horsted) had much in common with Mary Storey. They both testified for John Wallop, they prepared food on the plantation, and they both eventually landed in court accused of fornication. Their feelings for John Dyer, however, could not have been more different. Mary detested him as a self-serving complainer; Rachel may have loved him, at least for awhile.

Not as glib as Mary, whom the court questioned first, Rachel simply verified Mary's account of Wallop's food supplies and then added that she had overheard the men servants as they discussed someone who saw them "have meat enough last Sunday night." The servants conspired to claim it was a month's worth, even though they regularly enjoyed that much meat.[15]

Rachel also confirmed that Master Wallop did not hesitate to partake of his servants' fare. When a complaint was voiced about sour hominy, Wallop called for some and tasted it. Neither he nor Rachel found anything wrong with the hominy; in fact when Rachel ate some the next morning, she found it still was not sour.

Rachel, along with four of the grumbling menservants, was a comparative newcomer to Virginia. On 19 May 1681, several months after the servants first filed their complaint, John Wallop obtained a certificate for transporting Rachel, William Dixson, Harry Handson, Thomas Wheeler and Thomas Worslee, along with a Negro named Bess and a tailor named James. Though the individuals on this list had likely set sail a year or more earlier, the new certificate entitled Wallop to claim 350 acres of land, fifty for each person whose passage he had paid.[16]

Rachel was still in the service of John Wallop more than a year later, when she was summoned to answer for the sin of "fornicacon and haveing a Bastard Child." She appeared in court with a very unusual note from her master, who promised to pay her fine and pleaded with the court for her speedy return:

> May it Please ye Worships my Servant Rachell Hosted is sumoned to the Court for haveing a Bastard Childe. Please to doe me the favour to dispatch her Examinacon that she may quickly returne home. Her fine wth Court charges shall next yeare be paide by me, John Wallop Als
> 19th Febr 1682[/83] To ye worshipll Court of the County of Accomack.[17]

It is unclear why Wallop was so concerned about his servant's speedy return. He may have needed her help in preparing for his upcoming trip to England, he simply may have been reluctant to relinquish even a day's worth of work, or maybe Rachel was needed at home to tend to her hungry infant.[18]

Before allowing Rachel to hurry home, the court, ever hopeful of placing the burden of child support where it belonged, questioned her about the paternity of her child. Servant girls typically named a fellow servant, and Rachel was no exception; she swore that her infant's father was John Dyer. The court immediately ordered him summoned to the next court.[19]

A fortunate exception to the harsh custom of the time, Rachel's baby lived on the same plantation as its mother. Because women servants were required to work, they were rarely allowed to marry, and nursing an illegitimate baby was generally out of the question. Time-consuming infant care was given over to poor married women whose husbands would receive 1200 pounds of tobacco a year for their wives' trouble.[20]

But John Wallop, unpretentious enough to share his servants' food, must have also been compassionate enough to consider a servant mother's distress. Taking an especially enlightened stance for a 17th century master, Wallop arranged for his wenches' offspring to be raised on his plantation. Mary Storey, to be accused of killing her child, certainly must have had access to her baby, too. Court records clearly show that Rachel Hasted's baby remained on the Wallop plantation until at least January 1683/84, when it would have been around a year old.[21] True, Wallop collected child support for Rachel's infant, but such payments could not adequately compensate a master for his servant's lost time; if Wallop's arrangement had been financially advantageous, more masters would have followed suit.

Having served Wallop since at least 1680, Rachel was probably due to be freed sometime in 1684, after serving the customary five years, though her term may have been extended so she could work off the 500 pounds of tobacco Wallop had paid for her fine. All we know is that after 1684, Rachel and her baby vanished from the records; the baby's father, however, did not.

The same court entry that ordered John Dyer to reimburse the parish for a year's support of Rachel's infant, noted that Ann Fish, servant of Thomas Welburne, had "dyed in Child-bed." The justices further noted that "the sd Dyer is suspected by Circumstances appearing to yᵉ Court to be yᵉ Reputed father of yᵉ sd Fishes Bastard Child."[22]

The court accordingly ordered Welburne to turn Dyer over to the authorities when his term of service ended; Dyer was to remain in the sheriff's custody till he posted a bond for the 1200 pounds of tobacco already paid out for Rachel's infant, and also for "wt shall be alleadged agsᵗ him on yᵉ behalf of yᵉ p[ar]ish concerning yᵉ sd Ann Fishes Basterd Child."[23]

Less than a year later, in October 1684, John Dyer was a free man. But his freedom did not last; the next month he was taken into custody for not supporting the Fish and Hosted children. It took the prodding of the court, plus a number of years, before his child support was paid.[24] His impulsiveness would be a continuing source of trouble,[25] but it seems that John Dyer had harbored genuine feelings for Ann Fish. Evidence indicates that her motherless child, who was initially placed "at nurse" with John Melson, may have continued to enjoy the support of his father. When John Dyer died in 1721, his will named his wife Joan and someone called John Fish as joint executors.[26] Dyer bequeathed his entire estate to the two of them, stipulating that they should live together; the undivided estate was to go to the survivor. Fifteen years later, John Fish sold what had been Dyer's land.[27]

Elinor Hew
Death of a servant girl

Almost six years after John Wallop's men servants discovered that their women counterparts were willing, even eager, to contradict them in court, one of those same young men turned on a servant wench with deadly results. William Dixson,[28] barely a teenager when he joined the others to complain about their rations in 1680, was still Wallop's servant in the spring of 1686. By this time, however, William was nineteen years old and enjoyed a measure of authority over at least two other servants, a mulatto slave named Franck and a servant girl named Elinor (or Nell) Hew. Caught in a system that did not blink at physical punishment–even the abused girl seemed to accept it as normal–the three of them became leading actors in a tragedy; Elinor died in a tobacco field and the two young men stood accused of her murder.[29]

A newcomer to Virginia,[30] and the only wench working in the field at the time, Elinor probably held the lowest position in the servant hierarchy. To make matters worse, she had recently annoyed the other servants by shirking her work and by telling tales, apparently repeatedly. At least that was William's story, which may have been biased; it was in his own self-interest to cast the girl in an unfavorable light.

If Will was telling the truth, Elinor's stories were definitely a little strange. Less than a week before her death, he had Elinor describing a night time visitation. She told "everyone in ye house that there Came a black man to her and called her up and tould to get up and go to grind." The significance of this incident (or dream) is somewhat puzzling. Was William implying that Elinor was delusional, or was he suggesting that Elinor communicated with supernatural forces? Or was he hinting that she fabricated the story to justify her next move? Of course, it is possible that Will actually quoted Elinor, and, unlikely as it seems, she may have been telling the truth. At any rate, the next day she ran away.

Like many fugitive servants, she was not gone long. A lonely hair-raising night of hiding in the woods often motivated runaways to opt for the more predictable misery of servitude. When she came home the next day, Elinor was interrogated, and according to William, "being asked where she had been, she said wth a black man at a very fine house and he gave her victualls and drinke."

Elinor's story would have generated raised eyebrows, disbelief, and ridicule. She likely felt compelled to defend herself to the other servants and, according to Will, defiantly told them she would run away again. In fact, William claimed that she said it so often that "she made them weary."

A day or so later, on the seventeenth of June, Elinor set out for the tobacco field with William Dixson, Franck and her master's two sons, Samuel aged thirteen and John Jr., who was listed as "Aged fourteen years & upwards." They had been in the field for only a short time that morning when William began to find fault with Elinor's work. Accusing her of "cuttinge up plants & leavinge weeds," he took a stick about the "bignesse of his finger or thum at the great end" and beat Elinor over the back with it. Later that morning, after Elinor left some weeds, John Jr. watched as "Will Dixon gave Franck (A malatto boy) the stick & bid him drub her & he drubed her on ye back And another time for coveringe of weeds ye sd Will hitt her two or three times wth ye small end of his how helve." Young Samuel reported this too, saying that "Will struck her or puncht her with his how [hoe] helve." Later denying this last abuse, Will claimed it was Franck who used the hoe handle against Elinor.

The depositions, which were taken almost three months after Elinor's death, contradict each other in key points, but it was more than the passage of time that caused the discrepancies. William Dixson, whose version naturally minimized his own participation in the rough treatment of Elinor, accused the two Wallop boys of glossing over Franck's role because Franck, as a slave, was much more valuable than William. The Wallops had already suffered the loss of one servant; if they had to give up another as her murderer, they would much prefer to lose William, an indentured servant who would soon be free anyway.

When the workers returned to the main house for the noon meal, the Wallop boys told their mother that Elinor would not work. Mrs. Wallop was probably used to such complaints, and one can almost see her shrug as she turned to William and told him "y^t he must either make her worke or do ye worke himself."

Determined not to do another's work, and bolstered by the authority offhandedly given them by Mrs. Wallop, William and Franck took further action when they got back to the tobacco field after lunch. According to the Wallop boys, William grabbed a chunk of wood and threw it at Elinor, hitting her either in the back or the lower part of her clothing; he threw it again at her legs, but they could not tell if it actually hit her the second time. In the meantime, Franck broke off a peach tree switch, stripped it, and after giving it to William, "putt ye sd Nells shift away & loyd (sic) her back bare." Clearly visible on her back were "sevall markes of stroakes," but the fresh welts inspired no sympathy from her fellow servants. After Franck pulled Elinor's shift down, "Will beat her wth ye sd switch."

In his version, William completely forgot about throwing the chunk of wood and tried to make himself appear reluctant to hit Elinor even with a switch. According to him, after "goeing to worke againe ye aboves^d mallatto made her unty ye neck of her shift pulling it down of[f] one of her shoulders and haveing provided himselfe of one peach tree switch gave [me] ye switch and bid [me] beat her." William, who was asking the court to believe that he took orders from a slave, went on to contradict the boys' story by specifically denying that he beat Elinor. He swore that after he gave Elinor just one small stroke, he threw the stick down, but "ye mallato askeing why [I] beat her no more tooke up ye switch and beat it to peices upon her backe wch was all that passed y^t day."

Even after this abuse, Elinor's complaints were few, as though she expected this treatment and had become accustomed to it. While she complained of no soreness or injury to the elder Wallop boy, she was a little more open with his younger brother, who may have been closer to Elinor in age. He reported that "after all this she worked well & talked well and seemed to aile nothing onely she Complained of her arme and shewed it to this declarant & it was a little black & blew & there was a little blood."

The next day began as usual on the plantation. The slave, the two servants and the master's two sons trudged out to the tobacco field to work before breakfast. Elinor acted well enough and talked well enough, but John Jr. heard her complain "that she was soare where Will beate her." Nonetheless, Elinor accompanied the others as usual when they went in to breakfast.

Samuel testified that she did "Eat her victualls & Ayled nothing as this declarant perceived." After returning to the field Elinor worked well for two or three rows and "then she went & dranck a great draught of water & came to work againe and prsently afer (sic) she groaned & said she was not well & this declarant saw her shake & she had an ague."

Elinor was in severe distress. According to Samuel, she complained that "she had water or something that lay about her heart or Liver or Lights [lungs] & if she had a Knife she would cutt her belly or run it in her belly." John told the court that Elinor "said if she had a knife shee would run it here (pointing to her side) & said she hoped, or wisht, she might dye & she prayed God to save her soule."

Certain that the end was near, Elinor turned to the 13-year-old boy for a measure of comfort, appealed to God for a measure of hope and recalled the loving care of a mother that she would never see again. She told Samuel that she had been troubled with a distemper every year, and she was now "sure she should dye & cryed & prayed to save her soule to God & prayed Jesus Christ to save her soule Then she said that when she used to be sick her mother used to goe to ye Apothecaries & buy something for her wch. cost

Eight pence & now she was gone from her mother & her mother could not looke after her."

In Elinor's background lurks a sad story that we will never know. She spoke as though her mother were still living. Why, then, would Elinor, a young girl prone to yearly illnesses, leave her mother for the colonies and indentured servitude? Her family was not wealthy—eight pence seemed an impressive sum to Elinor—yet many families would not have had that much to spend at the apothecary's. It seems unlikely that Elinor would have voluntarily chosen to leave her home. Perhaps her family had fallen on hard times or she shared the fate of many other English youngsters who were kidnaped and shipped to Virginia, a bargain for their masters who would own them till they reached adulthood.[31] Or, like others, Elinor may have been ripped from her mother's arms and sentenced to servitude in Virginia as punishment for stealing a handkerchief or committing some other petty crime.

At about eleven or twelve o'clock, the workers again left the field, this time to "noon it" with the others on the plantation. Upon entering the house, Elinor lay down and seemingly fell asleep. When Mrs. Wallop came in to dine with the servants, she saw the girl lying there. Concerned, she felt Elinor's hands and declared that she was a little feverish. Shortly afterward, Elinor was called to eat dinner, but she only groaned and said, "Noe." After the others finished, Will approached Elinor, who was still lying down as if she were asleep, and ordered her to get up. When she did not rise, he picked up a small stick and gave her one blow. At that she groaned a little, but got up and went out with him.

By now even William was beginning to suspect that something might actually be wrong with Elinor. After accompanying her to the field, he left her to her hoeing near John Jr. while he went to work with the weeding plow. A short time later Will approached Elinor and asked if she were any better. After replying that she was neither better nor worse, she worked side by side with Will for about two rows. And she worked surprisingly well, even faster than Will. After making herself very hot she "went & dranke a great draught of cold water & then went fast to her work againe."

It is possible that Elinor's heroic attempt to work well was meant to ward off further painful blows, or maybe she was responding to the glimmer of concern shown by Will. She may have been going into shock, or perhaps she really meant it that morning when she cried out that she wished to die; maybe she was grimly working herself to death, a final running away from the world that had been so cruel to her.

After working only a little, she started "peckinge about ye Rowes as if [she] were distracted and Reeled & staggered & did not speake."

When William saw that Elinor had fallen down, he picked up a white stick and did what he did best—he struck Elinor, this time between two and four blows. When she groaned and would not get up, Will finally concluded that Elinor was not joking. He at last resorted to something other than a stick. In the words of John Jr., "Will ran home to [my] mother."

While the horrified Samuel watched Elinor, John Jr. took off after William. Rebecca Wallop had already come out of the house when John Jr. "mett her & told her that Nell dissembled or Else was a dyeing." He then turned and ran back to the tobacco field and "went to ye s^d Nell before his Mother & the s^d Nell was lyeing on her back & Ratled in ye throate as if there was water or some thinge that stopt her breath." When John Jr. took Elinor by the hand and turned her on her side, "there came watery ugly stuff out of her nosstrills & she was blewish or black on her lipps & when this depon[en]t[']s] mother came to her she Caused her to be sett up & then the said Nell dyed prsently."

Young Samuel confirmed the story, and when questioned by the magistrates, added a few details, "this declarant saith That he saw ugly mattery stuffe like that wch comes out of soares that had come out of her mouth & nose & before she dyed she seemed to be almost choaked & had much adoe to fetch breath And further saith that when ye abovesd Will struck ye sd Nell wth ye Chunck & how & sticks she did not fall downe neither did any blood appeare in her face when she dyed nor any blood in any parte of her body or coth[e]s before she dyed but a little on her arme."

So on 18 June 1686, Elinor died far from her mother and in the company of those who cared only about her deftness with a hoe.

Once the servant was dead, Mrs. Wallop had some decisions to make. Though her husband had been in the area both the month before and the month after Elinor's death, he was not at home when Mrs. Wallop needed him.[32] Since it was a warm day, Rebecca naturally wanted the body buried as soon as possible, but private burials, like private births, tended to raise suspicions; she decided to send Will to the Stockley plantation to fetch Thomas Worsley to come help bury Elinor.[33] Once a servant to the Wallops, the 22-year-old Worsley was also well acquainted with Will; together they had complained about the Wallop's food.

Will found Worsley, but his grim mission piqued the interest of several others on the Stockley plantation. Woodman Stockley, William Blake Jr. and John Blake, all returned with Thomas Worsley and Will. They went directly to where "Ellinor lay dead in Mr. Wallops Tobb° ground." While looking at the body, Stockley "tooke notice of a small stick that lay by her & some splinsters which Woodman shewed us." The visitors then left the field and went on to the house.

There Mrs. Wallop prevailed upon the men to bury the servant. Though other dead servants were washed and otherwise prepared for burial, it seemed that Elinor was to get nothing more than a hole in the ground.[34]

Accompanied by Mrs. Wallop, the four men walked back to the field where the body lay, but the observant Woodman noticed that the shattered stick was now missing. When he asked for it, Will replied that he had thrown it away. Suspicious, Woodman "bid him fetch it againe wch he accordingly did & then Woodman asked him how it came soe broke. Wm Dixson replyed he broke it beating of Cowes."

Cows in the tobacco field? Feeling that Will might have something to hide, the men took a closer look at Elinor's body. They found two or three marks on "one of her arms wch wee supposed to be strokes." And then Mrs. Wallop, who knew Elinor had been whipped but was likely unaware of the severity of her beatings, "bad us turne her over upon her belly." That was "when wee saw upon her back severall marks (made by stroaks as we supposed)."

Knowing that suspicious deaths had to be investigated by the coroner, the men "told Mrs Wallop we durst not bury her till some body else had viewer (sic) her."

In the heat of the afternoon sun in the middle of a tobacco field, the little group stood gazing down at the lifeless form of a servant girl. The laws of men demanded that her death be investigated; the laws of nature mandated a speedy interment. They discussed the options and eventually "unanimously concluded to putt her into the ground & putt some dirt upon her." Before they buried Elinor, however, they noticed a small spot of blood on her forehead, but speculated that it may have been done by a horsefly. The next day the men went to a magistrate "to acquaint him wth our proceedings therein."[35]

Summoned to look into Elinor's death, a jury had her body exhumed and rendered a judgment, but without the benefit of the coroner's presence or an inquiry. In spite of the glaring legal shortcomings of this report, John Wallop's "servants William Dixon and Franck a mallatto suspected to be ye death of ye said Elianor" were ordered to appear before the coroner and at the next court. Facing the loss of two more of his servants, Wallop maintained that the inquiry was not made according to law, and, at the court held 6 July 1686, requested that the coroner impanel a jury to properly inquire into the death of his servant.[36]

Three days later the coroner dutifully impaneled the same jury that had previously met without him; it was noted that the members had "formerly vieued ye body." They considered the "Evidences & what wee have seen that ye body of ye sd Ellenor was very much bruised by severall stroaks upon her arms back & sides & also we ye Jury afores^d did see a swelling bruise on ye left side of her head & also her Eare sweld, all wch bruises we doe think in our Conciences was ye shortning of her daies." Among those signing the coroner's report were Woodman Stockly and William Blake Jr. two of the men who helped bury Elinor.[37]

It wasn't until the seventh of September that Captain William Custis, the county coroner, presented the jury's decision and the evidence to the court; the report and depositions then were read in the presence of William Dixson "ye p[er]son suspected to be ye occassion of her ye sd Elianors death." The county court, which had no jurisdiction over cases in which the death penalty might be imposed, found Dixson to be "so farr Criminall as to bee no farther proceeded ags^t in this Court." They ordered the sheriff to take William Dixson into custody, detain him without bail and deliver him to the high sheriff of Jamestown for further trial. Thomas Worsley, John Blake and the two Wallop boys were required to post security for their appearance in Jamestown as witnesses.[38]

Franck, Wallop's valuable mulatto slave, was no longer under suspicion, and this development was not lost on the primary suspect. The next day, while being questioned by a court justice, William swore that "Samuel and John, Mr Wallops two sons tould him, they would lay it all upon ye prisoner and clear ye mallatto because he was a slave for his life."[39]

William admitted beating Elinor with a small stick a day before her death, but accused Franck of beating her with a hickory stick, with his hoe handle and then with a peach tree switch till it broke to pieces. Will admitted giving Elinor three small strokes on the day she died; he swore, however, that Mrs. Wallop and her son ordered him to beat Elinor, "which he much forbore to do." Instead he claimed that Franck took it "upon him most to do it after an unreasonable manner wch is all he know^th of ye sd Elinor Hugshs death."

The court listened to William Dixson's accusations and ultimately ordered Franck to be taken into the sheriff's custody as well; he would be transported to Jamestown for trial along with his accuser.[40] Though they both went to trial, it seems that neither of them was convicted of murder. In 1693, Wallop gave his son "my mallata Franck to serve him according to Law for Slaves."[41] And the name of William Dixson reappeared in the court records in the fall of 1692, six years after the trial would have been held at Jamestown. This William led a quiet life, paying his taxes and living at Widow Holliday's for a time. Years later his wife Ann stood accused of breaking the Sabbath, but William hired an attorney who managed to convince the court to quash the case.[42]

Thomas Worsley died just about a year after the girl he was called to bury. Though his grave is probably very near hers, his interment was not as unceremonious as Elinor's. When Thomas died with no will and no relatives, John Wallop provided a funeral for him. But this consideration was not a gift to the departed former servant; Wallop later entered a claim against Thomas's estate for 395 pounds of tobacco to pay for the funeral expenses.[43]

When Elinor felt sure the end was near, she attempted to identify the cause of her approaching death. Sometimes dying colonists would name the

When Elinor felt sure the end was near, she attempted to identify the cause of her approaching death. Sometimes dying colonists would name the person who "was the death of me," but Elinor did not name a person. She seemingly attributed her impending death to a distemper that had troubled her every year. Evidently she was so accustomed to whippings that she did not connect her present distress to the punches with the hoe or the repeated beatings.[44]

With the advantages of hindsight, we can conclude that Elinor was mistaken about the cause of her death. Her seasonal distemper, whether allergies, asthma or something else that affected her breathing, was probably not as deadly as being jabbed with the end of a hoe handle. According to a physician who kindly agreed to study the depositions, Elinor's symptoms, along with the timing of her injuries and death, strongly suggest that one of the punches from the hoe handle ruptured her spleen. Internal bleeding would have caused the increasing pressure she felt around her liver, lungs and heart; loss of blood would have made her thirsty and faint. The increasing accumulation of blood would have triggered pulmonary edema, which was indicated by her difficult breathing and the fluids expelled just before her death.[45]

So, the coroner's jury was correct; the injuries sustained by Elinor shortened her days. Though the conflicting testimonies ensure that we will never know if Franck or William delivered the fatal blow, a major portion of the guilt must belong to William Dixson. He incriminated himself by surreptitiously discarding the shattered stick, and even if he did not punch Elinor with the hoe, he was the dominant figure out in that tobacco field; he could have stopped the abuse of Elinor before it ever began.

Perhaps the Wallop servants came to the attention of the court more often than most because the Wallop family consistently maintained a comparatively large workforce on their plantation. Although John Wallop was taxed on seven tithables in 1680, Mary Storey mentioned that he had ten servants that year. Either number would have placed Wallop in the upper crust of servant holders; just seven residents of the county had more than seven servants in 1680, and only two had more than ten.[46]

John Wallop lived for only seven years after the death of his servant Elinor, but even so, he outlived most of his family. On Christmas Day 1677, a boy named William Wallop reached "up to a haw Tree wth y[e] Cock of a Gun Being Loaded wth a slugg." The cock caught in the branches causing the gun to go off, and the slug "entred the Belly of the Sd Wm & went Slanting down into his Thigh w[ch] caused the death of the sd William Wallop."[47] A daughter Sarah lived long enough to marry, but died a few years later, leaving her husband with two small daughters.[48] By the time John Wallop made his will a few months before he died in 1693, his wife Rebecca, John

Jr. and Samuel were all dead as well.[49] Only Skinner, the youngest son, survived to inherit the Wallop land.[50]

Life was not easy for anyone on a colonial plantation.

Chapter Three

Margaret Teackle

The minister's daughter

Some things have not changed since 1695. Parents who leave for the weekend still run the risk of returning home to find their teenager has hosted an unsanctioned party.

It all started on a Saturday afternoon shortly after Mr. Thomas Teackle, a wealthy widowed minister, left his daughter Margaret in charge. She probably began by flaunting her authority before the servants, the slaves and her younger siblings, and while such a display may have been gratifying in its own way, Margaret yearned to impress her friends.[1]

Her thoughts turned to a young married woman named Elizabeth Parker and three members of the Doe family who were about to embark on a trip. Summoning a slave boy named Cambridg and a pregnant 24-year-old indentured servant named Betty Ballard, Margaret directed them to go a few miles down the Chesapeake Bay to deliver the invitations.[2]

No one mentioned the mode of transportation, but it is likely that Cambridg and Betty launched a canoe at the mouth of Craddock Creek by the Teackle home,[3] paddled out into the waters of Chesapeake Bay, and after briefly hugging the shore of Scarburgh's Neck, turned up Occohannock Creek to the Scarburgh plantation, where Elizabeth Parker's father lived.[4] The servants understood that they were to bring the guests back with them, and that is exactly what happened.[5]

It seems a little odd that Samuel Doe at age thirty-eight and his forty-year-old wife Mary found their way onto Margaret's guest list. It is possible that they were related to Margaret, or perhaps the invitation was really aimed at Mary's daughter. Whatever the case, Margaret clearly hoped to see the Does; Samuel Doe later testified that the two servants had urged them to "come forthwith to Margret Teagles for she would speak with them before y^r depon[en]t & wife went away."[6]

Elizabeth, the wife of Phillip Parker, received the other invitation. Probably only a little older than Margaret, she was the granddaughter of Col. Edmund Scarburgh, the brilliant but erratic "Father of Accomack County," who almost 40 years earlier had accused Thomas Teackle, then a 26-year-old minister, of trying to poison him and committing adultery with his wife. Margaret and Elizabeth may have been oblivious to past inter-family tensions, but it seems likely that the minister's bitter memories had lingered.[7]

Though Elizabeth was anxious to accept the invitation, she dutifully refused to go until her father returned, and the servants settled down to wait. Judging by the sun, they figured it was about an hour later that Elizabeth's father came home, and she was ready to go.

Accompanying the guests up the bay was a Negro boy belonging to Elizabeth's brother-in-law, Richard Bayly.[8] It was the exceptional musical talent of this unnamed slave that helped turn a simple visit into a party. His skill with the violin even overshadowed his identity; in the many depositions regarding Margaret Teackle's party, manual laborers, servants and other slaves are mentioned by name, but Mr. Bayly's Negro boy was consistently identified only as "the Fiddler."

The Bayly family owned land adjacent to the Teackles, just up Craddock Creek; no doubt this was the Fiddler's intended destination.[9] Margaret, however, seized upon his fortuitous arrival and took pains to "desire & request $y^e s^d$ Negro boy to stay & play upon his fidle." Afraid of angering his master, and knowing he would have to go home to retrieve his fiddle, which didn't even have strings, the Fiddler at first rejected the idea. Determined to have her way, however, Margaret turned to her friend for help in convincing the reluctant slave. She "did desire Eliza: Parker to stay & Keepe $y^e s^d$ Negro boy."

"He is not mine, nor at my disposing," Elizabeth replied. "If he was, I would Keep him." But she then turned to the Fiddler and made an offer, "If you will stay, I will speak to my Brother [in-law] not to be angry."

With the further inducement of "silke to string his fidle & three or foure yards of ribbin & two or three yards of lace," the Fiddler finally agreed, and someone was sent up the creek to fetch his instrument.

In the meantime, supper was served; while no one thought to record the menu, the indignant minister later called it a feast. Margaret's guests must have enjoyed the best of the minister's liquid refreshments and the choicest fare from his larder. In addition to the visitors, the diners included Margaret's cousin Jane Hall and John Addison, a 40-year-old workman who had just finished some work at the house. Besides the Teackle slaves and servants, Margaret's younger siblings, a brother and two sisters, must have been present as well.[10]

They had finished feasting, the fiddle had arrived, and the fun had only just begun when James Fairefax came for the Fiddler. His master apparently had discovered the slave's whereabouts shortly after someone had carried the fiddle away. Facing the loss of their musician, Elizabeth laid aside her former qualms about the Fiddler not being at her disposal and put up a bold front. She told Fairefax that she "had borrowed the Fidler of her sister Ursula Bayly, wife of the said Capt. Richard Bayly, and he [the Fiddler] should not goe with her will."

Afraid that the mounting pressure might induce the Fiddler to hurry home, Elizabeth pulled "a bitt of Spanish money out of her pockett & gave [it to] ye fidler . . . to oblige him to stay, & thereupon the fidler stayed." Having convinced the Fiddler to defy his master, Elizabeth proceeded to persuade messenger James Fairefax to join the party, too.

With the Fiddler safely retained, the merriment resumed. Margaret's cousin reported that "after Supper they went to dauncing." The servant Betty claimed that "they danct about two or three houres," but workman John Addison, who was trying to get some sleep, complained that "Eliz. Parker & company continued danceing & merry most of the Saturday night whilest this depon[en]t staid up in the parlour of the Said Mr Teackles dwelling house." To the tired worker, the merrymaking downstairs probably seemed interminable; after arriving an hour late, the guests probably had dallied over their supper and likely didn't even start dancing till after Addison's usual bedtime.

It must have been well past midnight when the music stopped. If Addison rolled over and muttered a sigh of relief, it was because he was blissfully unaware of Margaret's next move. The party was far from over, at least for the womenfolks. Margaret urged her friends to follow her upstairs saying she would show them "her weding garters & her fine things." When the women entered the room where he was trying to rest, Addison beat a sleepy retreat down the stairs to a less populated part of the house.

Though Margaret was eager to show her finery to Elizabeth, Mary Doe, Mary Jones, her cousin Jane and even a slave named Sarah, she and her friends deliberately excluded Betty, the indentured servant. They not only closed the door, they locked it and plugged the keyhole. Margaret, whose father strictly controlled even the clean clothes she was allowed, may have feared that Betty would inform the minister of his daughter's forays into his secured trunks. Soon to become the mother of an illegitimate child, Betty would have had good reasons to curry her master's favor.[11]

Over the next two hours Margaret unlocked two trunks and a chest, emptying them of all sorts of luxury items. According to cousin Jane, Elizabeth asked Margaret for "fore Snips of Ribbon & two thread Laces." Margaret, who responded by giving half the ribbon to Elizabeth and the rest to Jane, also freely gave "a paper with something in it" to Elizabeth, who had not even asked for it.[12] Mary Doe reported that Margaret brought out a piece of ribbon and asked Elizabeth "if she would accept of a Girdel [belt] of ye Ribbin." Elizabeth said if it was for sale, she would buy it, but "Margaret Teagle desired her to accept of itt & cut of[f] a Girdle." Elizabeth, who had an impressive number of coins at her disposal, "put her hands in her pocke[t] & puled out a peece of mony for the Girdle" and offered it to Margret, who told Elizabeth to give the money to her cousin Jane.

Jane also recalled the incident, saying that "Margret Teackle opened a small Trunke in the Hall chamber and tooke a broad peece of Ribbon out & cutt of[f] about a yard & a quarter of it which she sold to ye sd Eliz Parker for a seven pence halfe penny peece wch money the said Margaret Teackle gave this Depon[en]t."

During Margaret's showing and selling, Elizabeth's disdain for Mr. Teackle became increasingly apparent; she advised Margaret to be more assertive in dealing with her strict father. Declaring "that she should not regard her father," Elizabeth encouraged Margaret to be generous with the expensive items stored in his trunks. According to Mr. Teackle's later accusations, Elizabeth had enjoined Margaret to ignore her father's wishes by "goo[ing] any where & comeing at her pleasure, making feasts in her fathers absence and giving his goods away, slighting his comands and reproofs and at any time if he was angry with her, to give him as good as he brought."

To prove that Mr. Teackle was unworthy of Margaret's trust and respect, Elizabeth broke some stunning news. She informed Margaret that her father was about to marry a woman even stricter than himself. Still grieving over the death of her beloved mother, Margaret was shocked, frightened and more than a little angry with her father.[13]

Elizabeth spared no details, telling Margaret "that her father was suddainly to be married to Capt. Wallop de[cea]sed his Kinswoman & what a proud woman shee was and wore fringes at the bindeing of her petticoate." With such a haughty and overbearing stepmother in the offing, Elizabeth suggested that Margaret "had best provide for herselfe by secureing what she could in friends hands."

The servant Betty had been eavesdropping. She heard "Eliza: Parker insinuate by way of advice to ye s^d Margaret yt ye s^d Mr Teackle . . . was a goeing to be married to Mr Wallops Kinswoman," who, she added, "was a Severe woman and y^t she would not let her [Margaret] have her cloth[e]s." Elizabeth then offered to keep Margaret's clothes for her "and further p[er]suaded her not to be obedient unto her s^d Father in any matter."

Distraught at the prospect of a cruel stepmother, Margaret readily complied with Elizabeth's suggestions. How else could she prevent her own clothes from falling into the clutches of that heartless woman? And while she might not be able to keep the interloper from taking her dead mother's place, Margaret could certainly hinder her enjoyment of the previous Mrs. Teackle's treasured possessions.

As Margaret's desperation grew, so did her generosity. Mr. Teackle, who came to hold Elizabeth Parker legally responsible for the giveaway, subsequently submitted a lengthy list of missing items to the court. He accused her of unlawfully taking gold and silver money, five pairs of kid leather gloves, an amber necklace that had belonged to Margaret's mother, a long black sarsenet scarf, twelve yards of black silk, fine holland cloth, two

broad laces, various trims, three kinds of thread, a white flowered gauze
hood, a dozen silk laces, three pieces of lawn and cambric, several parcels
of satin and taffeta ribbon, a piece of narrow red satin, silver ribbon, knots
of ribbon for decorating clothing, six small hanks of fine silk of several
colors, a new lace cap belonging to Margaret, enough lace to go three times
around another cap and a pocket handkerchief belonging to Teackle himself.

At some point in the giveaway, Cousin Jane left the little group and
"went downe & stayed a considerable time, and when she went up againe,
she found them all up staires as she left them." While she was gone,
Margaret had given Elizabeth "a muslin Cap with a broad Lace on it about
a yard" along with "another peece of smal Lace to put under that broad Lace
. . . to make a new fashion Cap for her."

After showing Elizabeth "her mothers Child bed mantle y^t she was a
working in Gould & Silver," Margaret opened a trunk and took out "some
bitts of old Ribbin."

Elizabeth came right out and said, "Give me sume of y^t, a bitt to make
me a Garter."

Margaret replied, "Take it all."

"A little will serve my Turne," responded Elizabeth, who nonetheless
accepted the ribbon, part of which she immediately gave to Mary Doe for the
use of her daughter.

Even though Margaret and her friends lived an ocean away from stylish
European girls, fashion was still paramount. Margaret requested Elizabeth
to "alter her sume head dresses for she had none but old fashen Skull Caps
to goe to church in." Elizabeth agreed, and asked Margaret "to change a
cupple of fine neadles for a cupple of corse ones" when she went to a trunk
to fetch thread for the task.

After Margaret and her friends had been in the upstairs chamber for
about two hours, Betty became curious and went up to see what they were
doing. "And when [I] came up found ye dore fast shut and the latch hole
stopped [so] y^t [I] could not see w^t they ye aforesd p[er]sons were adoeing."
Not to be put off so easily, the servant "askit them to let [me] in." Though
she could not exactly tell whose voice answered her, she thought it was
Elizabeth who told her to "goe down staires again for a little time, and then
[you] should be let in."

The servant did as she was told, "and some small time after came up
again and findeing the Doore open went in and found ye aforesd p[er]sons in
the same roome where [I] found one Trunck in the said roome open; all the
cloaths were taken out. [I] then and there saw ye s^d Eliza: Parker had in her
Lap in her apron some Ribbon & Spice, but Know not what Quantity of
Ribbon & Spice." The servant remembered what the ribbon looked like,
however. One piece was green worked in with white and another was yellow
and black.

Mary Doe saw "Marg[ret] Teagle take Some poore hores lace & give it to Eliza Parker to put upon Some drawn worke." Margret's next request provided a glimpse into her father's character and the tension that existed in the preacher's household. "Margret Teagle did importune Eliza Parker to cutt her Cusin Jane Hall a black hoode for she durst not give he[r] one of her owne for feare her father should know it. [Then] Margret Teagle & Eliza Parker went in a rume to take ye silk out of ye chest for to cutt itt out. After ye hood was cutt out Margret Teagle tooke ye remainer & put it into ye chest & in turning ye Key up & down she could not gett it out, the s^d Margret Teagle crying and saying y^t was part of her fathers text y^t made ye Key do soe bad." By this time it was Sunday morning and Margret's conscience may have been stirring.

Cousin Jane, whose room and board apparently depended on Mr. Teackle's reluctant hospitality, told a little different story, omitting the part about her own hood and shifting all the blame to Elizabeth. In her rambling and disjointed statement, Jane said she saw "Eliz: Parker receive a Key of a chest from Margret Teackle which chest shee unlocked and ye s^d Margaret tooke out a peece of black silke and ye s^d Eliz Parker desired her to give her as much of that black silke as would make her a hood and the s^d Margaret began to cutt it of[f] and said she could not cutt it even & gave it [to] ye s^d Eliz: Parker and she made an End of cutting it of[f] and tooke it with her." Next, "Eliz Parker asked Margaret Teackle to open a Trunck againe She opened overnight which Margret Teackle went to open and could not, but desired ye s^d Eliz Parker to open and accordingly she did but twisted the Key and Spoyled the Lock: and tooke in [my] sight a clove & a small blade of mace or Cynnamon out of the sd Trunke and then [I] went down staires and there left them and went up no more that morning."

Betty saw Elizabeth Parker "take out the s^d Ribbon & mace but did not see her take any of the cloth[e]s wthin menconed out of ye s^d Trunke." The servant went on to relate how she saw Elizabeth drop some silk thread and lace from her pocket. When Betty picked up the lace and thread and asked who they belonged to, Elizabeth said it was hers, reached out and "put it up."

After his fitful night's sleep, John Addison awoke that Sunday morning and discovered that, in his haste to surrender the upstairs chamber to the invading ladies, he had forgotten his belt. "Goeing up into ye parlour chamber of the said Mr Teackle, where he had layen, for his belt wch he had left in ye s^d Chamber," Addison came upon Margret Teackle "sitting by a Trunke crying bitterly, and the s^d Eliz: Parker & Mary Doe . . . with her." Addison, "pittying the said younge Gentlewoman . . . asked her the occasion of her lamentacon who replyed the Trunke was open and she could not lock it nor get the Key out and therefore wished her self dead for feare or dread of her fathers anger." No one made light of Margaret's distress; she may have been foolish and immature, but she was undoubtedly well acquainted with her father's disposition.

Her friends endeavored to put things right. "Striving to gett out the Key some of them were concluding to send ye Lock to ye smith takeing the Key to be broke in it." When Margaret said she had no money to pay the smith, Elizabeth offered to lend her a "bitt or two."

With the money in hand, Margaret turned to Samuel Doe, who testified that she came "with a Key and desired [me] to carry it to ye smiths to mend it and gett it mended before her father came home & she would pay [me] anything as [I] would axe, and alsoe Marget Teagle gave [me] two bitts of mony for the smiths pay." But he never got the chance to run the errand.

Margaret, in her desperation, suddenly remembered the workman, who was presumably adept with tools, and asked Mary Doe to call "John Addeson up to sea w^t he could doe about ye Lock."

In the confusion, Betty had returned to the upstairs chamber and "did see Mrs. Parker att a Chest pulling ye Key out y^t was broke within ye Lock and could not get it." Frustrated, Elizabeth asked Hugh Egleston, Mr. Teackle's mulatto servant, "to gett it out if he could." Hugh, who emerges as something of a hero in this crisis, managed to take "ye Lock of[f] and mended the Lock and wards of the Key and put it on againe and lockt it."

Hugh's work was not yet finished. During the trunk raid of the previous night, the women had broken two locks. "There being a Trunk in ye s^d same Condition, [Elizabeth] desired to have them both mended, which ye s^d Hugh with ye help of John Adison did as well as they could."

Hugh then offered Margaret some advice. "Hugh desired his M[istress] Margret to put up ye Keys till ye ould Devill came there himselfe to goe to ye chest." Clearly, Hugh Egleston's opinions of Mr. Teackle were not so different from those of Margaret, who immediately started "crying & saying y^t her father would not allow her nor her sister clen close [clean clothes] to put on, wch was not so in her mothers time."

In all fairness, it must be said that Mr. Thomas Teackle served the community for many years as a minister, and, aside from the apparently unfounded accusations of assault and adultery, he enjoyed the respect and admiration of his flock. In his public life he was perceived as an honest, learned man.[14] His parishioners and associates, however, could look only on the minister's outward appearance. Perhaps the members of his own household had gotten a glimpse of Mr. Teackle's heart.

Those who were part of his private life–neighbor Elizabeth Parker, daughter Margaret, and servant Hugh Egleston–apparently found little to admire. To them Mr. Teackle was aloof, intimidating, arbitrary, inconsiderate and unforgiving; character flaws rise to the surface when a man feels safely hidden from the public eye. Ironically, Mr. Teackle himself, by indignantly summoning witnesses to describe the pilfering in his home,

ensured that sworn testimonies would cast shadows on his character for
centuries to come.

On that first Sunday in February 1694/95, Mr. Teackle was probably
standing in some distant pulpit and well into his sermon before the party at
home came to an end. John Addison testified that Elizabeth and those with
her stayed till "Sabbath day after breakfast till about ten or Eleven a Clock
in ye forenoone."

One would have thought that, with the trunks repaired, Margaret could
have ordered the servants to clean the house while she enjoyed a peaceful
Sunday afternoon nap. But not so. Though Margaret's friends were leaving,
trouble had come to stay. After Addison had eaten "his breakfast and was
ready to come away with ye rest of the company, the s^d M[istress] Margaret
Teackle was lamentinge and crying as much or more then she did before. [I]
asket her ye reason & she replyed she had lost the Key of the Trunke wherein
her father put all his Keys." And that was the way her friends left her.

Apparently Margaret or one of the servants recovered the lost key, for
it was in one of Mr. Teackle's pockets a little more than two weeks later,
when Elizabeth Parker came for another overnight visit and again took
advantage of Mr. Teackle's absence. Several months later when he
interrogated Cousin Jane before the court, Teackle mentioned this visit and
claimed that Elizabeth had taken "the Key of his Trunke, where his other
Keys were, out of his pockett & a third time cause[d] his trunks & Chests to
be opened, out of which shee got an apron full of things & carried [them]
away wth her ye next morning."

Jane confirmed that Elizabeth had come on February 19, but claimed she
took "not an apron full but some things in an apron." Jane also admitted that
Elizabeth, seeking to keep her forays a secret, had requested Jane's
cooperative silence.

Although Elizabeth, Jane, and no doubt Margaret, took steps to keep
Teackle in the dark, he had learned the whole story by the first week in
March. We are not told exactly how he discovered the details of the dance
and the giveaway a month earlier, but it was probably the servant Betty who
enlightened the minister. She had nothing to lose and may have cherished a
hope that Teackle would reciprocate with kindness. Instead, a few months
later Teackle refused to provide any kind of support for Betty's newborn,
and took steps to place that burden upon the parish. As a result, Betty's baby
was almost certainly separated from its mother, nursed by a hired stranger
and sold into servitude till adulthood.[15]

No one gave a deposition describing Teackle's reaction when he was told
of the party, but there is no doubt that Margaret was right when she
predicted her father's anger. Considerably more upset about the vanished
finery than the dance and the broken Sabbath, Teackle sought out an attorney
and took steps to recover his losses.

On the 8th of March, he sent Cousin Jane to Elizabeth Parker to "bid her bring home all those things she had wrongfully taken, stolen and carried away out of y[e] said Teackle's house." The next morning Jane dutifully returned to the Teackle home with Elizabeth, who "brought several things with her in a white apron."

Mary Major, a 45-year-old neighbor, happened to be visiting Mr. Teackle in the parlor when the two girls arrived.[16] She noticed that Jane deserted Elizabeth and slipped into the kitchen, which would have been a separate building located near the main house. While making her way to the parlor, Elizabeth also noticed Jane's sudden absence, and nervously asked "several times why did not [Margaret's] cousin Jane come in."

Meanwhile in the kitchen, Jane beckoned to Margaret, who was also probably trying to stay out of her father's way. The two girls apparently concluded that Mary Major had no business witnessing Elizabeth's humiliation, and Margaret called out to her. Mrs. Major left the parlor and approached the girls to see what they wanted, but when Margaret let slip the purpose of Elizabeth's visit, Mrs. Major indignantly "turned about again" and hurried back to the house. She was not about to miss out on the drama in the parlor.

The distraction had cost her a few minutes, though. She testified that "before [I] came into the house againe, the goods was layed down upon a Trundle bed & [I] heard Eliza. Parker Say here is the things and wished she never meddled wth them."

Turning to Elizabeth and Mary Major, Mr. Teackle "bid them bring [the goods] to the Table." There the minister "made a pen & writ them down."[17] His calculated actions worried Elizabeth, who had simply expected to return the items and obtain the minister's forgiveness.

While Teackle was meticulously listing each piece of lace and ribbon, Elizabeth ducked out onto the porch with Mary Major and apprehensively asked her if she knew what Teackle intended to do. Choosing to believe the best about the minister, Mary, took a guess and erroneously assured Elizabeth that Mr. Teackle only "desired to have his things returned againe."

Elizabeth then said "she could sware by y[e] heaven" that she had returned all but "some poor whore's lace." By this time Mr. Teackle had finished his list and Jane, who had ventured from the security of the kitchen, was close enough to hear Elizabeth "begg with teares to forgive her fault & pass by the wrong she had done y[e] s[d] Teackle, desiring her father might not Know it & excuseing Mary Doe most vehemently and said the said Doe was as inocent as y[e] child that was unborne & had nothing."

Ignoring the tearful pleas for forgiveness, Teackle coldly told Elizabeth and Jane "y[t] he would take no Care of the things & y[t] they should take them."

Fearful of Teackle's intentions, Elizabeth and Jane appealed to Mary Major, saying "pray take them." Mary, "seeing the young women so penetent

& Mr Teackle['s] demand so reasonable," agreed and took the goods into her possession.

A few days later when Mary Major was visiting Major Bayly's house, a still worried Elizabeth again asked if she knew what Mr. Teackle intended to do. Mary, less sure this time, replied that she "thought Mr. Teackle onely desired his own." Elizabeth admitted to Mary that she still had a few "great pinns and some Thread & y^t she would carry them home y^t week."

Indeed a short time later Elizabeth gave Jane a few more items: "foure Rows of pins, three hanckes of thread, a paire of silke ferriting Ribbin shoe strings, & two snips of Ribbon about a yard & halfe & some whited browne thread." Jane took the trifles home and tried to return them, but Mr. Teackle, who was more interested in a lawsuit than ribbon and thread, refused to accept them.

Shortly thereafter Mr. Teackle, claiming damages of 500 pounds sterling, filed suit against Phillip Parker "for severall Goods illegally taken by the Defdts wife out of the possession of ye Pltff." Called before the June court, the Parkers failed to appear; it was therefore in September before the case went to trial.

The jury heard the evidence and decided that Elizabeth Parker had indeed illegally taken goods from Mr. Teackle's home. However, they did not agree with the inflated values the minister had assigned to the purloined articles. After reappraising ribbons and lace, hoods and silk, the jury awarded Mr. Teackle 29 pounds sterling, which was still a considerable sum. It would take a common laborer more than two years to earn that much.[18]

As it turned out, Margaret never had to endure the oppression of a cruel stepmother; instead she and her sisters and brother became orphans. A few months after winning the settlement against his daughter's friend, Mr. Teackle died. And there is evidence that his bitter feelings lasted to the end.

As his strength ebbed and the need for a written will became apparent, Mr. Teackle seemingly remembered Margaret's embarrassing party and found it difficult to forgive her assaults on his authority and his locked trunks. He certainly singled out his eldest daughter and slighted her. Teackle bequeathed an entire plantation to each of his younger daughters and the remainder of all his lands and houses to his son John. To Margaret he granted permission to live on a plantation on Craddock Creek only until her brother reached the age of eighteen years. If she happened to marry a man so poor that he owned no land, she could remain on the plantation for her natural life, but she would never own it.[19]

As the minister knew, it would have been laughable for a girl of Margaret's status to marry a man without land. Margaret, who was not assigned a guardian as her younger siblings were, was probably about eighteen years old at the time of her father's death. True to Teackle's expectations, it wasn't long before Margaret married. However, her marriage to John Stringer, a young man who had received 600 acres from his prominent grandfather, was brief and childless; by 1698, Margaret Teackle Stringer's husband was dead. The young widow next married Littleton Robins, the son of her father's cousin.[20]

In 1703, when Margaret's sister Catherine (then almost 15 years old) became dissatisfied with her guardian, she requested the court's permission to live in the home of Littleton Robins. Catherine had not made her choice lightly. Surely in her sister's home she would find someone sympathetic to her plight. Catherine's grievance had a familiar ring–she complained that her current guardian was not providing her with sufficient clothes.[21]

The records provide only a few clues regarding the rest of Margaret's short life. She died sometime before May 1708, when her second husband brought a suit for 4200 pounds of tobacco against Joseph Milby, who claimed "that the legacy left by Thomas Teagle of 1000 gallons of cider yearly to his daughter Margret is wholly extinct & determined by ye death of ye said Margret." Milby insisted that Robins had no claim to the 700 pounds of tobacco per year that Milby was formerly obliged to pay to Margaret. The court, however, ruled that the legacy was not terminated by Margaret's death and ordered Milby to pay 3500 pounds of tobacco to Robins.[22] If this was the amount due since Margaret's death, she may have died in 1703. The amount requested by Littleton, however, suggests that Margaret died earlier than that, maybe even before her younger sister echoed Margaret's love of fashion.

Chapter Four

Mary Calvert Supple

Clandestinely Married Servant

Not much is known about Mary Calvert directly, but clues in the records left by her father and her husband help flesh out her life. In the 1600's, women's lives usually were defined and overshadowed by their men. In this regard, Mary was typical.

In the late 1640's, when Mary's father was in his thirties, he began appearing in the court records on the Eastern Shore of Virginia; by the 1650's, Christopher Calvert was busily engaged in enlarging his land holdings.[1]

His daughter Mary was born in 1656,[2] just a year after her father patented 800 acres on which the historic town of Onancock now stands.[3] Calvert, who started his family later than most men of his time,[4] must have doted on Mary and her brother Charles.[5] They were still toddlers when he divided the Onancock property and gave each child half.

Baby girls rarely owned that much land, and it would seem that Mary was destined for a comfortable childhood and an early marriage to some ambitious planter. Her real future, however, was quite different.[6]

Beginning in the 1660's, Christopher Calvert's debts began to accumulate, and by the early 1670's the family's prosperity seems to have been eroding.[7] It is likely, however, that their attitude toward servitude had as much to do with Mary's destiny as their economic situation.

During Mary's early childhood, her parents owned a servant girl who was also named Mary.[8] This maid, who must have helped tend young Charles, Mary and their new brother John, was treated so indulgently by the Calverts and their close friends that she hardly seemed a servant at all. The Calverts repeatedly gave her leave to travel around the county to visit different ladies. In addition, Anthony Hodgkins, the godfather of baby John Calvert, singled out Maid Mary and gave her a ewe lamb, a gift generally reserved for a child whose future you cared about.[9]

It could be that Mary's frequent excursions were not merely pleasure jaunts. Especially after she became ill in the early summer of 1661, she may have been seeking medical attention. When George Parker inquired about Mary's health, Mrs. Calvert said that "She had little of a feaver after blooding." And then, not even sure of the name of the newly married lady that Mary was currently visiting, she added, "I know not how she now doth, for shee is gonne downe to one y' was Mrs. Clark." Unfortunately, Mary was not doing well; some time after this conversation, she succumbed to her fever, or perhaps her cure.[10]

After a brief court squabble over the dead maid's lamb, the original owner agreed to transfer possession to his Calvert godson, and Maid Mary vanished from the records without even leaving a last name.[11] It seems, however, that a general acceptance of Mary's favored status lingered with the Calverts and left them with views of servitude that others did not share. Because they had treated a servant so much like their daughter, it seems that they had few qualms about their daughter becoming a servant.

Mary Calvert was only five years old when the servant died in 1661; it was probably around a decade later when she became a servant herself in the household of George Parker, the neighbor who years earlier had been concerned about the Calverts' maid. During January of 1672/73, Parker was urgently arranging to purchase a wench still aboard an English vessel, "for I have att present more then ordinary occasion for her, my wife beinge neare her time of lyinge in."[12] It is possible that Parker acquired Mary Calvert around this time; the price he was willing to pay for a woman servant–2400 pounds of tobacco and a hog–might have seemed very attractive to Mary's indebted father.

Since their daughter's new master was a neighbor[13] and apparently a friend of the family, the Calverts no doubt expected that Mary would enjoy their own lenient brand of servitude. This may have held true for a while, but George Parker died in 1674, and Mary Calvert became the property of his widow Florence. With six underage children, Widow Parker needed all the help she could get, and she was unwilling to ease up on Mary's work load.[14]

Mary, however, was now eighteen years old, and she was focusing her attention elsewhere. She had fallen in love. The object of her affection was Garret Supple, a former servant with a rather colorful past.

In 1667, as a seventeen-year-old in Dublin, Ireland, Garret and two friends, the Murphy boys, may have been looking for adventure or perhaps seeking a brighter future. Unable to read or write, the boys did not understand the finer points of what they were doing, but somehow they found reputable agents who prepared documents stipulating that they were to serve Capt. Pitts for four years after arriving in Virginia.[15] Capt. Pitts did not abduct Garret and the Murphy boys; had he spirited them across the Atlantic into forced labor, he certainly would not have given them indentures limiting their terms of service.

The men who prepared his indenture obviously tried to impress Garret with the importance of the document they were handing him, but he boarded the *Dove* with only the vague idea that this paper was worth something.

For the times, Garret's term of service may have been a fair one, but the accommodations aboard ship, especially for the servant class, soon became unbearable. As the *Dove* made its way toward Virginia, the water supply ran short, and Garret craved the water allotted to the higher class travelers. In his desperation, the Irish teenager pulled out his indenture–that piece of paper that the men in Dublin had considered so valuable–and in an act that the more educated passengers must have considered naive and laughable, tried to trade it for something to drink.

More than four years later, one of those passengers, a tavern keeper and mariner named Ambrose White, well remembered Garret's indenture. White swore that he had seen it repeatedly because "Garrett Suple did often shew itt and proffer itt to sell on board ship for water."[16]

A very thirsty Garret finally arrived in Virginia on the 23rd of April 1667.[17] He recovered from his voyage, but he came to doubt the worth of his indenture; because no one else wanted it, he concluded it was not as valuable as he had been led to believe.

Consequently, when Ann Toft paid Capt. Pitt for the three young Irishmen and claimed them as servants, Garret didn't mention his indenture. Nor did he bring it up when she took him and his friends to court a month later to have their ages officially determined. Probably just happy to be alive with plenty of water to drink, Garret, when questioned by the justices, merely told them that he was seventeen years old. Completely unaware of the purpose of the proceedings, he failed to speak up or do the math when the court stated he came to Virginia with no indenture and then ordered him to serve his mistress till he reached the age of twenty-four. Of course, Garret wasn't alone in his oblivion; the Murphy boys didn't say anything either.[18]

During the next four years Garret learned about the rigors of servitude on a large plantation, and, when it became clear that he was expected to serve seven years, not four, he began to understand what was so important about that old piece of paper. Unfortunately, long before the document's real value dawned on him, Garret had carelessly lost it.

Desperate to avoid serving the extra time, Garret managed to capitalize on his former misery and ignorance. While the *Dove*'s water shortage had driven him into misguided attempts to sell his indenture, it had also ensured that the document was readily recalled by Ambrose White, who willingly came to court in November 1671, and swore he was certain that Garret had come to Virginia with a four-year indenture.[19]

By then Garret had served several months beyond the specified four years, so the court ordered his master to pay him 200 pounds of tobacco, that year's taxes, and court costs in addition to the corn and clothes that freed servants customarily received to help them begin a new life.[20]

A few months later, the administrators of his former master brought suit against Garret Supple in an apparent attempt to reclaim his service. Ambrose

White again appeared in court and, along with another witness, reconfirmed the existence of the indenture he had seen aboard the *Dove*. Finally, Garret Supple's freedom was assured.[21]

During the next two years the former servant maintained a low profile, but he did not wander far from the court that had set him free. And getting something to drink was still high among his priorities.

Unfortunately, Garret's proximity to the court became a problem in February 1673/74, when he and another colonist imbibed a little too freely. Because "Garret Sapple, riottinge & drinkinge, insolently behaved himselfe in presence of y° Court," the justices fined him 100 pounds of tobacco and took him into custody till he posted a bond for his good behavior and the payment of court costs.[22]

Three months later Garret petitioned to be released from his bond;[23] he had behaved himself well enough, so no objections were raised. Perhaps he was realizing that there was more to life than drinking and rioting. He had discovered Mary Calvert.

As 1674 began, there must have been plenty for Mary to do at the Parker place; her master was seriously ill and the newest Parker baby was not yet a year old. The sheer number of children and servants on the plantation, however, probably produced sufficient confusion for Mary to slip away now and again.[24]

We know nothing of how Garret Supple met and courted Mary Calvert, but they must have been seeing each other that spring and summer. They certainly knew that Mary's servant status was a problem; servants needed their masters' permission to wed. Married people could get down on their luck and become servants, but single servants were rarely lucky enough to get permission to marry. As a rule, masters were very jealous of their servants' time and did not like to compete with infants or spouses.

Garret and Mary must have been waiting for an opportunity to sneak away. It was probably no coincidence that they made their move around the time everyone's attention was riveted on the final illness, death and funeral of Mary's master. But their exact course of action remains a mystery.

Getting married in 1674, was not a simple thing in Virginia. Two years earlier a proclamation declared that a marriage would be valid only if the couple published their intentions three or more times in their local parish (fee: 40 pounds of tobacco) or if they obtained a license signed by the Governor (fee: 100 pounds of tobacco or more).[25] The only other option would be to strike out for parts unknown.

Garret and Mary's union clearly did not enjoy the Governor's blessing, so that avenue would have been ruled out. Nor could the two lovers have published their banns locally. Even if the Parkers were too preoccupied to notice, some alert gossip would have relished the chance to break the news.

Keeping abreast of your neighbor's business was one of the few sources of entertainment available in those days.

With a "clandestine" marriage their only option, Garret and Mary must have eloped to a community that did not know Mary was a servant. Although a fortune-seeking young man from the next county took a twelve-year-old heiress across the Chesapeake Bay and illegally married her within Virginia,[26] it seems most likely that Garret and Mary slipped across the border into Maryland, which was less than twenty miles away. In so doing, they were following a practice that occurred more often than one might expect.

By 1673, Maryland had become such a popular destination for Virginia couples that the Assembly requested a committee to negotiate with Maryland's Governor. They wanted their northern neighbor to prohibit clergy from uniting couples who found Virginia laws too restrictive.[27] Maryland, however, retained her reputation as a favored wedding destination for many years. Today, a historical marker at the state boundary on Highway 13, commemorates the "Marrying Tree," where couples from Virginia were married just a few feet over the line in Maryland, some of them without leaving their buggies.[28]

Though Garret Supple and Mary Calvert wouldn't have had the luxury of a carriage, they could have canoed to Maryland or merely walked the wooded roadways. Regardless of how they traveled, they returned home legally united as man and wife.

It would have been hard to keep a secret like that. Perhaps the new couple didn't even try. The news did not set well with Mary's mistress, who turned to the court in her displeasure; on 10 November 1674, she sued Garret Supple. With his attorney's help, Garret had the matter referred to the next court, so it wasn't until the following January that the justices found him guilty of clandestinely marrying Mary Calvert, the servant of Florence Parker. The court ordered that he pay his wife's mistress 1500 pounds of tobacco or serve her himself for one whole year.[29] The justices gave Mary no options; they ordered her to return to the service of Mrs. Parker according to the Act of Assembly, which probably meant that she, too, was to serve a whole year in addition to her original term of service.[30]

Garret Supple had known the sweet taste of liberty; just three years earlier he had entered court a servant and left a free man. Now his chagrin was compounded with freedom slipping away, not only for himself, but also for the one he loved. Naturally frustrated with the turn of events, Garret Supple appealed the court's decision in February.[31] Probably guessing that a favorable outcome was unlikely, he and Mary turned to their only asset, Mary's land.

On the 16th of March 1674/75, Garret and Mary Supple sold the land on which the Onancock school now stands.[32] The price they received for their

200 acres is not recorded, but it was probably substantially less than the 6579 pounds of tobacco paid four years later for the neighboring 200 acres on which the streets of Onancock were subsequently laid out.[33] One can only imagine how the Supples felt as they made their marks surrendering the land that should have been their home.

The next day the sheriff approached Garret Supple and made a demand that Garret flagrantly refused to obey.[34] Garret was probably ordered to deliver his wife and their tobacco into the possession of Mrs. Parker; he may even have been told, as another couple was, that he and Mary could not live as man and wife until she completed her obligation to her mistress.[35] Outraged by Garret's defiant attitude, the sheriff reported the offense to the court, and Garret's day became immeasurably worse.

He should have known better. The court had clearly expressed their disapproval of his drunken brawl the year before, but Garret now carried his defiance and anger into court, where it exploded in the faces of the justices. His rash actions elicited a swift and severe response. The court ordered that Garret Supple immediately receive thirty-nine lashes "upon the Bare Back well laid on." He was also taken into custody till posting security for his good behavior.[36]

Much is left unsaid in the old records, including the final details of Parker vs. Supple. It seems likely that the sale of Mary's land ensured Garret Supple's freedom, but the fate of Mary herself is less clear. A hint may reside in one obscure entry, however, which implies that Florence Parker felt she had been done an injustice. On 19 March 1674/75, just two days after Garret's traumatic day in court, Mrs. Parker brought a suit against Mary's father, who, of course, would have been the one who agreed to Mary's servitude in the first place. Could Mrs. Parker have been suing for breach of contract? Or was she accusing the old man of having a hand in planning the wedding? The timing suggests that she was going after Christopher Calvert to get Mary back. But, whatever Mrs. Parker's complaint, the court found no cause for her action, and the matter ended there.[37]

Garret Supple continued an active court life that year, returning three more times to answer suits against him, all of which were thrown out, including an accusation of assault and battery.[38] But apparently all was not going well financially. On 1 February 1676/77, Garret and Mary Supple sold another 100 acres.[39] A year later Garret, who tended to dally over his debts, still owed a total of 1396 pounds of tobacco, part of it to the tavern keeper.[40]

Five years to the day after they sold their first 200 acres, Garret and Mary sold the last 100 acres of Mary's land, getting 3000 pounds of tobacco for their home.[41] Subsequent records indicate that they moved onto a town lot in Onancock, not far from Mary's parents. Garret, who according to the deed was a sawyer,[42] would not have needed much land for a saw pit and would have found a ready market for his boards in a town where new lot owners were required to build a house or lose their property.[43]

Around this time both Garret and Mary, with their servant days well behind them, were called upon to serve as jurors. On rare occasions panels of women were appointed to investigate matters requiring female expertise, and in 1681, both Mary and her mother Elener Calvert served on the jury that viewed the body of Mary Burton's dead infant.[44]

Eighteen months later Mary made her last recorded court appearance in Virginia, and again, it was the suspected murder of an infant that drew her there. This time, however, there was no body, and the accused couple was trying to prove that there had never even been a baby. While testifying on their behalf, Mary revealed something of herself and the women of her time:

> The Deposicon of Mary Seple aged about twenty five yeares saith that yor Depont being in Labour about the seventh day of Septem[ber] last past, Margaret Pickering was at yr Deponts Labour very well in health to yr Deponts thinking likewise the Sunday following the said Margarett Pickering was at yr deponts house very well in health to yr Deponts thinking & yro [sic] Depont washing of her linnen some severall times did never see no more by her then might be seene by any other woman not being wth Childe at that time and further saith not
> August y[e] 18th 1681   Mary X Seple Her mark[45]

The first point of interest is the blessed event that had taken place nearly a year before. In her deposition, Mary referred to her "Labour" much as one would talk about a party or other social occasion, which, in fact, it was.[46] In colonial times a birth was an exclusively female event during which the midwife was joined by most of the neighborhood women at the home of the expectant mother. The ladies were there to support, comfort and commiserate with the mother-to-be, and, during the early stages of labor at least, to eat, drink and gossip as well. Women became well acquainted at these gatherings, which lasted for hours, and even days if the delivery was a difficult one.

Mary's neighbors clearly arrived well before Mary was distracted with pain; she took careful notice of her guests and eleven months later could swear to the health of Margret Pickering.

Another interesting point concerns how all-inclusive the community of women must have been. Their circle was not limited to upstanding matrons and ladies of good repute. Mary's guests who socialized with nineteen-year-old Margret Pickering could hardly have forgotten the scandal in her recent past. Married in Barbados the previous year and brought home to Virginia by her new husband, Margret had found herself living in close proximity to the other wife her husband had there. Margret continued to live in her "husband's" household, but was subsequently known as the "kinswoman."[47]

It would be natural enough for neighbors to periodically check in on a new mother, but it seems that a slightly selfish reason may have prompted Margret to visit Mary less than a week after the baby's arrival. Beyond the neighborly concern, was Margret wondering how long it would be till Mary was on her feet again and able work? And that brings us to another interesting point in Mary's deposition.

Mary was in a position to comment on Margret's maternal condition because Mary routinely laundered Margret's personal linen. Mary's statement lays bare her financial situation. Women whose husbands earned a comfortable income did not take in other women's personal laundry. Garret's earnings were so low, or his drinking tab so high, that Mary was forced to supplement the family income. Nearly seven years after her marriage, Mary was no longer an indentured servant, but she was still doing a servant's work.

Other things were not going well either. Shortly before Mary testified in court, Garret had committed some unnamed misdemeanor and had to post a bond.[48] The next spring he became involved in a "brabling and vexatious business occasioned by drink" and was accused of assault and battery. The case was thrown out by the court, but Garret still had to pay court charges and post another bond for his good behavior.[49]

The Supples, who had long since sold their town lot, went on to face other reverses over the next several years. Garret was sued, but failed to appear. Besides owing debts to the tavern keeper and the attorney, he was ordered to pay a cow and calf to a neighbor. He became bail for a debtor who failed to appear in court, and someone else sued him for unspecified damages. He had health problems, too; on one occasion, he sent a message saying he was so sick and weak that he could not appear in court.[50]

The only positive note appeared in June 1682, when Mary's father, Christopher Calvert, gave a cow and her increase to his grandsons Waitman and Garret Jr., the sons of Garret Supple. He did not mention Mary, the mother of the children, but such omissions were common in colonial documents.[51]

Years earlier, young love and restrictive laws had inspired the Supples to sneak off, probably to Maryland, and secretly marry; now motivated by debts and other problems, Garret and Mary again looked northward. By the late 1680's Garret was suing and being sued in Somerset County, Maryland.[52] Some years later, with the spelling of their name changed to "Sipple" the family had settled on Murderkill Neck in Kent County, Delaware.[53]

There is no neat ending to the story of Mary Supple. She may have lived only long enough to settle down in Delaware, even though she certainly carried genes for longevity. Throughout the years her father swore to wildly conflicting ages, but there is no doubt that he attained a respectable age for the times. Depending on which deposition you believe, Christopher Calvert was between 65 and 82 years old when he gave his grandsons the cow.[54] Mary's son Waitman outdid his grandfather by dying at the reputed age of almost 99 years, though there is the possibility that he also inherited his grandfather's tendency to lose track of time.[55]

What little we know of Mary's life was marked by oppressive toil and poverty punctuated by her husband's drunken riots. Yet, that was not her whole story. She could also look back on the glow of new motherhood, the joy of gaining freedom and the thrill of running off with a reckless young Irishman.

Chapter Five

Susan Johnson

The African Lady

Because of who she was and because of what she did, Susan Johnson was unique. She was an African who sidestepped slavery and instead married into a family of free Black plantation owners. And though her husband proved unfaithful, Susan had the courage and poise to rise above it all.

Though she was sometimes called Susannah, it seems likely that she was the "Susan Negro" who first appeared in 1661, in a list of transported persons along with "Johne Negro," who would have been her husband John Johnson. Her father-in-law "Tony Negro" was listed with them;[1] otherwise known as Anthony Johnson, he had a history nearly as old as Virginia itself.

Upon arriving in Virginia in 1621, Anthony was purchased to labor on the Bennett plantation on the south side of the James River. He had been working there for less than a year when the infant colony suffered a staggering blow. On March 22, 1621/22, in a carefully coordinated attack, Indians massacred more than three hundred and fifty Virginians. Of the fifty-seven people on the Bennett plantation, only Anthony and four other men survived.[2]

Anthony's good luck in war was matched by his good fortune in love. Later that same year "Mary a Negro Woman" joined the laborers on the Bennett plantation, and, in 1625, was listed as the only woman living there. Anthony may have taken his time wooing Mary, but, in view of the scarcity of women, he probably did not dare waste much time. Their union was a long and apparently happy one. They had at least four children and lived together for more than forty years[3] in an era that saw the average marriage survive only ten years or so before death overtook one of the partners.[4]

His master Richard Bennett undoubtedly influenced Anthony's move to the Eastern Shore. The Bennetts and Johnsons both arrived about the same time, but while Anthony and his family settled in, Bennett moved on to become the Governor of Virginia. We do not know when the Johnsons took their surname or the details of their freedom; the couple either fulfilled their time as indentured servants, or, if slaves, they were freed by Bennett. However it played out, there was clearly a congenial connection between the two families. Anthony and Mary named one of their sons Richard, and when he reached young adulthood, Richard Bennett gave his namesake a cow.[5] It is likely that their ties to the Governor played a role in the Johnsons' economic and social progress.[6]

By 1645, Anthony was well on his way to independence. A bystander observed Anthony and Capt. Taylor going into a corn field, and when they returned, Anthony announced that, "now Mr. Taylor and I have devided our Corne And I am very glad of it now I know myne owne, hee finds fault with mee that I doe not worke but now I know myne owne ground I will worke when I please and play when I please." Upon Taylor's inquiry, Anthony "answered saying I am very well content with what I have."[7]

Anthony Johnson may have been content, but that didn't mean he was complacent. He accumulated herds of cattle and hogs,[8] and in 1651, he obtained a certificate for transporting five individuals[9] and laid claim to 250 acres of land on Pungoteague Creek. This promising start was interrupted two years later, however, when much of Anthony's plantation was destroyed by fire. Devastated, the Johnsons petitioned for relief from the court, which duly noted that Anthony and his wife Mary had lived in Virginia for more than thirty years and were known for their hard labor and service. Because the loss was deemed so great, the justices excused Anthony, Mary and their two daughters from paying taxes for the rest of their lives. Since men, indentured servants and Negroes were taxed, but not white women, the conflagration at the Johnson place effectively gave Mary and her girls the legal status of their white female neighbors.[10]

The Johnsons had at least one other thing in common with their white neighbors. They were slave-owners. John Casor had been purchased by Johnson on the western side of the Chesapeake Bay about 1640, and like slaves everywhere, Casor wanted to be free. After serving Johnson for about fifteen years, Casor claimed he was actually an indentured servant, not a slave, and enlisted the aid of some neighbors eager to obtain Casor's service for themselves, and for a while it looked like Casor's freedom was a sure thing. Anthony, who feared the outcome of this trouble, initially allowed his wife, two sons and a son-in-law to talk him into setting Casor free. A short time later, however, Anthony had second thoughts, and upon his petition to the court, the justices lined up behind their fellow slave-holder. They sent Casor back to serve Johnson and ordered the meddling neighbors to pay court costs.[11]

Anthony's eldest son John was almost thirty in 1652, when he patented 550 acres of land near his father's plantation.[12] A white man who shared John Johnson's name tried to fraudulently take possession of the property, but Anthony's son successfully defended his rights. Demonstrating an understanding of legal procedures, human nature and county politics, John made it appear that the white Johnson questioned the competence of Col. Scarburgh, who had surveyed the land. Indignant, influential and outspoken, the Colonel saw to it that the rightful owner prevailed.[13]

John, who could sign his name, had managed to obtain some education,[14] but he still had no wife. A few years after John's brother Richard was punished for committing fornication with a local Black woman named Mary Gersheene in 1654,[15] John became acquainted with Susan, who, unlike Mary, apparently did not live nearby. The fact that he and his father were listed as headrights in 1661,[16] for re-entering the county with Susan implies that they made a trip to get her. It is possible that John, with his father's help, sought out a wife to purchase and take home to live on his plantation. Even if she shared the family's cultural background and mother tongue, it would have been a lop-sided way to start a marriage, and John may have persisted in viewing Susan more as his servant than his partner. Whatever the situation, by 1664, the marriage of John and Susan Johnson was in trouble.

On 16 February 1664/65, John was called into court and accused of fathering the infant of Hannah Leach, an English indentured servant belonging to Anne Toft. Though John did not deny paternity, he must have offered the court a rebellious attitude. We are not told exactly what transpired, but John could have lashed out against the severe fines imposed on biracial fornicators, or perhaps he balked at paying child support and the damages that Hannah's mistress claimed. Whatever he said, it was defiant enough for the justices to decide that "John Johnson hath appeared incorigable to ye Court in comitting ye sin of fornicacon It is therefore ordered y^t hee bee comitted to Bridwell their to be imployed in ye Worke of Bridwell tell ye further pleasure of ye Court."[17]

John was likely hauled off to prison immediately to begin the work ordered by the court. Susan was surely at work that evening, as well. When threatened by the loss of their slave, the Johnsons had called a family counsel; it is easy to imagine Susan's in-laws gathering around her during this new crisis to offer support and to help formulate a strategy. If she harbored any bitterness against her cheating husband, Susan set it aside in favor of doing what was best for the family.

The next day, after the justices' tempers had cooled, Susan appeared before the court to plead for her husband's freedom. "Upon ye peticon of susanna Johnson wife of John Johnson negro desireing ye Court will please to Release him from his Comitment, Whereupon ye Court doe order y^t if ye sd John Johnson shall put in security to save ye parish harmless from a base Child begotten on ye body of hanah leach and shall pay & sattisfie all such damages & charges as is by Law awarded & promise a nurse for ye sd Child & bond for his good behaviour all these Injunctions to bee performed wth paym^t: of Court charges Then ye sd John Johnson to bee released from Bridwell."[18]

Security, child support, damages, fines and a wet-nurse—it was a tall order. Susan did not have sufficient resources on hand, and it would take some time to meet the court's demands. Meanwhile John remained in prison to work and ponder his future, which now depended on the woman he had betrayed.

When the court convened on 14 March 1664/65, a man named "Morris Mathews entered himselfe Security for ye good behavior of John Johnson Negro, as also to save ye parish harmless from a base Child begotten on ye Body of Hanah Leach by ye sd Jno: Johnson and pay Court charges."[19] Susan's respectful petition and financial arrangements had rescued her husband from the full consequences of his impulsive and careless behavior.

Her husband's lover was not so fortunate. Because Hannah Leach had crossed racial lines to commit fornication, her punishment was doubled; she was sentenced to spend an extra four years in servitude and to pay a fine of 1000 pounds of tobacco instead of the typical 500. Hannah would have been whipped if her mistress Ann Toft, along with Ann's friend Col. Scarburgh, had not agreed to pay Hannah's fine.[20] This was not a gift, of course; Toft and Scarburgh, who were the reputed parents of three illegitimate daughters themselves, expected Hannah to repay the debt by adding one or more years to her term of service.

Hannah was still their servant five years later when an indiscretion with an Englishman produced another baby. Ann Toft again agreed to pay Hannah's fine, but things were getting complicated. At Hannah's request, the court clarified her obligation: she had to serve five years to complete her original term of service, four years for having Johnson's child plus one year to repay the associated fine; she had to serve another two years for having William Gray's child and a half year to pay her fine for that offence. Her obligations, which amounted to twelve and a half years of service, would be completed on 16 December 1674.[21] Unfortunately, two years before her extended term expired Hannah Leach gave birth to a third child.[22]

While Hannah was anticipating that third birth and dreading the consequences, John and Susan Johnson freely returned to court to confirm the sale of their 550 acres. On 17 July 1672, Anthony signed his name and Susan made her mark, a cursive squiggle.[23] They must have made a special effort to be there, for they had been living in Maryland about six years by then. John and Susan, their two sons, the elder Johnsons and their slave had moved to Somerset County, where Anthony Johnson leased a plantation that he named "Tonies Vinyard." When Anthony died shortly after the move, his wife Mary renegotiated the lease for 99 years.[24]

John Johnson, his widowed mother and his wife Susan began turning up in the county records of Maryland.

In December 1666, "Susan the wife of John Johnson" was subpoenaed as a witness in a paternity suit. John Cooper had sold his servant Susanna Brayfeeld for two years; when she gave birth, Cooper was accused of fathering the child, but both he and Susanna claimed it was another man. Susan Johnson's unrecorded testimony helped convince the court that Cooper and his servant were telling the truth, but Cooper's subsequent actions cast doubt on that conclusion–he refused to release Susanna's child to its "father" and two months later married the mother.[25]

In March 1667/68, John and two white friends were charged with stealing corn from an Indian named Katackcuweiticks. The following June they confessed the crime and reported that they had returned the corn; the court ordered them to deliver an additional two barrels for the Indian's use.[26]

The Somerset commissioners expressed no qualms about taking Susan's testimony in 1666, but in a 1670, land dispute they accepted her husband's testimony only after they interrogated him: "And before the takeing of his Oath the Commissioners asked him whether he has been baptized the said John Johnson made answer he was baptized; Afterwards they asked him if he did rightly understand the takeing of an Oath the said John Johnson gave them A Satisfactory answer & was permitted to Swear in the Cause depending."[27]

On 3 September 1672, "Mary Johnson negro of sommersett County in the Province of Maryland widowe the relict of Anthony Johnson" assigned power of attorney to her "wellbeloved sonne John Johnson." That very same day she drew up a deed of gift in which she gave a "Cowe Calfe" to John's son Anthony and additional cattle to her son Richard's two boys.[28]

One of the witnesses to her deed of gift was "John Cazara negro." He was still serving the Johnsons after more than thirty years, but it seems that Mary was treating him more like a trusted friend than a slave. She allowed him to record his own mark for livestock in 1672,[29] and four years later purchased a mare that she assigned to him. [30]

In 1677, John, the son of Susan and John, purchased property of his own in Somerset County, Maryland, and, in a nod to his heritage, named it "Angola."[31] The elder John and Susan and Mary, however, relocated to Delaware. It turned out to be Susan's last move.

Like most married women, Susan had remained in the background, and as long as she lived peaceably, the court basically ignored her. It was only after she died that she received any notice. Then, during the summer of 1683, the Sussex County Court focused its attention on Susan Johnson as the subject of a murder investigation.

Soon after Susan's death, John Johnson was implicated by two neighbors, one of whom swore he saw John strike his wife in the ear with the end of a rope. Suspected of murder, John was hauled before the court, but when a jury of women inspected Susan's body, and the neighbors' depositions were reexamined, the case began to fall apart. The twelve women reported that they had "endeavored to view the body of Susan Johnson and we could not discover one Sign of Murder." Perhaps realizing that his testimony was not supported by the findings of the women, the witness wavered and changed his story. When he denied "that he saw the Roapes End strike her on the Burr of ye Ear which was one affirmation of his Oath," the Court "accounted his Oath of No Vallew." Noting that the women of the jury and the coroner had cleared John Johnson, the justices accepted his promise to appear at the next court, where they too intended to clear him if no other evidence materialized.[32]

So many questions linger about the circumstances surrounding Susan's death. Did those twelve women really have any idea what to look for? Did the witnesses actually see John beat his wife with a rope? How well did John Johnson usually treat his wife, anyway? We will never know the real answers, but we do have a few clues.

Many colonial women dabbled in doctoring and could no doubt recognize bruising and other injuries, but they would likely have had very little experience investigating crime scenes. Justices generally appointed women juries because it was deemed more appropriate for women to examine a woman's body. It may be significant that the jury said they "endeavored" to view the body; it was summer, and we are not told how long after death the examination occurred.

While the witness reversed himself on one detail, there may have been an element of truth in other parts of his testimony. John's willingness to cheat on his wife and the shameful way he later treated his elderly mother suggest that Susan may have endured emotional, if not physical, abuse at his hands. About ten years after Susan's death, Mary Johnson went to court complaining against her son John, who had agreed to care for her, but instead had made off with her goods and cattle. John may have been cleared of murdering his wife, but the court did not let him get away with cheating his mother.[33]

While the typical colonial woman simply disappeared, Susan's mysterious demise ensured that we have at least a little information about her death. It is regrettable that we do not have more details regarding her life. We can guess that she was kidnaped in Angola and purchased as a bride in Virginia, that she told her sons stories of her homeland and, with her mother-in-law, clung to certain traditions that her English friends did not share. All we really know, however, is that Susan Johnson earned the trust of her neighbors, repaid her cheating husband with kindness and won over a panel of haughty justices with her intelligence and courage.

Chapter Six

Mary Beadle Cole

Serving the judges, winking at the law

Mary Cole had a front row seat at the county court. Married to the innkeeper who catered to the court trade and provided a place for the justices to meet, she literally lived at the courthouse and helped her husband serve food and drink to judges, jurors, constables and criminals.[1]

The thirsty gentlemen who thronged the inn on court days to purchase cider, wine, rum, ale and other drinks provided John and Mary Cole with a respectable income.[2] But Mary nourished little respect for the court or the law. She may have assumed that her friendship with the justices and her husband's generosity to the court rendered her immune to the penalties inflicted on less well connected lawbreakers. She was almost right.

Showing uncommon cunning for a 13 or 14-year-old,[3] Mary had wasted no time in gaining the upper hand in her relationship with John Cole, then a 28-year-old tailor,[4] behavior that may have arisen from her unsettled home life. The court was convinced that Mary's parents, Richard and Anne Beadle were still married, but Anne had taken her adolescent daughter and had moved in with William Satchell. William and Anne, who had just faced charges of adultery and bastardy, were soon to go their separate ways, however, and Mary's welcome in the Satchell home was tenuous at best.[5]

Even in her insecure situation, Mary was much less interested in marriage than John was, and, though he denied it, he attempted to buy her affection. In the late summer or early fall of 1663, he secretly approached 24-year-old Mary Bostock, a servant on the Satchell plantation, with several items wrapped in paper. He instructed her to give the things to "Mary Beadle and tell her I doe not give them any waies to buy her Love, but I freely give them unto her."[6]

The servant dutifully relayed both John's words and his gifts to Mary Beadle, who took John at his word and accepted the package. When she removed the paper, she must have been pleased at what she saw: two hoods, a round scarf and a long scarf complete with a skein of black silk thread for hemming it.

Mary's acceptance of the gift led John to assume that the two of them "were made sure togeather," but Mary did not see it that way, and when she failed to bestow the expected affection upon John, he wanted the hoods and scarves back.

When Ann Mellinge and her husband William accompanied John Cole to the Satchell plantation, William knew there was "some difference, betweene Mary Beadle & Jno Cole" over the things John had given her, but William was unprepared for the length of the confrontation. He waited "an hower or two on horseback for ye sd John Cole, who demanded & Required" Mary to return the gifts. Maintaining that Mary had "prov[en] herselfe falce," John was "very urgent for ye things."

Mellinge's wife Anne may have arrived on horseback, as well, but if she did, she dismounted and went inside where the real action was. She later reported that when John demanded the items, "Anne Beadle and her daughter Mary Beadle both of them denied y^t ever they had any things of ye said Coles" except for some linen that they had already returned.

Exasperated, Cole left the house and called the woman servant as a witness. The ensuing quarrel was summarized by Anne's statement: "Soe they haveing all many words."

Ultimately, "Cole said he never geave anything to her but upon ye acc[oun]t y^t she was sure to him."

Mary replied that "if she had thought he gave them to her upon y^t intent then she never received them of ye sd Cole."

Finally convinced that Mary was playing games, William Satchell stepped in and put an end to the squabble in his house. He turned on Mary and said, "Hold yor tonge you Jade, and gitt y^u out of ye house to worke."

Still waiting on horseback out in the yard, William Mellinge then heard Mary's mother tell "John Cole hee should not have ye things now, but he should have them an other tyme, or ye vallew thereof in tobacco." The court felt that was fair and ordered Anne Beadle to return the goods received by her daughter or to pay for them.

Once he got the items back, however, John realized that he wanted Mary, not the hoods and scarves. After rethinking his strategy, he gave the gifts back to Mary and then sought out the servant who had served as intermediary in the first place. Finding her in her master's corn field John confided, "I have given unto Mary Beadle ye things once againe, and if she will not accept of ye giver as well as ye guift let it be to her owne Conscience."

The servant answered that "It was well done, for in giveing of things and taking of them againe, you play ye foole wth her, and yor selfe two."

Mary Beadle eventually married her anxious suitor, but it was apparently only after she had legally taken possession of some very substantial gifts, a step that gave her a measure of financial independence enjoyed by very few married women of her time. More than ten years later in 1674 and 1675, she passed on to her daughter Frances and son John a horse and some cattle that her husband had apparently deeded to Mary before their marriage.[7] The children were well prepared to receive such a gift. Their cattle marks had been registered in 1673, when Frances was only two years old.[8]

During the late 1660's and early 1670's, when Mary was raising young children, the activities swirling around her had to be a concern. John had called himself a tailor in May of 1669, but an incident more in keeping with a tavern than a tailor shop occurred at the Cole house later that summer.

Mary testified that as John Wiltshire sat in the doorway, he exposed himself to Sarah Gilbert,[9] who immediately flung a porringer of water at him. Calling him a "nasty roague" and screaming at him to cover himself, she ran into the woods. Giving chase, Wiltshire rudely assaulted Sarah in the forest. Incensed at his behavior, the court ordered that Wiltshire immediately "receive upon his naked shoulders thirty nine Lashes well laid on."[10]

By 1671, small crowds were finding the Cole house a convenient place to drink and brawl. In November of that year, three men were arrested there for unlawfully drinking and fighting, and on a Sunday no less. On this occasion the crowd at Cole's house included nine named individuals and an unknown number of anonymous bystanders.[11]

An incident during the summer of 1673, must have given Mary further reason to fear for her own safety and for that of her children. Several men had come to Cole's tavern; many of them arrived on horseback, others on foot, but all of them were drinking when a shot rang out. A little later, someone noticed that John Stockley's horse had suffered a head wound. "Informed that his horse was shott hee stript of[f] his clothes sayinge that if hee did know who had shott his horse he would either strike him or beate him." Bystanders intervened, and a fight was averted, but John Fenn, the careless gunman, was later ordered to pay 300 pounds of tobacco for the cure of the horse, which did ultimately recover.[12]

A few months later Richard Southerne stole a sheathed knife from John Cole and "played some other pilferringe tricks att his house." Aware that the culprit was ordered to receive "Tenn lashes on his naked shoulders as a just reward," Mary likewise must have taken mental notes when he petitioned the court and got his punishment suspended.[13]

Immediately after they dealt with Southerne, the court turned its attention to John Cole and the boisterous behavior in his tavern during the recent Christmas celebration. Roundly condemned for suffering "rude and disorderly Actions in his house by sellinge of drink on the feast day of the nativity of our Lord," Cole was ordered to pay a fine of twenty shillings or to construct a new pair of stocks and have them set up at the courthouse before the next court session.[14]

Maintaining an establishment near the seat of justice may have been lucrative, but living there had its own disadvantages. Mary couldn't help seeing "John Stratton lay violent hands on [prisoner] William Norton pullinge of him by the haire of the head & strikinge of him in a violent manner." Afraid of lengthening his jail time, William didn't dare defend himself, but he found a champion in Mary, who reported Stratton's abusive behavior. Stratton retaliated by bringing action against Mary, who was then forced to defend herself in court, but the justices believed Mary, not Stratton, and dismissed the suit.[15]

That same year John Cole was accused of selling liquor without a license and at prices differing from those set by law;[16] he managed to refute both charges, but life at the ordinary continued to be stressful.[17] Open as their house was to the public, the Coles were vulnerable to thieves,[18] and there was always the pressure of providing food for guests, servants and even inmates. In the spring of 1674, John, the appointed jailer, complained that he was unable to find food for the prisoners. Recognizing the "Extreame want of provision in the County," the court ordered all plaintiffs to supply funds for feeding anyone they caused to be arrested.[19]

During the late 1670's business at the ordinary continued to be brisk. In fact, on one Sunday in 1678, the Coles attracted a larger congregation than the minister. An unnamed supporter of the church complained to a grand juryman that during the sermon there were very few in the church but more than twenty individuals drinking at John Cole's.[20]

A year later the payment of a routine fine for fornication hinted at the unusual financial independence that Mary Cole enjoyed. In fact, it seems likely that she was more capable with money—or tobacco—than her husband. When Ann Harrison could not pay her fine for bastardy, she appealed to several individuals for help. Among those who assisted her were John Cole with 60 pounds of tobacco and his wife Mary, who saw fit to provide 100 pounds.[21]

As the years passed, the Coles acquired more servants, some hired, some working off debts.[22] Mary assumed the responsibility of managing these workers, and this was when some trouble began.

In September 1679, one of their servants, Richard Johnson Jr., was seen to "kick Mrs. Cole withall giving her daring words."[23] The cause of Richard's outburst is not recorded, but later documents indicate that around this time the Coles were pressuring their servants to steal their neighbors' hogs, a crime that wise servants avoided.

A few months later there was more trouble with a Cole servant. An orphan in the custody of John & Mary Cole since 1666, when he was four years old, John PettiJohn eventually proved to be an eager hog thief and general hellion.[24] We can only guess what he may have done to antagonize a group of mariners—all we know is that they made a "Riot" and assaulted PettiJohn "in yᵉ Kings high way." Hoping for compensation, Cole filed charges, and it seems he was not disappointed. Victims of a shipwreck, the sailors had salvaged a considerable quantity of goods from the *Batchelours Delight*. The ship's master asked them to guard the merchandise, which they did for a month, and though they later swore they had sold nothing, it is quite possible that they managed to transfer some of the goods into Cole's possession in exchange for dropping the suit. Cole, who had already had the sailors apprehended, suddenly "for Severall Consideracons best Known to myself" dropped the charges and acknowledged himself to be fully satisfied.[25]

During the 1670's and 80's the court was held in various locations, sometimes at Cole's, sometimes not, though Cole eventually lured the seat of justice into a more permanent relationship with his establishment.[26] With the monthly influx of business somewhat uncertain, hard times descended upon the Cole household, and surreptitious hog hunts on surrounding plantations became commonplace.

In May 1681, John PettiJohn was found guilty of killing a hog belonging to a neighbor named Christopher Thompson. Since Thompson was both the hog's owner and the court's source of information, PettiJohn was ordered to pay him 2000 pounds of tobacco. It was only fitting that John Cole presented himself as PettiJohn's security, for even though PettiJohn had actually killed the hog, Mary Cole had instigated it all.[27]

The morning of 8 April 1680, had dawned as usual on the Cole place. Folks were expected to work before breakfast, so William Thorton, John Terry, John PettiJohn and William Yeo were out laboring in the woods when Mary Cole beckoned. She invited the servants to "to come & sitt downe & pip[e] it." When the men gathered around her for a smoke, she revealed the true purpose of her visit. She said, "Come let us contrive & get a hog."[28]

Though such a conspiracy obviously required secrecy, Mary further justified her furtive behavior by saying, "I am afeared y^t hore Terris wife well [will] tell if she should Know it." How John Terry reacted to this insult aimed at his wife went unrecorded; servants undoubtedly learned to bite their tongues.

The men followed Mary in to breakfast and after the meal met to conspire again, this time "under ye houseside whare she Dwell." By now Mary had selected John [Jack] PettiJohn as her primary hog thief, and was seeking a willing accomplice to assist him. Looking at the cluster of servants, she demanded, "Who will goe wth Jack to get a hog?"

Yeo and Terry refused, but Thorton finally agreed to go. His cohort's weapon of choice was an axe, and they all watched as PettiJohn cut the handle to a more manageable length. With that detail out of the way, PettiJohn and Thorton "sd one to ye other wch way shall we goe?"

Mary was ready with a suggestion: "Y^t blind dog Tomson & y^t ould knave or Rog[u]e Boman hath good hogs. See, get one of thires."

So, off they went, one toting the axe and the other carrying a rope or bridle, as if they were out looking for horses. Arriving by way of the woods,

PettiJohn approached a hog bed near Christopher Thompson's pasture fence where there "lay foure lusty barrow hoggs." Rousing the animals, PettiJohn threw corn among them and lured them as far as a small tobacco patch. He tried striking at the hogs but missed, so he resumed enticing them with corn. After the hogs were a good distance from home, he set his dogs on them.

The "doggs seised a whitish hogg whereupon the sayd PettiJohn tooke the said hogg by the hinder Legg and Knocked him on the head." That accomplished, "PettiJohn stuck him and opened his belly and pulled forth his gutts, and so halled him to the roote of a tree and threw junks of wood on him."

Three or four hours after they had started their hunt, Thorton and PettiJohn returned to work and informed their fellow servants that they had gotten a hog.

About an hour before dark the two hunters left on horseback to fetch the meat. "When twas darkish in y[e] Evening," they neared home, one of them carrying the hog before him on the horse. Cautiously leaving the road, they went down to the creek side near the Coles' house and threw the carcass to the ground. Until they knew who was in the house, they were taking no chances.

When PettiJohn "saw y[e] house cleare of Company only Wm Steavens in ann inner rome," he asked for someone to go with Thorton to get the hog. Cognizant of the penalty for stealing hogs, Yeo and Terry backed off, just as they had when Mary first suggested her plan. Finally, with a little help reluctantly given, Thorton managed to bring the hog into an inner room of the kitchen. There Mary Cole joined the group and noticed the unwilling attitude of her servants.

"What a pox is y[e] matter wth y[u] all?" she snapped. "Y[u] shall all help to hold it, for we will be all as deep in the dirt as in the mire." Accepting her logic and her position as their mistress, the servants obediently helped scald the hog, carry it into the milk house and dump its hair into a hole by the root of a tree.

The next day part of the carcass was dressed and served to William Stevens, who was presumably unaware that he was eating purloined pork.[29] John Terry's wife, however, was not fooled. She discovered the truth when she chanced by the tree and noticed the hog's hair.

That same morning, while the servants were working around the fence, Christopher Thompson happened by. William Yeo asked the others "if theire harts did not ake for killing y[e] mans hog & to see him ride by." Keenly aware of the crime he had committed, Thorton replied that "all the blood was in his face."

After agreeing that they were glad Thompson had been so far out of the way the day before, the conversation turned to the Coles, who appeared to handle their guilt remarkably well. Yeo summed it up when he said that "it is so comon wth ye sd Coles family y^t thay [do] not dred it at the sight of any man home [whom] they have wronged in the like kind."

It took some time, but word of the stolen hog got out. In spite of Mary Cole's apprehensions regarding Elizabeth Terry, it seems that Thorton, the accomplice, was the one who divulged the shameful secret. At least he was the first to testify about the details of the crime. His revelations only served to goad Mary Cole into attempting a coverup.

Approaching Elizabeth Terry and her husband in the kitchen, Mary said, "This will be a bloddy [problem] about [what] this rog[u]e Thorton had dun." She entreated the Terrys to be good–which of course meant be dishonest–and tried to bribe the couple into perjuring themselves. "Let us stick altogether," she begged, and promised that what they owed would be forgiven. "Terre," she declared, "y^u and y^r wife shall be free, y^u shall not pay a pound of Tobacco & I will p[er]suade Cole that y^u shall Pay none." And as a final temptation she proclaimed, "I will give y^r boy a mare Coult."

Unfortunately for Mary, her former assessment of Elizabeth's character was the more accurate one, and a matter of days later, Elizabeth Terry, John Terry and William Yeo all told the truth. Their testimony was instrumental in convicting John PettiJohn as a hog thief, but incredible as it seems, Mary Cole's role as his inspiration was totally ignored by the court. Her rapport with the justices was apparently paying off.

That is not to say that the Coles escaped all responsibility for hogs that went missing in the area. Less than two months later, on 12 July 1681, John Cole was forced to pay 1000 pounds of tobacco to Edward Revell, who had informed the court about a hog that Cole had killed.[30] Just two days after that, Cole had cause to regret posting security for the good behavior of John PettiJohn, who was arrested for urging his dog to harass or "sowl" a sow by tearing at her ears.[31]

That fall and winter the Coles and their servants were called into court again. Edmund Bowman apparently took inventory of his hogs and, after a little investigation, determined that he was the lawful owner of five or six hogs and a sow killed by the Coles two or three years earlier. But Bowman was unable to name the exact month and day of the crime, and John Cole got the case dismissed on that technicality. The testimony is still revealing, however.[32]

Forced to help dispose of evidence, Elizabeth Terry gave a deposition filled with glimpses of life in the late 1670's.[33] PettiJohn and another servant cautioned her not to "rid the gutts" but told her to throw them a long way from the house so they would not stink. Regretting this waste, Richard Johnson said he "wished the fatt that was upon the Gutts were at his home, for it would serve him to eate wth homine all ye yeare."[34]

With everyone working on fresh pork, the hogs' feet and ears had been stashed in the house and overlooked. After three or four days Mary noticed

this incriminating evidence and said, "Come Betty, lets put these feat &
Eares out of the way for feare y^r master should see them." John Cole was
certainly aware of the stolen hogs; it was just that he would take a very dim
view of a dozen or so hogs' ears in his house, especially when they bore
Bowman's identifying marks.

Accordingly, Elizabeth "tooke the Buckett on her head & went wth her
sd Mistriss to ye branch [creek], and wee kneeled upon an old tree and w^t
Eares [I] thrust into the ground were cropt on both eares & a hole in the left.
And further [I] heard Alexander Dun say y^t they were Majr Bowmans
hoggs."

Richard, who had looked longingly at the fat on the entrails, remembered
that Mary Cole ordered the cheeks of one of the hogs to be boiled and they
ate it for breakfast.

It is doubtful that the Cole servants were being fed so well a few years
later. At least we know their clothing was dreadfully inadequate. In February
1683/84, Henry Hansome, a hired servant of John Cole, complained that he
was not provided with clothing and proper lodging. The court agreed, finding
that "he was bare of cloathing being allmost naked." If Cole did not remedy
the situation immediately, Hansome was to go free. The Coles, however,
managed to bend justice. A year later the poor servant was still without
"necessaries." But instead of letting him go free as promised, the court only
asked Cole to find a "Rugg and Blancket" among other things or forfeit a
bond of 1000 pounds of tobacco.[35]

In November 1684, John PettiJohn was back at his old tricks, making "it
his continuall practice to hunt and range the woods & Killing of a hog or
hoggs." There was no question that PettiJohn had recently killed a hog and
brought it inside Cole's house where he left it bleeding on the Sabbath day,
but because the hog's ears were unmarked and no owner could be identified,
PettiJohn escaped with only a small fine for breaking the Sabbath. As usual,
the Coles received no punishment at all.[36]

By 1685, the Coles had fallen deeply in debt with 38,000 pounds of
tobacco due to John West.[37] Facing the loss of all their property, they started
hounding Lancelot Jacques for certain debts that he owed them, but he too
was short of cash. Like the Terrys, who were forced to work off their debt
to the Coles, Jacques became a servant, albeit not a very compliant one.[38]

What triggered the incident is not recorded; perhaps Mary Cole
unleashed her tongue upon Jacques. At any rate, he became violent with her
in front of her children, both of whom testified that Jacques struck their
mother "viollently on the face & flung her with his armes violently agst y^e
Chest & bedstead." John Jr. signed his name to the document, while his sister
Frances made her mark. Their story was verified by Katherin Hanning, a
servant woman who reprimanded Jacques by asking "if he was not ashamed
to misuse his mistriss soe bad." For some reason Jacques was judged not to

be within the compass of the law cited by John Cole, and the case against him was dismissed.[39]

Though it seemed the favor of the court that Mary had long enjoyed was finally eroding, her next escapade proved otherwise. In an age when even mildly defiant words were punishable by heavy fines or worse, Mary brazenly defied the court and received what amounted to a slap on the wrist for an act that even the court called "most notorious & insolent" and "in contempt of his Majesties Lawes & authority."

It was only natural that Mary Cole felt drawn to Micah Warder. He was her kind of servant. After suffering financial reverses (a fine of 500 pounds of tobacco for fornication),[40] Micah had become a servant and then a hog thief.

In September 1688, he appeared before two justices and confessed killing a hog belonging to Richard Cutler. Shortly afterward, when Warder confessed to killing another of Cutler's hogs, the court threw the book at him.[41]

Because Warder was a servant and unable to pay fines, the court ordered that he receive twenty lashes for each 500 pounds of tobacco assessed against him for his first offense. The justices did not specify the size of Warder's fine, but at the going rate of 2000 pounds of tobacco for one hog, Warder was in for eighty lashes.[42]

The court did not stop there, of course. They had a repeat offender on their hands. Citing an Act of Assembly made in 1679, entitled "an additionall act for ye better preventing Stealing of hogs," the court ordered that "the Sherriff forthwith cause him to stand two hours in the Pillory and have both his ears nailed thereto an[d] at the expiracon of the Said two hours to have his Ears cut loose from the said nails being a Second time convict of hog stealing."[43]

It was in the midst of this phase of Warder's punishment that Mary Cole found him. Long familiar with the court, Mary certainly knew how seriously the justices took their directives, how grave a matter it was to oppose them and how cruel their punishments could be. Sympathizing with a prisoner whose hair had been yanked by a constable was one thing; showing compassion for a thief nailed to the pillory by order of the court was clearly something else. Nevertheless, when Mary laid eyes on poor Warder nailed to the pillory, something stirred within her.

She walked up to that pillar of shame and probably spoke a few hushed words to the miserable lawbreaker. Two men standing nearby then saw "Mary Cole take up the haire of Michaell [who] was fastnailed to ye pilory and with her hand pluckt ye naile which he was fastened wth out of his Eare." She then calmly laid the nail on a plank and declared, "Here it is."[44]

In spite of the original order, which called for the piercing of both ears, the witnesses implied that Mary removed the only nail that held Warder fast.

Perhaps the sheriff was short of nails, or found it impossible to nail both ears to the same board.

Of course the court could not tolerate such a challenge to their authority. After noting that Mary Cole had pulled the nail fastened to Warder's ear, the justices sought a punishment that would penalize her for her offense and deter others from following her example.

Nailing Mary's ear to the pillory may have been suggested, but in the end the justices took a more merciful approach. Instead they ordered that "she stand two houres tyd fast to ye Pillory with her back thereto & her face to ye Cort house." The nature of her crime would be proclaimed by "a Paper fastened to her breast written in Capitall Letters viz for her contempt of authority." Mary was to remain in the sheriff's custody till she posted security for her good behavior and the payment of court charges.[45]

Though her two hours of shame probably seemed interminable, Mary walked away without nail-pierced ears, without scars on her back and without taking a dip on the ducking stool. The justices knew Mary well, though, and her punishment may have hurt more than we know, for at age 39, Mary Cole was cured. She wanted nothing more to do with the court, or for that matter, her husband's tavern. She took her youngest children and moved to the Folly, the nearby 500 acre plantation that she and her husband had lost to John West.

Seventeen-year-old Frances apparently shouldered her mother's responsibilities at the inn; she also proceeded to match her mother's talent for coaxing gifts from her father. In March 1688/89, less than six months after his wife was untied from the pillory, John Cole placed several items in trust for his daughter. The gifts included a side-saddle and bridle, a gun, iron pot, feather bed with bedding, a chest, a small grindstone, cattle, sheep, a mare and two gold rings. Frances, who no doubt enjoyed her mother's assistance in negotiating the details, was to share the mare's increase with Mary Cole.[46]

It wasn't long before Mary was busy arranging a transaction of her own. How she managed it is unclear, but on 10 February 1690/91, John West released "ye Folly where Mary Cole liveth" to John Cole on the condition he confirm the land to Mary for the future support of the Cole children. One week later, John Cole dutifully assigned the land to his wife and youngest children.[47]

The wording of the document reads like a will or a divorce settlement. In addition to the plantation, Cole was to supply his wife with a feather bed and bedding, a new "Square turned Table," iron pots and pans, six sheep and a spinning wheel. He promised to pay her a barren cow and 1000 pounds of tobacco for the current year; the following year she would receive 500 pounds of tobacco and a bull. The third year she would get only a bull or barren cow.

It may have looked like the Coles were parting ways, but the records indicate otherwise. Mary and John clearly had some kind of understanding. Established on her own plantation, Mary subsequently signed documents with her husband[48] and, at age forty-two, gave birth to another of his children.[49]

After her many stressful years at the tavern and courthouse, Mary must have appreciated the quieter pace of plantation life where the only "rude and disorderly Actions" were the childish squabbles of William and Robert, the twins Richard and John, and the cries of baby Angellica.[50]

Though Mary may have retired from tavern life, she did not drift out of the picture entirely. On 12 September 1693, when she and her husband sold their tavern at the courthouse to Gervas Baggale for 40,000 pounds of tobacco and then agreed to operate it jointly with Baggale's tavern at Onancock, Mary was very much a part of the negotiations. In their lengthy contract, Cole and Baggale agreed to purchase meat and liquor together, to allow themselves free drinks, to hold the "brewing Copper" and shuffleboard table in common and to provide four beds at each establishment for accommodating strangers. The joint venture became somewhat lopsided, however, when Baggale promised that his wife would do her part to run the tavern for the next seven years; any offer of Mary's help was conspicuously absent.[51]

Even so, Mary sought certain concessions. She carefully inserted clauses that would allow her to continue using the hand mill, the horse cart and the "copper" to brew beer for her family. She also insisted on a lifelong right to the pear and cherry trees on the old property.[52]

The fruit, however, was only part of Mary's attachment to the spot. A few years earlier the Coles had buried their eldest son John among the trees of this orchard. Now that the property was no longer theirs, they took pains to reserve the right to build a fence around the grave site and to be buried near their son.

After signing this document, Mary Cole quietly retired to her plantation and disappeared from the records. Tavern life had not been easy, and she had earned a rest from serving liquor, procuring pork, managing servants, outmaneuvering the justices and manipulating her husband. The date of her death is unknown, but somewhere not too far from the present courthouse in Accomac, Virginia, Mary Beadle Cole still rests among the moldering roots of a colonial orchard.

Chapter Seven

Mary Watson Hope Bonwell Mikell Hubancks

The lady who married a pirate

Mary Bonwell's first appearance in the records was typical enough. Her husband James, who was old enough to be her father,[1] had died, and Mary had come to court in July 1667, asking to be named the administrator of his estate. The court granted the young widow's request and ordered that James Bonwell's earthly goods be appraised the next week.[2]

The officials, tightfisted as they were, took such inventories very seriously; the property a man left behind was all that stood between his orphans and their need for public assistance. In Mary's case, the fatherless children and step-children were both numerous and from a tangled chain of widowed and remarried parents. The dozen or so orphans were born of four different couplings, bore three different last names and ranged in relationship from full siblings to no blood relation at all. About five years earlier, Mary, a teenaged widow with a child, had married James Bonwell, a widower with children as well as step-children from his first wife's previous marriage. Mary and James Bonwell had gone on to enlarge the family with children of their own.[3]

Even though she knew that most of her dead husband's estate legally belonged to the children, hers and otherwise, Mary surreptitiously took steps to augment her own share. Five months later she stood accused of "covertly and fraudulently" deceiving the heirs of her husband by giving an "imperfect inventory."[4]

Selling a few yards of cloth would seem like a trifling offense today, but Mary lived in an age when fine linen was guarded along with the family silver. No one mentioned how much she was paid for the linen she liberated from the Bonwell estate, but the amount was substantial; one of her customers offered 1000 pounds of tobacco for the remainder of the cloth. Though Mary had wisely refused that offer, she went on to prove that making wise decisions was not something that came easily for her.

The cloth sale had been only part of her scheme for circumventing the appraisers, and she couldn't resist gloating over her shrewdness to one of the linen buyers. Mary bragged that she had prepared for the inventory by making her own bed as "rich as she could" by placing one pair of sheets on the bed and another pair on the canopy; she had also hidden some new cloth in her chest beneath her clothes.[5]

When word of her deceit got around, Mary was called before the justices, but she was smart enough to behave with "humble submission" in the presence of those who questioned her. Considering her humility and lack of prior offenses, the court did not mete out the "severity of censure due" but only voided the first inventory and made Mary pay the court charges.[6]

Mary's appreciation of nice things and her willingness to defraud her own children, however, may have caught the attention of Roger Mikell, a local pirate in the making. Mary appeared to be his kind of woman, and less than four months later, in the early months of 1668, they were married.[7]

Mary's devious dealings and her affinity for Roger Mikell[8] would have been unbecoming for a proper young widow, but obstinate and self-serving, if not shady, behavior appeared to be something of a tradition in her family. Mary's father was Robert Watson, a schoolmaster with a penchant for collecting land certificates.[9] The statutes of Virginia encouraged immigration by offering fifty acres to anyone transporting a person into the colony, and Watson, who recognized opportunity when he saw it, took full advantage of that law. In 1672, he came to court, declared that he had transported himself into Virginia no less than eight times, and claimed a certificate for 50 acres for each time he had reentered the colony. This loophole was not illegal, and many colonists got a little extra land upon their return from a vacation or business trip in England, but eight times?

Watson eagerly acquired chunks of Virginia soil, but he was not enthusiastic about serving in the militia to defend it or working on the roads to improve it. He habitually failed to show up for musters and road repair duty.[10] Clearly preferring the more sedentary pursuits, Watson willingly served on several juries[11] and taught his daughter to read and write, though he never did bother to show his wife how to sign her name.[12]

Robert Watson looked quite virtuous, however, when compared to his daughter's choice of a third husband. Agreeing to marry Roger Mikell was one of the worst decisions of Mary's life.

In Mary's defense, we need to consider the man involved. Several recorded incidents suggest that Roger had something, whether uncommon good looks, an engaging manner, leadership ability or convincing lies, that proved especially alluring to women. It could also be argued that Roger's background, though somewhat unsavory, gave only a hint of what was to come. Before their marriage, Roger's brushes with the law had been limited to Sabbath-breaking,[13] a sharecropping venture that turned sour,[14] and fornication with the maid of his sharecropping partner.[15]

It was about a year after being fined for fathering the maid's illegitimate child that Roger won the hand of Widow Bonwell[16] and, at the age of 25,[17] went from a quibbling sharecropper to a landowner in charge of a considerable estate. About the same age, Mary was a matron with sufficient status to serve on a woman's jury called that December to investigate the death of an infant.[18] The outlook for the Mikells seemed good, at least on the surface.

It wasn't long, however, before the real Roger Mikell began to make himself known; he was fearless, forceful, and cruel. Probably powerfully built, Roger was especially given to violence. The year after his marriage, upon discovering two servants chopping a tree on disputed land, Roger boldly accosted them and violently wrested axes from both men.[19]

In spite of his brawling behavior, or perhaps because of it, Roger Mikell was made a constable.[20] If this position was intended to enlist Roger's fervor on the side of law and order, it did not work out well. Inside of a year, Roger had made an enemy in high places. Not only was he delinquent in paying large debts to Justice John West, Roger had allowed a prisoner of West's to escape. With West pressuring him for payment and questioning Roger's ability as a constable, Roger lashed out saying "if he meet Capt. West in the woods alone, he would pay him off and bang him." This threat to West's safety landed Roger in jail, but even as the court was arranging a bond for Roger's release, they were getting reports that what Roger threatened to do in public, he was already doing at home. In their very next breath, the justices ordered two men to investigate Roger Mikell's abuse of his wife.[21]

This first public awareness of their marital strife came to light on 17 March 1669/70, two years into Roger and Mary's marriage.[22] If the investigators prepared a report, however, it was never recorded. Perhaps they dropped the matter when Mary again fell under Roger's spell and returned for more abuse. It was an unfortunate decision that she repeated time and again.

A little over a year later, on 19 July 1671, Mary filed a petition complaining against her "husband for sundry great and unsufferable abuses." The court, which was also unhappy with Mikell for ignoring a summons, cited both charges and sent the sheriff out to apprehend Roger Mikell.[23]

The next day Roger was hauled before the court where it was stated that he had "contemptuously absented himself" when summoned for jury duty. The justices fined him 100 pounds of tobacco and went on to address his domestic behavior. Although the court noted that Roger had "inhumanely abused" his wife Mary, and even though they condemned his arrogance, finding "him nothing inclining to reluctancy or sorrow for the same," Roger received a lighter punishment for beating his wife than for skipping jury duty. He was merely ordered to remain in the sheriff's custody till posting security for his good behavior.[24]

Mary found refuge with her stepdaughter Ann, whose husband Phillip Quinton detested Roger and began plotting revenge for Mary's mistreatment. By the first week of August, Quinton had almost perfected a strategy by which he and his stepmother-in-law could effect Roger's arrest and imprisonment, but Mary squandered the opportunity by abruptly returning to her abusive husband. Disgusted, Phillip said, "for my own part & them that is with mee I will not take Roger Mickaell wives part any longer for shee is flown from Us & turned to him again, for just as wee had brought our business to a head, she hath left us and I will warrant that she will never have him at such a Lock againe: But for all that wee will have him to Prison to morrow for I will have revenge Upon him in behalfe of his wife yu shall see."[25]

In spite of his boast, Quinton failed to attain his goal. A friend probably voiced the sentiments of the justice system when he said, "That should be a Warning to him for ever medling atwixt man & his Wife." As if to show how completely Mary's loyalties had shifted, one witness reported hearing "Rogers Wife miscall [Quinton] in ugly groese Names severall Times."[26]

With Mary back home and under his control, Roger spent the next few months managing his growing wealth, collecting debts, acquiring servants and even serving on a jury,[27] but the domestic scene was not going smoothly. Roger's unmarried stepchildren, who undoubtedly shared in their mother's misery, began escaping from Mikell's clutches. In April 1672, George Hope, Mary's eldest son, went to court, petitioned to be freed from his stepfather, and asked that Robert Watson (Mary's father) be appointed his guardian instead. The court agreed and ordered Roger Mikell to turn over the boy's estate.[28]

It seems that the boy's upcoming petition had been a matter of contention in the Mikell home. On the very same day, Mary also came before the justices and swore "that shee stands dayly in fear: & danger of her life by reason of the Threats and frequent Abuses of her said husband Roger Mackell." And the familiar ritual was repeated: the court listened to Mary, took Roger into custody, made him post security for his good behavior and then released him.[29]

The next child to flee was a Bonwell daughter named Hickman; in June 1673, Roger was ordered to relinquish her inheritance. Then two years later, James Bonwell successfully shed Roger's guardianship.[30]

As the children broke for freedom, their estates were supposed to go with them, but their stepfather would surrender control only when forced by the court. Although Roger certainly must have found such reverses aggravating, it seems that the years were becoming slightly more tranquil for Mary. Of course, she may not have been seeing much of her husband. Many things were vying for his attention, such as the church (where he was a vestryman),[31] the court (where he repeatedly served as a juror),[32] the highway (where he was an inspector),[33] and the tavern (where he just drank).[34] However, the lion's share of Roger's time was likely consumed by a project dear to both his and Mary's materialistic hearts.

Roger Mikell was building a house. Situated on 1500 acres just north of Onancock, it was no ordinary home.[35] This brick edifice was still under construction eight years later.[36]

There was something about Mikell's house, maybe its grand scale, peculiar style or perpetual construction, that made it a source of amusement among the neighbors. In early 1675, John Parker enlivened a winter day by composing several verses about Mikell and his brick house, which he then read "in a Laughing Jeareing manner" to a number of friends. Word of this poetic endeavor got back to Mikell, who caught up with Parker at the tavern and accused him of libel. Parker denied the verses were libelous, but admitted "he had Enough to make a Booke of." When Mikell expressed a desire to see them, Parker obligingly agreed to sew them together and bring them to the next court.

That's when Mikell hit Parker with a lawsuit. The gentlemen of the jury, who apparently enjoyed a good chuckle as much as Parker did, found no cause for action, and the suit was tossed out. Still seething about the verbal attack on his brick house, however, Mikell appealed to the General Assembly in Jamestown, and Parker's little book was undoubtedly sent across the bay as evidence. Unfortunately, no copy of the verses was made for the county records.[37]

Mary's children, who weren't interested in living under Mikell's roof, grand or not, kept on leaving and squabbling with their stepfather. Roger unsuccessfully accused George Hope and Phillip Quinton of theft, claiming, among other things, that they were taking stockings and drawers "by my wife's order."[38] Quinton, whose wife's inheritance had been illegally detained by Mikell for more than four years,[39] turned around and sued Mikell for the estate. Coincidentally or not, a few months later, Roger and Mary Mikell signed a document deeding 200 acres to Phillip Quinton.[40]

Little things like family strife, lawsuits and debts continued to plague Mikell,[41] but by the spring of 1676, Mary's complaints of abuse ceased as Mikell began disappearing from the records, and presumably from the county as well, for several months at a time. He was absent until almost a year later when he was subpoenaed as a witness; on that occasion he refused to swear and was thrown in jail until he complied.[42] He vanished again and a few months later unwillingly returned to court in the company of the sheriff.[43] Gone again, he returned in November 1677, to say he still wanted his job clearing the roadways,[44] but the next month, Mikell, who was facing a lawsuit over a debt, sent someone to inform the court that he had urgent business elsewhere.[45] Then he was gone for a year and nine months.[46]

During his absence his taxes fell delinquent,[47] he was dismissed from his highway job,[48] and one more stepson selected another guardian.[49] Both the stepson and the tax collector told the court that Roger Mikell had left the country, and though Mary and her remaining children had not yet moved into the new brick house, they were almost certainly enjoying peace and quiet in the old one.

In the late summer of 1679, when Roger was expected to return, Mary no doubt became apprehensive, but she had no way of knowing how traumatic the occasion would be. For when Roger arrived home, he came with a vengeance and a new teenaged wife.

Mikell wasted no time making it clear to Mary, both in word and violent action, that she had outlived her usefulness. Terrified that he "would beat wound or kill her," Mary fled to a magistrate who recorded her complaint "of divers great & Sundry abuses from her said Husband insomuch that she went in manifest danger of her life by his inhuman & tyrannous actions & desperate cruelties & that she was necessitated for yᵉ preservacon of her life to absent herself from his house."⁵⁰

Acting immediately, the magistrate issued a warrant commanding Roger to appear before a justice, but Roger claimed he was sick and refused to come. Instead he sent two men, who (in exchange for a counter-bond of 40,000 pounds of tobacco payable by Mikell) agreed to post a bond of 20,000 pounds of tobacco to ensure that Mikell would appear at the next court and keep the peace till then. While accepting the bond, the court took pains to caution Roger against bothering Mary and ordered him to pay for her upkeep while she lived apart from him.⁵¹

Returning to her temporary quarters, Mary began seeking witnesses and accumulating evidence against her illegally remarried husband. It is difficult to keep such activities secret, however, and in the first week of November, Roger reacted with predictable fury.

Scorning the no-contact order and the hefty penalty for disobeying it, Roger mounted his horse and tore off toward the Ewell home, where Mary was in the company of two other women. Probably alerted by the pounding hooves, Ann, the lady of the house, watched "Roger Mikell leape his horse into yᵉ yard." Without dismounting, he "came to yᵉ Doore & called his wife whore & Bitch." Roger "then lighted of[f] his horse & came in & further threatned her & sayd yᵗ he would have her home & beat her worse then ever he did." Though terrified, Mary may have found the courage to reply, for Ann recalled that "other words passed." Whatever the words were, they did nothing to ease the situation, for "then hee Came and Struck her wᵗʰ a Cane severall Blows wᶜʰ is the truth."⁵²

Roger's violent assault provided Mary with two more witnesses eager to testify against him, and the bruises he left on Mary's person also must have furnished mute testimony in court a few days later.

That's when Mary appeared before the justices and informed them that "Roger her husband did actually marry in yᵉ Island of Barbados a certain woman named Margret here allso prsent in Court & the sd Margret did owne use & cohabit wᵗʰ as man & wife dureing their voyage & allso untill this prsent time ye s^d Mary y^t alive." To prove her accusations, she presented letters and depositions in which Roger's shipmates told the sordid tale.[53]

In April 1679, Margret Pickering Anderson was an eighteen-year-old widow who, though a resident of Barbados, had set her eyes on Virginia. Her father approached the master of the ketch *Unity* and promised to pay for the passage of Margret and her slave girl, Betty.[54] However, three weeks later, when the ship was about to sail, Mr. Pickering confided to the captain that he had no money and suggested that Margret be liable to the laws of Virginia once she got there.[55]

During this time, Roger Mikell, who was moving in the highest social circles on Barbados, met Margret and caught her eye. A wealthy Virginian would have been quite appealing to a girl in Margret's financial situation, and she hastily decided to marry the dashing stranger twice her age.

Before setting sail, Roger Mikell, James Gey and others were headed up to the Governor's when they met Margret on the path. "Roger saluted her & after him James Gey and in these words said, God give you Joy Mrs Mikel." Gey actually knew that joy would soon be in short supply. Acquainted with Mikell and planning to sail with him on the *Unity*, he told a fellow passenger that "Roger Mekell was married to ye s^d Margret Pickring & that he had the Lycence for their marrige in his hand." Gey then went on to predict "that when they came to Virginia he the s^d Roger would be troubled for he had certainly a wife alive there."[56]

In reality, the trouble started well before they reached Virginia. Having heard that Mikell was already married, the other passengers and the crew sailing aboard the *Unity* spent their idle hours watching the Mikells and gossiping about them. Among other things, there was considerable speculation about whether the couple had really gotten married, though it was commonly agreed that "during the terme of their voiage they did night & day ley togeather as man & wife in one Cabbin when they pleased." By the time the ship reached Jamaica, one young man, a little bolder than the rest, resolved to find out for himself.[57]

After nearly all the sailors and passengers had gone ashore, John Remney found himself alone on the ketch with Margret. They fell into conversation over a cup of punch, and he bluntly asked her if she was really married to Mikell. "Margret answered me she was married to ye s^d Roger & had her Certifficate to show." John did not reveal the rest of their conversation, but chances are good that Margret found out why he was asking.

Still blissfully unaware of Roger's violent temper, Margret confronted him with the rumors about his other wife. The exchange became heated, and Margret called Roger a "Cuckall." Though the term did not precisely apply, the slur was enough to infuriate Roger, who reverted to his old ways and fell to beating his new wife just like he had battered his old one.

From Roger's viewpoint, this display of violence had the desired effect; Margret was completely intimidated. Carried out as it was on a small ship, the "falling out" between Roger and Margret had been no secret, and the captain became concerned for Margret's safety. He privately approached her and told "Margret that if she desired it, he would p[ar]t them, upon which ye s^d Margret answered that could not be, for they could not be parted."[58]

In an attempt to quell the gossip swirling on deck, Roger would pointedly call Margret his wife, but that only seemed to fuel whispers about his *other* wife. And as they neared Virginia, things intensified. One young man recalled, "When wee arrived at Point Comfort & report came that his old wife was alive, he the s^d Roger proffered to lay a 1000 l[bs] to[bacco] that his wife was dead aleven months before."[59]

One wonders what Roger was thinking, bringing a new bride home while his first wife was still living there. In spite of his bluster and his bet, he surely knew that Mary was still alive. If James Gey knew it while they were still in Barbados, Roger certainly would have known, too. Did Roger think he could browbeat Mary into complete submission and maintain two wives in his new brick house? Perhaps he thought no one would notice if Mary disappeared shortly after his arrival. Or was he already accumulating enough wealth, ill-gotten or otherwise, that he felt he could pay his way out of any difficulty?

Though Accomack County was known to tolerate and even offer assistance to unsavory pirate types,[60] Roger's behavior was beginning to irritate the court. After considering his recent assault on Mary, the tumultuous history of their marriage and the evidence pointing to an illegal second union, the justices decided there was a possible felony involved and ordered Mikell and those testifying against him to appear before "ye Govr & Councell at James Citty ye 4th day of the next Genll court." Roger Mikell was to post a bond for his appearance in Jamestown and for his good behavior, but because he had previously disregarded the court's order by assaulting his wife, he was to forfeit the earlier bond he had posted.[61]

Mikell's debts were piling up in a big way. On 7 November he admitted owing 40,000 pounds tobacco to the bondsmen; the next day, the court decreed that Mary should live with George Hope and ordered Mikell to pay Hope for Mary's "accomadacon & such necessaries as she shall have occasion for according to the Quallity of the said Roger & proportionate to his Estate." Though the court did not set the amount, Mary could have expected about 150 to 200 pounds of tobacco a month.[62]

The next month, the court determined that Mikell, by his stubborn refusal to release his stepson's inheritance, had failed to properly administer the Bonwell estate. Mikell denied he had signed the counterbond intended to prevent this eventuality, but when Mary and another woman swore that he had, the court ordered Mikell to pay the penalty of 500 pounds sterling.[63] By

January 1679/80, these and other debts that Mikell owed the court and individuals would have hovered around a staggering 150,000 pounds of tobacco.[64] A man working at the average wage would take about 24 years to earn that much.[65]

In addition to the debts, Mikell still had a brick house to finish and a wanton lifestyle to maintain. And the fact that he apparently avoided punishment for bigamy may indicate that he also had made some rather quiet and expensive arrangements. Somehow, the authorities failed to notice that Margret Pickering continued to live with Roger Mikell.

Though Roger may have already experimented with piracy, his pressing financial situation in early 1680, probably stimulated his career. It seems he left the area for a time, returned during the summer long enough to witness Griffith Savage's will and vanished again.[66] Then in October, perhaps visualizing a time when his possessions would increase, or foreseeing further difficulties with his first wife, he made a legal agreement with Mary.

On 19 October 1680, "for divers causes and Consideracons" Roger and Mary Mikell "mutually agreed & Concluded & consented to part each of us from ye other and live asunder wthout Claiming any further maintenance or any other duty belonging to each of us to ye other."

Roger, who discharged Mary from "all offices and duties of a wife," promised not to "Compel her to live wth me any more" and granted her liberty to "trafique or deal" with others as she wished, provided Mary would "save me of & from all manner of troubles y^t have happened heretofore." She also was not to demand support, meddle in Roger's affairs or claim any part of his estate.

Mary listed what Roger had already given her: a three-year-old gray horse branded with RM and PZ; two cows with two calves by their sides; a feather bed, a bolster, two pillows, a pair of sheets, a rug, a blanket, a set of curtains and valance; her clothing; a side saddle; a chest; a round table; six hogs; an iron pot, two pewter dishes, a pewter cup and a pewter flagon; a looking glass; a spit; two barrels of corn; a Bible; a pair of cards; and three yards of new bed ticking. With these things "I the said Mary am now and at all times hereafter fully satisfied."

With its curious mix of first person statements by both Roger and Mary, the agreement may have been put together at home; even the witnesses were homegrown, one a servant, the other Mary's son. Two days later the Mikells went to court to acknowledge the document, "this being the full and finul end of all differences that ever hath beane or to prevent any y^t ever may in any waies happen hereafter."[67]

Their optimism was unrealistic; the peace lasted just over six months. And Mary, though she remained in the background, apparently played a major role in plaguing Roger with further difficulties.

At the court held 17 May 1681, Roger, claiming that his servant Patrick Michell had run away almost five years earlier, requested the servant's penalty to be determined by the justices, who complied by ordering Patrick to remain a servant for an additional four years.[68] One wonders why Roger waited till Patrick's term of service was almost over. Perhaps Roger simply let the matter slide, or maybe he took a twisted pleasure in snatching Patrick's freedom away at the last moment.

Any perverse satisfaction that Roger felt, however, vanished in a matter of seconds. Availing himself of his moment in the limelight, Patrick informed the court that Margret Pickering had been "privately delivered of a Child." Because unattended births often spawned infanticide, Margret's empty arms looked all the more suspicious to the court, which immediately appointed two justices to investigate the matter.[69]

The next day they took a deposition from Patrick and questioned Margret's slave girl Betty; the day after that they interrogated Margret herself and empowered a jury of matrons to physically examine her.

According to Patrick, he, James Bonwell and the Negro girl Betty were "picking out" pegs in the barn one night about the first of September. In the course of the evening, Betty had promised to help the following night as well, so when she failed to appear in the barn on the second night, Patrick went to see why. "Comeing wth in sight of y[e] window [Patrick] did see a light in y[e] house," which was strange, because he had seen "hardly any light when [I] and James Bonwell went to pick out peggs." He also knew that Roger Mikell and Margret Pickering "were both gone to theire beds" before he and James had left for the barn.

The barn was apparently some distance from the house, for Patrick "went over y[e] stile into the orchard" and then up to a window. There he "did see my master Rodger Mikell take a Child from Margret Pickering al[ia]s Anderson and y[e] Negroe Gearle Betty held the light." Roger headed toward the door with the child, which Patrick never saw again. Weeks later, however, he did see some linen, foul with blood; interestingly, this linen was laundered by his "Dame," by which he meant Mary Mikell.[70]

It was highly unusual for justices to seek testimony from a slave girl, but they were aware of Roger's proclivities, and she had light to shed on a possible murder. They actually questioned her twice, once privately and again before the entire court. Her detailed but disjointed story undoubtedly reflects the order that the questions were put to her: One cold night during apple time, she was making a fire when she saw her master Roger Mikell stand by her mistress Margret's bedside "wth a naked child in his hands whispering wth her." They sent Betty out for water, and Roger later washed his hands in it, making it bloody. Betty warmed a clean shift for Margret, who folded the one she took off, thereby preventing Betty from seeing its condition. Betty did not see what happened to the child; before she fetched the water Roger left with it and was gone less than an hour. That night James Bonwell and Patrick were stripping tobacco or making pegs. It was about midnight when they came in to bed, the door being locked. The next morning, Roger and Margret warned her not to say anything, threatening that "they would Kill her [even] iff there was noe more Negroes in the world." Betty saw no sign of life in the baby, nor did she hear it cry. When asked if any means was used to hide the signs of having a child, Betty answered that a red rug was laid under Margret. Like Patrick, Betty also recalled that the linen was washed by Mrs. Mikell, who came the next day and carried it to Quinton's.[71]

The court next questioned the 20-year-old Margret, who denied ever having a child:

Question 1: had you ever an husband:
Answere: Yea
Question 2: how long were you married to him or lived with him
An: About a quarter of a yeare he lived wth me
Quest– is he liveing or dead:
Ans   He is dead & hath bin dead for about 2: or 3 years
Q had you evever (sic) a Child or ever were wth Child
A: [unreadable] had a child nor ever I was with child.[72]

The justices then appointed six matrons, and swore them "to the best of yor skill & Judgment by the usuall waies & means in such cases used, find out and discover whether you in y^r judgments doe believe that Margret Anderson al[ia]s Pickering ever had any child, miscarryed of child, or hath been wth Child." After examining Margret, the women returned to court and declared that Margret had had "one Child if not more, but know not whether ye Child or Children were at there full time or not."[73]

The court had impaneled a jury of inquest, which had heard all the evidence. This jury returned their verdict, saying they "vehemently suspect ye sd Roger Mikell" as well as Margret "to bee guilty of concealing ye birth of a Child borne one [on] the body of Margret Andrson al[ia]s Pickering." Because the charges against Roger and Margret were "so farr Criminall," the local court could not proceed against them; they would have to appear at the General Court in Jamestown. The court took the pair into custody till Roger could arrange a bond of 100 pounds sterling to ensure that he and Margret would personally appear across the Bay to answer the accusation. Since the court also suspected that Roger and Margret were living in adultery, they required an additional bond of 40 pounds sterling to ensure that the pair "shall not cohabit nor unlawfully accompany togeather." In both cases, the bonds were posted by other individuals, who could hold Mikell accountable for double the amount if he missed the boat to Jamestown and failed to send Margret packing.[74]

In debt, in trouble with the court, and with nefarious activities likely in the works, Roger must have realized that he could never safely settle down in his still unfinished brick house. It would be much wiser to keep the authorities guessing at his whereabouts. Less than a month later, he liquidated his assets by selling his property to one of the bondsmen; Roger accepted 60 pounds sterling and 5000 pounds of tobacco for his celebrated house and the 1000 acres on which it stood. True to her promise in the separation agreement, Mary dutifully signed the deed as "yᵉ lawful wife" of Roger Mikell and made no effort to claim any part of Roger's estate.[75]

Ironically, Roger intended to do one more thing before he became a full-time criminal. He set out to clear his name, and Margret's, of the murder charges brought against them. Though he disappeared immediately after signing the deed, he returned the next month to ask the court to examine *his* evidence.

Some of the testimony he presented had the ring of truth, like the account of the servant woman attacked by Patrick Michell, Roger's prime accuser. And some of it rang hollow, like the description of Roger's gentle questioning of the slave girl Betty. It is interesting to note that the court did not throw out the original case but merely ordered that the new evidence be sent to Jamestown along with the suspects and the old evidence. They probably did not know what to believe, and one look at some of the characters involved might indicate why.

–Mary Mikell, deceptive and unpredictable, had compelling reasons for seeking revenge against her husband.

–Roger Mikell, a liar, bigamist and violent wife beater, was already known as a thief and pirate.

–Patrick Michell, a disgruntled servant, was a liar and attempted rapist.[76]

–John Tankred, Mikell's long-time friend and attorney, had once been debarred for arrogance, ignorance and trying to coerce witnesses to lie.[77]

–Edward Brotherton, a hotheaded future counterfeiter, was the current adulterous lover of Roger's sister.[78]

–Anthony Delopar, a foul-mouthed slacking servant, had violently attacked a lame overseer.[79]

–Betty or Bess, the slave girl, was at the mercy of her violent master and intimidated by the other servants.[80]

The first of Roger's evidence was supplied by John Tankred, who had been associated with Mikell for more than six years, served as his attorney and was known to spend the night at Mikell's house. Tankred's description of Mikell's mild behavior toward the slave girl is so contrary to Mikell's known penchant for violent retribution that it is immediately suspect. Tankred asked the court to believe that Roger, a violent wife abuser who beat his "bride" for calling him "Cuckall," gently interrogated a slave girl who had accused him of murder and then had run away.

According to Tankred, he went home with Roger on the Thursday evening after Roger and Margret had been accused of murdering Margret's infant. Upon their arrival, "Roger Mikell did Immediately soe soone as he went into ye house, Aske ye Negro girle in faire smooth Language wth out any Austerity or severity either in words or Countenance wt made her Run Away when she went from Court on Tuesday & where shee was while she was away."[81]

The slave girl, who may have been the first person to sleep in Roger's unfinished mansion, answered that she "lay in ye bricke house y^t night & went Early in ye morning to Lt Coll Wests." According to Tankred, after Roger gave Betty "many good & Godly Admonitions," he said, "Now Betty all is over. Neither yor mestris nor I are angry wth y^u. Declare ye truth before God & these men heere, doe you know any of y^t y^u said in ye Court to be truth; Speake freely."

This is when Betty's story changed. She answered that "she Knew nothing but [what] Patricke bid her say."

And this is when Roger's piety, patience and understanding soared to incredible heights. "Doe not belye Patricke," he said, "for allthough he be a villeine and a Rogue to me you must not tell a lye of him. Have not I taught y^u your praiers & doe y^u know wch is best a truth or a leye?"

Betty answered that "he had taught her her prayers, & truth was better then a Lye," and then the slave girl went on to tell what appears to be the real story. But it must be remembered that Betty's words are second hand and reported by a lawyer with a history of composing testimony for unwilling witnesses and forcing them to sign. Tankred's testimony was corroborated by Edward Brotherton, who was best known for counterfeiting money, viciously biting off a man's nose in a fight, and brazenly committing adultery with Mikell's sister Bridget while her husband lay sick in the next room. Also present was an unknown, illiterate woman named Elizabeth Bennet, who had come home with Mikell, Tankred and Brotherton; what she was doing in the company of these men is hard to say.[82]

At any rate, according to them, Betty then revealed that "Patrick did on munday morning at ye oven at ye bricke house tell her y^t he was goeing to Court to see to be free, but if his master tooke ye Law of him for his Running away he would say Mrs. Margarett had a Childe and hee see it in his masters hands, and bid her say soe too." Patrick predicted that the sheriff would come for Betty "to bring her to Court and bid her Remember w^t he bid her say & be sure to say it."

Tankred took pains to claim that Mikell had not spoken to Betty "from her Coming from Court untill she came to ye house (onely she was bid to make fast ye Canoe we went over ye Creek in)."

Edward Brotherton and the mysterious Mrs. Bennet were able to "further testifie y^t when ye s^d [Tankred] was a bed wth Roger Mikell ye Negro Girl said y^t on munday—at the oven when they were putting bred ye said Patrick bid her say w^t she said about ye said Roger Mikells threatening to kill her."

Unlike John Tankred, a servant named Anthony Delopar gave his statement three months after the incident he was describing. Though he was known for his laziness, rough language, rebellion and violence, Anthony had no real history of lying, and the detailed story he told, if not true, was at least cleverly crafted. His tale put the blame squarely upon Mary Mikell's shoulders as the originator of the plot to frame Roger.[83]

While he was living at Roger Mikell's, Anthony said he paid a visit to James Bonwell's house. James was not at home, but his mother Mary Mikell was there, and Anthony overheard her talking with Roger's servant Patrick.

Anthony claimed Mary began by saying that "she was lying on the Coutch a sleepe at Rodger Mikells house & that then ye said Rodger Mikell waked her and asked her if she would wash the Cloathes for to put the Child in & a shift for Margret Anderson wth them." Surprised, Mary asked, "What? have she goten a Child?" Roger apparently then vanished and the conversation was taken over by Margret, who calmly replied, "Yes." Then Mary said she "asked her is it by my husband & the said Margret answered noe, but let me beg y^u not to speake of it to any body." Mary promised she "would not wth out anyone els did."

Anthony then heard Mary "bid the said Patrick say soe too that Mrs. Margret had Child."

Warming to the idea, Patrick then "sayed that he stood at the fore windoe of the house & saw the Childe & then went Round the house & went in at the shead dore and went to bed to sleape."

Fleshing out the details, Mary and Patrick went on to say that "ye negroe Girle held light in the Chimney when the Child was borne for them to see wth." Mrs. Mikell advised "Patrick to bid ye Negro Gearl say so too y^t her mistriss had a Child borne of her body that wee all three may agree in one story."

When Anthony got home, he asked the Negro girl about what he had just heard, and "she tould me y^t she knew nothing of it & y^t it was all lyes that they s^d." She added that "she was never called up upon any occasion."

The testimonies of Sarah Dyer and her friends shed no light on any baby that Margret may have had. Instead they spotlighted Patrick's integrity, or rather his lack of it.

Apparently a newly arrived indentured servant, Sarah knew neither the roads nor the people when she arrived at the Mikell place one summer evening with a fellow servant. Her friend was busy with cattle, so when she wanted to go home, she asked directions of Patrick, who "willfully lead me out of the way as I understood afterwards by his wicked intent." After they were in the woods, Patrick pulled a knife

and laid violent hands upon y[r] Depont & threatning me wth death & that he would cut my throat if I would not [y]eild to his wicked intent as to let him ly wth me but I y[r] Depont utterly denied him altho in great feare and perrill did youse my best indeavoour to Keepe him of[f] from me a considerable time and when I did see that I could not wth stand his comitting a Rape upon my Body I being allmost spent wth striving and after much blood shead betwixt us I did Chry out wth all the might I could & then y[e] s[d] Patrick yoused his best indeavor to stop my mouth wth one of his hands but at last I was heard by some of our family w[ch] was allmost a mile off & they answered and was cum allmost too the place where I was then the s[d] Patrick left me and Ronnaway.[84]

The next morning, noting that Sarah's clothes were all bloody from the previous night's attack, one of her rescuers went to inform Roger Mikell of what his servant had done but found that Mikell was not at home. The rescuer, who made a point of finding Patrick, observed that he was still wearing a bloody shirt.[85]

Aside from giving insight into Patrick's character, Sarah's experience helped pin down the whereabouts of Roger and Margret during the critical last week of August or first week of September, when Patrick claimed the murder took place. According to Sarah and her rescuer both Roger and Margret were gone from home, presumably together, at the end of August.

That left the first week of September, and that's where Mary Seple [Supple] comes in. About the seventh of September, Mary went into labor, and as was customary, the neighborhood women gathered around. Among them was Margret Pickering, who appeared "very well in health" both then and the next Sunday when she paid another visit. Mary, who washed Margret's linen several times, saw nothing to indicate that Mary had recently given birth.[86]

It is unlikely that Roger and Margret accompanied the evidence to Jamestown for the final determination of the case, even though they probably would have been cleared of murder charges. And while Mikell's name continued to appear in court, like when Patrick ran away and was captured more than thirty miles from home[87] and when various suits were brought against his estate, he came to court only one more time, in October 1681, when one of the Bonwell orphans pressed for his estate. After that, Roger never darkened the county courthouse door again.[88]

That does not mean that he vanished entirely, however. Residents of Maryland as well as Virginia all up and down the Chesapeake were painfully aware of Mikell's presence as he devoted himself to full-time piracy. During the early 1680's Mikell and his band of "Pirates and Robbers" kept busy "violently assaulting plundering and robbing" the people of Maryland "and others passing to and from the same both by land and water." Nor were Indians immune to his raids; Mikell would rob them of guns and furs.[89]

Though one report implied that Mikell no longer lived in Virginia, he returned to his home area for at least a while, setting up operations on Watts Island, a spot also associated with Mikell's old friend Edward Brotherton.[90] It was here that a boatload of tobacco fell into Mikell's clutches.[91]

Just before the 20th of January 1684/85, Richard Stevens and two others headed south from Maryland in a 16-foot boat loaded with 20,000 pounds of tobacco. As night approached, they made the mistake of putting ashore on Watts Island, where they built a fire. As they warmed themselves, they were suddenly surrounded by Roger Mikell (with whom Stevens was acquainted) and several other men, all well armed with guns and swords. When Roger commanded two of his men to board the tobacco boat and put off, Stevens tried to stop them, but Roger violently knocked him into the water for his efforts. As their tobacco sailed away, Roger guarded his victims for nearly two hours, during which time he offered them "many threatning words, and daunting expressions."

When his cohorts returned, Mikell handed his prisoners over to them and left to spend the night at a nearby house. The next day when Stevens and his fellow prisoners were taken there, they found Mikell and his friends "drinking and feasting with Rumm or Brandy, mutton turkeys &cª but would not entertaine or releive whom they had robb'd." After detaining his prisoners for two days and two nights without food, Roger ordered two of his men to row Stevens and his friends to the mainland. Upon "landing them in a remote place upon Marishes, [the pirates] immediately returned, but exacted from them some of their clothes for their soe doeing." Though only partially clothed and very hungry, the men all survived their wintertime trek through the marsh, and Stevens was able to file a report with the authorities.

Only a week later, Roger again tried his luck with a boat that anchored near the island and sent two men ashore. "With many large Invitacons" Roger invited all the men to come ashore and refresh themselves with freshly killed beef and mutton. The weary sailors must have been tempted by the offer, but they escaped Roger's treachery when Thomas Ley, who was "wind bound" by the island in a poor sloop loaded with lumber, informed the strangers that Roger was a pirate.[92]

By early 1685, the gentlemen of Maryland were ordering Mikell's arrest, complaining that he and his accomplices "have for some considerable time, and yett doe frequently infest this Province as Pirates and Robbers." Supporting this action was William Anderson, who testified that "Roger Makeele hath been a person of not onely evill fame, but certainly of very bad life and conversation," all of which Anderson knew "by at least Sixteene or Seaventeene yeares acquaintance."[93]

In early March, by sailing to Virginia's Isle of Wight County, robbing a home and disappearing, Mikell convinced the Virginia authorities that he was a serious threat in their area as well. Governor Howard reacted by ordering three ships to "saile into ye bay and cruze about and search all parts therein for ye aforesaid Roger Makeel and ye other his Complices."[94]

With both Maryland and Virginia alert to his activities and issuing orders for his arrest, Mikell sought refuge in North Carolina. Though Virginia's Governor did not specifically order his pirate hunters to invade the neighboring colony, he did suggest that if the pirates' haunts were discovered, his men should strive to bring the pirates back to Virginia for trial.[95]

Unfortunately, we have no record of Mikell's capture or trial, but we do know that he had met his end sometime before 11 March 1685/86, when the court noted that Roger Mikell, a witness to Griffith Savage's will, was deceased.[96] Governor Howard almost certainly had been referring to Mikell in the latter part of 1685, when he reported that "some Pilfering Pyrates have done damage to the Inhabitants, but I have taken the Chiefest and executed them."[97]

While we do not know the details of Roger's last moments, we can safely assume that they were not pleasant. His execution could have paralleled that of three other pirates captured in Virginia fourteen years later. Taken to points along the shore overlooking the scenes of their crimes, each was hung upon a sturdy gibbet "by the Neck till he be dead dead dead." As a warning to other would-be pirates, the bodies were to be left there "hanging in a good strong Chaine and Rope til they rott and fall away."[98]

The fate of Margret Pickering is unknown; she simply vanished. But we can speculate. Financially dependent on Roger Mikell, intimidated by him, known to accompany him on his travels and accused of murder with him, Margret almost certainly sailed off with Roger when he dropped all pretenses of gentility and devoted himself to a life of crime. Even though she likely accompanied Roger on his pilfering raids, she was no more successful at taming Roger's roving eye than Mary had been. In early 1685, one Lydia Baldwin alias Bitterson was arrested in Northampton County for "goeinge aboard" with Roger Mikell "a Knowne Pyrate and Robber."[99]

With the separation agreement protecting her from Roger's many debts, Mary must have felt a sense of profound relief when she learned that Roger Mikell would never return to abuse her again. Rebounding from her association with such a high profile scoundrel, Mary next selected a husband blessed with comfortable obscurity.

She must have been approaching fifty when she married Henry Hubanck, a man of modest means and a comparative newcomer to Virginia.[100] Life with Henry was probably not very exciting, but it wasn't dangerous, either. Mary never found it necessary to run for her life or accuse Henry of abusing her. Hubanck wasn't perfect, but his scrapes with the law barely merit mention; aside from committing fornication shortly after his arrival and neglecting to plant corn as required by law, his crimes were limited to using ten barrels of corn, a hoe and an earthen jug without permission and failing to appear in court when summoned.[101]

Henry also helped Mary in the continuing administration of the Bonwell estate, which for some reason was still unsettled thirty-five years after Bonwell's death.[102] It seems likely that the avarice Mary exhibited as a young widow in 1667, never really went away.

Even after Mary was widowed for the fourth time,[103] she stubbornly maintained her struggle to control the Bonwell estate. And as she entered her eighties, Mary made it clear that she valued money more than good relations with her son John, who in the early part of 1723, invaded his mother's space and apparently took what he considered to be his.

As she had done so many times with Roger Mikell, Mary turned to the court. This time she sued her son John for 100 pounds sterling for trespass and assault. The jury did not believe that John had assaulted his elderly mother, nor did they find him guilty of trespass.[104] John was just reclaiming his own from a stingy old lady.

Although her children and grandchildren were numerous, Mary's last years may have been lonely ones. In her long life she had gathered goods to herself, consorted with a pirate and hoped to live in a mansion, but faced with stinging abuse, rejection and disappointment, she had retaliated with lawsuits, bitter accusations and conspiracies. Mary Watson Hope Bonwell Mikell Hubanck was close to ninety years old when she died in 1732, an astonishing age for the time.[105] She had outlived children, grandchildren and four husbands,[106] but she never did outgrow her greediness, and if that left her to live her last days alienated and alone, it was a shame. Think of the stories that old lady could have told.

Chapter Eight

Joanna Michell Matrum Smith

The lady who married a monster

Hard as life was in the 1600's, few women faced as much tragedy as Joanna Michell Matrum Smith. It was common enough for a colonial woman to look death in the eye, to lose loved ones, to suffer privations or even to be at the mercy of a cruel husband or master. But the intensity of physical and emotional suffering endured by Joanna was exceptional. It was almost equaled, however, by at least eleven other women who also fell into the clutches of Joanna's second husband, Henry Smith. Even the court justices were convinced he was "more like a monster then a man."[1]

Unlike most of the other women abused by Smith, Joanna had been traumatized before she even set foot in Virginia. As a young wife and mother in London during the mid-1660's, Joanna had been jolted by two of the most horrific events to befall that city. The plague, which began in London in 1664, and lingered on into 1666, claimed almost 100,000 lives.[2] Among the dead were Joanna's husband, Joseph Matrum, and at least two of their children.[3]

The Great Fire that swept through London in September 1666,[4] was somewhat kinder to Joanna than the plague had been; her remaining two children, her maidservant and her possessions survived.[5] The combination of catastrophes, however, left Joanna toying with the idea of leaving London behind.

She was not the first member of her family to consider the colonies. Bridget Mikell Savage, Joanna's wilder, more daring sister was already living in Virginia.[6] She likely sent Joanna glowing accounts of a society where widows could have their pick of landed gentlemen. Bridget must have prevailed upon her neighbor, a merchant named Devorax Browne,[7] to contact her sister when he sailed for London in the fall of 1666. Over the next few months Browne repeatedly approached Joanna, urging her to come live in Virginia.

Once he made the appeal in her "chamber" and another time in a tavern on Bishopsgate Street, which was close to the horrible destruction, but had been largely spared by the Great Fire.[8] Browne persisted while Joanna demurred on the grounds that she lacked the funds to make the trip. No doubt under the assumption that a colonial suitor would reimburse him, Browne became magnanimous. He "severall times did promise" to give Joanna free passage for herself, her children and her possessions; she need only pay for her maid's passage.[9]

When Joanna finally agreed to accept his offer, Browne instructed her to "put his name D:B: upon her severall packs of goods that they might goe aboard of ye shipp as his goods." Joanna accordingly marked her trunks, her furniture and her packages before traveling with them to Gravesend, where Browne's ship, the *Marygold*, was lying in port.

When Joanna arrived, Devorax Browne took one look at her baggage and began to regret his generous offer. The lady had more of this world's goods than he had been led to believe. Browne retreated to the house of Robert Pitt, a sea captain and fellow Virginian, to complain "that Mrs Joanna Matrum was at Gravesend and that hee promised her to give the fraight of her goods but did not thinke she had neer so many as she then brought to Gravesend and shipped aboard ye Marygold."[10]

One can only imagine what thoughts were going through Joanna's mind as she and her maid bundled little Sarah and Mary onto the deck of the *Marygold*. She may have felt a certain smugness in arranging free passage, but the decision to leave England had not been an easy one, and Joanna still may have been harboring doubts. Unfortunately, she had no way of knowing that she was embarking on yet another tragic chapter in her life.

At first Virginia must have been exciting—the relief of completing a safe voyage, the reunion with her sister, the new sights, the new foods, the expanse of untamed land and, of course, the number of gentlemen eager to meet a young widow with so many possessions.[11]

Among the wealthiest of those gentlemen was a master of manipulation, a greedy deceiver who would stop at nothing to obtain what he wanted. Before Joanna met Henry Smith, probably in the early spring of 1667, he was already guilty of murder, rape, theft, sadistic abuse and, naturally, lying to cover his tracks.

Henry Smith's recorded crime wave began in March 1662/63, when he violently raped Mary Jones, one of his servants,[12] in a tobacco house. When she resisted subsequent rape attempts, Henry had her whipped by the magistrates, beat her himself, had her "tyed neck and heels," deprived her of food and clothing and ultimately, when she had almost served her term and was about to go free, imprisoned her on an island.[13]

Mary may not have been his first victim. Henry's first wife, (probably named Margery)[14] whom he brought to Virginia some time after the summer of 1662, was so weakened by Henry's beatings that she died an early death a few years later.[15] Before she died, Henry transported Joan and Samuel Holbrooke, Margery's sister and brother-in-law, to Virginia, along with Rachel Moody, his wife's niece.[16] But any joy this might have afforded Margery was short lived. Henry repeatedly threatened to sell the niece as a servant[17] and flagrantly committed adultery with Joan Holbrooke. "It was the breaking of his former wifes hart," when Henry was "so kind to her sister & unkind to her selfe."[18]

Henry also had a maidservant named Eliza Carter, who, beguiled by Smith's promises of marriage, had become Smith's mistress before his wife even reached Virginia. Margery may not have known about Eliza, but her sister Joan Holbrooke certainly did. On one occasion, "Smith being in naked bed wth [Eliza] & his former wifes s^d sister Mrs Holbrooke . . . Smith put his hand over ye s^d Mrs Holbrooke & felt [Eliza], Whereupon ye s^d Mrs Holbrooke his wifes sister fell into fits."[19]

Why were Eliza, Margery, Mrs. Holbrooke and ultimately Joanna attracted to a man like Henry Smith? They were likely lulled by lies and dazzled by his wealth. Not only was he the master of a number of plantations, he also owned an island in the Chesapeake Bay; by 1667, he held title to 3,800 acres.[20] For a colonial woman seeking security in an uncertain environment, an advantageous marriage did not so much mean finding someone you loved as it meant finding someone with money.

Though he had several free-ranging hogs himself, in early 1666, Henry killed one that belonged to a neighbor.[21] The resulting lawsuit did not go well for Henry, and in a pattern that he later repeated with Joanna, he took out his anger on those under his control. Smart enough to know that his brutalized and starving servants could get him in trouble with the court, Smith developed a devious plan to discredit the servants most likely to alert the authorities.

He feigned kindness for two days, then gathered five of his servants, put them in a boat and took them to Capt. Bowman, a court commissioner who had the authority to administer whippings. On the way he duped his two most educated servants, both skilled blacksmiths, into believing that their treatment was about to improve. For this the two men were "very glad hoping to have victualls enough for ye future."[22]

Once at the commissioners, Smith accused Mary Jones, the rape victim, of running away. He wanted her whipped. Mary defended herself saying that she had been starved, ill-clothed, hard worked and forced to go barefoot in the snow. The other servants knew this was true, "But there sd Master told his tale so fair," and the servants, hoping for better treatment "said nothing to contradict their Master hoping to have his future regard." A servant named Old John, who had left the plantation a few days earlier in an unsuccessful attempt to report his own mistreatment, also "held his peace and did not complain" for fear that the commissioner would grant Smith's request that he too be whipped. As it was, Bowman declared that the old man had more need of a nurse than a whipping, and refused to punish him, but "Mary Jones was whipped by Capt: Bowmans order & ye Depon[an]^{ts} terrified but hoped still for better usage, so returned wth their master."[23]

Back at home, Smith immediately reverted to his abusive ways. Recalling their master's promises, the blacksmiths requested better treatment, but Smith "called them Rouges & asked them why they did not speake before Capt: Bowman, and then to[o] late they knew ye ill consequence of being soothed to silence when their tyme was to speake."[24]

Many pages of the old records are filled with heartrending accounts of the cruel treatment suffered by Smith's servants before he met and married Joanna.[25] Not only were his people kept almost naked, winter and summer, they were starving and would have died if a neighbor widow had not fed them.[26] The widow's charity could go only so far, however; most of the servants were so hungry that they ate a diseased and rotting dead sheep that Old John found in a field. And after working all day, the servants were forced to grind corn for their master at night.[27]

Besides imposing the daily misery of hunger, fatigue and cold, Smith inflicted emotional anguish as well. The servants never knew when their master's anger would boil over into rapes and beatings. The assaults are best described in the servants' own words.

– Mary Jones testified: "About ye middle of March 1662[63] . . . beeing not sensible of ye Evill intentions of [my] master did goe to ye tobacco house wth him & there [he] did throw [me] downe . . . [I said] yowe will undoe mee. [He] replied If I undoe yow I am able to Maintaine yow. Upon y^t [I] cried out for Releife & [he] pulled out his Handchercheife out of his pockett & tyed it about [my] mouth & Ravished me." For telling others about this incident, "Smith beat her greviously." One morning that same month, Smith sent the other servants away, and "did rise out of his bed & tooke [me] in his Armes . . . whereupon yor Depon^t rushing from her master cryed & [he] Come out & did beat [me] wth a great tobacco Stick." Another attack occurred where Mary slept, "in a little hole Called the Cuddy." Mary tried to hide from Smith's "Cruellties of whipping beating Laying neck & heele & such like for takeing bread or Hominy to sattisfie hunger & speaking truth." She was also beaten for eating oats and not grinding fast enough.[28]

– Elizabeth Nock: "Henry Smith did attempt a Rape upon [me] but y^t time & place did not serve him to overcome [my] resistance." Smith " Called [me] into ye great howse & went into ye Inner or Middle Roome before this Depon^t & told [me] [I] should make ye bed, But we^n [I] came there . . . Smith threw [me] downe on the bed & said nothing, But [I] gott away from ye bed, & [my] Master ran after [me] & gott [me] by ye arme but [I] forced from [him] & ran out of doores. [Smith] following [me] Saw Jno Higgs & Roger coming, so for y^t tyme left [me] & went to get Corne topps for his horse." Elizabeth also would be beaten if she failed to "card two pounds of wool each day & milk thirteene Cowes and doe all ye worke about ye house." For a missing piece of bread, Smith "whipt [me] tell he had broke a whole handfull of rods." Henry Smith "ordered [me] to winter hoe a peece of ground for wheat w^{ch} [I] did . . . but the wheat being sowed by his Brother came not up, for wch cause [my] master whipt [me] so long as a great handful of Rods would hold." Elizabeth "long suffered under his Cruellty of hard Labour by neight & day, ill diet & hardly Clothes to Cover her nakednes in sumor & to keepe warme in ye winter, wth many & often blows Kicks & Whipping."[29]

— Jean Powell: for making a cap, "Hee beat me three tymes over tell my armes was as black as ye shooe and my back ye same." Jean also was beaten for wrapping her feet in cloth to protect them from the snow, eating an apple, asking for a piece of candle and simply because she was there; when she came home from the fields while her fellow servants were receiving a beating, her master "beat her foure or five blowes, saying she should have some for company."[30]

— Rachel Moody: "[I] Came in a freeweoman & for Love of [Smith's] wife [my] Aunt," and "hath had very Little or noe Cloathing from ye s^d Smith & [am] at this tyme all most naked & hath bin so [for some time]." Rachel was "proved to be often Cruelly beaten to ye Danger of her Life & Continuall hard usage." Once Smith beat Rachel so badly that she fainted and would have "fallen on ye ground if Richard Francklin had not held her up . . . The weapon y^t he beat her wth was a hard ropes end."[31]

As much as Smith misused his women servants, he reserved the worst treatment for Old John, "an aged man at least Sixty yeares of age his beard & haire of his head all grey." Although Old John did "his Labour according to his abillities," Smith abused him, kept him ill-clothed and barefoot, often beating him "wth a Bulls pizle & [Old John being] hungrey for want of foode was less able to doe his worke."[32]

Commissioner Bowman's refusal to whip Old John along side of Mary Jones angered Smith, though he contained his rage until he got back to his own isolated plantation. There, Smith ordered Old John's hair cut off "from ye one side of his head. Hee having a very coml[e]y head of hair was much greived thereat." What followed is best told by Elizabeth Nock, Jean Powell and the blacksmiths, who were eyewitnesses:

Y^e depon^ts Master . . . tyed him to a Mulberry tree when hee was stripped & their was a great Swelling under his arme . . . and ye depon^ts Richard Chambers & W^m. Nock were in their Shopp & William Nock was doing Some worke, & Richard Chambers when hee heard ye old Man cry looked out at ye window a long tyme & saw his sd Master Smith a whipping ould John. At last he stopped, or tooke up more Rodds & Richard Chambers & W^m: Nock sd one to a nother what, will our Master never give over whiping ye ould Man, Let us count ye blows and ye sd Chambers & Nock did after count fourty seaven or forty nine lashes and doe judge ye tyme [Smith] was whipping ye ould man before was much longer then ye tyme hee was whipping when they accounted ye lashes. After the Whipping a plough chein was fastned to ould Johns legg & so large that it reached over his

Shoulder to ye ground, The same night ould John, Eliz^a. Nock & Jean Powell were apointed to grind, but Ould John was soare wth whipping & also had a great swelling under his arme wch hee sd came wth his Masters blowes wth a bulls pizle and hee shewed ye Swelling to Jean Powell & Eliz^a. Nock & ye place was much Swelled & looked very red wch had so disabled him hee could not grind. Then Eliz^a. Nock & Jean Powell ground ye Corne and after[wards], whilest ye ould man lived (wch was not longe), The Servants did beare out his worke to keepe him from more blows. Ould John was not sick of any apparent disease but languished wth greife & Suffering of blows & hunger & would often weepe bitterly complaining of his inSupportable Misery Saying that ye blows his Master had given would bee his death & was so weake that ould John would often reele & stagger & fall downe as hee went & was lodged in an open tobacco house remote from ye dwelling house & had only straw to lye on and three or foure yards of Virginia Cloth for his Covering in ye cold of winter. Ould John was still forced to worke & our Master Smith would feele of his wrist & call him dissembling Rouge & that continewed about Sixteene or twenty daies after hee was whipped. One Satterday Morning ould John was forced to thrash & about breakfast tyme came up, and Jean Powell was sitting at worke neere ye Chimny Corner in ye dwelling house & ould John came in & reeled as hee went by ye fier ready to fall in ye fier and if Eliz^a: Nock had not catcht him by ye arme hee had fallen into a kettle of hott water, and our Master called him disembling Rouge saying hee could find [it] in his heart to throw a bed staffe at him. Old John sd truly hee could not helpe it, but Spake so that wee could scarce tell what hee sd. His eyes were sunke in his head & his countenance changed so^c that wee sd surely ould John would not live longe, neverthelesse our Master called him dissembling Rouge. At breakfast ould John would eat noe homine, but satt in ye Chimny corner neere Jean Powell where she was carding of wooll. At Dinner o^r Master gave ould John a peece of meat wch hee did eat. Then o^r Master said it was asigne by his eating hee was not sick & that hee dissembled. Ould John answered hee had not eat so much [in] a great while. At night ould John went downe to his ill lodging in ye tobacco house upon straw & in ye way going, Rich: Chambers meet ould John to whome ould John complained y^t ye blowes given by his Master would bee his death, and this being a Satterday night about ye 25th of 9ber [November] 1666 John Butt al[ia]s ould John died in ye night alone in ye tobb house & was found dead in ye Morninge, Then Eliz^a: Nock & Jean Powell on ye Sunday was put to stripp ould John who was so ghastly a sight they could ill indure it, and they ye sd Eliz^a: Nock & Jean Powell doe declare that ye dead body of ould John was all ye back & sides full of ye ma[r]kes of ye blows given him by their Master wch. they could not but see they were so apparent, but ye horridness of the sight did divert their search to view ye bruise & Swelling under his arme w^{ch}: some tyme before his death was broke & run blood & water. The sd ould Johns corps was so lean that wee might see each bone & joynt & so lowly that ye sd depon^{ts} could not touch him but were covered wth: lice. . . . On ye Monday Morning Eliz^a: Nock & Jane Powell put ye Corps of ould

John in a peece of ould saile . . . & when ye corpes were put in ye ground
our Master would not allow tyme to fully cover ye Corps wth earth but
hastned ye Servants to work, So left ye grave but halfe full or thereabouts &
so it was a long time if not to this Day.[33]

James Hinderson, who had just helped launch a nearby sloop, helped
carry Old John to his grave, and noticed the fresh blood on the old sail. He
commented that since "ould John died in a tobacco house so remote &
amongst hoggs & after such a Manner alone, it was not fitt hee sould bee
buried untill a Jury had passed on [examined] him [for evidence of foul
play]."[34] No one acted on these suspicions, however, and Henry Smith, who
might well have been convicted of murdering his servant, blissfully went on
to win the hand of Joanna Matrum, who arrived in Virginia a few months
later.

Besides visiting her sister, tending her small daughters and attracting
suitors, Joanna had at least one other concern that summer. Devorax Browne
still felt she had taken unfair advantage of him, and by the fall of 1667, he
was apparently trying to recoup the cost of bringing Joanna and her
possessions to Virginia. That December, Joanna, who appeared in court as
Joan Michell alias Matrum, presented the testimonies of her maid and Capt.
Pitts, both of whom recounted Browne's pledge to pay her passage.[35] By this
time Joanna had almost certainly agreed to marry Henry Smith, so he may
have been the one so anxious to ensure that Browne kept his word. Still,
Henry must have paid Browne something; two months later it was Smith, not
Browne, who obtained a 50-acre certificate for transporting Joan Smith to
Virginia.[36]

It would be interesting to know how much Joanna actually knew about
Henry Smith, and how much she chose to ignore. Could she have been totally
taken in by Smith? Her sister must have heard gossip about Smith; what did
she tell Joanna? Did Henry's wealth so awe Joanna that she chose to
overlook the dark rumors?

She likely knew that the Governor had stepped in to absolve Henry of his
hog problems, and that Henry was now required to pay only for the purloined
pig, without the hefty penalties usually levied on hog thieves.[37]

She may have known that a woman named Mary Jones was working on
Henry's island, but she probably wouldn't have known that the poor woman,
though legally free, was being held a captive servant there. Rumors about the
rape in the tobacco house had circulated a few years earlier, but they
eventually died away, and Joanna may not have heard them.[38]

Joanna (along with every other woman in the county) had probably heard
the story of Ann Cooper, Smith's former servant,[39] who had come back to
coax Smith's niece and the other servants into giving her wheat for pancakes,
butter for chicken pies, pepper, salt and several pieces of clothing that had

once belonged to Smith's first wife and her sister. Taken to court in May 1667, Ann was convicted of her crime and got the very public punishment of 25 lashes on her bare back.[40] On the other hand, Joanna would not have known about Ann Cooper's other transgression–she and Henry Smith had committed fornication a few months before Joanna married Henry, and Ann was expecting Henry's child.[41]

Joanna would certainly have known that Henry was in the process of moving his main residence north to Oak Hall. The house at Occohannock, though fitted with glass windows, was of humble "wattle and daub" construction, a framework filled with interwoven sticks and daubed with mud and clay. The Oak Hall plantation, however, boasted a new main house imposing enough to be termed the "Great House" as well as other buildings including a servant quarters with at least two rooms and a loft.[42]

Joanna probably even looked forward to living at Oak Hall, but she certainly was not aware of what was going on there before she moved in.

Eliza Carter, whose indenture had expired in June 1666, was no longer Henry Smith's servant. She was now his mistress, who, with Henry's blessings, wielded control at Oak Hall. Corrupted by the power and perhaps cherishing the hope that Henry might still marry her, Eliza had been taking a Henry-like pleasure in seeing the servants abused. She later admitted in court that she was "so much his prostitute y^t she allwaies served his Carnall desires & to please him had bin so Rigorous y^t she had ye hate of all his servants."[43]

That August, Eliza was about to join Henry at Occohannock when a wolf-bitten steer had to be slaughtered at Oak Hall. For a week Eliza stayed by to eat her share, and then hearing that Henry was ill, she rushed to his side. In her absence the other servants continued to eat the meat, which for the lack of salt, was beginning to spoil anyway. Upon the return of Henry and Eliza, Elizabeth Nock was singled out and given "forty lashes on ye bare back" because so much of the meat was gone. Shortly afterward, at Eliza's urging, Elizabeth was whipped again for not carding enough wool; later when Eliza accused her of taking a piece of bread, Elizabeth was beaten with rods.[44]

On a January morning in 1667/68, as her wedding festivities swirled around her,[45] Joanna probably had no idea that she was going home to a plantation where the servants were cold and hungry and that her new husband habitually beat them "only for [the] pleasure & humor of himselfe & wench Eliza Carter."[46] Joanna probably did not know that Eliza Carter was even then expecting Henry's child, but she soon found out.

Joanna's first disturbing sight might have been the shabbily clad servants shivering in the cold. That spring Henry threatened to beat Elizabeth Nock when she tied cloth around her cold bare feet.[47] And though we have no record of it, Henry probably found more than one occasion to slap his wife around during the early months of their marriage. The real trouble, however, did not begin until summer. That June, Jean Powell summoned her courage along with the testimony of her fellow sufferers and complained to the authorities, who could not deny that she had been severely whipped; her scars bore silent witness. It was further shown that Jean was forced to sleep on the ground and had been given only one shift that year. Although the court had already heard of Smith's cruelty by "common fame," they only admonished him to treat his servants better.[48]

Disdaining the court, Henry continued to beat his servants, his disposition darkening as Eliza Carter's pregnancy advanced. Upon the arrival of that child, Henry would be faced with another embarrassing court visit. Eliza didn't want the baby either and repeatedly told the other servants that "she had a frogg or Snake in her belly," and that "shee would goe downe to Occahannock & gett some Physick & make either a hogg or a dogg of it."[49] With the servants gossiping and Eliza growing larger by the day, Henry sent her away from Oak Hall, a move that may have been suggested by Eliza herself. She later admitted that she did not want to be around Joanna.[50]

Trapped in the turmoil of this unhappy home, Joanna and her small daughters caught the brunt of Henry's anger. About the middle of August, when Henry found four-year-old Sarah Matrum in the yard, he commanded her to "ride upon a stick, saying to the Child, gallup." Dressed in a thin blue frock, Sarah replied that she couldn't do it. She had not yet learned that no one said "no" to her stepfather. His anger flaring, Henry said he would make her gallop, and beat her with a stick. Sarah ran behind the storehouse crying, but Henry caught up with her and viciously beat her again.[51]

A matter of days later, Henry, upon seeing Sarah go into the milk house, looked through the window in time to see Joanna "give her finger to ye Child to Lick." With that Henry stormed into the milk house, dragged "ye Child out of the roome & whipped her, saying [to Joanna] y^t her bastard & shee would eat all ye Creame."[52]

The recipient of beatings herself, Joanna was powerless to alleviate her own suffering or that of the servants, but when her child became the victim, she had to do something. Probably forbidden to leave the plantation herself, Joanna quietly sent word to her sister, most likely by Mary Hues, the trusted maid servant she had brought from London. So, in September, about two or three weeks after Sarah's first known beating, Griffith and Bridget Savage came to Oak Hall to rescue the battered little girl.[53]

Joanna, who had probably not seen her sister for some time, warmly greeted the Savages, telling them how glad she was that they had come for Sarah. Joanna must have wished that she could escape, too, but she dared not go. Instead she made sure that Bridget and Griffith knew of her plight. Before Henry was aware of the visitors' arrival, Joanna "pulled up her sleeves & shewed her armes how her husband had beat her wch they saw as also her face to be black & blew & sore bruised."

Heeding Joanna's plea, Griffith went to ask Henry "if he might have one of his wifes Children to keep." Fully aware of the anguish the separation would cause Joanna, Henry "gave his free Consent & said he had nothing to doe wth ye Child."

As Joanna stood there watching the Savages preparing to depart with little Sarah, she turned to Henry and asked, "Will you not give the Child a cow calfe?" Henry, who was perfectly happy to give away his wife's child, was not about to relinquish the child's inheritance. He "answered very Churrlishly, bidding her hold her prating & mind her busines."

Joanna's request indicated that she was not anticipating a brief separation from her child. The calf would eventually produce milk for the child, but that was not its primary purpose. Colonists gave cow calves to children for starting a herd as an investment for the future. Clearly, Joanna's daughter was going away for a very long time.

And Henry's answer spotlighted his greed. When Joanna married, the ownership of her many possessions passed to her husband. Henry did not legally own the children's estates, but he was hereby notifying Joanna that he was taking what belonged to the children, too.

In fact, Henry had established a pattern of ridding himself of dependents while keeping their property. He had done it with his first wife, her sister (intentional or not) and very nearly with her niece. Joanna and her daughters were next in line.

As the summer of 1668 wound down, the pressure on Henry increased. Eliza Carter's baby was almost due, and so far it had resisted both Eliza's and Henry's attempts to abort it. Eliza had found lodging with Jean the wife of Robert Hill, Henry's former overseer, and that is where Henry found Eliza at the beginning of September.[54]

Concerned about her choice of refuge, Henry asked, "Wherefore didst thou come hether in ye hands of thy Enemies? Thou knowest they owe y^u noe good will, nor I neither." Then he added, "Where dost thou intend to goe? Thou was not best to stay heere."

When Eliza replied that she thought she was provided for, Henry changed the subject, and suggested that an abortion was yet possible by asking, "Dost thou intend to have that old fellow still?"

Eliza's reply, if there was one, was not recorded, and Henry reverted to his former line of thought. Though he had earlier sent Eliza away from Oak Hall, he now urged her to return there. Eliza "made answer and sd noe, She was to neere his wife." Henry then "asked her to goe to ye Island & bee there, and then she [would be] out of ye noyse of her Enemies."

Henry clearly feared that Eliza would bear a live child, be convicted of fornication and implicate him. That would mean court visits, fines and child support. And he also feared the Hills, who could not be trusted to keep quiet about Eliza's pregnancy and abortion attempts. If Eliza returned to Oak Hall, which was, after all, very isolated, he might be able to hide a birth, abortion–or infanticide. His island, which was even more remote, would serve his purpose even better.

For once, Eliza did not do Henry's bidding. She may not have had time. A matter of days after Henry urged her to flee, she gave birth to a child with only Jean Hill present.[55] Such an arrangement, with no midwife or attending cluster of neighborhood matrons, was against the law and highly suspect. Bad things often happened to babies entering the world at "private" births. And something bad did happen to Eliza's infant.

Jean Hill's husband knew a suspicious situation when he saw it, and he also knew what was required by law; he called in a witness. When Elizabeth Taylor arrived at the Hill home, "there lay a dead new borne child upon a Chest." It is not clear if Eliza was still in the house, but Jean Hill freely shared Eliza's name with Mrs. Taylor, who then set about examining the child. She "found it to bee all black athawrt ye body, the head of ye child haveing a fine ragg upon it." Mrs. Taylor, "putting of her hand upon the childs head, found it to bee soft and the ragg to bee bloody."[56]

Perhaps at the insistence of her husband, Jean Hill also went out and found a witness. She asked Ruth Bunduck to come "to her house to see a child of Elizabeth Carters that was still borne." Ruth also examined the child and reported that "The flesh of ye child was black and ye skin stript of[f], and ye scull very soft, and ye Cloath that tied up ye mouth was bloody." This was clearly not your typical stillbirth.[57]

Though he was not present at the time, it was at the court held on 26 and 27 October, that Henry Smith's world began to implode. Not one, but two, women named him as the father of their illegitimate children. Although the court had known of Ann Cooper's indiscretion for some time, she had waited till now to identify the father.[58] The court ordered that Henry Smith appear at the next court to answer Ann's charges and then they moved on to the much more serious case of Elizabeth Carter.

She had "secretly brought forth a bastard Child w^{th}out ye help of any weomen except her confederate Jane (sic) Hill & ye said Chld being dead & bruised in ye head was suspected by the court & Country to be Murthered."[59]

In an attempt to distance herself from the suspected murder, Jean Hill told the court that "Eliza Carter did often times take phisick when she was with child & did bruse her body & belly to the danger of destroying the said Child bastard borne." To support her allegations, Jean requested that two servants, Elizabeth Nock and Mary Jones, be called to testify about the "former practises of the s^d Eliza Carter & her suspected being wth child." She promised their testimony would show that Smith "did frequently lye wth the said Eliza Carter & gave her phisick."[60]

Accused of murdering her own infant, Eliza swore that Henry Smith was the father of her child and "most greviously wth teares complained" that he had "brought her to this ruine by getting her wth child & deserting her in distress." She asked that Smith "might face to face the next court appeare, where he could not deny her just accusacon."[61]

The justices consequently ordered that a special warrant be issued for the personal appearance of Henry Smith at the next court. The two servant witnesses would also be there, along with a jury of "the most grave . . . and Judicious weomen" prepared to invesitgate the birth of the dead child. Eliza Carter was committed into the sheriff's custody till the next court; Jean Hill could go free if she gave security for her appearance.[62]

The county court was rarely called upon to preside over such scandalous proceedings. Though it sometimes dealt with fornicators, the court's patrons were usually dispassionate men, and the topics were usually debts of tobacco. Although gossip must have already been circulating, one can only imagine how fast it spread after the October court. And if the gossip did not push Henry Smith over the edge, the special summons certainly must have.

Shortly after the court appearance of Jean Hill and Eliza Carter, Smith visited with Jean and told her that the "Cour^t had proceeded illegally & unjustly, and done more then they could answer [for], and hee would make them ashamed of it before ye Govno^r & Councell."[63] One had to be very angry, or foolish, or very well connected to criticize and threaten the most powerful men in the county.

Only a matter of days later, Henry, who was conducting an investigation of his own, had Joanna with him when he visited the house of Ruth Bunduck, one of the witnesses who had examined Eliza's dead infant. Ruth and Marrian Fruin later reported the details of the Smiths' visit.[64]

Henry told them that one of the justices had become so ashamed that he "rose from ye table" during the questioning of Eliza: "Coll Scarburgh did often urge her whether it was her Master or her Mistris that sent her for Physick to Mrs. Ann, and she sd her Mistris but hee urged her still whether it were not Master Smith."[65] In this one accusation, Henry was accomplishing three things; he was insulting the justice by implying he was easily embarrassed, he was accusing Col. Scarburgh of being biased against him, and he was naming Joanna as the one who promoted Eliza's abortion attempts.

It may have been this comment, or another, that touched off the trouble, but whatever it was, Henry and Joanna "fell out about Eliz^a: Carter." Right there in front of Ruth, Smith told Joanna "that all this was long of her and that damd whore, her sister." Frustrated and powerless to get back at the justices and his accusers, Smith grimly added "that hee could not bee revenged of them, but of y^u I will, y^u damd whore."

Marrian recalled that Henry spoke "very discontentedly to his wife about Besse Carter & ye trouble hee was to expect, calling his wife whore, damd whore & impudent whore, Bitch, and very often her Sister whore."

Henry raged "that whores and Rouges were admitted to Swear against him, but hee could have noe Justice, and hee would goe els where. Hee would have Justice, and ever & a non called his wife whore & bitch, and shaking his fist at her said hee would bee revenged of her."

While Joanna wept silently Smith raged, "All this is long of y^u, you whore." Then he threatened her again saying, "I will take my revenge of y^u, and y^u shall rue it. I will make y^u to rue it, for I cannot bee revenged of them y^t doe it, but I will be revenged of you, you whore." To further emphasize his point, Smith was "holding up his fist & shaking it att her very often."

Weeping, Joanna asked, "What have I done? Why is it long mee? What have I done?"

At this point, Ruth Bunduck boldly confronted Smith and said, "If I were yor wife I should bee afraid to goe wth y^u in ye woods."

In a "very surly" manner he replied, "Then y^u were best to keepe her."

The tirade continued for about an hour, and then Smith suddenly "was in hast[e] to be gone." He probably stomped out of the house to get the horses, for Marrian turned to Joanna and said, "It Snows & Rains & is very cold. Why will y^u goe?"

Joanna answered, "I must goe, or hee saith hee will dragg me at his horse taile."

Meanwhile, Henry was beginning to notice the weather himself. The rain and snow did not cool his anger, but it did dampen his haste to leave the warmth of the Bunduck home. He decided to stay the night, but his conversation hardly improved: "a great deale more of such railing . . . was his continuwall talke."

Among other things, Henry accused Joanna of improper conduct with Eliza's interrogator, Col. Edmund Scarburgh. Smith alleged that Joanna "told him The Coll sent for her."

Joanna said, "It was not so, That ye Coll never sent for [me] to [my] knowledge."

"Thou didst so good as tell me so," he shot back.

"Noe it was not so," she countered. "The Coll never sent for me."

Then Henry said he "would not keepe a wife of his to bee a whore and so Coll Scarburgh should know, nor would hee bee a pimpe."

For the second time Ruth came to Joanna's defense, saying, "I am very confident y^u need not troble yor selfe about ye Coll and keepe yor wife at home for all him." Ruth knew what she was talking about; she did not live far from the home of Ann Toft, the Colonel's young and extremely close friend.[66]

So it continued that evening: "More words very bad, ... wth his shaking his fist, stamping & grining [grimacing] at his wife, were his talk while hee staid."

Early the next morning, "In a cold day hee would bee gone, and hurried his wife away wth him." Not only was Joanna "very thin clothed," but Henry would not even wait long enough for her to lace her bodice. According to Marrian, Joanna was "so scared & distracted . . . that she knew not what she did. His lookes were so divelish & feirce on her & others that if [I] had bin alone wth him [I] should have feared [for my] Life." Under ordinary circumstances, Joanna might have had time enough to dress that morning, but Henry's continued threats and scoldings scared her so badly that she "could not dress herselfe, But wth a flux upon her went away wth him in a very cold Day enough to endanger her Life."

Joanna survived the trip back to Oak Hall, but she was not well; "the flux" was still upon her when the next one-sided confrontation occurred.[67] The day started normally enough, with Joanna walking over to the "quarter house" where the servants lived and asking the maids there to make lye for the washing. Later that same day, towards evening, Joanna's own maid, Mary Hues, arrived from Occohannock. Anxious for news, Joanna asked "ye wench how her Sister did and ye Maid sd y^t she was well." In a voice too soft to be easily heard, Joanna then began plying the maid with other questions, perhaps about her daughter.

Maybe Mary noticed Henry glaring at them, for she suddenly told Joanna that she would not tell her now. Later Mary asked Joanna to come outdoors, where Joanna "stood & talkt but two or three words" with her maid. The two then parted with Mary heading toward the quartering house and Joanna walking to the great house. That is where Henry accosted her.

He "called her damnd whore & asked her if she could never leave playing ye whore wth every Rouge in ye Country."

When she asked him "who she was playing ye whore wth," he cursed her again and said that "Higgs & every Rouge must bee her companion."

She replied that Higgs was not around, "for ye fellow was upon ye bed a sleepe." She added that if Henry "went about to follow any whore well & good, but she did not follow any Rouge."

The servants heard a few more heated words and watched as Henry "fell a beating her, & she cryed out for some of us to come in, but wee durst not."

Later, Joanna came out to the quarter and admonished the servants "saying that she might have bin killed for none of us would come out to helpe her."

The servants replied, "Wee durst not come in for he would beat us."

Joanna then asked "John Higgs to give her a pipe of tobacco and ye fellow did give it her, and while she was taking it, she desired me to stand &

watch y^t yor deponts master did not come, for if hee should come hee would beat her againe."

So there sat the master's wife, in the servant quarters, fearing for her life and smoking a borrowed pipe. "After she had taken [smoked] it, her Maid desired her to goe in againe, but she was loath to goe in for feare that hee should beat her, But wee all prayed her to goe in; because their was noe bed for her to lye in."

Eventually Joanna agreed to return to the house with Mary, her maid. Although Henry had previously ordered Mary to bolt the door, she had only pretended to obey and later sneaked out to the quarter. Joanna entered the great house with Mary and meekly asked Henry "whether she should come to bed to him."

He snarled, "Noe, and called her damnd bitch & sd y^t she should not," so Joanna "went to goe to bed wth her maid & her Children."^{68}

Henry then "came out of ye Roome & beat her, and pushed her out and boulted her out of doores." So, for the second time that night, Joanna "came into ye Quarter." Although it was a very wet and cold night, she "had nothing upon her but one thinn under coate & under wastcoat, bare legged only her slippers on."

As Henry was angrily bolting the door himself, Mary headed off to bed. She had been troubled with a pain in her side, and as she lay there in bed with one of the children, Henry "came to ye bed side & felt her wrist awhile & Suddainly leaped into the bed to this Depon^t & said he would Cure the Paine in her side, & then attempted to force her, but she gott over ye Child & lapped her selfe in the Blankett and lay so on her belly." Because of the child, and the blanket and the number of people around the houses, Mary escaped that time.

Meanwhile, out in the quarter, Joanna asked a servant to make a fire, and then huddled there in front of it. Since there was no bed in the Quarter for their mistress, Jean Powell and Elizabeth Nock sat up with Joanna and listened while she recounted how she had suffered at the hands of her husband. Jean later recalled how Joanna told her "that I could witness how gross hee had abused her & her Children."

In full agreement, Jean replied, "I would speake ye truth if I died for it." This was not hyperbole. Jean had seen Old John's beating; she had helped bury his broken body. She knew the depths of Henry's cruelty. She just did not know that he was eavesdropping on her that very moment. Smith had sneaked out of the big house under the cover of darkness, had crawled up to the servant quarters and "lying under ye house, & harkning, heard me say these words."

Fearing nothing so much as the truth, Henry immediately slithered from his hiding place. Charging inside he "fell upon John Higgs and gave him a box on ye eare & a cuff on ye chopps and bid him goe out of ye house & hee went out." With the lone man servant out of the way, Henry turned his attention to the terrified women.

He started by asking Jean why she "satt up at y^t tyme of ye neight." "I satt up to beare my mistris companye," answered Jean.

Henry then "tooke ye shooe of[f] his foot & beat me about ye house wth ye heele of it. . . . I was so sore y^t ye next day I was not able to lift my hoe."

Henry ranted that the three servants had been sitting up to "combine" against him with "a whore." As they denied his accusations, Joanna cowered in the main room and Jean made a break for it. In her words:

> I runn into ye Roome where I lay [slept], and hee came after me & beat me againe. Then I runn out of doores and Elizabeth Nock went up into ye loft. Then hee followed her gropeing about on his hands & keenes (sic) but could not find her. Wth y^t hee came downe againe & sd y^t she should have it in ye morning, and then againe beat my mistris in ye Quarter wth ye heele of his shooe & flung her downe. When she gott up againe, he pushed her before him into ye great house and said that hee would have us two whores slasht [like] never was whores slasht, and she should come to ye whipping post wth us for Company."[69]

The next day Henry went out to the field to question the women servants. They denied scheming against their master, but he refused to believe them. He said the "three theeves of us did sitt up to combine wth a whore, and that wee did consult wth her to cutt his throat." In Henry's opinion, his servants were thieves, his wife was plotting his murder, and the justices were biased against him. Though his views were exaggerated, they were not entirely groundless. The starving servants actually had been stealing food, his wife really was soliciting witnesses to testify against him, and the justices, who had already felt the sting of Henry's insults, were definitely in a hostile frame of mind.

Even though he vowed to go over the heads of the county judges and get justice in Jamestown, Henry could not escape dealing with the local court. He still had to appear at the December session to answer the charges of fathering the two infants born to his former servants. And if Henry thought his violent threats could contain the trouble brewing at home, he was badly mistaken. Though Joanna may have felt like cutting his throat, she had settled on a less violent plan. When Henry's court date arrived, neighbors, relatives and servants flooded the court with a barrage of complaints and depositions that could have been orchestrated only by Joanna.

True to the promise she had made in the servants' quarters, Jean Powell appeared before a commissioner to recount Henry's mistreatment of little Sarah Matrum.[70] The next day, on the third of December, Griffith and Bridget Savage related how they had come for the abused little girl.[71] Four days later, when the justices took their places for that month's session, another eighteen witnesses appeared to give their evidence against Smith.[72] Ultimately the overwhelmed justices voiced a complaint against Henry themselves, accusing him of causing "three dayes trouble to ye Court."[73]

Some of the court's troubles are not readily apparent in the records, but politics lurks between the lines. Though the connection is not clear, the Governor was known to favor Henry, whose repeated threats to get justice in Jamestown were not lost on the commissioners. Col. Edmund Scarburgh, the leader of the court, had a rather rocky relationship with the authorities in Jamestown, and he could hardly afford to generate further displeasure on account of Smith.[74] The court therefore proceeded carefully, making every effort to justify their actions and seeking the Governor's advice at every turn.

The justices first addressed the damage done to the dignity of the court. They were incensed by Henry's allegation that their questions about "physic" had embarrassed one of their number. Calling Smith's words "altogether false & a Knowne notorius Lye," the court sought the Governor's counsel in dealing with "Smith for his Scandalous reporting Such words to ye Dishonour of the Kings Court Members."[75]

They also turned to the Governor for guidance in dealing with Smith's second offense, in which he, with "great rage and fury," had made many "insulting boasts" concerning the action against Eliza Carter for murder. He claimed the proceedings were "in Malice to him threatning y^t he would have revenge of his Wife if he could not be revenged of them y^t did it, wth many other insolent & unbeseeming words." The justices, deemed this to be a crime against the power and dignity of the government, but did not dare to proceed "untill ye Honable Govnor can be fully informed of ye s^d Henry Smith, his wicked Life & demeanor."[76]

Then there was the matter of Joanna and the formal complaint she filed. The court began examining the witnesses who could shed light on "Henry Smiths tirannical using his Wife." Even "Mrs. Browne whom ye s^d Smith did call as Evidence for him did evidence agst him." She related how Smith took up a plate to throw at his wife, how he used "scandellous words often," and how she had seen the marks of "blows on ye s^d Smiths Wifes bruised body."[77]

Even a casual observer could see that Joanna was "very sick and in a weeke Condicon of Body." But if any doubts lingered, Mrs. Fookes, "a motherly Weoman & of good Repute," confirmed Joanna's affliction "by Such symptoms as are not fitt heere to recite."[78] Joanna supplicated the court to save "her from utter Distruccon by her cruell Husband, & did declare she had Rec[eive]d so many & heavy blows y^t hereby her prsent & Long Lingring Sicknes was Occasioned wch in a Yeares tyme or Less would bring her to an untimly death."[79]

To further support her allegations, Joanna produced servants Mary Hues and Jean Powell, both of whom had repeatedly heard variations of the following exchange:

After receiving a beating at the hands of her husband, Joanna would say, "I thinke yu will kill me before you have done."

Henry would reply, "If I had given my other wife so much I thinke I had killed her, but I thinke yu have a hart of stone & nothing will kill you."[80]

With the damaging testimonies mounting, Smith angrily charged everyone with plotting a conspiracy against him. Yet, when he had occasion to use some of those same witnesses to advance his own position, he would declare them "unblamable." The court noted that the many servants testifying against Smith "did most Cautious & Concienciously declare ye truth, & when by ye s^d Smith denied, they would most cleerly instance ye tymes places & circumstances of words & actons." Though even "the most Subtill" person could not have predicted the justices' questions, the servants' stories matched, and the "Court & Country (of wch were many pr[e]sent) did & doe Conclude the Evidences to be of great integrity."[81]

The court further concluded that Henry Smith was "most Notoriously impudent in Denying truths sufficiently proved & was so arrogant as to tell the Court they suffered a Combinacon ag[ains]t him." The justices, reprehending Smith for his rudeness and unseemly words, warned him his accusations would only aggravate his situation and threatened to censure him if he did not show better manners. "Never ye less ye s^d Smith did againe in the heat of his Rage charge ye Court with suffering a Combinacon ag[ains]t him." Upon this second affront, the court had Smith committed to the sheriff's custody, yet for the record they cautiously refused to punish him, preferring to wait "untill ye Hon[ora]ble govnor may be informed & give further Direction in Censuring ye s^d Smith according to his desert."[82]

Other matters, however, would not wait. The fate of Joanna had to be decided. As they usually did in such cases, the justices made an attempt to reconcile the quarreling couple; surprisingly, the main objection came not from Joanna, but from Henry, who repeatedly answered, "No way so good as a seperacon. I beseech y^u, a Seperation."[83]

Finding that Henry was so "verry Stuborn & perverse no Reason could rule him," the court struggled to come up with "some expedient" of their own to save Joanna from Smith's tyranny and provide for her support. Their efforts were happily cut short when Henry himself proposed a compromise which was "accepted & Consented unto by Joanna his Wife for their greater quiet [and] Satisfactorye liveing." The agreement:

That y^e s^d Henry Smith did propose to his s^d Wife her Choice either to live at his plantacon at Oaken Hall or Occahonnock & y^t she shall at either of

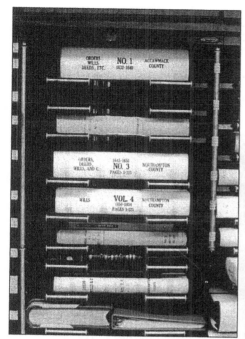

The court record books of Accomack and Northampton Counties in Virginia are among the oldest continuous records in the United States. The earliest entries date from 1632.

"'The Bear and the Cub' - Probable site of Fowkes Tavern where the first recorded play in English America was performed August 27, 1665." The husband of Rhodea Fawsett (Chapter 11) arrested the men who performed the play, and the tavern itself was later owned by John and Mary Cole (Chapter 6).

The humble home of Alice Boucher (Chapter Thirteen) had a single room with an upstairs loft, a floor plan it shared with some of the better homes of the time. Pear Valley (right), a house still standing in Northampton County, features one room with a large fireplace on the main floor and two tiny rooms beneath the steeply sloped roof. Recent dendrochronology indicates that the house was built about 1740.

Alice Boucher and her family did not own land, but the hogs that frequented the swamp near their home were owned by men who lived on Hack's Neck (Chapter Thirteen).

After she separated from Henry Smith, Joanna Matrum Smith was granted permission to reside on his plantation on Occohannock Creek. Elizabeth Rackliffe, who saved Smith's abused servants from starvation, lived on the land to the left; the Smith land lies in the distance. (Chapter Eight)

The mansion known as Arlington was situated on this site; it was the home of Tabitha Scarburgh during her marriage to John Custis, about 1680 through 1696 (Chapter Ten). In the foreground may be seen the bricks marking the outline of the mansion which was excavated in 1988 and 1994. The tombs of John Custis and his grandson lie a few steps from the mansion site.

The tomb of John Custis, the third husband of Tabitha Scarburgh, was probably constructed several years after his death. The inscription reads in part: "Here lies the body of John Custis Esqr one of the Councill and Major Genarall of Virginia who departed this life the 29th of January 1696 Aged 66 years."

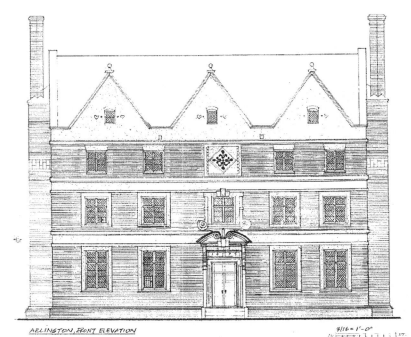

ARLINGTON, FRONT ELEVATION

3/16 = 1'-0"

The conjectural appearance of Arlington, the home built by John Custis, probably in the early 1670's. In 1676, during Bacon's Rebellion, Gov. William Berkeley fled to Arlington, where he set up temporary headquarters. Tabitha Scarburgh Custis lived at Arlington during the 1680's and 1690's (Chapter Ten). --*Drawing by Edward A. Chappell is used with the permission of the Association for the Preservation of Virginia Antiquities.*

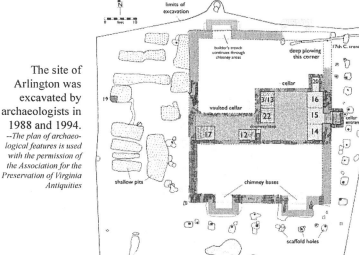

The site of Arlington was excavated by archaeologists in 1988 and 1994.
--*The plan of archaeological features is used with the permission of the Association for the Preservation of Virginia Antiquities*

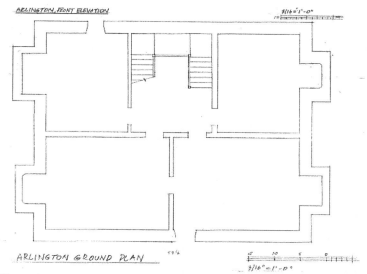

ARLINGTON, FRONT ELEVATION   3/16"=1'-0"

ARLINGTON GROUND PLAN   3/16"=1'-0"

The conjectural floor plan of the ground floor of Arlington. It is thought that the room in the upper left may have served as a kitchen; the room below it may have been the dining room. *--Drawing used with the permission of the Association for the Preservation of Virginia Antiquities.*

Archaeologist Jamie May cleans the masonry block with an incised heart that probably once decorated the facade of Arlington. *--Photos used with the permission of the Association for the Preservation of Virginia Antiquities.*

Found at Arlington, the fragments of a small deftware bowl with a pale blue background date to the 1680's. *--Photo used with the permission of the Association for the Preservation of Virginia Antiquities*

Found in the basement of Arlington, the six-inch high glass wine bottle (dating from about 1670-1690) bears the monogram of John Custis. *--Photo used with the permission of the Association for the Preservation of Virginia Antiquities*

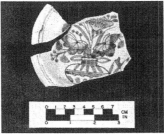

The neck portion of a Rhenish stoneware "pear-bellied jug" was found in the cellar entrance at Arlington, the home of Tabitha Scarburgh during her marriage to John Custis (about 1680-1696). The jug, which has molded decorations on a dark blue background, was probably used for drinking rather than serving beverages. *--Photo used with the permission of the Association for the Preservation of Virginia Antiquities*

Tabitha Scarburgh probably posed for her portrait in London in the late 1660's or early 1770's, during her marriage to Devoarx Browne (Chapter Ten). *--Tabitha Scarburgh, attributed to Sir Peter Lely (British, 1618-1680), oil on canvas, 28 1/2 in. x 23 1/2 in. Given by Mrs. Lewis McLane Tiffany in memory of her father, 6 January 1929. Collection University of Virginia Art Museum.*

ye s^d places be sufficiently accomadated wth meat drink and needfull Cloathing agreeable to his fortune & as her Condicon doth require

That she have a Weoman servant to attend her & her Child & a man servt to doe such Offices as are needful for her occasion

That he ye s^d Henry Smith will not come neere his s^d Wife unless by her desir[ed] nor then give her any abuse or unkind treaty

That his Wife have Liberty at her pleasure to goe See her sister and friends

Henry Smith

Joanne Smith[84]

Mary Hues, Joanna's long time maid, would have seemed the logical choice to be Joanna's promised servant, but Henry appointed Elizabeth Nock instead. Aside from being perverse, Henry had other reasons for this choice. Elizabeth, whose indenture would expire in less than ten months, was not worth as much as Mary, who had about two and half years yet to serve.[85] And though both women had recently foiled Henry's rape attempts, Elizabeth was by far the most vigorous and successful in her self defense. The first time she had twisted from his grasp and run, and in the most recent attack, which had occurred in the servant quarters about a month earlier, she had fought Henry off for fifteen minutes before she tricked him into believing that she heard Joanna coming.[86]

While she did not choose the servant, Joanna got her choice of where to live. Though the house was old, she selected the Occohannock plantation. Not only was it in a more populated area, Joanna had probably never lived there, so it was not haunted by terrifying memories. It was also closer to her sister, and as the last clause of the agreement implies, Joanna was eager to escape the isolation from loved ones that Henry had forced upon her.

The court ordered Henry to abide by the agreement and to provide everything necessary "both for use & ornament for his wife & child & for ye man & maid servant" that were to live at his Occohannock plantation. The court continued:

And in Respect ye s^d Joanna is at this tyme weake Sick & much impaired in body & mind by ye Cruell blowes & hard usage of ye s^d Henry Smith her husband, The Court doe allso order y^t ye s^d Smith provide for his Sickly & weake wife Comfortable drinke & Nourishing food fitt for a weoman in her Condicon & in Respect of ye great dread and horror she is in y^t ye s^d Smith will take some Occasion or frame pr[e]tenses of Occasions to Come to her & use his Accustomed Cruelty of beating her or stabb her (as she makes oath he threatened) or endanger her life (as by the Evidences is manifest he hath endeavored) The Court doe strictly order y^t . . . ye s^d Smith Come not at his wife unless by her desired.[87]

If for some reason it became necessary for Smith to visit Joanna, he was to take two commissioners with him–or one commissioner and two honest neighbors. This measure was to prevent "his feared attempts of murthur or beating his wife & also to Moderate their Extreame of Discontent."

The "impairment" of Joanna's mind noticed by the court correlates with the behavior observed by the women who reported that Joanna was so distracted by fear that she could not dress herself. Although the dread and horror of her situation had clearly traumatized her, Joanna's reasoning was still intact. She was rational enough to seek provision for her future sustenance in case Henry left Virginia for Maryland.

It was an insightful prediction and a sensible request, so the court ordered Smith to post security for the support of Joanna and her child before he moved anything else into Maryland. Then, still mindful of Smith's relationship with the Governor,"The Court did further ordr y^t in case ye s^d Smith be Refractory & Continew Obstenate to his Own proposalls or disobey & Contemne this ordr, then ye s^d Smith to be Secured in the Sherr[iff]s hands untill ye Honble Govnor be made acquainted wth this whole Case & ye Evill Life & ill fame of the s^d Smith y^t such farther Course may be severely used as ye Honble Govnor shall please to direct & in ye meanetime ye s^d Smith pay all Costs in ye suit occasoned by his shamefull and Cruell Dealings."[88]

When the court turned from Henry Smith's wife and focused their attention on his mistress, Smith openly scorned Eliza Carter's sworn testimony and "impudently denied" that he was the father of her dead child. Eliza replied by recounting how he had lured her to his bed with the promise of marriage and "other notorious & shamful imputacons." After substantiating her claims by citing times, places, persons, circumstances and even witnesses, Eliza accused Henry of deserting her to the "Hazard of her Life & perpetually infamy." She insisted that Henry be made to swear whether he was "not ye father of her Bastard Child & had very often Carnally known her."[89]

Henry was in a bad position. Everyone knew he was guilty, but if he admitted it, he would be convicted as a fornicator and open himself up to charges of abetting a murder. If he swore to his innocence, he would be adding perjury to his list of offenses. Consequently, Henry refused to swear at all. Given that response, it did not take the court long to condemn him as Eliza Carter's partner in fornication, fine him 500 pounds of tobacco and charge him for court costs.[90]

If Eliza's baby had lived, she would have gotten away with a fine, too, but since she was suspected of killing her infant, the investigation continued. If the evidence pointed to deliberate murder, the local court would not have jurisdiction, and the case would have to be sent to the Governor and his council for trial.

The jury of women impaneled for the inquiry found that Eliza had indeed sent for and had twice taken a purgative hoping to induce an abortion. While they faulted her for taking the physic, they cleared her of absolute murder. In their judgment, though it may have done harm, "it was not ye physick wch shee tooke y^t did murther ye Child, it being taken so Long before ye production." Nor did they conclude that the baby was murdered during the birth; instead, the women found that the infant "received its wronge by ye fall wch ye s^d Carter receivd three weeks or there abouts before." These ladies generously assumed that Eliza's injury was an accident, even though Jean Hill had earlier testified that Eliza would bruise her own body and belly with the intent of killing her baby.[91]

The gentlemen subsequently ordered that Eliza receive thirty lashes on her bare back at the next court for taking physic to destroy her child and to pay 500 pounds of tobacco for her act of fornication, or receive twenty additional lashes. Eliza was to post security to ensure she would appear for her whipping and any other punishment the court might deem proper.[92]

Jean Hill, who had made the mistake of helping Eliza deliver the ill-fated child, made subsequent mistakes as well. At different times and places before several people, she had "behaved herselfe as a wild weoman reporting — slanders & Clamorous Speeches both of ye Court officers & private p[er]sons" including, as it turned out, Mrs. Browne. It is interesting that the court considered Jean's gossip to be more punishable than Eliza's attempts on the life of her child. They gave Jean the choice of receiving thirty-nine lashes at two consecutive courts or of becoming the "Comon whipper for one whole yeare . . . to punish ye incorrigeable whores" as she would periodically be commanded. She preferred to give rather than get the whippings, so a few months later she was ordered to start giving four fornicators a monthly whipping of twenty lashes each.[93]

The justices then turned to the case of Ann Cooper, who had also sworn that Henry had fathered her child. Her oath was all they really needed. The court convicted Henry and ordered him to pay court charges as well as the past and future costs of rearing the child.

Though the justices were quick enough to assign responsibility for child support, they harbored some nagging doubts about the pregnancy's timing and the mother's reputation. Henry, who had been at Patuxant, Maryland, had returned home five days after the calculated conception of the child, and the court freely acknowledged that Ann was "of evill fame, openly accompanying one John Cross & had before this tyme a bastard Child wch might Render her of Less repute." Because of their uncertainty, the court decided not to impose the usual fine. However, lest their leniency be misunderstood, they took pains to point out that they had not concluded that Smith was innocent "of Carnally knowing ye s^d Ann Cooper."[94]

About Ann's guilt, there was no question, and a whipping was decreed. Ann, however, beseeched the court's mercy, pleading for a fine instead. Unable to pay 500 pounds of tobacco herself, she said she would solicit contributions from kind people. Curiously, though she had no apparent claim to it, she also asked for the estate of John Cross as well as any wages still due to him. In an unusual move, the court agreed. They probably figured that the estate would soon be sitting in the county coffers, anyway, as payment for the fine. Besides, the man who thought enough of Ann to free her from the clutches of Henry Smith surely would have wanted her to inherit his estate.[95]

The beleaguered court next contemplated the plight of Smith's abused servants. This was, of course, not the first time that Henry's vicious treatment of his servants had come to the court's attention; he had been warned before. In view of the severity of their abuse, the justices debated whether the servants should be set free from such a cruel master. After pondering the matter, however, they backed off, noting that servants were men's estates and expressing the fear that such a precedent might "be of worse Consequence then intended."[96] They probably visualized most of the servants in the county–including their own–rushing to court with tales of woe in hopes of gaining freedom.

Instead the court ordered Smith to quit striking his servants. If any of them required correction he was to bring them before a justice. The servants, however, expressed an additional concern. They were terrified of being transported against their wishes to Smith's island or to Maryland where Henry would "use his Cruellty in a place where he is not so well known & understood." To allay their fears, the court further ordered that none of the servants be removed from the main part of the county. After a few other admonitions about food, clothing and work, the court sent the servants back to Smith with the warning that noncompliance with the court's orders would result in a report to the Governor and a request that the servants be freed or sold to other masters.[97]

Finally, Henry's most helpless victims, Joanna's little girls, received the attention of the court. Out of "pitty to ye distressed," Daniell Foxcroft filed a complaint on behalf of four-year-old Sarah Matrum. He described how Smith had taken possession of the estates of both children, how he had so cruelly treated Sarah with "blows & hard keeping" that the Mother was forced to seek charity from Griffith Savage. After praising Foxcroft for undertaking "so pious & Charitable endeavor," the court heard other testimonies which made it clear that "Henry Smith did inhumainely beat y^e

S^d Infant & deny fitting sustentacon being also willing to part ye Child & Mother whilst he could keepe ye Estate."[98]

Concluding that Smith was not fit to have Sarah under his care, the court commended the charity of Griffith Savage and his wife and ordered that Sarah's estate be entrusted to them. Joanna was to "recollect her best thoughts" and at the next court give an account of any part of Joseph Matrum's estate that had fallen into the hands of Henry Smith. All such goods were to be collected, appraised and then divided into three parts, one each for Sarah and Mary Matrum, and one for Henry Smith. Though he had a legal right to Joanna's portion of the estate, there was some question–upon further "advice in ye law" the whole estate might be granted to the children. In the meantime, the Savages were to control Sarah's portion, and some other person would be entrusted with Mary's.[99]

After three hectic days, the court finally wrapped up with a summary of Henry's misdeeds. He had defied the court with scandalous and threatening words. He had fathered illegitimate children with Eliza Carter and Ann Cooper. His abuse of his wife had resulted in "her prsent maime desease & danger of death." He had burned her clothes and had beaten her innocent little children. He had cruelly whipped, beaten, ill-clothed and strenuously worked his servants. He had engaged in other notorious and wild actions offensive to God and in contempt of the law and the King's officers.[100]

After considering the "insupportable greiffe Suffering & Callamities of his Wife her Young Children & his poore & painfull Servants," the court ordered that Henry Smith be placed in the sheriff's custody, but only until he could give security for his good behavior. Henry Smith, the Governor's friend, had barely gotten a slap on the wrist.

Although Joanna agreed to live at Smith's Occohannock plantation, she did not go there immediately. It was not ready for her, and she was still too weak and sick to live alone. And if she ever was tempted to set up her household there with two servants and two small children, that thought certainly evaporated with Henry's next move.

After the grueling court session, Joanna retreated to the mansion of Edmund Scarburgh's special friend, Ann Toft. Located at Gargaphia, less than ten miles from Henry's Oak Hall, Ann's vast plantation was tended by more than forty servants.[101] Joanna was recuperating there when Henry suddenly shattered the serenity of a quiet winter day. He brazenly forced his way into Ann's house and then, finding the room where Joanna was in bed, forced his way into it, too. Fortunately other people in the house realized what was happening and stopped him in the nick of time. Joanna had been wise to select a well-staffed refuge, for it would have been to the "great Hazard of her p[er]son if people neere [at] hand had not prvented" Henry.[102]

Unfortunately there was no such safety net for Joanna's maid, Mary Hues. When the other wenches and Joanna left Oak Hall, Henry moved Mary from the servant quarters into the great house, where Mary at first shared a room with Henry's children. The weather became cold, however, and Henry insisted that the children sleep with him. Therefore, on Sunday night the 27th of December, Mary was sleeping alone when Henry entered her room, threw off her covers, violently leaped onto the bed and declared his intentions. Terrified, Mary screamed, begged and fought with all her might, but her efforts fell short. Henry raped her anyway.[103]

Besides violating Joanna's no-contact order and raping Mary Hues, Henry had been keeping himself busy that December with other unconscionable behavior. He made only a paltry attempt to provide for his wife and little Mary Matrum. Out of spite he removed a pane of glass and the only good chair from Joanna's intended home. In contempt of the court's orders, he sent Jean Powell to his island and refused to provide clothes to "cover ye Nakednes & keepe warme his servts this Cold weather." And he failed to bring in the Matrum estate "whereby much Loss is hapened."[104]

At the court convened in January, Joanna petitioned for relief for the second time. Although Henry had pretended he had provided for his wife at Occohannock, two men appointed to investigate found otherwise. In their opinion, neither the house nor the accommodation was fit for a woman in Joanna's condition. In fact, Henry had committed many "willful & mischeivous actions . . . done to ye prejudice of his s^d wife & her Children" there.[105]

They described a 25 or 30-foot house with a leaky roof and an open hole over the bed where the windowpane used to be. The furniture consisted of a bed with minimal bedding, a trundle bedstead with no mattress or bedding, an empty chest of drawers, a trunk, an old table and four old chairs. There was an assortment of kitchen utensils, some of which were hardly serviceable. The food consisted of the meat of one steer, barely salted, and a bushel and a half of wheat. There were other rooms in the house which could not be examined because Henry had locked them.

Joanna was ordered to accompany two commissioners to the home to view the situation; if she was satisfied with the place, she could "possess & Live upon ye same." If not, she was to enumerate the things needed. The sheriff would "speedily" give a copy of her list to Henry, who was ordered to amend the situation before the next court. If he failed, the justices vowed to procure the needed articles from Henry's estate and censure him for contempt.

Though it was not mentioned in Henry and Joanna's written agreement, Henry had promised to provide Joanna with the "mare & side sadle y^t she did usually ride on." Instead of producing them, however, Henry spitefully got rid of Joanna's saddle and flatly refused to let her have the mare. When the court demanded to know why, "He stubornly answered y^t he had better Considered & would not Lett his wife have ye mare & sidesadle."[106]

Deeming this obstinacy to be in contempt of the court's authority, the justices empowered the sheriff to require Smith to deliver the items. If he refused, the sheriff was to forcibly take the mare and saddle and deliver them to Joanna himself.

At this juncture, Henry dropped a bombshell. He suddenly declared that he would need to live at the Occohannock house, the same one where Joanna was to stay. The move was necessary, he said, because the great house at Oak Hall had burned down.

The ashes of the ruined mansion had barely stopped smoldering when Henry made the announcement in court on the 6th of January, a Wednesday. The house had been standing ten days earlier, on Sunday night the 27th of December 1668, when Henry raped Mary Hues in one of its bedrooms. It was intact when he left to visit a neighbor on Monday morning, as it was on Tuesday when Rachel Moody dressed his children, and as it must have been when Henry returned home that Friday, the 1st of January. It is possible that the house burned that evening, or on Saturday. Mary (who was seeking an excuse to get away to report the rape) vainly pleaded to go see Joanna on Sunday about her indenture, since her own copy was burned. Whether she lost her indenture in the house fire or on another occasion is unclear. It does seem odd that none of the servants specifically mentioned the fire that destroyed their master's house.[107]

The destruction of Oak Hall stunned the justices, some of whom quietly asked Joanna if she wouldn't let Henry and his children have the Occohannock house. Having just reviewed a list of the home's shortcomings, and probably fearing that Henry would return to attack her there anyway, Joanna gladly offered to find lodging elsewhere, provided she be given a hogshead of tobacco per year for the purpose.

Pleased with themselves for engineering such a speedy solution to the housing problem, the justices were unprepared for Henry's response. When told that Joanna had agreed to live elsewhere, "It appeared y^t what he Complained of before was but a pretence to some other unknowne ends."[108]

We will never really know exactly what Henry was scheming, but incredible as it seems, he may have been willing to burn down his own house in an attempt to manipulate the outcome he desired. To be fair, there is no proof that he set this fire, but he had certainly used fire before. Though the servants do not mention the house fire, they twice mention the time Henry burned Joanna's clothes. Even if he was not the arsonist, Henry was at least trying to play on the sympathy of the court to attain his own questionable goals. But Henry, the cruel manipulator, had been frustrated in his attempt to rejoin Joanna, the woman he had promised to kill.

Smith's obstinate behavior was beginning to wear on the justices, who suddenly realized that they had neglected the "needfull inquiry into some p[ar]ticulars" because they had previously assumed that Henry could not possibly be as "Cruell & impious" as he was made out to be. Though they were still careful to desire the Governor's advice, the court now concluded that "Smith appeareth to be one of the most wicked of men & therefore, in duty to ye Courts trust, doe ordr y^t stricter inquiry be made into ye truths of the s^d Smiths alledged guilt."[109]

Consequently, the January court began to look something like the marathon session the justices had endured in December. Depositions were read, witnesses were called and more sordid details came to light. Henry and his lawyer had tampered with witnesses by trying to force Mary Hues and Rachel Moody to give false testimony. Henry had tortured and raped Mary Jones and imprisoned her on his island for fourteen months after she was legally free; she had suffered whippings, cruelty, starvation and lack of clothing. He had beaten Rachel Moody, his first wife's niece, with the hard end of a rope, intimidated her into silence and threatened to sell her as a servant.

Although the court acknowledged that Mary Jones was a free woman and had "suffered many Crueltys" at the hands of Smith, including rape and a fourteen-month imprisonment on his island, they harkened to Smith's plea that Mary had run away, had used some wool, and burned an old tobacco house. Depriving her of the wages she was due, the court awarded her only the corn and clothes that a freed servant customarily received.[110]

Rachel Moody received more sympathetic treatment. She never had been a servant, though Henry claimed her grandmother in England had made her one. The court ordered Henry to obtain legal proof from Bristol; if he failed, he would have to pay Rachel for her service and sufferings. Fortunately for Rachel, a letter from grandma arrived a few weeks later. Deploring her granddaughter's treatment, she unwittingly proved that Henry was a liar. She had written, "I had been better [to] put y^u serv^t to yor Uncle then have y^u so used." Rachel was ordered released from her uncle's service.[111]

Because Henry and his lawyer had intimidated Rachel into swearing "for his Advantage & nothing to his p[re]judice," the court began to wonder how much false testimony they had accepted as truth. They therefore ordered an investigation to see if they had committed any errors in judgment. And, for the future, they would reject any evidence presented by Smith or his attorney unless the witness could be examined before the court.[112]

The testimonies all had a familiar ring, and Henry's penalty did too. The sheriff was ordered to take Henry into custody, but only till he provided security for his good behavior. Naturally, the court was obligated to inform the Governor of "such Monstrous pceedings as hath bin very Comon wth ye s^d Smith," and, as always, they would ask for his Honor's advice. With that the justices moved on to decide other matters.[113]

Henry, however, did not move on so readily. Only a fool would bet his tobacco on the future good behavior of a man who had defied the orders of the previous month's court. Very few people probably cared to have him running loose anyway. Because even Henry himself refused to post the needed security, the county experienced a period of tranquility. No one attacked Joanna, no houses burned, no servant was raped. Out of his "Obstinate & Refractory Stubornes," Henry had chosen to "lye in prison before he would give Security to performe ye Orders of Court."[114] This response greatly irritated the court. They hated to be disobeyed as much as they loved to enrich the county coffers.

So Henry retired to the jail until the February court, where he was once again the primary focus. The justices reviewed the rapes of Mary Jones and Mary Hues along with the attempt on Elizabeth Nock and the recent information about the deaths of two of Henry's abused servants, Old John, who died from beatings and Richard Webb, who was "very hard used by his Master Smith & died madd." The court resolved to inform the Governor about these matters and ask for his direction.[115]

Having carefully deferred to the Governor throughout the proceedings, the justices were incensed when Henry petitioned to appeal to the Governor himself. Not only was this a slap in the face, in the court's opinion, Smith was attempting to delay justice. True to form, the court had this exchange recorded as well for the Governor's benefit.

Joanna was ready with a petition, too. In this, her third appeal, she complained that her husband had perversely added to her misery and sickness by withholding funds for her support and relief. She again asked for a sum of money to be allotted to her, and "also to be out of ye Noise of all his Clamours."[116]

It had been two months since Joanna had lived with Henry, yet the court still noted the "apparent weaknes & infirmity of ye s^d Joanna Occasioned by ye blows Maimes & Vexacous Usage of her husband Smith." Though the idea seemed incomprehensible, they further observed that Smith "is soe invetterate, y^t to Distroy his Wife he Contracts his owne Ruine."[117]

Eight men, including Col. Scarburgh, had just revisited the Occohannock plantation to inspect what Smith had provided for his wife. What they found was deplorable. Not only was the house leaky, it had a very smokey "Chimney where no fire Can be safely kept, it being undaubed & many holes burnt in it." Smith had ordered that the servants also be provisioned out of the stinking beef, inferior pork and two and a half bushels of wheat left there for Joanna; there was no beer, malt, or Indian corn. The house contained a dirty feather bed, rug, blankets and a pair of course sheets–no table linen, pillow cases, regular sheets, towels or anything else fit for a healthy woman "much Less for Smithes weake & Sickly Wife." Nor were there suitable utensils or any accommodations for the man and maid servants that Joanna was to have. Two panes of glass had been removed, and the other window was broken and full of holes. The walls were also broken, with the daubing fallen off. According to the servants, when it "Raines they are forced to put bowles & traies to keep the Raine from ye bed." The eight inspectors concluded that the "Defects of the howse is not in One, but all places."[118]

Indignant at Smith's defiance of their orders, the court granted Joanna a yearly allowance of thirty pounds to be paid by Smith. They also cited the separation agreement that Henry had signed and freely gave permission for Joanna to "goe to her freinds in England or elce where" in order to "secure her Life and recover her health." It is unlikely that Henry had Joanna's English friends in mind when he agreed to let her visit, but, in the court's view, this was about the only way the cruelties that had hastened the death of the first Mrs. Smith might be prevented from happening again. It was "ye Evill she [Joanna] truely feares."[119]

Joanna's children, who were now forced to depend on the charity of others, also needed what rightfully belonged to them. Refusing to surrender anything, Henry whined that "there is noe proofe what Estate ye said Children had, but only by his wife their mother." He maintained that Joanna's accounting of the estate was illegal because a wife could not give evidence against her husband. Furthermore, her first husband had died in England, and Henry contended that the case should be handled there.

The court retorted that Joanna had "lost her Husband & other Children in ye tyme of visitacon in London" and had been granted administration of the estate. Because of the "pestilential times in England," a formal inventory had not been taken, but the duty still needed to be done. As the mother of the children, his wife "may & ought to be Evidence for ye Children." Justice itself required her to do it. The court went on to condemn Smith's other evasion, saying that the children's estate was a matter of right, not fact, and could be tried in any court of law, "But more Especially in ye same County where ye Estate is."[120]

In exasperation the court resolved to send Col. Scarburgh across the Bay with a copy of the court's proceedings so he could inform the Governor about Smith's activities and seek advice in person. The court clerk prepared the document with the Governor in mind; he deliberately included even "triviall" details so the Governor might be informed and give commands accordingly.[121]

The court summarized the misdeeds of Henry Smith, among which were rape, adultery, lying, threatening the court, tampering with witnesses, cruelty, maiming his wife, abusing his step-children, whipping and overworking his servants, starving them, failing to clothe them, and even killing them. The mistreatment was so severe that "those Left Alive were forced to seeke Releife from Justice." In the court's opinion, Henry had "the marke of Gods Desertión by his pride & Arrogance." He was not at all humbled by God's apparent judgments, such as the death and loss of his creatures and the burning of his house. Instead Henry was obstinate and impenitent.[122]

After reciting his crimes, viewing the evidence and considering Henry's deformed character, the court concluded that he was a suspect in the death of his servant and guilty of rape. As they were considering the course to take, John Tankred (Smith's attorney) who was "standing by in ye hearing of all ye people . . . interrupts ye Court & tells y^m all this would come to Nothing." Because of his behavior, the leading judge threatened to have Tankred "throwne Over ye barr."[123]

At the end of the tumultuous February court, Henry was deemed a felon and sent to prison where he was to remain until the Governor could give directions concerning him.

While we know where Henry was staying, it is unclear where Joanna was living during this time. Although she may have moved in with her sister, it is likely that she continued to reside at Ann Toft's spacious plantation. Joanna, who had paid for her maid's passage to Virginia, was entitled to fifty acres of land, one of the few assets she had. In apparent gratitude, or as payment for hospitality, Joanna assigned her rights to Ann, who that March obtained a certificate for transporting Mary Hues.[124]

By the March court, Joanna had been married to Henry for a little more than a year and separated from him for three and a half months. For all that time she had been known as Mrs. Smith. Now, however, she signaled a further split from Henry. She had already expressed the desire to return to her old home in England, and it seems that she wanted to return to her old name as well. For the first time since before her marriage, her name appears as "Mrs. Joanna Motrum," and then as if in afterthought, the phrase "now ye Wife of Henry Smith" was appended.[125]

Some things, however, had not changed. Joanna was still destitute, she was still in a "sickly & maimed Condicon," and Henry was still refusing to help her in any way. Nothing–not friendly persuasion, harsh admonition nor court orders–would move Smith, who continued to be "stuborne & refractory."[126]

Having tried everything they knew, the court finally appointed the sheriff to go and search through Smith's goods. In addition to finding the clothing that belonged to Joanna and her children, he was directed to seize and immediately deliver to Joanna "one good feather bed & furniture of Rugg blanketts boulster pillow Curtaines Vallence & two pair of sheets out of ye Estate of ye sd Smith." It is curious that so many of the possessions in Henry's control had escaped the fire that had burned down his house.[127]

The sheriff was also to speedily inquire into Smith's finances and discover what tobacco was due to him, so three thousand pounds of it packed in casks could be delivered to Joanna for her support. The pilfered estate of Sarah and Mary Matrum was to be placed into safe custody, as well.[128]

In light of Henry's continued allegations of a conspiracy and false evidence given against him, the justices again called into open court most of the witnesses that had previously testified. They were "strictly" reexamined, and though every effort was used to discover any lies or plots, the court found each witness to be "cleer & untainted, declareing ye truth wth manifest integrity of Conscience." They all confirmed their former testimonies.[129]

Eager to present a true and orderly account of Old John's treatment to the Governor, the court ordered the clerk to meet with the witnesses and assemble the various depositions into "One Gen^{ll} testimoniall." Because they were aware of Smith's craft, impudence and willingness to deform the truth, the court was especially careful.[130]

Having returned from his mission across the Bay, Col. Scarburgh relayed the Governor's directive: Proceed according to law. Therefore, because Smith was suspected of raping Mary Jones and Mary Hues as well as causing the death of Old John, all crimes too serious for the local court to try, the justices ordered that Henry remain in custody until the next General Court held at James City. For the trip, the sheriff was to provide two boats, one to carry Henry Smith as the prisoner and another to carry the seven witnesses, who, along with the documents prepared by the clerk, were to be presented to the Governor. The group would sail on 16 April 1669.[131]

They should have left sooner. A spring wind came up against them, and by the time the two little ships arrived in James City, the General Court was over. The Governor, who had been planning a trip across the Bay, ordered that the evidence, the accusers and the prisoner return home. Henry Smith would be tried in Accomack County when the Governor got there.[132]

That arrangement didn't work either. The Governor arrived as promised, but without even discussing Henry's trial, he cut his stay short, attributing his speedy departure to intemperate weather. Though he did not say so, the Governor's actions made it clear that he was loath to bring Smith to trial. Col. Scarburgh, however, boldly ignored his superior's nonverbal communication and, as the Governor was hurrying off, inquired about Henry Smith. The answer was curt: take bail for his appearance. And then the Governor was gone.[133]

The local officials were left to wonder just exactly where Henry was supposed to appear, and when. Unsure of the course to take, and reluctant to incur the Governor's displeasure, the justices prepared a bond obligating Smith to appear for trial at the pleasure of the Governor, which they ultimately took to mean at the next General Court. And then they released Henry Smith.

For nearly eight months Henry had been behind bars. His incarceration had made his underhanded activities more difficult, but not impossible. No doubt assisted by his shifty lawyer, he had managed to direct the removal of his entire estate–and that of his step-children–to Maryland. He had hampered the sheriff's inventory by refusing to relinquish keys to chests and doors, and he had succeeded in keeping his tobacco out of the hands of the authorities.[134]

The items that the sheriff did collect for Joanna were few and pathetic. He had been ordered to seize 3000 pounds of tobacco and a bed from Smith's estate, it "beeing A Small part of much she brought him."[135] But Joanna never got the tobacco. Nor did she ever receive the promised yearly support of thirty pounds sterling. The only items the sheriff found were a "mean bed" with bedding and Joanna's clothes.[136]

Joanna was not only destitute, she was now painfully certain that she would never reclaim even a small portion of the wealth that she had brought to Virginia. And though Henry was still in jail at the time, he wasn't far away, and the terror he kindled was her daily companion.

So sometime that summer Joanna left for the safety of England, her passage paid by Col. Scarburgh. She had come to Virginia as an elegant lady with a mountain of possessions, a maid servant and two young daughters. Two years later she departed with only a shabby bed and the clothes on her back. Henry Smith had deprived her of her fortune, her peace of mind, her health, her servant and probably even her children.[137]

The records are vague, but more than six months after Joanna's departure, a court summary of the Smith case mentions that Joanna's daughters, abused and robbed of their estate, had been left to the charity of others. If Col. Scarburgh had paid for their passage to England along with their mother's, that act of generosity would surely have been mentioned. Suffering lingering, if not permanent, disabilities from Henry's beatings, it is likely that Joanna was incapable of caring for her two young daughters and so left them in the care of others in Virginia.[138]

Joanna's fate in England is likewise unknown. In December 1668, she had attributed her "prsent & Long Lingring Sicknes" to the "many & heavy blows" that Henry had given her. At that time she predicted that this abuse "in a Yeares tyme or Less would bring her to an untimly death."[139]

We do not know if this sad prophecy was fulfilled, but we do know that the other prediction Joanna made that day came true. She told the court she feared that Smith, "out of his Surlly humor shall forsake Virginia & goe to live in Maryland where he is now intended, prsuming of more Licentious liveing & Liberty of useing his Tirany to all under his power."[140]

Henry did just that.

His case appeared in the General Court held in April 1670. Incredibly, the evidence against Smith was found to be insufficient, and the charges against him were dismissed. Justice suffered another blow when both of Smith's accusers, rape victims Mary Hues and Mary Jones were victimized a second time. After freeing Henry, the court ordered them to serve "double their time they have been from him." That amounted to four years five and a half months for Mary Hues and four years for Mary Jones. Their only consolation was that they were sold to other masters.[141] The county court must have had a premonition of what was coming, for in February 1669/70, they assumed an extremely humble stance and made an effort to defend their previous actions against Smith. While referring to their own "weake judgments," they enumerated Smith's "Barbarous Cruellties," and cited lengthy passages from law books to support their decisions. They were reduced to pleading that they "had done no more than their duty."[142]

Henry, along with his ill-gotten gain, was soon comfortably ensconced in Maryland.[143] A mere four months after his trial, he was himself made a justice in the court of Somerset County.[144] He served in this position for several years in spite of his devious behavior in Maryland and the dark rumors from Virginia. Several of his unsavory activities are recorded in the Maryland records. Henry, as despicable as he had ever been, lapsed into stealing both horses and land.[145] In 1671, he successfully defrauded Maryland out of fifty acres by claiming that he had transported his wife "Jonah" into the colony.[146] That same year, an angry neighbor vowed to make Henry eat the trees he had deliberately mismarked for a property line, and though the neighbor threatened to rout Henry out of the county like he had been routed out of Accomack, it never happened.[147]

Henry married again, probably not knowing or caring if Joanna was still alive in England. This third marriage may have been no happier than the first two, but at least it was longer.[148]

And Henry continued to have children, both by his wife and by his servants.[149] Raped six times by Henry in early 1673, a maidservant named Dennis Holland gave birth to a little girl named Hanna, who at the age of eleven months was relegated to servitude, just one more victim of Henry Smith.[150]

Before he died at age 69 in 1703,[151] Smith lived to reap a little of what he had sown. Henry's own arrogant disregard for the law reared its ugly head in the character of his son Henry Smith Jr., who stole horses, fathered an illegitimate child, swindled his father out of 1680 pounds of tobacco and then exchanged lawsuits with him.[152] Even so, the younger Henry Smith was not even a shadow of his predecessor—the Henry Smith whose cruelty had made the plague-ridden, fire-swept ruins of London seem like heaven to Joanna Matrum.

Chapter Nine

Bridget Savage Baggale

The wanton woman

In the middle of the road in the middle of a fight, Bridget Savage burst onto the scene and into the court records. She defended her husband that day with a passion that characterized almost everything she did for the rest of her life.

Formerly an indentured servant,[1] Griffith (or Griffin) Savage had settled down on his own land with his wife Bridget by 1668.[2] The Savages seemed to get along well enough with many of their neighbors. At least most of them joined Griffith in his fight with Martin Moore.

His land nearly surrounded by that of his antagonists,[3] Moore had fought with Griffith Savage before. Why they first came to blows is unknown, though it seems that Moore initiated the disagreement. Maybe he disputed a property line, or flung a few insults and punches, like he did with someone else two years later.[4] It is also possible that the trouble involved one of the neighborhood wives, three of whom were opinionated and outspoken, if not violent, themselves.[5] Martin's wife Margaret had just been cleared of uttering scandalous words against Teage Miscall, who had brought charges against her.[6] Likely still smarting from this defeat, Miscall eagerly joined the group planning to thrash Martin.

Griffith, who blamed poor health and the heels of his shoes for his miserable showing in his first fight with Moore, eventually started to feel healthier and started to plot revenge. In the spring of 1668, he altered his shoes, secured his hair and invited his neighbors to join him on the road not far from Moore's house. Teage Miscall, who agreed to act as messenger, found Moore and delivered Savage's challenge to fight. Moore may have doubted his ability to win this second fight, for he took his time while his challengers sat down to wait.[7]

Two men who happened to be passing by reported that they were "neer yᵉ Dwelling of Martin Moore and there they saw Griffith Savedge, Lawrance Robinson & Teage Miscall sitting on an Ould Tree neere yᵉ path side." Others were there as well; a young Frenchman named Sebastian Delastatius[8] arrived on the scene just ahead of Martin Moore, and though Bridget Savage may not have been sitting on the log with the men, she was certainly lurking nearby.

Initially unaware that a fight was in the offing, the two passers by continued on their way, but they had barely resumed their journey when they heard Moore command the intruders to get off his land.

The travelers, who then heard Savage call Moore a "Rogue & Knave," turned to watch as "Griffin Savdege fell upon Martin Moore & beate him very sore and kept him Downe in ye Cart Rutt & shewed Martin very foule play."

Moore cried, "Let me rise!" but Savage had no mercy. He "kept Martin Downe & beate him so y^t when Martin Moore did rise he was blind wth blood."

It was at this juncture that Bridget took over. She "flew at Martin & kicked him," apparently repeatedly, for he asked her five or six times to keep off. But Bridget showed no more compassion than her husband. She next "ran upon Martin & tore his haire wth other vehement & quarelling behavior."

Martin made his retreat with Bridget still attacking him. She may have continued with him around a bend in the path, for the two witnesses were not sure how the two came to be parted.

Eventually, when the confrontation was over, Griffith and Bridget joined the two travelers, and as they walked together down the road, Griffith proudly analyzed his victory. He told the men that "he had cut of[f] ye heels of his shooes then for y^t when he fought wth Martin before, his heeles of his shoes threw him downe." Besides taking measures to prevent stumbling, Griffith had taken precautions with his hair, for the two witnesses remembered that they "saw Griffins hair bound up behinde." The farther he walked, the more Griffith's bravado grew. He ultimately "bragged y^t now he had his health he would beate two of Martin, but when he fought wth him before he had a fevour & ague."

When Martin Moore brought action against Griffith Savage for assault and battery, the court heard the depositions of the two impartial witnesses and decided that Griffith Savage, Lawrance Robinson, Teage Miscall and Sophet Delastatius were all guilty of unlawfully meeting together, quarreling with Martin Moore and disturbing the peace.

The four neighbors admitted their mistakes, repented, pleaded for mercy, and claimed that they were ignorant of the law. Since it was their first offense of this nature, the court fined them 100 pounds of tobacco each, sentenced them to prison for one day and charged them for court costs. After their initial jail time was satisfied, they were to remain in custody till they found security for their future good behavior.

The court also concluded that Martin Moore was not an innocent victim. He could have avoided the fight, had he wanted to. Under oath Moore admitted that messenger Teage Miscall, "did tell him that his message to him was to fight wth Griffith Savedge." The court therefore awarded no damages to Moore, but instead committed him into the sheriff's custody till he paid his share of the court charges and posted a bond for his good behavior.[9]

Bridget, as a wife acting in the presence of her husband and therefore ostensibly under his control, was not punished by the court for her part in this fracas.[10] A little more than a year later, however, Bridget had begun acting on her own. She was taken into the sheriff's custody for threatening Lawrance Robinson's wife, who swore that she went "in danger of her Life by ye threats of Bridgett ye wife of Griffeth Savage." Coincidentally, Bridget's incarceration occurred on the same day her husband sued his old enemy Martin Moore for defamation, assault and battery.[11]

Though the Savages were known for their vehement talk and forceful actions, evidence indicates that Griffith, at least, was making a change for the better. In fact they both overcame their turbulent backgrounds to provide a safe haven for one little girl.

Only a few months after the Savages confronted Martin Moore in the middle of the road, they received a message from Bridget's sister Joanna, the wife of the abusive Henry Smith. Fearing for the safety of her children, Joanna implored Griffith and Bridget to come and take four-year-old Sarah home with them.[12]

So, in September 1668, Griffith, who was then 29 years old, and Bridget, who was 23, turned up at Smith's house at Oak Hall with the intention of becoming foster parents.

Joanna, who had not informed Henry of her plans, apparently had a little time alone with the Savages. In their sympathetic company Joanna showed them the marks of her husband's abuse and told them that "she was glad they were come for ye child." When Griffith approached Henry, he readily agreed to part with Sarah but made it disdainfully clear that no support for her would be forthcoming.[13]

So, in an age when parishes bent over backwards to avoid doling out child support, the Savages took in Sarah with no expectation of remuneration. Their generosity did not go unnoticed.[14] Informed of the Savages' willingness to aid Sarah Matrum, the court noted that they did "much approve & Comend ye Charity of Griffeth Savedge & his Wife," and promised to put Sarah's estate in their care, even though they had not asked for it. Unfortunately, with Sarah's estate disappearing into Maryland, it was a promise the court could not keep.[15]

Bridget retired into the background for the next several years. Perhaps she was busy tending Sarah and Griffith Jr. and pondering the transformation in her husband's character. During this time Griffith Sr. busied himself with the typical concerns of colonial life.[16] He served on juries, owed debts, paid taxes, assessed wheels, examined a ship, visited the tavern–and began to frequent church. Elected as a vestryman in March 1672/73, and publicly recognized as a supporter of the church in 1676, Griffith began coming to court on behalf of the parish.[17] It may not have been a change that Bridget welcomed.

Sometime in 1675, Griffith and Bridget opened their home to a boarder named Henry Sadbury. It was a decision that Griffith probably later regretted, for this may have been when Bridget fell into the habit of becoming overly friendly with her husband's associates. Perhaps Griffith took one look at Sadbury, whose nickname was Harry Half-legs, and decided he posed no threat. In spite of Sadbury's physical shortcomings, however, he and Bridget became very close.[18]

Naturally, the neighbors were no kinder to Sadbury than they were to anyone else, and it wasn't long before someone made some derogatory remarks. While visiting a neighbor's home, Griffith and Bridget heard John Onions imply that someone had stolen a neckcloth and given it to the ferryman in exchange for a ride. When Bridget asked Onions about whom he was speaking, Onions replied that "he meant Harry halfeLeggs that lived at [Savage's] house." And that was not the only time Onions made such an accusation; Bridget also heard him use Henry's proper name and accuse him of being a thief.

The Savages must have reported the insult to Henry, who took the matter to court. Both Griffith and Bridget gave depositions favorable to Henry, and when they affirmed that he was also known as Harry Half-legs, the court sent the matter to a jury. After "a serious debate" they awarded Sadbury ten pounds of tobacco in damages plus court costs.[19]

Henry repaid the favor in 1678. The Savages had two servants, John Welsh and Elizabeth Pursill, who ran away to Maryland. Returned to Virginia, they complained of bad usage and overwork, but the court, after hearing the evidence, decided that they had "small cause to complain." Clearly disagreeing with the court, the two ran away again. This second time Henry Sadbury pursued the servants to Maryland and brought the fugitives home.[20]

It must have been about this time that the Savages sold part of their property to Sadbury, though the transaction was never properly recorded.[21] Henry probably began living on his own place, but he continued to visit the Savage home, especially when Griffith was absent. By January of 1679/80, Henry and Griffith were disputing unspecified debts, perhaps the expense of retrieving the servants or payment for the land.[22] Bridget, however, remained strangely unaffected by their rift.

A planned absence, perhaps related to church business, during the summer of 1680, might explain why Griffith, though in perfect health,[23] made his will; he may have considered the risks of travel and decided to put his affairs in order.[24] He also may have thought Bridget could use some companionship, or someone to watch her, while he was gone. Or maybe he was just performing another charitable act. Whatever the case, in May of 1680, the Savages again opened their home. This time it was to Mary Burton, a teenager whose stepfather had sexually abused her and then ostensibly killed her child. Ordered removed from her home situation by the court,[25] Mary was still considered guilty of fornication herself and therefore did not enjoy a very good reputation. That fact probably did not bother Bridget much, and the attractive young fornicator living on the Savage plantation seemed only to intrigue Henry Sadbury.

He probably already knew about Mary when he mounted his horse for the short ride to the Savage place. Short legs aren't so obvious when their owner is on horseback, so Henry must have played the part of a dashing Virginian as he rode up to the rail gate. Mary, who was apparently home alone, took him for a stranger there and came over to see what he wanted. She soon found out. According to the deposition she gave several months later, Henry at first made small talk and then asked if she would "marry" him behind the house next Saturday. Mary did not record her immediate answer, but her subsequent actions indicated that she was not really interested in the suggested tryst.[26]

Griffith was gone,[27] but Bridget was home, the next Saturday evening, when Sadbury came into the yard and paused near the front door. Bridget, knowing nothing about the rendezvous Henry had in mind, spoke to him "free & Softly" and invited him into the house.

Sadbury answered as though he might not come in, saying he had been warned against it. At this Bridget petulantly "stept to ye doore herself and said she hopt she might be Master of her house and Spoke to Sadbury to come in wch he accordingly did."

With apples plentiful on the Savage plantation,[28] Bridget could afford to be generous with cider. She and Sadbury began drinking just after milking time and continued all that evening till it got very late. When Mary crawled into bed, Bridget and Henry continued the party out in the barn. Dawn was just breaking when Bridget came to bed and told Mary that "she had been wth Hen: Sadbury in ye barne." Bridget went on to confide that she had been "Speaking a good word in [Mary's] behalf." Henry must have been inquiring about Mary.

A little later that morning some unexpected visitors arrived, and Bridget deemed it advisable to cover her tracks from the night before. Knowing Henry was still out in the barn with his horse tied among the oats, Bridget instructed Mary "to goe to the barne & tell Hen: Sadbury there was Company in the house & that he should stay there." Safely warned, Henry did not stumble into the house for breakfast.[29]

By this time, Bridget's wandering eye had fallen upon Edward Brotherton, one of the men who had witnessed her husband's newly made will. Maybe this new interest explains why she warmed to the idea of sharing Henry Sadbury with Mary and began trying to arrange private time for them. One evening, Bridget "drest her self very fine just at night," and under the pretext of visiting Mr. Mikell, tried to persuade Mary to go with her. Even though Mikell was a "knowne pyrate and Robber,"[30] such a visit would have been socially acceptable; it seems likely that Roger Mikell, the godfather of Griffith Jr. was a relative.[31] Bridget and Roger may not have been brother and sister, but they certainly acted like it. Only two years apart in age,[32] they possessed kindred personalities and shared a markedly similar viewpoint when it came to extramarital affairs. If Bridget really went to Mikell's house that night, it was only one stop on her itinerary. When she returned home, it was very late, and she had Henry Sadbury with her.

Some time later, on a Saturday night, Bridget suggested that Mary send for Sadbury herself. Mary demurred, but Bridget kept at it and finally "over persuaded" the girl. Bridget then sent a young servant to Henry with the message that Mary wanted to see him.

Sadbury didn't come immediately, and Mary, apparently relieved, went to bed. Bridget, however, stayed up to welcome Henry and then went to rouse Mary, who later complained that Bridget "would not let me alone pinching me by my feete untill I did rise up & I staid wth them till I was weary." Mary then returned to bed, and left Bridget to entertain Sadbury.[33]

On the fourth of August 1680, after Mary had been with Bridget for about two and a half months, the court suddenly ordered that she be removed from the Savage home. Perhaps rumors of Bridget's unconventional behavior had reached the magistrates. Insulted and angry at the turn of events, Bridget addressed some unrecorded, but obviously derogatory, words to the court. Ordered taken into custody for her contemptuous behavior, Bridget later "submitted herself to y[e] Court" and was released after paying court costs.[34]

About a year later Bridget's friendship with Sadbury was definitely over. Her husband had returned home, at least for awhile,[35] but there was another reason for Henry's fall from favor. Bridget had openly taken up with Edward Brotherton, who, at the age of 32, was about four years her junior.[36]

Upset and jealous, Henry Sadbury confronted or threatened Bridget, who complained to the court in the spring of 1681. Henry, who had to post a bond for keeping the peace, waited for the time to expire and petitioned to be discharged, but he hit a snag when Edward Brotherton objected, swearing in open court that "he went in danger & feare of his life by the threats of the sd

Henry Sadbury." The court arrested Sadbury and ordered him to post another bond, this time to keep the peace to everyone, but especially to Brotherton.[37]

This setback did nothing to improve Sadbury's disposition. One can only imagine the words that flew between Henry and Bridget the next time they met. In fact, Sadbury may have deliberately antagonized Bridget to make her say something so *he* could complain to a magistrate. Col. Jenifer listened to Sadbury's grievance and signed a warrant for Bridget to appear before a justice, and then he directed Constable Francis Wharton to deliver it.

With Henry Sadbury tagging along, Wharton obediently headed for the Savage home. As he tried to serve the warrant, Bridget suspiciously asked what it was and who sent it. When Wharton told her it was a warrant from Col. Jenifer commanding her to appear before a magistrate, Bridget immediately knew who was behind it all, and she was incensed.

She grabbed the warrant, and according to an onlooker, "threw it one [on] the ground & said Coll Jenifer should Kiss her arss & she bid Henry Sadbery tell him soe."

Henry did her one better. He reported the affront to two other justices. Bridget was consequently bound over to the court held in June 1681, for contempt of authority and vilifying Jenifer. Rather intolerant of attacks on one of their own, the court considered Bridget's "contempt and intollerable abuses and contemptious behaviour" and fined her 500 pounds of tobacco. For her scandal to Col. Jenifer, she was to be ducked immediately and then stand two days at the next court, one hour each day, with a sign on her breast in capital letters: "FOR HER CONTEMPT OF JUSTICE." The sheriff was ordered to keep her in custody till she found security to ensure her good behavior and the payment of court charges.[38]

It must have been around this time that Bridget's husband died. Griffith's will, which was written in July 1680, wasn't presented to the court until 1685,[39] but two court entries indicate that he probably died in 1681, when he was about 42 years old.

In November 1681, a young servant on the Savage plantation ran away. When he was caught, the court noted that he belonged to Bridget Savage and was apprehended about eight or nine miles from her house.[40] Had Griffith been alive, he would have been named the owner of the servant and the house, not his wife. Married women were not usually referred to as property owners, but widows were.[41]

The other evidence is much more compelling. Just a little over a year later, on 4 January 1682/83, the grand jury presented Bridget Savage for bastardy.[42] Considering the delays inherent in the legal system, Bridget must have been a widow for at least a year at that point. The other young women presented with her for the same crime eventually appeared to answer their charges, but Bridget did not. She may have slipped through the cracks by getting married in the interim. She did not marry Edward Brotherton, though she probably should have.[43]

Instead Bridget married Jarvis [or Gervas] Baggale, who at age 25, was about thirteen years younger than his bride.[44] Though Bridget seemingly would have had something in common with a man interested in tavern keeping, the marriage was not a happy one. Before the fall of 1684, the honeymoon was definitely over.

By September, when Jarvis became so sick that it was necessary to hire Abraham Dorton to attend him, Edward Brotherton had developed the habit of turning up at the old Savage place to visit Bridget. Baggale warned the intruder to get off the plantation, but Brotherton had nothing but scorn for Bridget's new husband. According to Dorton, "Edward Broderton often said he had more to doe there then Mr. Baggale had & gave the sd Baggale many ill words bidinge him begon out of doores & if he ye sd Bagale was not lame, hee would Knock his braines out."[45]

And there was more. While Dorton looked on, Brotherton arrogantly turned to his ailing rival, pointed at Bridget and said that she "was his wife & none of Mr. Bagalles."

To emphasize his point, Brotherton added, "Doe not you Know that Child on her lapp is my Child?"

"Noe," answered Baggale.

"But it is and y^u Knew that well Enough," Brotherton shot back.

The next morning Dorton "saw Edward Broderton came out of the Bed from Bridget Baggale onely in his shirt."

Brotherton was not joking when he ordered Bridget's husband out of his own house. In November, Jarvis Baggale complained that his wife Bridget "& Edward Brotherton did illegally accompany togeather and Keep him from his habitacon." When Baggale asked for the court's protection, they ordered Edward Brotherton and Bridget Baggale to appear to answer the complaint.[46]

What the magistrates said on that occasion is not known, but the sight of Bridget must have jogged their memory. They noted that she, the widow of Griffith Savage and "now wife of Mr. Jearvis Bagale" had neglected to provide the court with an inventory of Savage's estate as directed by law. In January, they ordered that the situation be remedied. At this juncture Baggale petitioned for the Savage estate to be divided so that young Griffith could have his share and so Baggale, as the widow's husband, could have his.[47] Baggale's claim may have been technically correct, but Bridget was in no mood to assist him.[48]

The situation at home continued to deteriorate, though Baggale was apparently feeling a lot better physically. In February, he again attended court and, like most of the other attendees, sought refreshment at the nearby tavern. Unfortunately, his rival was drinking there too. The controversy swirling around Bridget, Baggale and Brotherton was no secret, of course, and the gentlemen at the bar probably encouraged a confrontation.[49]

That is when the sarcastic side of Jarvis Baggale emerged. He announced that "Edward Broderton was a very Courteous man, for when [Baggale] could not lye wth his wife himself, [Brotherton] would."

The tavern probably erupted in laughter, and it was above the tumult that Brotherton addressed Baggale with his caustic reply, "[I] lay wth her before you did & since, And whats that to you?" Brotherton then brazenly added that he planned to do it again.

While the men in her life were talking, Bridget was taking action. On the 11th of March, she submitted Griffith's will to the court.[50] In this document, Griffith was surprisingly generous to a wife that he must have known was fooling around. It was written in July 1680, the month after someone—undoubtedly Griffith—had warned Henry Sadbury to stay away. In the will Griffith three times referred to Mrs. Savage as "my dearly beloved wife Bridget" and decreed that she and their son should equally divide the cattle, horses and personal estate. Unlike many of his less considerate contemporaries, Griffith declared that his widow could live on the home plantation her entire life, not just during her widowhood. She was given full custody of Griffith Jr. till he was nineteen, and made the sole executrix. If Griffith Jr. were to predecease Bridget, the entire estate would go to her and her heirs.[51]

There was one other unusual aspect of Griffith's will. Three witnesses had signed the original document, but when it was presented to the court, two of them, Roger Mikell and William Prettiman, were dead.[52] The only living witness just happened to be Bridget's lover.

Edward Brotherton swore that he saw Griffith sign the will, and the court "well Knowing the hand of the said Griffith," believed him. If the gentlemen of the court accepted the will as genuine, we should probably not second guess them. But still, certain suspicions arise. It is interesting to note that both Brotherton and Bridget were literate, and possessed both the ability and motive to forge a favorable will. Also, Bridget may have known Griffith's hand better than the court did.[53] And, unlike the magistrates in 1685, we have the advantage of examining Edward Brotherton's subsequent brushes with the law. For instance, in December 1698, the court judged Brotherton to be "guilty of a great misdemeanor" when they found him in possession of several pieces of counterfeit money.[54]

Besides taking care of the will, Bridget took measures to hamper the appraisers sent to do the inventory. Going over the heads of the local court, she complained to the Governor, who commanded the proceedings to halt and ordered Baggale to appear at the next General Court. Whatever Bridget said in her complaint did not hold up entirely, however. In the absence of a clear directive from the Governor, the local court, held 12 May 1685,[55] ordered her to prove the will of Griffith Savage (though they had accepted it two months earlier) and take inventory so the estate of Griffith Jr. could be secured.

At the same court session Baggale informed the magistrates "that he went in dread and feare of his life by Edward Brotherton." This was the second piece of bad news for Bridget, and when the court ordered her lover arrested and kept in the sheriff's custody till posting a bond for his good behavior, she lost control.

After her outburst, the court fined her fifty pounds of tobacco "for prophanly Swearing in open Court." And she was ordered to join Brotherton in the sheriff's custody till she too could post a bond for "ye good behaviour for misdemenrs & threats used in open Court ags^t ye Court."

Bad as things were, they were about to get worse. Baggale went on to complain that Edward Brotherton "doth indecently accompany together wth Bridget ye said Beggalles wife." He added that he had reasons to distrust his wife and believed that "Bridget Begalle & the sd Edward Broderton have had carnal Knowledge together."

Noting that the accounts of various witnesses were confirmed by "comon fame," and that circumstantial evidence strengthened their suspicions, the court cracked down. They again ordered that Brotherton be taken into the sheriff's custody and remain there till he posted another bond "wth Sufficient Security that he forthwth refraine and Shunn (and allwaies hereafter) ye said Bridgets company." They ordered another bond for good behavior and the payment of court charges as well.[56]

That summer Bridget began preparing for the inevitable inventory. At least it seems she started liquidating some of the assets. A debtor was seen transporting cattle, which could presumably be sold to satisfy his obligations. However, when the court discovered the cattle belonged to Bridget Baggale, the widow of Griffith Savage, they backed off, noting that the Governor had halted all proceedings relating to Bridget. The justices preferred to wait "untill his Excellencys Pleasure bee farther Known."[57]

Bridget, however, was still concerned with her own pleasure. In December 1685, Gervas Baggale went to a justice and reported that Edward Brotherton had broken his bond. Because of a technicality, however, the court dismissed the suit, and no details were given.[58]

It wasn't until the summer of 1686, that Bridget produced an inventory of the Savage estate. By then her split with Baggale must have been recognized by the court, for this time they did not refer to her as Bridget Baggale at all; instead they called her Bridget, the relict of Griffith Savage. As specified in Griffith's will, she was granted sole custody of her son's estate.[59]

We don't know much about how Bridget died, but we do know about when. It was in the winter of 1686/87, when she was about 41 years old. By that March, the court was again concerned about the inheritance of young Griffith Savage. Because of his mother's recent death, it was feared that some greedy person would waste or embezzle the estate. Other records indicate that the court had Edward Brotherton in mind; they had no qualms about Jarvis Baggale, who was among the five men ordered to go immediately to the Savage plantation and take an "exact Inventory." To head off anticipated trouble, the court ordered two trustees to take possession of the estate. If they met opposition from "any evill minded p[er]son" the sheriff was ordered to use "such means as ye occasion may Require."[60]

That summer the five appraisers submitted the inventory, along with a list of goods at the plantation claimed by Edward Brotherton. With Bridget out of the picture and the Savage estate still unsettled, Brotherton experienced a temporary reformation, becoming a constable in September 1688. He must have done an acceptable job, for two months later, at the request of Sheriff Daniel Jenifer, he was sworn in as deputy undersheriff for the county.[61]

Three years later, however, the old Brotherton was back. On "New Year's Day during the night," he assaulted Robert Davis in his own house and during the struggle bit off Davis' nose, which was left hanging "by some small matter of skin or flesh." It wasn't till almost a year later that Davis, by then "cured" by Dorothy Bell, brought suit against his attacker.[62] Forced to pay damages of 1000 pounds of tobacco and court costs, Brotherton may have spent the next few years trying to make money, but his efforts backfired when the authorities discovered it was counterfeit.[63] Found guilty of a "great misdemeanor," Brotherton withdrew from his life of crime and contented himself with harassing Griffith Savage Jr., who repeatedly filed suits against his mother's old friend.[64] When Edward Brotherton died in 1721, he had attained the age of 72 years, a long life for those days. Irascible to the end, he left his wife Mary no means of support in his will,[65] thus forcing her to go to court to set matters right.[66] The fate of the child he had with Bridget is unknown.[67]

Jarvis Baggale recovered from his brief marriage to Bridget, moved to town and made something of a career out of providing security for people needing to post bonds. In 1693, Baggale purchased the tavern where he and Edward Brotherton had had their memorable confrontation eight years earlier.[68] For many years he was proprietor of the tavern where the court was held, and in 1699, became jailer as well.[69] About nine years after Bridget died, Baggale was presented to the court for committing fornication with Elizabeth Skinner, to whom he insisted he was legally married. Lacking evidence to prove otherwise, the court acquitted them, and the couple stayed together.[70] After having enjoyed close ties with the court for many years, Jarvis Baggale became a justice himself in August 1704. He never served in that capacity, however, for he died just over two months later.[71] His wife, who in some ways was similar to the first Mrs. Baggale, regularly turned up in the court records, especially after becoming a widow.[72]

Henry Sadbury, responsible for the warrant that Bridget found so repugnant, was eventually himself bound over to court for contempt of a warrant. Taken into custody, Sadbury convinced two men to post his bond and then made himself scarce, leaving the bondsmen to pay the penalty.[73]

Griffith Savage Jr., who probably came of age not long after his mother's death, remained on his father's plantation. Since Griffith was at first suspected of possessing some of Brotherton's counterfeit money, it is possible that Brotherton made a bogus payment to Griffith or tried to include him in criminal activities.[74] Though Griffith had some minor scrapes with the law—detaining a lady's horse in 1699, and refusing to serve on the grand jury in 1705—his reputation suffered no real damage;[75] he went on to dispute with Edward Brotherton,[76] to serve on several juries[77] and to sell part of his land.[78]

After the death of his first wife,[79] Griffith married a second time,[80] and when he died in 1739, he named eight children in his will.[81] From all indications he had enjoyed a fairly long and peaceful life, quite different from that of his mother.

Unconventional as she was, Bridget Savage had been ahead of her time, although in a rather negative way. Whether she intended to or not, Bridget demonstrated the level of equality that one brazen colonial woman could achieve. If men could fight and drink, own property and appeal to the Governor, sleep around and use profanity, then so could she.

During her forty-one years, Bridget attracted lovers, broke hearts, fought with fury, swore at justices, defied the law, spoke without thinking, married the wrong man, committed adultery, threatened the lives of her neighbors and tried to improperly influence a teenage girl. Her single shining moment occurred when she helped rescue an abused four-year-old, and even that generous act really wasn't her own idea. Everything considered, Bridget probably led a rather unhappy and wretched life. But it certainly wasn't boring.

Chapter Ten

Tabitha Scarburgh Smart Browne Custis Hill

The Virginia Aristocrat

Wealth could provide painted dishes and monogrammed bottles filled with elegant food and imported wine. It could dress you regally and house you in mansions, but it could not protect you from grief. Disease and accident were traumas that everyone suffered, but the very presence of riches seemed to attract additional attacks by anyone–rich or poor–who coveted your possessions. Though she grew up to live in one of the grandest houses in Colonial Virginia, Tabitha Scarburgh's life was scarred not only by violent illness, but also by hostile servants lurking on her own plantation, Turkish pirates on the high seas and a vindictive minister who had her thrown into prison.

Born in Virginia in 1639, Tabitha, as the eldest daughter of Col. Edmund Scarburgh,[1] had a childhood of privilege and luxury; even the Governor himself gave her one of the best ewe lambs in the county.[2] Her social status would have guaranteed an abundance of eager suitors, and by the time she was fourteen years old, she had become the wife of John Smart. About nine years older than his bride, John had gained the favor of Tabitha's father, who, on 12 July 1653, gave the young couple a plantation at Maggattey Bay complete with houses and cattle.[3]

We know very little about John and Tabitha's marriage, except that it was short. John died young leaving Tabitha with a daughter who bore her mother's name, maiden name and all.[4] Perhaps John, if he was still alive when his daughter was born, was so enamored with his young wife that he wanted to name his daughter after her. It could have been a nod of gratitude for the plantation, or maybe the elder Tabitha Scarburgh Smart, in an early show of her forceful personality, insisted that the baby be named after her.

As a wealthy widow, probably not yet out of her teens, Tabitha again would have had her pick of landed gentlemen. This time she smiled upon Devorax Browne, a wealthy merchant who could boast of extensive land holdings and political prominence.[5] Tabitha's father was the only person in the county who paid more taxes and owned more servants than Devorax Browne.[6]

Devorax, Tabitha and little Tabitha settled in on their Nandua Creek plantation,[7] which had easy access to Chesapeake Bay. Not far away was a mill in which Browne had part ownership. In addition to shoemaking workshops where many of Browne's servants labored, the plantation buildings included a milk house, a small house sturdy enough to imprison troublesome servants, a lockable clapboard store, the servant quarters and the master's house which boasted at least one interior door fitted with lock and key.

Little Tabitha was probably about six years old in 1660, when she was joined by a half-brother named Edmund. While his childhood may have been tranquil, his parents' lives during these years were complicated by recurring servant problems.

When Stephen Warren ran away during the summer of 1663, Browne saw to it that Warren received twenty-five lashes on his naked shoulders. At the same court Browne complained about his servant Ruth Colledge, who steadfastly refused to name the father of her unborn child. Called into court, Ruth behaved obstinately and was sent to the house of correction for a month. The following March, when another of Browne's servants was sent on an errand but went farther than authorized, he was lashed 28 times on his bare shoulders.[8]

The servants also pilfered goods from the Browne plantation, often relieving their master of half a dozen bottles of liquor at a time. During the winter of 1664/1665, they stole a hundred pounds of tobacco, a pair of shoes, a case of liquor, an Indian basket of nails and a case of brandy. Placed on the back of a mare, the goods were transported to a neighbor's house after dark.[9]

In May 1667, a servant named Henry Permaine made a legal bid for freedom by going to court and claiming he had served his time, which was six years according to his indenture. Upon Browne's denial and Henry's failure to produce documentation, the court declared that Henry was 18 years old–which meant he would be obligated to serve another six years.[10] A few months later Browne brought another servant to court and accused him of unnamed "trespasses." After begging for mercy, this servant agreed to serve Browne for an additional two years.[11]

This unrest among the servants ensured a stressful life for Tabitha, especially during her husband's long absences. And while she apparently sometimes went with him to Jamestown and joined him on at least one of his trips to England, where she sat for her portrait, there were other times when she remained behind to manage the plantation. And she had trouble maintaining control.

While her husband was in England, probably in 1666 or 1667,[12] Tabitha complained to John Wise that her servants had broken up her storehouse. This information came as no surprise to Wise. He had sipped the contraband himself. He told Tabitha he had seen a bottle of English spirits or brandy in the window of Mihill Ricketts, who "takeing ye Bottle in his hand said Come Neighbour I will make bould of my freinds drame to drink to y^u." Wise did not know who the friend was, but he did recognize the taste. Immediately after commenting on the drink's good quality, Wise said "he beleived it was Mr. Brownes."[13]

When Browne returned home, he sued his thirsty neighbors and recovered a total of 3000 pounds of tobacco for his losses and 1500 pounds of tobacco for their "Entertaining his Servants."

One December night in 1670, the lure of Devorax Browne's brandy played a part in unraveling a daring plot.[14] Confident that they, along with several colleagues, would soon escape from the oppression of Mr. Browne, three servants persuaded another servant, 17-year-old Alexander Swan, to squeeze between some broken boards at the back of Browne's store. As instructed, Alexander shoved a cask of brandy up to the broken wall and then hid while his co-conspirators held the boards aside and bored a hole in the cask. The brandy was spouting out nicely when Devorax Browne made his move.

It is unclear whether he had been tipped off to the activities planned for that night or whether he was just there guarding the goods that had been systematically disappearing. Whatever the case, Browne had been waiting inside the store, and he was prepared. About a gallon of brandy was sloshing in the servants' kettle when their master raised a pistol and fired. Though he undoubtedly realized that one of the thieves was inside the store, Browne rushed out to capture the three servants with the brandy. Alexander, who had dropped to the ground at the sound of the shot, crept out of the building and hurried off to bed.

The captured servants were locked in a small house, where Alexander saw them the next morning pacing back and forth, vowing to be free. But that did not happen. Instead, the incident sparked a thorough investigation, and Browne learned of not one, but two escape plots. One had already failed; the other was about to take place.

A few years earlier, an 18-year-old carpenter named Isack Medcalfe had been earning thirty pounds of tobacco a day working on board Captain Pitts' ship, the *Dove*.[15] When Pitts died, Devorax Browne was left in charge of the estate and somehow acquired Isack as a servant.[16] It was not a congenial arrangement.

Taken to Browne's plantation, Isack found conditions there to be deplorable and complained bitterly to the other servants. He said that he

"never saw any people kept soe in the country before, and if he had soe long
to serve hear as some of us had, he would hang himselfe before he would
serve itt." It wasn't long, however, before Isack abandoned the idea of
suicide and began promoting another option: "He wondered that wee would
live as wee did and not indeavor to make an Escape and run away." When
asked how that could be accomplished, he replied, "Doe as four did at
Pocomock, take a boat & runn away."

Little more was said until October, when their master was called away
to the assembly at Jamestown. Because Tabitha's father had been summoned
to answer serious charges there, she and the children probably went too.
With such a window of opportunity, the servants hastily developed plans to
"take the Boat that belonged to the Ship." Besides providing the inspiration,
Isack fashioned oars. Another servant stole sails from the loft of Browne's
storehouse and helped cut them to fit the smaller craft. Mary Warrener, a
servant in Tabitha's kitchen, baked bread to provision the voyage and also
assembled meal and linen.

Although she had been planning to escape with the men, Mary did not
join them when the time came. An unwed mother of an infant daughter,[17] she
may have had second thoughts. Perhaps Margery Gary, her fellow servant,
persuaded Mary to miss the boat. The mother of two young children herself,
Margery steadfastly refused to have anything to do with the plot, even though
her husband was one of its leaders.

After dark on a blustery Saturday night, the six men servants gathered
to load the boat with the tools, linen, clothing and food. They then climbed
aboard and attempted to sail the little craft out of the "gut" and into the wide
creek that emptied into nearby Chesapeake Bay. Their hasty preparations
had been adequate, but their timing could not have been worse. The wind,
now gusted violently in exactly the wrong direction and "blew soe hard at
Northwest as [we] could not stirr out of the gutt."

Realizing that it was impossible to make their escape that night, the men
quickly turned their attention to hiding the evidence of their failed attempt.
Before returning the boat to its accustomed place, they pulled up at a point
of land and threw their provisions and tools ashore for later retrieval. "Soe
Mary fetched the Linnen & such things as shee had there & said she never
saw such fooles in her life to loose such a opportunity as that, for there was
in the milke house a great deale of Butter & 14 or 15 Cheeses that she
ordered for our voyage."

By the time Browne returned from Jamestown, all evidence except for
the mutilated sails had vanished, and one of the servants devised a ploy to
take care of that, too: "Wee will fetch the sayles downe again & lay them by
the Creek side & then come & call [everyone] by and swear [we] saw men
come from towards Bedlam [the storehouse], but when we come to the Creek

none of us should find them." As planned an innocent man discovered the ruined sails, and the next day, after their scheme had succeeded, and unknown thieves had been blamed for the damage, the wily servant couldn't help boasting, "Was it not well turned? Let [me] alone for a scurvy Trick at any time."

Having come so close without arousing suspicion, the emboldened servants broadened their scope and started to plan anew. Word of the intended escape spread from plantation to plantation, and the conspiracy quickly grew to include at least fifteen servants from six different masters. With so many involved, confusion crept in, and a more unruly faction grappled for leadership. This time they would forego Browne's small boat and would steal his sloop instead. Some wanted to arm it with John West's gun. It was so heavy it would ruin the horse that carried it, but they didn't care, for its noise "would make people afraid to follow us." They would have "Black James yᵗ came downe with Cornelius a dutchmans wife . . . to be our Pylott to goe for New England." Or, on the other hand, someone would steal a compass, and they could go to Venice to live. To ensure their plans stayed secret, they swore they would "knock that person on the head who should first reveale" the plot. The more daring conspirators impatiently urged that the attempt be made at Christmas, even though the weather might be inclement and the master and his family would be at home.

One of the more cautious servants who had participated in the first attempt when the Browne family was gone could not imagine any other scenario. To his impatient cohorts, however, the solution seemed obvious. They would simply tie up everyone in the house.

Two of the servants vowed "that they would bind my master Browne & Mrs Browne & M[istress] Tabitha Smart," who by then was a teenager. Another servant said "that he would Hock my Mastr browne and when they had soe done they would take the Keyes and take what liquor & other necessaryes they had occasion for out of the store and carry with them to accomodate our intended Escape."

Even this was not enough for one would-be runaway with bitter memories of the pampered Tabitha Smart. Intoxicated with his impending freedom, Robert Milner added a final defiant touch by saying "that he would have M[istress] Tabitha Smarts Read [red] Taby [taffeta] petticoat for to carry with us for our Colours."

Such talk of hocking and binding and stealing petticoats certainly would have alarmed Tabitha. Even with her husband at home, she and her daughter were not safe on their own plantation. What might happen when Devorax was off attending to business or politics?

Though undoubtedly angry about his pilfered goods, concerned about the possible loss of so many servants, and disturbed at the threats to his family's safety, Devorax Browne took his time in filing a suit against the culprits. He eventually claimed that they caused damages amounting to 13,260 pounds of tobacco. In addition to the ruined sails, they had stolen other goods including almost thirty yards of linen, more than a hundred gallons of brandy, a hogshead of white wine, 300 pounds of sugar, and eleven pair of fine worsted stockings worth seventy pounds of tobacco a pair. Devorax Browne's ten guilty servants, including Mary Warrener, were each ordered to pay an equal portion of the losses suffered by their master.[18] Naturally, the penniless servants would have to satisfy their debts by serving extra time.

The schemes of the discontented servants had only been the crowning stress in a very unsettling year for Tabitha. Though she would have been troubled by the servants' threats, she must have been even more worried about her father. In spite of his brilliant mind, his wealth and his powerful connections, his life was imploding.

On a Sunday night that spring on the plantation of Edmund Scarburgh's lady friend, a disgruntled worker had assaulted Scarburgh, throwing him down twice and then giving him a "desperate blow" with a heavy wooden lantern. To make matters even more uncomfortable, the attacker's words were quoted in open court and placed on record: He had said "hee would worke no more for Scarburgh & his whores and bastards."[19]

A few months later, Col. Scarburgh found himself in more serious trouble, this time for flying in the face of the Governor's policy of maintaining peace with the Indians. Not only had he stirred up the Native Americans, his actions had been so horrific that he had offended the sensibilities of a society that considered court ordered whippings a form of entertainment.

The October trip to Jamestown that the Browne servants had found so convenient coincided exactly with Col. Edmund Scarburgh's summons from the Governor. The Brownes must have accompanied Scarburgh to Jamestown to lend what support they could. On 12 September 1670, Governor Berkeley had sent a directive to the sheriff of Northampton County beginning, "Whereas I am informed by persons of known worth and Integritie and by some of the Officers of both the Counties on the Easterne Shoare Thatt Collonel Edmund Scarburgh hath contrary to my order and the peace long since established betweene us and the Indians unjustly and most Tiranously oppressed them by Murthering whipping and burning them, By taking their children by force from [those] who are their parents and many other waies to the apparent hazard of the said peace."[20]

Local tradition fills in a few details, accurate or not, of one incident that happened that summer. Scarburgh, who was known as "The Conjurer," had called the Indians together, promising them they would hear the voice of the Great Spirit. When they arrived, Scarburgh seated them in a ditch. Hidden at one end was a carefully aimed "cannon which 'spoke' at the appropriate time." This atrocity has come to be known as the "ditch murder."[21]

Since such actions clearly undermined the peace, the Governor commanded the sheriff to "Arrest the Body of the said Coll Edmund Scarburgh and him to cause personally to appeare before mee and the Councell and Assembly on the Seaventh Day of October Next." Scarburgh was arrested the 24th of September, but he managed to avoid the shame of arriving in Jamestown in chains; declaring he had been summoned four days earlier to represent Accomack County, Scarburgh crossed the bay as a burgess instead of a prisoner.[22]

His brother Charles, as the personal physician to Charles II, was in a position to influence the King, so Edmund Scarburgh was accustomed to a measure of immunity.[23] Perhaps even now his connections provided some protection, but the Governor was not inclined toward leniency. Only six months earlier, Henry Smith, one of the Governor's favorites, had appeared in General Court to fight charges of murder and rape. And though Smith (probably thanks to the Governor's clout) ultimately went free, the Governor would not have forgotten that Scarburgh was responsible for marshaling the strong accusations leveled against him.

In fact, Tabitha herself had made an enemy of the Governor's friend. Demonstrating that she had inherited some of her father's wiliness, Tabitha had allowed Smith to believe that she would testify in his favor during the county trial. Instead, "Mrs. Browne whome y[e] s[d] Smith did call as Evidence for him did evidence ag[st] him & wth Relacon of most Notorious behaviour of the s[d] Smith in takeing up a plate to throw at his Wife with scandollous words often by the s[d] Smith repeated & allso y[t] y[e] s[d] Mrs. Browne saw y[e] markes of blows on y[e] s[d] Smiths Wifes bruised body."[24]

No such details have survived from the trial of Tabitha's father. The verdict was not as harsh as it could have been, but "touching the complaint of the Indians and other matters contayned in the said charges," it was ordered that "Coll Edmund Scarburgh shall from hence forth stand suspended from all offices as well military as civill untill by his future obedience and fidellity It shall please the Right Hon[ble] the Governo[r] to Restore him."[25]

The most forceful man in the county now had no legal power at all. It is not surprising that Scarburgh faded quickly. By May 1671, he was sick,[26] and in a letter to London dated the 23rd of that same month, Governor Berkeley noted that "Scarborough is Deade."[27] Along with his legitimate children, the colonel left a tangled web of debts, the special woman friend who was almost certainly his mistress, and her three daughters. A year later, Tabitha, who apparently harbored no resentment against her father's second family, witnessed the document that gave her three young half-sisters possession of a good share of the wealth that Scarburgh had helped their mother accumulate: 5000 acres of land, livestock, silver, linen, furniture, kitchen ware, corn, wheat and Negro servants.[28]

During this time Tabitha probably expended a good deal of energy on her father's estate. Her brother Charles, brother-in-law John West and her husband had been named administrators, but since Devorax was again away on business, Tabitha was acting as his legal "agent and attorney." It took more than a year and a half to iron out the differences between Scarburgh's legal heirs and his former mistress.[29]

Meanwhile, Tabitha was dealing with another difficult servant. In late 1671, her husband had received credit for transporting one Edward Grindley, an educated "gentleman" for whom Browne hoped to receive a high price.[30] When a well-heeled buyer did not materialize, Browne put Grindley to work on his own plantation where the new servant soon became as disgruntled as the old ones.

Aware that such a servant could use his learning against the interests of his master, Tabitha, who was increasingly in charge of affairs at home, confiscated Grindley's papers and locked them in her chamber. Later that summer Grindley acquired an urgent reason to escape; he would soon be facing the consequences of fathering the child of another of Browne's servants. Grindley was looking for an opportunity, and he soon found it.

The incident was reported by the same woman servant who had provisioned the escape attempt two years earlier. In spite of Mary's past mistakes, Tabitha, who was gone from home, sent the key of her chamber to Mary so she could "doe some Necessary buisnes there, it beinge after your declarants mistresse had taken the writinges from Edward Grindley, the said Edward Grindley seeinge the chamber doore open, thrust himselfe in, went to a chest where the writinges were, hee the said Grindley tooke out of the chest many writinges, some hee putt in againe & some writinges he the said Grindley carried away with him to the Quantity of two sheets of paper."[31]

That September Tabitha went to court and complained that "her pretended servt Edward Grindley" had absented himself from her service and had not tended to his work as he had been trusted to do. Though the runaway clearly was not present, the court ordered that he return to Tabitha's service and pay all damages, or be placed in the sheriff's custody.[32]

To hamper her servant's flight, Tabitha posted a note on the door of the courthouse at Pungoteage: "These are to give Notice to all persons within this County & Collony that they neither Transport out of this County Deale bargaine or entertaine or have any manner of Comerce upon any pretence whatsoever with my Servant Edward Greenly as they will answere all damages that may or shall acrue thereupon according to law in such Case provided witness my hand this 17th of September 1672. Tabitha Browne."[33]

Grindley successfully evaded his obligations as both a servant and a father, at least for a while. The following March, when Anne Peale swore that Grindley had fathered her child, the court again ordered that he be taken into custody. That apparently did not happen,[34] and nearly a year later he still had not paid the woman employed to nurse Anne's child, even though Anne swore that he had promised to pay her fine and support their child.[35]

Some time later Tabitha located Grindley and started proceedings against him in the General Court at Jamestown. While the judges rejected her claim that Grindley was still her servant, they did ultimately make him pay Tabitha 4 pounds 13 shillings and 700 pounds of tobacco.[36]

With Devorax Browne off on another trip during 1672, Tabitha resumed her leadership role. That November, she was in court promising to train a servant as a shoemaker in exchange for two extra years of service.[37] To legitimize her actions, she produced a power of attorney signed by her husband, who had been gone since the previous January.

It is possible that Devorax Browne never did return home. A matter of months after Tabitha agreed to train the shoemaker, Browne was dead. On 16 June 1673, Tabitha presented his will for probate, but the court rejected it on the grounds that there was not enough evidence and testimony to prove it was his real will.[38] It could be that the witnesses lived so far away that they could not conveniently swear to its authenticity, or the will may have been hastily prepared under difficult circumstances. Because there was no legal will, Tabitha was granted administration of the estate the next day.

This time the new widow was in no hurry to remarry. Her marriage to Browne had amounted to an apprenticeship in business, and she had become more skillful at acquiring and managing servants, witnessing documents, filing suits, handling finances and administering estates. Not only did Tabitha go on to manage the estate of her dead husband, but upon his death she took over his duties as administrator of the estate of Captain Pitt as well.[39]

Though probably still reeling from her recent loss, Tabitha was not incapacitated by her grief. A few months after her husband's death, she was in the market for a pair of wheels, and she wanted the best. Mathew Shippe offered her a cart and wheels for 500 pounds of tobacco, but Tabitha wanted only wheels, insisting that they "do me good service." When Shippe offered to warrant a set of wheels for the same price, she agreed. Nine months later, Tabitha saw Shippe at court and when told that her wheels were ready, her response was, "Are they good?" There was nothing second rate about Tabitha.[40]

By the mid 1670's, Tabitha's children were striking out on their own. Her daughter Tabitha Smart had married William Whittington and together they produced a third Tabitha.[41] Though only a teenager, Edmund Browne had probably acquired considerable experience helping his mother manage affairs and was already calling himself a merchant. It was apparently in this capacity that he made a trip to England in 1677.

In the course of looking for goods to take back to Virginia, Edmund found something else he wanted to take home. Her name was Martha Davis. This young lady welcomed the attentions of her seventeen-year-old suitor, and they were married on the 27th of June 1677, in Surry County,[42] but she wasn't ready to sail for the colonies just yet.

When Edmund Browne boarded a ship bound for Virginia, his bride elected to stay behind in England. It was fortunate for her that she did. Captain John Martin's ship had probably not gone far when it was attacked by Turks. The details are scant, but the passengers and crew were captured, and at least three of them, including Edmund, were taken to Turkey. It was there in 1678, that Edmund Browne died in captivity at the age of eighteen. Eventually Captain Martin and another Englishman named Timothy Law made their way back to England with "Capt Jno Martin Rep[o]rting that He [Edmund Browne] Died and Timothy Law, Saying, He Carried y[e] said Browne to his Grave."[43]

A half a world away in Virginia, when Edmund did not return as soon as expected, Tabitha's first twinges of worry must have escalated into dread and then anguish as it became clear that something terrible had happened to her son. She probably waited for a year or more before her worst fears were confirmed.

Maybe Tabitha felt especially alone after Edmund's death, maybe her loss sucked the excitement out of her shrewd business deals, or maybe her grief drove her into the arms of a third husband. On the other hand, Tabitha may have recognized an offer that was just too good to pass up.

John Custis II, who lived in neighboring Northampton County, was extremely wealthy and politically prominent. At one time or another he had been county justice, sheriff, member of the Governor's council, surveyor, coroner, vestryman and a major general in charge of all the militia on the Eastern Shore. Not only that, a few years earlier he had put the finishing touches on the original Arlington, one of the most magnificent mansions in Virginia—a large house fine enough to serve as the capitol in 1676, during Bacon's Rebellion, when things were not going well for Governor Berkeley around Jamestown.[44]

Archaeological excavations done at Arlington in 1988 and 1994, show that the house was 54 feet wide and 42½ feet deep with a vaulted cellar below and two large chimney bases on each end. Built of brick, it was decorated with recessed masonry hearts. Old documents indicate that the mansion, surrounded by gardens and orchards, was "three stories high besides garrets" and possessed one of the first dining rooms in colonial Virginia.[45]

One possible drawback for Tabitha might have been the personality of the great home's owner, who some considered to be as pompous as his mansion. In the 1660's, a woman, forced by Custis to pay the same debt twice, had repeatedly defamed him and pledged to "post him for a knave at James Citty."[46] Several years later when the people of Accomack County attempted to present their grievances against him for his arbitrary actions as the collector of customs, Custis became "exceedingly angry and 'presuming on the dignity of his place, and great authority,' threatened the people, took away that paper and demanded a view of any other they might draw up. 'The people being terrified and affrighted drew up no other grievances at that time.'" On behalf of the citizens in Custis' district, the House of Burgesses petitioned "that the inhabitants might not 'for the future, by the power of greatness of any person, be hindered or molested in giving in their just grievances.'" The Governor "stated he would so caution Colonel Custis for the future that no anger should carry him into any such acts of heat."[47]

About the same time, Mary Tilney heard some of her sarcastic in-laws "sayinge the severity and Rigidnes of the said Coll Custis was soe greate that they could doe noe lesse then give him the Honor to call him Kinge Custis." The fact that Mary felt comfortable enough to quote her husband's relatives in the presence of Custis himself, might suggest that there was another side to the Colonel–perhaps even a sense of humor, caustic though it might have been.

Why Mary was visiting Arlington is unclear, but not long after she had shared her gossip a "Younge Lad Named William Lewis" arrived with a message from Mary's husband. Young William, "after hee had delivered the same, Saucily clapt himselfe downe in A chaire with his hatt on his head in the said Coll Custis dineinge Roome before & in prsence of him, w[ch] hee the said Coll lookinge about & takeinge notice of, hee said to this Boy, how now Sirrah, don't you Know that I am Kinge Custis, Jokingly as yor depont apprehended . . . reprehendinge the said Boy for his Rude unmannerlines."[48]

By this time, Tabitha was a formidable personage too. About forty years old, she had fended for herself for the past six or seven years and had managed her absent husband's affairs for years before that. Self-assured and independently wealthy herself, Tabitha was probably up to the task of handling "Kinge Custis."

It is not clear exactly when they married, but in May 1679, Tabitha Browne's lawyer came to court regarding her servants and her money. After that, Tabitha, whose name had been appearing so regularly, all but vanished from the court records. The next March, it was noted that John Custis was the current owner of a servant who had recently belonged to Tabitha Browne. Whether the transfer of ownership resulted from purchase or marriage is unknown, but the two may have wed as early as 1679. They probably had been married for some time by 16 August 1681, when the records mentioned that Custis was married to Tabitha Browne, the administrator of Devorax Browne.[49]

So, Tabitha was probably newly married and living in a mansion when her widowed daughter-in-law arrived in Virginia. The young lady may not have been particularly welcome, for it is unlikely that Tabitha had approved of her son's marriage. Married at fourteen herself, Tabitha was in no position to criticize a seventeen-year-old groom, but other issues were involved. Tabitha would naturally be reluctant to release her son's estate, especially to someone like Martha Davis, who may have been pretty, but who was probably not aristocratic. Jonathan Davis Jr., a witness to the nuptials and probably Martha's brother, was a 30-year-old dyer by trade.[50]

By the summer of 1679, Martha had learned of her husband's fate. As his wife, she had not been especially anxious to go to Virginia, but as his widow, she had found the prospect of that trip more agreeable. Before leaving for the colonies, Martha carefully laid the groundwork for proving that she had legally married the wealthy young Virginian. First, in August 1679, she obtained a copy of the marriage record as it appeared in the parish church of "St Mary Newington Butts in the County of Surrey." The document, which certified that the two were married just over two years earlier, was signed by the parish clerk. Then, in October, with that certificate in hand, Jonathan Davis Jr. appeared before officials in London at the "request of Martha Brown the Widow and Relict of Edmond Browne Merchant who lately in his voyage to Virginia was taken by the Turks and (as is advised is Since deceased)." When Davis swore that he had been present and had seen Edmund Browne and Martha Davis joined in wedlock, the officials wrote out his testimony and affixed the seal of London.[51]

Armed with her legal documents, Martha arrived in Virginia during the summer of 1680. That August she went to court and petitioned for administration of Browne's estate, which the court granted,[52] but it is unclear if she remained in Virginia to pressure for possession of her share. John and Tabitha Custis were certainly in no hurry to hand it over, but when they faced the inevitable four years later, Martha was there. In May 1684, the Custises settled with Martha by deeding her the 850 acre "Andewy Plantation" that had once belonged to Devorax Browne.[53] The Custises retained the title to another 3700 acres, that had once belonged to Tabitha's son. By claiming that Edmund Browne had "deserted" the land, Custis had obtained a patent for it. [54]

Martha was still around, but anxious to be off, ten months later, when she submitted an inventory that included 48 head of livestock, an assortment of table linen, several kitchen items, two tables, twelve chairs, a cart and wheels, 1500 pounds of tobacco, two beds with bedding, a looking glass and two chamber pots. In the estate were also three men servants, but Martha was planning to leave Virginia before their terms of service could be calculated, so John Custis agreed to send that information to her at the next shipping.[55] Martha held onto the land for fifteen years as an absentee landlord, and then she and her next husband, a mariner, sold the plantation to the man who had been renting it.[56]

During the 1680's and into the 1690's, Tabitha reigned at Arlington with "King" Custis. Just as their mansion far exceeded the typical colonial home in splendor, the fabric of their daily lives contrasted sharply with that of their poorer neighbors. The number of artifacts recovered during the archeological excavations of Arlington was disappointing, but the few that came to light illustrate the luxuries that the Custises enjoyed.[57]

In the cellar entrance was found the neck portion of a Rhenish stoneware "pear-bellied jug." Originally about eight inches high with a three-inch wide rim, the jug was likely used for drinking rather than serving beverages. On a blue background it has molded floral decorations joined by curving stems, a pattern typically produced between 1675 and 1700, a time period that meshes neatly with Tabitha's tenure at Arlington. Another artifact, a small English Delftware bowl, thanks to its pale blue background, can be dated more precisely to the 1680's.[58] Hand painted with a jug of blue flowers, this dish must have brightened Tabitha's dining room before it shattered, and, becoming worthless to her, was relegated to the trash, where the passage of 300 years transformed it into archeological treasure.

While the jug and the bowl may have added a touch of elegance to Arlington, they did not shout upper-class like John Custis's monogrammed wine bottle. Made of glass in England, such bottles with names, initials or seals identifying the owners were popular with wealthy Virginians; only the very rich could flaunt such status symbols. The fragments found in Arlington's cellar, when pieced together, formed a nearly complete bottle, six inches high, with a rounded body and a short tapered neck. Just below the neck is an impressed seal containing John Custis's initials, an "I" (which is the 17th century equivalent of a J) overwritten on a "C." Custis's little wine bottle, which was probably made between 1670-1690,[59] may have slipped from the fingers of a careless servant before Tabitha arrived, but even if it did, she must have admired others like it, if not every day, then certainly on special occasions like the celebration that surely accompanied her marriage to John Custis.

Though the new couple's wealth enabled them to shun home-grown cider and crude eating utensils, it could not fend off all misfortune. By 1680, John Custis was suffering from a lingering illness. Finding it necessary to repeatedly defer court actions, he sent a message to the court saying that "Gods hand haveing a longe time layne heavy on me and now through his great mercy hath raised me up but not yet to that strength as I dare to Attempt goeing abroad soe farr as yᵉ Court, Knowinge it will not only hazard my health but my life, for that I desire yᵉ Court will please to lett it bee referred a little longer till I can recover strength." John Custis signed the note at Arlington on December 29, 1680.[60]

Custis's convalescence may have been slow, but he did eventually grow strong enough to be out and about. A few years later, on the way to a neighbor's house, he lost a key. When he discovered it missing, Custis, along with his servants no doubt, returned to search the roadway. When they failed to find the key, Custis concluded that someone else had picked it up, and anxious to get it back, he turned to the colonial bulletin board. For two court sessions during the summer of 1684, he had his son post a notice at the courthouse door: "A Key of 6 inches in length or thereabouts belonging to Coll Jno Custis was lost on Wednesday yᵉ 18ᵗʰ of this instant June between his owne house & yᵉ house of Joseph Benthall Whosoever may have taken it up are desired to make informacon there of to Capt John Custis now prsent at yᵉ Court."[61]

Col. Custis's poor health continued to plague him. Not only did he have his son post the notice at court, he also sent Tabitha to court in his place. On the first of May 1684, he gave her power of attorney; the next day they both signed Martha Browne's release which freed them from any further claims on the part of Edmund Browne's widow. That same day Tabitha went alone to acknowledge the document in open court.[62] Later that fall, Tabitha joined her husband as they cited their "love and affection" and gave their kinsman Joseph Webb 500 acres in Accomack County.[63]

In spite of his health issues, Custis actively promoted his commercial interests with a merchant in Boston, sending him tobacco, hides and wheat. One of the five known letters that Custis wrote to John Usher shows that Tabitha also entered the picture. In his letter written 2 April 1686, Custis noted that his wife was sending Usher's lady a tree of rosemary in a tub.[64]

In 1691, when Tabitha was about fifty-two years old, her mother died. Mary Scarburgh, who had modified her will to reprimand Tabitha's brother Charles for neglecting his ailing mother, may have been opinionated about Tabitha as well. Perhaps feeling that Tabitha possessed ample earthly goods, Mary Scarburgh bequeathed her daughter only spiritual treasure, a single large Bible. [65]

But then, it may have been a wise bequest. Tabitha had good reasons for seeking comfort in its pages. By the spring of 1692, her husband was petitioning the Governor to be released from his civic duties, explaining that for "some yeares past" he had been troubled "with extreame violent sicknesses insomuch that in his own Judgment and the opinions of most others that saw him he could not live, and altho it hath pleased God in some measure to restor his health, yet is he sometimes afflicted with very violent fitts to such a degree that were not extraordinary Care taken of him in them he should be in great danger." The council commended Custis's past contributions and released him from his civic duties, noting that his "very great sicknesses which have caused him to be very weake and being yet afflicted with very violent fitts one of which may be expected in a small time will carry him out of this world also it being Evident that his memory and hearing are both very bad."[66]

It couldn't have been an easy time for Tabitha. She was probably constantly alert, watching for the first signs of a seizure and then hurrying to provide the "extraordinary Care" that was required. Nor would it have been easy watching her husband slip into forgetfulness and deafness. And these were not the only burdens Tabitha had to bear.

It was probably around this time, or earlier, that her daughter died leaving a son (also destined to die early), and a daughter named Tabitha, who followed in her grandmother's footsteps by marrying a Custis.[67] The husband of Tabitha III was Edmund Custis, the nephew of her step-grandfather. Pleased with the match, John and Tabitha Custis cited their "Love and affection" in 1693, and signed a deed of gift granting 1700 acres to "our well beloved Nephew and Grandson Edmund Custis of the County of Accomack in Virginia aforesaid, Gentleman, and Tabitha his now wife our Granddaughter." The young couple, who settled down on their new land, produced two children, Thomas and yet another Tabitha.[68]

John Custis, who was approaching his mid-sixties, and Tabitha, about ten years younger, probably welcomed the first great-grandchild together, but Custis was living on borrowed time. Four years after the councilmen predicted that his convulsions would carry him out of this world, John Custis died. He was buried a few steps from his mansion, where his tomb (likely erected several years after his death) may still be seen. The inscription reads in part: "Here lies the body of John Custis Esqr one of the Councill and Major Genarall of Virginia who departed this life the 29th of January 1696 Aged 66 years."[69]

In his will Custis bequeathed the mansion at Arlington to Tabitha for her lifetime, after which it was to go to his grandson, John Custis, who was attending school in England. Custis bequeathed Tabitha her clothing, her jewels and her pocket watch along with sixteen slaves and four servants in addition to the thirteen slaves she was to manage for the benefit of his grandson's education. He also enumerated some of the furnishings that graced his mansion: a Russian leather couch and twelve Russian leather chairs, the square table in the hall, the cedar and black walnut press (what now would be called an armoire) in the great parlor, and the large Dutch press and gilded looking glass in the dining room.[70]

Tabitha had lived at Arlington for fifteen years or more, and she could have spent the rest of her days sheltered in its luxury, but she barely spent nine more months there.

A widow once more, Tabitha was again attracting suitors. She was fifty-six years old, but her wealth and status would have more than compensated for any wrinkles or added pounds. In fact, Tabitha was in such a strong position that she could make demands and set her own rules.

On 26 September 1696, Tabitha negotiated a favorable prenuptial agreement with a prominent planter who lived on the other side of Chesapeake Bay. Colonel Edward Hill, the new man in her life, agreed to give and grant "to the said Tabitha Custis in case she survives me after this my Intended Marriage with her the full and just Sume of five hundred pounds Sterling." Not only did he pledge a large sum of money, he promised she could "hold and enjoy to her owne proper use and behoof her bed and furniture thereunto belonging and all her Rings, Jewells, Locketts, Necklaces and wearinge Apparell of what kinde soe ever to bee wholly and Solely at her free and absolute disposal."[71]

It is noteworthy that Tabitha thought to get her future rights down in writing. Had John Custis, the man who had bullied the citizens of Accomack County, also overstepped his authority with his wife's personal possessions? Or, as his will implies, did he indulge Tabitha, who had become so accustomed to managing her own affairs that she was loath to relinquish control? Whatever the case, Tabitha was heading off any misunderstandings that might occur in her new relationship.

When she wed Edward Hill II, Tabitha left Arlington for another impressive home, Shirley Plantation in Charles City County.[72] The mansion that now stands at Shirley Plantation, however, was built after Tabitha's time. Information about its predecessor, the home Tabitha shared with her fourth husband, may one day come to light as archaeologists continue their work at the site.[73]

During the 1670's Tabitha had traveled across Chesapeake Bay to spend time in Jamestown at various General Courts. Now she was living conveniently close to the heart of the colony, but she probably was still making trips across the Bay. Only now she was going the other direction to see her great-grandchildren and perhaps to oversee the management of Arlington and shuffle workers between plantations. Soon after Custis died, she had hired Benjamin Robinson as an overseer. It wasn't long before he was working for Tabitha's fourth husband instead, looking after his "Negroes for the sole use and benefit of said Hill, making considerable crops every year both of corn and tobacco."[74]

As it turned out, Tabitha's marriage to Edward Hill II of Shirley Plantation lasted just four years; he died on 30 November 1700.[75] It was just one in a series deaths that must have jolted Tabitha to the core. Some time after 1696, her grandson Smart Whittington died before reaching adulthood. Then his sister, the third Tabitha, died leaving her husband, Edmund Custis, and their two small children. Then Edmund Custis died too, about a month after the death Edward Hill.[76] Tabitha did not linger at Shirley Plantation. Her granddaughter's orphans needed her.

Tabitha could have settled in at Arlington, but she did not. Instead, in 1701, she relinquished Arlington to John Custis IV, her step-grandson. Though this young man eventually made his home in Williamsburg, he asked to be buried beside his grandfather at Arlington, the ancestral home he grew to love as much as he grew to detest his wife. Many believe he referred to his troubled marriage in the sentiments he had engraved on his marble tomb: John Custis IV died "Aged 71 Years and yet liv'd but Seven Years Which was the space of time He kept A Bachelors house at Arlington on the Eastern Shore of Virginia."[77]

When Tabitha's grandson-in-law, Edmund Custis, died in the early days of 1701, he left the bulk of his estate to his children, Thomas and Tabitha Custis. He appointed Francis Makemie and his wife Naomi as "Executors in trust to act And doe with the advice and directions" of Tabitha Hill, the children's great-grandmother.[78] Probably intending to relieve Tabitha of the burdens of executorship, the dying father put his faith in the integrity of a minister and the love of a grandmother. Though it may have seemed a good idea, this rather unusual arrangement blighted the lives of everyone involved.

Francis Makemie, the founder of Presbyterianism in America and an able businessman, had arrived in Virginia in 1683, when Tabitha was living a county away at Arlington. He obtained his license to preach in his Onancock home in 1699, when Tabitha was living across the Bay. He therefore may not have been well acquainted with her and probably felt he could simply ignore, or at least override, the wishes of an old lady. He had no idea what he was up against.

Newly widowed, Tabitha had the time, the know-how, and apparently still the energy, to ensure that no one took advantage of her great-grandchildren. She was watching closely, and she did not like what she saw. On 5 August 1701, she came to court and petitioned that "Mr ffrancis Makemie hath entered into the said Estate and hath and still disposeth of the Estate contrary to the good likeing of this peticonr which if not prevented would be to the ruine of the Said Children." Tabitha asked that Makemie submit an inventory of everything, including what he had removed, and then give oath in court to its accuracy. Makemie countered that he and his wife, as executors, were not required to render an account to anyone until the children arrived to lawful age. After rereading the will, the justices came down in favor of Tabitha and ordered that Makemie turn in a "true &

perfect" inventory at the next court. Two men were to inspect the accounts of Edmund Custis as they stood at his death, and Tabitha was to give an account of the estate that had come into her hands as well.[79]

The next December, when the court asked for Makemie's list, he claimed he had taken an inventory, which he had with him in court, but because Madame Tabitha Hill had a large portion of the estate in her possession, he could not give a "perfect" inventory. The court ordered that he submit the inventory at the next court and that Tabitha submit one, too. This was not a task to be taken lightly. The inventories that were eventually submitted to the court consumed several pages in the record books and included everything from slaves and jewels to wigs and knitting needles. The men who had inspected the books were to be present to ensure that everything was properly done.[80]

A few months later, on 3 March 1701/02, it was noted that Tabitha had not completed her inventory of the Custis estate. The Makemies may have reasoned that this lapse on Tabitha's part would excuse an intentional omission of their own. The next day, as Custis executors, they sued one John Stanton, who had the presence of mind to protest that Tabitha Hill had not advised the action. Called into court, Tabitha "utterly denied that She gave them such advice & directions to sue ye s^d Stanton, and did not Consent thereto." The Makemies stood rebuffed, and the court dismissed their suit.[81]

A month later the Makemies sued Tabitha herself. When she failed to appear in court, two of her well-placed relatives posted bail for her appearance at the next court.[82] While the records are silent about whether she made that appointment or not, the Makemie-Tabitha Hill feud did not quietly disappear. Instead, it escalated. The Makemies appealed to the General Court and obtained an order against Tabitha in the fall of 1703. A year later at her request, the General Court stopped their previous order and demanded that the Makemies post security for the delivery of the children's estate when they reached adulthood.[83]

The Makemies reacted in kind. They persuaded the General Court to order Tabitha to give an account of the Custis estate and the profits it had generated. The penalty for noncompliance would be a hefty 500 pounds sterling. Tabitha may have felt that her previous order against the Makemies still stood, which is probably what the Makemies were hoping for. They waited for a while, and on 5 February 1705/06, they appeared in court to collect some ammunition. They requested the local court to certify that Tabitha had not complied with the higher court's order. If they could wave such proof in the face of the General Court, they could bring their nemesis to the brink of financial disaster and enrich themselves in the process. Naturally hesitant to comply with such a request, the justices found a way to dodge the issue. Too few judges were present, they said. The decision would have to be postponed till the next day.[84]

On the sixth of February, when the justices reread the original order, they "Could not any way find that ye s^d order did request any such Certifficate."[85] The justices had wiggled out of a tight spot, but Tabitha was not so fortunate.

An old lady fighting for the rights and property of her great-grandchildren, Tabitha may have felt insulted at the suggestion of an inventory, which, of course, implied that she might be squandering the goods she held for the orphans. She knew her motives were pure, and she likely could not understand how anyone, be they a minister or a judge, could suspect otherwise. It is unclear why she stubbornly continued to ignore court orders for an accounting of the estate in the face of such severe consequences. Perhaps she thought the Makemies, if they knew what she had, would lay claim to it somehow. This may have been her way of preventing the "ruine of the said Children." She was risking her own fortune and freedom to save that of Thomas and Tabitha, who by now were in their teens. Perhaps she planned to hold out till they came of age.

There is so much that the old records do not say. Though we know that the Makemies were responsible for sending Tabitha to prison,[86] we do not know exactly when or how long she was incarcerated. But there are a few clues. Her imprisonment began when John Wise was sheriff, no doubt shortly after the Makemies sought the certificate to prove Tabitha's contempt of the General Court's order in February 1705/06. Her incarceration lasted on into the administration of the next sheriff, Tully Robinson, who served in that office from June 1706 to June 1708.[87]

While we do not know the exact circumstances of Tabitha's imprisonment, we do know that all prisoners were not treated the same. Much depended on the nature of the crime. Twenty years earlier, a piece of land around the prison, about eighty poles on a side, was laid out "for a place of liberty and privilege for each prisoner not committed for treason and felony."[88] A few months before Tabitha was committed, Sheriff Wise had complained that the old prison had become "insufficient" and requested something more secure. The court ordered him to use the former clerk's office as a prison till the situation could be remedied, so it is possible that Tabitha spent some time in the old office or perhaps in the new prison which was in the works by the late summer of 1706.[89] There is also a chance that Tabitha was allowed to find other accommodations within the prison bounds. Whether she slept in the prison proper, in a crowded ordinary or even in a rented room, Tabitha's path had taken her a long way from Arlington.

It is unclear if Tabitha ever submitted an inventory or paid the penalty of 500 pounds sterling. It is also unclear how Francis Makemie, a respected clergyman, could justify his actions against her. Tabitha may have neglected to turn in an inventory; Makemie, who, it will be remembered, also balked at submitting an inventory, was responsible for sending a widowed great-grandmother to prison.

Tabitha did not appear in the records for more than two years. Whether she received sympathy and support or endured ridicule and privation during that time is anyone's guess, but in early 1708, she was back in court to verify a certificate.[90] Then, on 2 June 1708, she came back to verify something else.

Many years earlier, Tabitha's brother Charles Scarburgh had given 2000 acres to his twelve-year-old nephew Edmund Browne, but when young Edmund died, Uncle Charles took the land back, and after Charles' own death, the land was sold.[91] The new owner, apparently to clear up any question about the title, asked Tabitha, her sister Matilda West and another woman to verify Edmund's age and the circumstances of his death.[92]

Tabitha's son, had he lived, would have been forty-eight years old when his mother came into court and swore "upon y[e] old Bible." The passage of time had not dimmed her memory, and the old anguish probably stabbed her anew as she told of Edmund's birth in the year 1660, and of his death in Turkey in 1678. She still knew the names of the ship's captain and of the young man who helped carry her dead son to his grave.[93]

At this point Tabitha had outlived four husbands, both of her children and both of her grandchildren. She also outlived Francis Makemie, who died sometime during the summer of 1708.[94] His widow Naomi remarried shortly afterward, and it was she and her new husband, James Kempe, who finally agreed to end the squabble over the Custis estate.

By, this time the Custis children had likely attained the ages their father had specified in his will, but before Naomi and her new husband consented to relinquish the administration of the estate, they wanted to be sure of one thing. The imprisonment of Tabitha haunted them, but it was apparently not so much a threat to their consciences as their pocketbook. Tabitha's incarceration had probably stretched into a lengthy stay, and Naomi and her new husband were afraid they might have to pay for it. This possibility was probably the subject of negotiations, and on 7 March 1709/10, the two sheriffs, under whose terms Tabitha had been imprisoned, came to court and promised that "they never would ask or demand any fees of Mr. James Kempe or Naomie his wife as Executrix of Mr Edmund Custis & of Mr ffrancis Makemie or their heirs Executors or administrators for or by reason of y[e] Imprisonm[t] of Mad[m] Tabitha Hill."[95]

Satisfied, James and Naomi Kempe came to court two days later to discharge Tabitha and Thomas Custis from any debts or claims. The Kempes turned the administration of the estate over to Thomas Custis and his sister Tabitha, who by this time had married Henry Custis. The Custises, for their part, agreed to discharge Naomi Kempe and her husband from "all manner of Clames" as well as for "Intermedling with the Estate."[96]

The battle was finally over, and Tabitha must have breathed a sigh of relief. The struggle may have hampered her style and diminished her wealth, but she still had resources, both financial and emotional. Between 1702 and 1714, Tabitha made several land sales,[97] and there are hints that, at least after 1709, she may have lived with John Baily and his wife, who had many ties to the Scarburgh family. Tabitha was probably staying at their home in November of that year when she accepted thirty-six drumfish "for the use of John Bayle."[98] Years later when he died, Baily generously gave Tabitha permission to live on his plantation if she liked and enjoy its profits after the death of his wife.[99]

As Baily implied, it must have seemed that, while others might die, Tabitha would surely keep on going. She did live to see her great-grandson Thomas Custis become sheriff of Accomack County in August 1713.[100] She also lived to see him suffer the death of his first wife and marry again, the second time to Anne Kendall,[101] a girl whom Tabitha apparently came to love.

At least Tabitha remembered Anne in a special way when she wrote her will on the 23rd of August 1717.[102] By now in her late seventies, Tabitha still had some finery, and she wanted Anne to have her wearing stays embroidered with gold, her black suit and silk clothes, her black stays set with bugles and her cloth of silver petticoat. Tabitha did not mention the rings, jewels, lockets or necklaces that she so carefully reserved for herself when she negotiated her marriage contract with Edward Hill, nor are any of those items mentioned in the inventory taken after her death.[103] It is possible that Tabitha had already given these valuables to her great-granddaughter Tabitha, who was not mentioned in the will either. Or, Tabitha could have sold some of her jewels to ensure a measure of comfort while in prison or as old age approached.

Within a few months after writing the will, Tabitha Scarburgh Smart Browne Custis Hill went to sleep for the last time. In her nearly eighty years she had lived in mansions and prisons, had fought ministers and servants, had defied court orders and governors. Over the years she had gained her share of treasure but had lost nearly everyone she held dear. In the end she relied on Thomas Custis, the great-grandson she had defended with all her might and for whom she had sacrificed her liberty. On 7 January 1717/1718, he brought her will to court and swore to it as the executor of Madam Tabitha Hill, deceased.[104]

Chapter Eleven

Rhodea Lamberton Fawsett Franklin

The alluring widow

During the 1660's, when marriageable ladies were in short supply, teenaged girls could have their choice of well-to-do older gentlemen, who often then died and made their wealthy young widows more desirable than ever. Most of these suddenly single women remarried in a matter of months. One noteworthy exception, a widow named Rhodea Fawsett, remained unmarried for more than fifteen years. This unusual delay was not caused by the lady's physical shortcomings, however. Though apparently blessed with good looks and a captivating personality, Rhodea was cursed with a total disregard for propriety. When her own husband died, she merely took up with someone else's.

Even her first marriage was not exactly typical. On the second of June in 1661, when she was sixteen or seventeen years old,[1] Rhodea Lamberton married John Fawsett,[2] an up and coming colonist who was almost twice her age.[3] It is possible that John Fawsett was a widower and brought a motherless toddler named John and an infant named William to this marriage, but he called Rhodea the mother of both boys when he wrote his will, so he left us to conclude that Rhodea's first two children simply arrived inconveniently early. John was born before May 1660, and his younger brother William claimed a birthday in 1661, the same year his parents were married.[4]

While Rhodea was home tending to her growing family, John Fawsett began accepting work in the public sector, becoming an undersheriff,[5] arms dealer[6] and attorney general[7] for the county. Charged with prosecuting criminals, he even became involved in a minor milestone of American history. At the complaint of another colonist, he arrested three men who, on 27 August 1665, had performed a play called "The Bear and the Cub." It was the first recorded theatrical production in the colonies. John probably had missed the first performance, but he surely attended the second–the court ordered the actors to don their costumes and reenact the drama. When they found no fault in the play or the actors, the justices turned an accusing eye on Fawsett, who quickly dodged responsibility for troubling the court. He shifted the blame to the informant, who was then ordered to pay all court costs.[8]

Even though John subsequently resigned his position as attorney general, claiming it was more trouble than it was worth,[9] he continued to prosper with the addition of land[10] and servants. Fawsett also took in an orphan girl in 1669, but it was no act of kindness on his part.

The three Colston daughters had been forced to serve two different masters after the death of their father. When the two who were serving together committed "small thefts" for which their master neglected to punish them, one of the girls was removed from his care and placed with her non-pilfering sister. Perhaps unwilling to see the upright sister corrupted, or maybe unwilling to see her master receive the benefit of both servants, John Fawsett requested that the innocent girl be reassigned to him. The court obliged and ordered Sara Colston to serve Fawsett until she reached the age of 24 years.[11]

Sara endured the Fawsett home for three years. By the summer of 1672, she had gathered enough courage and evidence to complain to a magistrate about "her harsh usage by Rodia ffawsett," who by this time was the 28-year-old mother of several children. The court believed the girl and had John Fawsett post a bond to ensure that "Sarah Coulston shall by Noe wayes bee abused." He signed the document on 1 August 1672. Twenty-five days later, when Sara's body was again beaten and bloody, Fawsett was forced to appear in court and admit that he owed the county 5000 pounds of tobacco, the penalty for the broken bond.[12]

His embarrassment and financial loss were Rhodea's fault. In the habit of lashing out for trifling misdeeds, she may have considered Sara's visit to the magistrate a major offense. Or it could have been something else entirely that triggered the incident, but, whatever the cause, Rhodea's fury had known no bounds, and nothing, not human compassion nor the loss of 5000 pounds of tobacco, could hold her back. She brutally beat the orphan girl, covering the child with welts and gashes from the waist down.

As soon as an opportunity arose, Sara made her painful way to a neighboring plantation where she showed her wounds to Gertrude Cropper, who later testified that "Sarah Colston came to my house on Saturday night being ye night after she was whipt by her Mrs. [mistress]. And I viewed her & saw ye greatest p[ar]t of her body beaten in a most inhumane manner, Especially from ye waste downewards." The girl had been "whipped in such manner that the blood lay dried up where it had trickled downe the length of her ffinger & on her hipps Bumps like scabbs with ye vehemency of the blowes."[13]

A week later Elizabeth Tayler and Susannah Watson also viewed Sara's body, and it still "appeared soe inhumanely beaten that from her thighes downewards they could not p[er]ceive any p[ar]t ye breadth of a finger but was black & blue & yellow." In addition, "the forepart of her body was all blacken and yellow & several colours & ye back p[ar]t from her thighes downewards was full of stripes with scabs att ye end of some of them."[14]

In view of such mistreatment, the court immediately removed Sara from the Fawsett home, assigned her to John Wise and shortened her term of service by three years, making her free at age twenty-one. So John Fawsett lost not only the penalty of his bond, he lost a servant as well. His wife's passionate nature had cost him dearly.[15]

Though Rhodea then faded into the background, at least as far as the court was concerned, the following year or so was eventful for the Fawsetts. That November Sara Colston's sister accused John of neglecting the Colston cattle in his care, and though they stopped short of removing the animals, the justices warned Fawsett to take better care of them.[16] In April 1673, John (calling himself a merchant) and Rhodey finalized a sale of 200 acres.[17] In June they bought 245 acres at the head of Occohannock Creek from John Cropper and his wife Gertrude, who had given refuge to Rhodea's abused orphan girl.[18] And then on 15 August 1673, when he was 43 years old,[19] John Fawsett drew up his last will and testament.[20]

In the preamble of his will, he thanked God that he was in "perfect sense and memory," and though Fawsett mentioned no illness, he must have known the end was near. On the same day that Fawsett signed his will, he was able to testify about a slander,[21] but that was the last time he appeared in court. Within two months he was dead.

At the next court, which was in October, John Fawsett's will was proved and copied into the court records where it filled five pages. By the standards of the day, Fawsett had been a wealthy man. Among his five children (John, William, Charles, Thomas and Elizabeth) he divided 1232 acres of land, his stock of wooden planks, four guns, five beds with bedding, two chests, a table, a large copper kettle, five iron pots, seventeen pewter dishes and plates, a silver sack cup, nine horses and numerous sheep and cattle. He left a bed, two horses, six cattle, seven sheep and the rest of the household goods to 29-year-old Rhodea, who was enjoined to care for the children till the boys turned 18 and the girl 16. As long as she stayed a widow, Rhodea could live on the home plantation.

Although Rhodea did remain a widow much longer than anyone would have imagined, she was far from lonely. Rhodea had probably known John and Gertrude Cropper a good while before the abused orphan sought Gertrude's aid in 1672, and though relations between Rhodea and Gertrude must have been strained, Rhodea did not let that little unpleasantness interfere with her affection for John Cropper. An accommodating neighbor, John began doing everything he could to comfort the attractive widow on the next plantation.

Rhodea actually was facing difficulties. After shedding the responsibility of keeping the Colston cattle in early 1674,[22] she became embroiled in a controversy over a cow and calf that her dead husband had owed to Mathew Shipp. That spring Rhodea tried to pay Shipp a cow whose calf she had killed, but he predictably refused that offer. Reluctant to part with her own cattle, Rhodea bought a cow to give him, but when that animal failed to have a calf, that plan fell apart too. Probably concluding that Rhodea intended to swindle him, Shipp offered "sevrall assaults & abuses" to Rhodea, who that September filed a complaint, saying she was "affraid to be Deprived of her life by ye said Mathew Shippe & dare not goe about her Lawfull occasions for feare of meeting with him." Shipp, who had to post a bond for keeping the peace, successfully sued Rhodea for his animals two months later. When a friend urged her to pay the cow and end the trouble, Rhodea petulantly replied that "shee would have paid him had hee not abused her."[23]

Finally, more than a year and a half after her husband's death, the court noted that Rhodea had satisfied the debt with Mathew Shipp.[24] That problem was finally behind her, but Rhodea's real trouble was just beginning. The very next day, on 17 March 1674/75, the church warden appeared in court to present Mrs. Rhody Fawsett and John Cropper for fornication.[25]

Both of them were summoned to the next month's court to face the charges. When they failed to appear on the 16th of April, the sheriff was ordered to "bring the bodies of ye s^d Rhodea Fauset & John Cropper p[er]sonally" to court the next morning.[26]

Once there, John and Rhodea were confronted with the testimony of Mary Wells, a young woman who swore "That I have often seen John Cropper & Rhodea Fauset lye togeather in naked Bed and further that I have often seen her goe to Beed (sic) to John Cropper and John Cropper likewise wth her."[27] Years later John's scorned wife would recall that her husband John, "through the allurements of one Rhoda Fassitt, betook himself unlawfully to her company." [28]

Convinced that "John Cropper & Rhody Fausset doe undecently accompany together," the court ordered Rhodea to remain in the sheriff's custody until she could post a bond to ensure her good behavior, which of course included "not unlawfully accompaning (sic) of the said Cropper."[29] Clearly, in the court's opinion, the alluring lady was responsible for her own downfall as well as that of her lover; John Cropper did not receive so much as a reprimand.

After posting her bond, Rhodea was released to busy herself with tax problems, debts, lawsuits[30] and a maid servant named Jone Bud, who like her mistress, had committed fornication. This common bond, however, did not generate any sympathy in the heart of Rhodea, who refused to pay her servant's fine.[31] It was therefore ordered that Jone immediately receive corporal punishment according to law, which meant that Rhodea stood by while her servant was stripped to her waist, tied to the whipping post and given twenty-five lashes on her bare back.[32]

No doubt still haunted by the loss of the 5000 pounds of tobacco her husband had posted to ensure Sara Colston's safety, Rhodea was careful not to forfeit the bond she had posted for herself. While it is possible that she called a year-long halt to her affair with John Cropper, it is more likely that the lovers simply became more discrete and deceptive, especially in the presence of servants. Whatever the tactic, their scheme worked. Rhodea appeared in court on 19 April 1676, asking to be released from her bond for good behavior, and after the customary proclamation was made three times with no objections raised against her, she was discharged from the bond.[33]

For the next year John Cropper and Rhodea Fawsett continued to maintain a low profile, probably arranging clandestine meetings and sneaking between their plantations. While that activity might have been exciting at first, it eventually lost its luster, and the lovers began to consider the advantages of sneaking off to Maryland instead. The border was not far away, and crossing it offered a fresh start among strangers. In Maryland they could carry on their affair unhindered by Virginia officials and unobserved by Gertrude. As an added bonus, if they hurried and made their move before the Fawsett sons came of age, the lovers would also be able to abscond with a good share of their estate.

In March of 1676/77, John Cropper set their plan in motion by ordering his servants to bring nineteen of Rhodea's cattle to the head of the Fawsett land. There Cropper met them and helped drive the herd part of the way to Maryland. Knowing that it was illegal to transport cattle out of Virginia without permission, Cropper "gave order that if any prson should stopp or hinder them," the servants were "to make what resistance and oposicon they could." About the same time, bedding and household items were loaded into a shallop and carried away by night.[34]

The cattle quickly made it across the border, but other things like crops took longer. John Cropper was still in Virginia and busy topping his tobacco that August when he got involved in another shifty enterprise.

Armed with a large club, a runaway servant named Richard Price unexpectedly accosted two servants and two of the Fawsett boys, who were working together in Cropper's corn field. Claiming he had business with their master, Price followed the servants' directions to the tobacco patch and shortly afterward returned with Cropper, who sternly commanded his servants and the Fawsett boys not to tell anyone that they had seen Price. It was a crime to hide a runaway, but Cropper, who saw an opportunity to obtain Price as his own servant, fed him, cautioned him to stay out of sight and "told him he might goe into the Barne & lye there upon the wheat & that he should have Victualls."[35]

The next morning Price begged Cropper to attend court and purchase him from Thomas Hall, the master he hated. Anxious to secure a bargain for himself, Cropper promised to try. When he returned home that evening, however, he had bad news. A hue and cry had been issued for the capture of Price, and Hall, suspicious of Cropper's offer to buy a missing servant, refused to sell.

Distraught, Price vowed "he would never serve Tho Hall but would goe as farr as a paire of shooes would carry him or hang himselfe first." Cropper assured Price that a settlement might yet be made; in fact, Hall had agreed to come see Cropper. Then, exhibiting strange behavior for someone expecting a guest, Cropper announced he was going to the southern part of the county and left the plantation.

Upon his return a few evenings later, he asked his maidservant about the runaway. When she reported seeing him in the orchard, Cropper "went towards the barne into the orchard & as soone as he had bin there, he went away imediately to goe to Mrs. Fossets."[36] The maidservant, who casually noted that Cropper returned home the next morning, treated her master's night-time excursion as though it was a common occurrence. It probably was.

As the move to Maryland approached, John Cropper grew more and more indifferent to the laws of Virginia. He had begun by spiriting cattle out of the colony, and then progressed to openly cohabiting with Rhodea, hiding a runaway, attempting to bribe his maidservant into silence and ordering his servants to lie.

By telling a blatant falsehood himself, he ultimately managed to trade his maidservant for Price, whose skeptical master, before sealing the deal, asked some pointed questions, saying he would bet 500 pounds of tobacco that Cropper knew something about his missing servant. Cropper, however, firmly denied the charge and offered to go before any commissioner "to take his oath that he did not know anything of [Richard Price] or had ever seene him since since (sic) his running away."[37]

After hearing all the testimony in the case a few months later, Hall probably realized that Cropper had done him a favor by taking Price off his hands. He learned that Price, who had seen Hall on the Cropper plantation shortly after running away, "went out of the barne into ye woods & cut a good Cudgell & was resolved to bang his sd M[aste]r if he had come neare him.[38]

Out of ignorance Hall had not been afraid, but with Cropper's wife, it was a different matter. Entranced by Rhodea's endearments, and busy smuggling both his own and his lover's assets out of the colony, John Cropper rarely came home to Gertrude at all, but when he did, it was not a happy scene. Gertrude knew she was in her cheating husband's way, and she feared for her life.[39]

Sixteen-year-old William Fawsett was also concerned. Working with Cropper's servants as he did, he was in a position to observe his inheritance disappearing into Maryland. So, in September 1677, he alerted the authorities by filing a complaint against Rhodea and John Cropper. The sheriff, who had already seized part of Rhodea's estate, was ordered to hold it till she posted security to ensure that William would get what his father's will bequeathed to him. The authorities were also very interested in young William's account of Cropper's surreptitious cattle drive and his purchase of the runaway servant.[40]

After William's complaint, things began to get very uncomfortable for John and Rhodea. On 23 November 1677, the same day that William left Rhodea's house and chose a new guardian, proceedings were initiated against Cropper for illegally transporting cattle. It was probably no coincidence that Cropper had three friends check the ear marks and brands on the next twenty-four cattle and nineteen hogs destined for Maryland. The court clerk recorded the list on 5 December,[41] but Cropper's change of tactics did not change the minds of the justices, who were still intent on prosecuting his previous infraction.

On the 20th of December, William Fawsett's new guardian went to court to help William retrieve his estate. Although Cropper proclaimed his willingness to comply, the court issued an order for him to immediately deliver the boy's estate, including anything that had been taken from the county.[42]

The next day, perhaps out of love (like he claimed), or possibly out of guilt, but certainly with the knowledge of his imminent departure, John Cropper went to court and made provision for two of the daughters that he would soon be deserting. He gave Elizabeth and Sara Cropper each a mare, and he gave his wife Gertrude the liberty to sell the mares' offspring if she deemed it necessary for the benefit of the children.[43]

After handing the reigns of authority to the wife he detested, Cropper may have departed for Maryland immediately. Even if he did, however, he returned to Virginia the next February to face two trials. Found guilty of both charges, Cropper was fined 1300 pounds of tobacco for fraudulently deceiving Thomas Hall, the master of the runaway servant, and another 19,000 pounds of tobacco for conveying Rhodea's nineteen cattle out of the county.[44]

While it is not clear exactly when they escaped the confines of Virginia, John and Rhodea were definitely residents of Maryland by the spring of 1778. In May of that year, when the eldest Fawsett son John initiated an action concerning his estate, Rhodea could not be located, and the court granted him an attachment of 5000 pounds of tobacco against Rhodea's estate wherever it could be found in the county.[45] Though she was not around, her attorney was; later that summer representatives of the court were sent to assess the damages done to the Fawsett plantation, but when they submitted their report that fall, Rhodea's lawyer requested a delay, putting the judgment off for a month.[46]

Hampered from taking possession of his deteriorating plantation, young John naively signed a covenant agreeing to live and work on a neighbor's plantation. Soon afterward, upon finding himself living in "inconsiderable & unreasonable condicons," he took steps to void the agreement. He assigned power of attorney to John Tankred, who went to court, claimed that John was still a minor and accused the neighbor of taking advantage of Fawsett's "ignorance & tender yeares." The suit was dismissed, however, precisely because John was a minor; he could not legally bring action without his guardian.[47]

Meanwhile, Rhodea's lover had been arranging for some legal transactions of his own. John Cropper sold his 355 acres in Virginia for 16,000 pounds of tobacco. Whether he shared any of the tobacco with his estranged wife Gertrude is not known, but she did dutifully sign the deed with an X.[48] About the same time Cropper bought 1200 acres in Maryland, a property he came to call Rixsom.[49]

Cropper's land dealings may have inspired Rhodea to suggest a similar solution to her son John. That fall she empowered her attorney to release her interest in John's inherited land, and a few months later on 16 March 1679/80, John sold the home place with the written consent of his mother.[50]

Rhodea, who had signed John's document the same day it was presented to the court, could not have been far away, but she had compelling reasons for not appearing in court herself that day. Her trip to Virginia had had a dual purpose. She had crossed the border to help one son sell his land and to give birth to another. Maryland didn't like bastardy any more than Virginia did, so John and Rhodea had orchestrated a plan to avoid trouble with the court system in their new home. In fact, by the time her signature was read in open court in Virginia, Rhodea was probably on her way back to Maryland, but without her baby.

Juicy gossip travels fast, however, and the next day Thomas Osburne and Edmund Allen were hauled into court and forced to post security to save the parish from supporting "a Bastard Childe: wch by comon fame Rhodea Fauset is reputed to be the Mother of, wch said Bastard Child is now at

Nurse at Mary Marriners." The magistrates all knew that Rhodea had illegally left her child in their county, but they still wanted Osburne to swear to the mother's name. When he refused, they placed him in the sheriff's custody for concealing the child and made him post further security to ensure his good behavior.[51] The fact that Osburne had known John Cropper for years and was probably his brother-in-law helps explain why he was willing to go to such lengths to hide Cropper's child.[52]

While others cared for Rhodea's infant, life returned to normal back in Maryland. John Cropper obtained a certificate for transporting several individuals including the runaway Richard Price,[53] William Fawsett turned eighteen and started clamoring for his inheritance in Virginia,[54] John Cropper registered his cattle mark,[55] and a servant became pregnant with an illegitimate child of her own.

Joan Garrett was about five months along in February 1682/83, when Cropper, much like the authorities in Virginia, became concerned about potential financial losses. He demanded 2500 pounds of tobacco from Oliver Berry, the baby's father, "for what Damadges the Said John Shoulld Sustaine by the Said Joans being with Chilld." After some controversy, a jury found for Cropper and awarded him 2150 pounds of tobacco.[56] That June the baby arrived, and six months later the mother was taken to court and charged with bastardy.[57]

That was exactly the type of unpleasantness that Rhodea hoped to avoid, so that winter she again packed her things and made another secret trip to Virginia. This time she refined her strategy a little by staying with a different family, by choosing a different nurse and by calling her baby Peregrin Johnson. Though she probably concocted that alias to mislead the authorities, it didn't work for long. By February 1683/84, Guslin Venettson's wife,[58] had been observed with a strange infant, and the authorities, ever curious about such matters, summoned her "to answere for haveing a base Child at nurse, wch sd Child she acknowledged to be named Peregrin Johnson & borne of the body of Rhodia ffawset."[59]

Mrs. Venettson also shared information about a Cropper relative named William Tayler Jr.,[60] who had ignored the law prohibiting aid to certain strangers. Because Tayler had "occasioned much trouble and Charge to ye p[ar]ish," by entertaining Rhodea, he was summoned to the next court.[61]

When Tayler failed to appear as ordered, he was taken into custody, and then, at the court held 4 June 1684, he finally admitted to "entertaineing Rhodia ffauset contrary to Law an Inhabitant of Maryland who was brought to bed at his house of a Bastard Child." The court subsequently ordered Taylor to post a bond of 5000 pounds of tobacco to ensure his future good behavior.[62]

It is not easy to imagine a mother so willing to leave her newborns in the care of others, and though the babies were not far away, Rhodea surely would have hesitated to risk the wrath of the Virginia authorities with regular visits. On the other hand, by the time "Peregrin" arrived Rhodea was almost forty years old, and she may have welcomed a respite from child-rearing. It is also possible that her Virginia offspring, when they were a little older, simply appeared on Cropper's plantation and blended into the company of children and servants already living there. As long as local midwives and neighbors were not called to assist Widow Fawsett in childbirth, and so long as no indigent child required aid from the local parish, the Maryland authorities could afford to shrug and look the other way.

John Cropper's illicit second family was growing, and so were his debts. Not only was he buying land and paying taxes, Cropper was managing plantations, directing servants, paying various court fees and indulging an appetite for cider, sugar, wine, flip and rum.[63] The life of a 17th century gentleman was stressful and fraught with health-threatening perils. John Cropper became sick and weak, and then in September 1686, he summoned a friend from Virginia to write his will.[64] Two months later, at the age of forty-one, John Cropper died.[65]

In his will he bequeathed his 3800 acres[66] to ten different individuals including his "brother" Thomas Osborne, Rhodea's eldest son John Fosset, Thomas Morris, six children with the last name of Cropper and Rhodea Fossett. Since John called his children, whether by Gertrude or Rhodea, by his own last name, the modern reader is left to sort them out.[67] Two of the six, the girls Elizabeth and Sarah, certainly belonged to Gertrude, who was to manage the mares Cropper gave them before he departed for Maryland. Two others, Edmund and Nathaniel were also Gertrude's, being named as grandsons in the will of her father.[68] That leaves just two sons, John and Ebenezer, who can be attributed to Rhodea.

These two boys may have been the nurslings that caused the Virginia authorities such headaches, but it appears that John, at least, was somewhat older. Rhodea's recorded incursions into Virginia for birthing purposes occurred in early 1680 and the winter of 1683/84, making those children around six and three years old when their father died. A six-year-old may have been too young to care for the horse, saddle and bridle that Cropper bequeathed to his son John, directing that he "Imediately after my decease be possessd with them." Rhodea Fawsett and John Cropper were proven fornicators by early 1675; if the first few years of their affair produced an infant (which fact they somehow hid from the authorities), the child would have been approaching ten years old, which would be more in keeping with the responsibilities of horse ownership.

Since John Cropper's wife Gertrude testified that her husband's illicit affair with Rhodea had produced "several" bastards, it is quite likely that three or more children were born to them. They just did not publicize how many times they stole across the border, left a deceptively named infant with a wet-nurse and then successfully slipped through the chain of gossip and constables that twice tripped them up. Some of these children probably fell victim to the high infant mortality of the times or were simply ignored in their father's will.

As it was, Cropper specified that Rhodea and her children receive a total of 1850 acres of land, most of the household goods, and half of the horses, sheep and cattle. Rhodea was to get the remainder of all the "utensils y^t belong to my Estate" in addition to all the hogs and all the male animals born to the other livestock. Cropper did remember four of his legitimate children with 1450 acres and some of the livestock, but he was careful to limit Gertrude's other unnamed children, giving "Each of them one shilling sterling money & noe more." And in the very next sentence, though sick and weak and lying on his deathbed, Cropper inflicted one last humiliation on their mother by naming "my beloved friend Rodea fossett my whole & sole Executrix."[69]

Upon learning of her husband's death, Gertrude, who had barely managed to support her family by her own labor and the charity of relatives, requested her share of her late husband's estate. Rhodea, however, citing the will in which Gertrude got nothing, flatly refused the request.

Frustrated, Gertrude turned to the authorities in Maryland, and in a frankly worded appeal, requested that probate of Cropper's will be delayed until she could prove her dower rights. She recited how she had married John Cropper about 1670, in Accomack County, Virginia, and how she had had several children with him in the six or seven years they lived together. During that time, however, Rhodea Fawsett's allurements had so enticed John that he hardly lived with Gertrude, preferring instead the endearments of Rhodea.

Gertrude recounted how she feared for her own life as her husband, anxious to enjoy Rhodea's favors, secretly moved his possessions and his lover into Maryland, where they lived in adultery for about ten years and had several bastard children together. Gertrude complained that Cropper had now left the bulk of his estate to those illegitimate children, whose mother he had made sole executrix. Facing "great want and poverty" herself, Gertrude had demanded her rightful share, but Rhodea "utterly refuseth to give to Gertrude anything of her said husband's estate." Touched by her plight, the Maryland justices approved Gertrude's request on 4 March 1686/87.[70]

As administrator of Cropper's considerable estate, Rhodea was facing some complicated challenges with the claims brought by Gertrude and scores of others seeking payment for debts. Gertrude had an attorney,[71] and it was probably through his efforts that the women in John Cropper's life reached an agreement. On 20 April 1687, Gertrude, in exchange 5000 pounds of tobacco, surrendered all her rights to her husband's estate.[72] Twenty months later, Cropper's will was finally proved in open court by three of its witnesses.[73]

One of those witnesses, Dr. John Vigerous, probably hoped that crossing this hurdle would open the way for payment of the medical bills that Cropper had incurred during his last illness. Rhodea, however, had other ideas, and she stubbornly refused to pay the doctor in spite of his frequent reminders. Vigerous eventually took her to court, and on 13 June 1689, he was awarded 1000 pounds of tobacco, though he had originally sought more than five times as much.[74]

Rhodea's "allurements" may not have had anything to do with the reduction of the medical bill, but she still had some charm left. A few months after her court appointment with the doctor, the claimants to the Cropper estate began craving orders against Rhodea's new husband John Franklin. A capable widower who eventually represented Somerset County in Maryland's General Assembly,[75] Franklin may have met Rhodea when his daughter married Rhodea's son William.[76]

Rhodea had been in no hurry to settle down. More than sixteen years a widow and bereft of her lover for three years, Rhodea was now forty-five years old. Likely tired of sneaky trips across the border, bastardy charges, gossip and complex finances, Rhodea must have sighed with relief as she turned the court battles over to her new husband. He could handle the folks clamoring for a share of the estate. He could take care of the land, the servants, the livestock, the horse-powered grindstone and collect the nearly 97 pounds sterling that others had owed John Cropper.[77]

Rhodea drifted into the background over the next few years. She did come back to court for four days in early 1693, when her testimony helped convict a woman of stealing four yards of cloth worth a hefty 200 pounds of tobacco,[78] and later that year, she no doubt gave moral support to her sons John Fawsett and John Cropper when they petitioned for their inherited land,[79] but all was not going well.

Rhodea was supposed to appear at St. Marys that summer, probably to clarify some aspect of the Cropper estate, which was still unsettled. But she was not feeling well. On 22 August 1693, her husband's attorney asked that Rhodea's absence be excused, as she was "incapacitated to make the voyage over the bay."[80]

Though her name occasionally surfaced in the following years,[81] Rhodea's defiant servant-beating, husband-stealing, bastard-bearing life was behind her. But it has not been forgotten.

In fact, the gossip about Rhodea that once swirled along the border of colonial Virginia and Maryland still circulates today. It enlivens genealogy forums on the Internet as Rhodea's many descendants and admirers recount her scandalous activities. It seems the passing centuries have made Rhodea more alluring and shameless than ever, and sometimes the stories get quite colorful.

For instance, there are reports that during their ten-year affair both Rhodea and John Cropper produced illegitimate children with other people. Rhodea's maternity forays into Virginia have apparently led some to believe that her benefactors there were responsible for more than sheltering Rhodea for a few weeks. The magistrates never accused Thomas Osbourne or William Taylor Jr. of anything other than enabling Rhodea to enter their county for the purpose of giving birth to a child the local parish hoped to avoid supporting. John Cropper's unwed maidservant Joane Garretts gave birth in 1683, but the baby's father was Oliver Berry, not John Cropper.[82]

There are also reports that Rhodea, while fighting Gertrude for Cropper's estate, enchanted and married Gertrude's lawyer. Rhodea may have fascinated William Whittington and his assistant Robert Carvile, but she married John Franklin. The rumor is patently untrue.[83]

Even so, the current embellishments focus on what made Rhodea remarkable; she *was* alluring, and she *did* live a life outside the accepted boundaries. That her story is drifting into the realm of legend would probably make Rhodea proud if she only knew.

Chapter Twelve

Dorothy Williams Watts

The outspoken abuser of servants

For more than three decades Dorothy Watts wove her way through the court records, flirting with trouble and speaking her mind. Willful and outspoken, she faced the court for infractions ranging from fornication, slander, breach of agreement and cheating her own children, to servant abuse, assault and contempt.

In 1658, when she was about 23 years old,[1] Dorothy appeared in the court records as the widow of Walter Williams,[2] a bartender who had likely died the year before.[3] Much older than his wife, Walter had been the proprietor of the tavern, or ordinary, where the county court often met.[4] So, during her marriage, at least, Dorothy had been in the center of it all. She likely served magistrates and miscreants, heard learned arguments and crude gossip, and witnessed whippings and barroom brawls.

The insights and skills that Dorothy acquired during her courtroom days stayed with her the rest of her life. Preferring to live on the edge, she became quite adept at dodging trouble. Her actions showed her to be impulsive, aggressive and sometimes downright mean, but she also must have possessed a measure of charm, especially when appearing before the justices. Time and again they were inclined to deal with her gently.

Unable to read and write,[5] and probably unaware of the dismal state of her late husband's finances, Dorothy made generous funeral arrangements.[6] If she thought she had become a well-to-do widow, however, she was sadly disappointed. Williams' debts consumed so much of the estate that reserving 800 pounds of tobacco for the funeral required an action of the court.[7]

In December of 1658, the court acknowledged that Dorothy had nothing left from Williams' estate and released her from further trouble with creditors.[8] Dorothy, however, was already in trouble of a different kind.

Only a month after that court appearance she was back again, accused of fornication. Before the magistrates, Dorothy Williams and John Watts openly acknowledged their guilt. It was "therefore ordered y[t] y[e] said Doretie Williams shall after delivery (shee apearinge to bee wth Childe) receive twenty Lashes on her bare back and y[t] y[e] said Watts shall Receive y[e] same punishment or pay 500 lb: of Tobacco for his said finne . . . and forthwith put in securetie for keepeinge ye parish harmless from any Charge for a Basterd y^t ye said Dorethy may and is like to have."[9]

There were probably no lingering doubts about Dorothy's impending motherhood when, just over two months later, she was referred to as "Dorithy Watts formerly the Wife of Walter Williams."[10] Whether she ever received her twenty lashes is unclear, but at least her child was born in wedlock.

That's how Dorothy came to marry John Watts, a tailor turned planter,[11] who like Dorothy, may not have always thought things through. Two years after their marriage, John and Dorothy Watts with a friend named John Milby set out to cure a servant of scurvy. Unfortunately, as a result of the cure "ye s^d Servt came to his hasty & imediate death."[12]

Thomas Evans had sought refuge at the house of a neighbor who described the poor man as being "lame & very ill haveing Swellen leggs very soare & broake out in blisters." Watts, who claimed Evans had caught scurvy by running away, first bathed him in boiled herbs. When that brought no relief, Watts asked Milby to help sweat the servant.

Though Watts claimed the first sweating treatment was effective, Evans could not have disagreed more. When a neighbor girl told him that a second treatment was planned for the following day, he "answered y^t would be ye last day of his life." His prophecy might lead one to wonder about the part he played in his own death, but such ominous predictions were fairly common. Dying servants regularly attributed their imminent deaths to people they considered responsible.[13]

With other duties requiring his attention that day, Watts put Dorothy and Milby in charge of the second sweating. The treatment had only begun when Evans "cryed out he was scalded. Jno Milby made answer you are not so foolish to scald yor selfe & imediately ye s^d Servt fell into ye water & was scalded." The neighbor girl was sent after some lard to anoint the servant,[14] but within three hours Evans was dead. Watts, who signed his deposition with his tailor's mark–a pair of open scissors–buried the servant that night.

Though Dorothy had participated in the fatal treatment, the court, following the customary practice, held her husband responsible. Though they realized the servant was not intentionally killed, the magistrates elected to send a message to other amateurs who might be contemplating medical experiments. They fined Watts and Milby 500 pounds of tobacco for their "Negligence Ignorance or both." The court then prohibited anyone from applying "Midicine as a phisition" unless he was approved and qualified by England, James City or the county court.[15]

The scalding incident was just the beginning. Throughout the years both Dorothy and John Watts established a pattern of abusive behavior to a number of their servants. There was only one servant who did not complain about the Watts, and even as he attempted to defend his master and mistress, he acknowledged their forceful personalities.

In the spring of 1663, a nearby landowner who suspected a neighbor was stealing cattle asked Watts' unnamed servant if he knew of John Die's thieving ways. The servant, who was searching for Watts' cattle at the time, replied that he knew, and so did his master and mistress. The servant went on to brag that "hee and his Master & Dame" would see that justice was done. It was very unusual for someone to rank a lady with her husband in such matters or imply that she might dispense justice or wreak vengeance, but apparently if you knew Dorothy, you would understand.

On this occasion, however, Dorothy's involvement was not necessary. The boastful servant had barely disappeared into the woods when he met the suspected cattle rustler. After they exchanged words like "thief" and "rogue," the servant bloodied John Die's face and threw him to the ground. The servant then made the mistake of straddling Die, who seized his opportunity, kicked the servant off and headed home. Watts, who was apparently conducting his own search for the missing cattle on Die's property, happened to be at Die's house when Die came home, his face still covered with blood. When Die informed Watts that his servant had beaten him, Watts retorted, "If [I] had been in [my] man's stead, I would have done better."[16]

Dorothy may have given the servant the impression that she was tough enough to handle a cattle rustler, but she did not always move in men's circles. Dorothy also relished the world of women's gossip. In the summer of 1663, when she was about 28 years old, she heard a juicy tidbit, and repeated it, not just to friends, but to the authorities.[17]

Dorothy, who had gone to visit Mary White and her husband late in the evening, was invited to spend the night. While there, Dorothy heard Mary say her aunt had stolen a hood and scarf in England and would have been arrested if she had not left when she did. Warming to her subject, Mary went on to accuse her aunt of stealing a case of doctor's instruments as well. These were very serious allegations in an age when stealing a petticoat and shirt could get you thirty lashes on your bare back.[18]

Dorothy's deposition helped convince the court that Mary White was spreading scandalous stories about her aunt, who was fortunate the magistrates took her side. They ordered Mary to ask her aunt's forgiveness before the court and in front of both church congregations in the county.

During the next four years or so, Dorothy's husband paid taxes, exchanged two fur mantles and a shirt for rights to Indian land, disagreed with his neighbor, served on a jury, tried to increase his land holdings, purchased servants and served as a substitute constable.[19] Busy with a growing family, Dorothy remained in the background until she crossed paths with William Onoughton.

Somewhat deranged and prone to violence, Onoughton had become so unbalanced by 1665, that he thought enemies were out to get him.[20] Two years later, after encountering Dorothy Watts, he was right.

Facing court fines for infractions like fathering an illegitimate child, breaking out of prison, assaulting a young woman, firing a gun at a woman's house, stealing a cutlass and deliberately killing twenty-three pigs committed to his care,[21] Onoughton also owed a number of debts.[22] In financial straights by the spring of 1667, he apparently agreed to work for John Watts in exchange for a share of the corn crop. When a young man arrived for work at the Watts' place, Onoughton took him to a spot near the house to begin weeding. Exhibiting his typical disregard for the property of others, Onoughton tromped right into the planting bed. Dorothy Watts, who saw what was happening, came over and told Onoughton to get out of there. When he refused, Dorothy stepped over and pushed him out. Angered, Onoughton retaliated and "thrust her down," according to the young hired man.[23]

John Dixes, an older man working at the saw pit near the Watts' home, testified that he "heard a great noise, and thought that ye said John Watts wife might bee beating her maid." Reluctant to interfere with a servant's punishment, John "tarried after [I] first heard ye noise while one might take a pipe of tobacco, and hearing ye sd noise continew went to ye house and at ye Dore was William Onoughton, and the said John Watts wife." When Dixes approached, Dorothy told him that "Onoughton had pincht her by the throat and almost Strangled her."

Dixes then turned to Onoughton and demanded, "What if you had killed ye Weoman?"

Dixes reported Onoughton's reply: "'Why,' said hee, 'what if I had? It had been noe great Matter.'"

After saying that, Onoughton "tooke her by the armes and through her downe on ye ground upon her Child, So that ye Child bleed both at nose and Mouth, and after[ward] told her hee could find [it] in his heart to kike [kick] her, wch was not beating." After this violent assault on his wife, John Watts sued Onoughton, who was ordered to pay damages of 1000 pounds of tobacco plus the cost of the suit.

Given the tension that must have lingered, it seems odd that Onoughton, after harvesting his corn, would want to store it at the Watts' place. Accompanying Onoughton when he gathered his corn, Teague Andrews asked if he would take it to a neighbor's. Onoughton "said he would not If goody Watts would give him house roome."

When asked about storing the corn, Dorothy was surprisingly polite. Perhaps she sensed an opportunity to detain her enemy's grain, or was seeking her own brand of revenge. In light of subsequent events, it seems unlikely that she had suddenly become considerate and attentive to Onoughton's needs. At any rate, she "replied She had noe place but ye quartering house flower [floor], and if you will put it their you may." Onoughton took her up on the offer, and though the storage conditions were less than ideal, he dumped more than two barrels of corn on the dirt floor of the quartering house.

That October, William Onoughton returned to the Watts plantation and demanded his corn from Dorothy, whose attitude had turned quite hostile. Maybe she considered the corn to be part of the payment she deserved, or perhaps she wanted to prevent Onoughton from seeing how much his grain had deteriorated. The intensity of her actions, however, seems to suggest her motive had more to do with retaliation.

According to Thomas Pettit (a servant who tagged along with Onoughton) Dorothy "would not lett him have ye Corne nor see it." Instead she "took up a fier brand and struck ye s^d William Onoughton wth it and when ye s^d Onoughton came to my Masters house hee shewed me his arme, wch was bloody. Then she presently run & fetcht an Iron Spitt and run at him, but hee stepped back [and] saved himselfe from ye thrust."

Onoughton may have had a tenuous grasp on reality, but he knew when it was time to leave. His departure was encouraged by Dorothy, who "drove him over ye fence and then she tooke up a stake and struck at him againe but did not hitt him, and called him Irish Rouge and said Hhee [sic] should have noe Corn for hee had none their, nor none hee should have."

Onoughton brought action against John Watts for the assault perpetrated by his wife. Dorothy did not remain in the background, however. When it appeared that Onoughton's bill of complaint had not been properly filed, it was Dorothy who requested that the suit be dismissed. The court agreed and awarded her court costs as well.

Of course Onoughton did not forget his corn crop. Neither did Dorothy. When she asked John Jenkins to come view the pile of corn on the quartering house floor, he found "that it was grone musty and decaied & horid & Sprouted." Shortly afterward, Dorothy was ordered by a justice (undoubtedly at Onoughton's request) to get two neighbors to appraise the corn. Just before the appraisers arrived, Dorothy told a friend that Onoughton had been there for his corn. She described a very civil exchange, significantly different from Onoughton's version. She said "that she bid him take his Corne so hee would pay her what hee owed."

When the appraisers examined the corn and sorted it, they found about two barrels of ears to be "poor indifferent Corne" valued at 150 pounds of tobacco; there was also a quantity of corn that was worth "little or naught." The court ordered John Watts to pay Onoughton for the spoiled corn.

For the next several years, Dorothy stayed out of court for the most part. The whole family was probably busy establishing their new plantation on the Sea Side near the Maryland line.[24] Four years later, in 1672, John and Dorothy sold their old homesite near the present town of Onancock to William Benstone.[25]

Five years after that, for some unknown reason, Dorothy insulted Benstone's wife Rebecca and was bound over for breaking the peace. Appearing before the court as she had done during her clash with Onoughton, Dorothy requested to be discharged. After noting that she "stood upon" her statement, the court ordered proclamation to be made three times. When no one raised an objection against her, the court acquitted Dorothy.[26]

Colonial Virginians incised their personal pattern of slits and nicks in the ears of hogs they owned and then turned the animals loose to forage in the woods. The populace, though largely illiterate, proved to be adept at reading earmarks. The owner would hunt for his hog or capture it when it wandered home, unless, of course, some unscrupulous neighbor had beaten him to it. Everyone knew all that pork running free in the forest presented a powerful temptation, and anyone caught with a dead hog whose ears had been removed was immediately suspected of hog stealing.[27]

In March 1680/81, Dorothy happened by a neighbor's kitchen and was one of several people who saw three dead hogs, at least one of which had an ear missing. The depositions given by Dorothy and the other visitors helped to clear up a misunderstanding about a pig whose ear had been marked by mistake.[28]

A few months later, Dorothy made a mistake of her own, this time while visiting in the house of Elizabeth Osburne. Also present was a neighbor's talkative servant named Mary Storey, who seemed to get around in spite of her servant status.

During the course of the conversation, Dorothy asserted "that Sarah Price Carryed a Basterd Childe about for Woodman Stokely."

"You cannot prove that," replied Mary.

Dorothy answered "that she could prove it and soe Could somebody elce alsoe if need Required."

Probably with Mary's help, the gossip soon reached Woodman, who considered the shame, calculated the child-support payments and filed charges of defamation against Dorothy and her husband, whose only mistake had been his inability to control his wife's tongue.[29]

The characters involved in this incident illustrate how intertwined colonial lives could become. As his first legal step, the disgruntled Woodman appeared before a magistrate to register his complaint. The nearest justice was Mary Storey's master, a man named John Wallop, whose land adjoined that of both Woodman and the Watts, and whose daughter would in time marry the son of John and Dorothy Watts.[30] Upon Woodman's complaint, Wallop issued a warrant for the nearest constable–who happened to be Dorothy's husband–to bring Dorothy before Wallop or another justice to answer the complaint. Wallop gave the warrant to Woodman and directed him to deliver it to John Watts.

John Watts was not at home when Woodman arrived, but Dorothy was there, along with the ubiquitous Mary Storey. Somewhat smugly, it seems, Woodman informed Dorothy that he had a warrant. He then proceeded to read it to her.

Dorothy may have been illiterate, but she was not ignorant. She knew what was required, and she made it clear that she was not about to appear before the justice that was her neighbor. "I will not goe before Mr. Wallop," she vowed, but then added that she would appear before another magistrate instead.

The situation rapidly deteriorated, however, when Dorothy refused to accept the warrant, and Woodman began to plead with her. "Dorothy," he said, "pray take yᵉ warrant."

Dorothy's heated reply landed her in court for contempt. Disdaining Woodman's piece of paper, she sneered, "Give it to me, and I will wipe my Arse with it."

"Whereupon," Woodman reported, "I profered her the warrant, but she would not take it."

Not only did Dorothy refuse to accept the warrant, she also failed to appear before a justice. At the next court the sheriff was ordered to take her into custody until she produced security for her appearance at the following court to answer for the defamation of Woodman and for the contempt of a warrant.

It was a more agreeable Dorothy that appeared before the magistrates that August. They examined the evidence and found that "Dorothy Watts is guilty of a misdemeanour in contemning and abuseing his Majesties authority." But Dorothy then "supplicated the Courts mercy," and they reconsidered. Since it was "yᵉ first Crime of this nature" that she had committed, the magistrates ordered that Dorothy be dismissed without further censure. She was, however, ordered to post security for her future good behavior and the payment of court charges.

As for Woodman's original complaint, the magistrates considered Dorothy's scandalous comments, and then somehow found her words "not actionable." They therefore dismissed the charges and ordered Woodman to pay court costs.[31]

Bad blood between the Watts and the Stockley families lingered for a long time. During the next few years Woodman and his kin, hoping for a reward, repeatedly informed the authorities that John Watts was removing livestock from the county without a permit. The complaints were eventually quashed, and instead of a reward, Woodman had to pay court costs again. But Woodman was not one to forgive and forget. In fact, years after John Watts' death, Woodman and Widow Watts were still quibbling, repeatedly appearing against each other in court cases. In 1687, when the authorities were trying to settle an estate, Woodman informed the man taking inventory that Dorothy Watts had 19 ½ pounds of feathers belonging to the deceased. In turn, Dorothy reported that Woodman owed the dead man ½ barrel of corn and 300 pounds of tobacco. The next year Woodman spent three days testifying against Dorothy in a case that she ultimately lost.[32]

John Watts, who had been seriously ill and under a doctor's care in 1677,[33] wrote his will in 1680 and died four years later.[34] Widowhood suited Dorothy well. She now headed the household, controlled the family finances, and could sue anyone she wished. Taking advantage of her new status, Dorothy often appeared before the justices both as plaintiff and defendant, collecting debts, obtaining non suits, and generally getting her way, except with members of her own household.[35]

When dealing with her children, who could be as greedy and inconsiderate as their mother, Dorothy did not fare as well. In the spring of 1686, she appeared before her old neighbor, John Wallop, and complained against Thomas Conway for "Pilfering [and] taking Severall things privatly" out of her house. After examining the matter, the court came to the conclusion that Dorothy's daughter Jennet was the principal person removing the items, and that Thomas was merely an accessory. Since Dorothy had not named her daughter in the accusation, the case was dismissed. The court, however, took care to show that they had not gone soft on thieves; they took Thomas into custody until he could post a bond for his good behavior and pay the costs of his incarceration.[36]

But persistent servant abuse, not thievery remained the big problem on the Watts plantation. Years earlier Dorothy's husband had "most inhumanely and brutishly used" a servant named Anne Dupper. Dressed only in a few rags and forced to go barefoot in the snow, the poor woman died before the court could take action.[37] Dorothy could have aided Anne, but there is no indication that she ever did.

When she was a young wife, the nearby sawyer took it for granted that the shrieks he heard were the result of Dorothy beating her maid. As a widow, Dorothy carried on that cruel tradition—and even encouraged others to do the same.

In September 1687, the whole family got in trouble with the law. An indentured servant named Margery Williams, filed a complaint with the authorities. She had suffered abuse at the hands of Dorothy, Dorothy's son John and Dorothy's slave named Black Will. Though she was not directly involved in the incident, Jennet Watts supported her mother and brother by refusing to testify against them.

Margery accused Black Will of "Sundry great abuses in an indecent manner offered her." While the records do not specifically say so, it is almost certain that the "indecent" abuses were of a sexual nature. The court further noted that "Dorothy Watts may be Suspected to abett and incourage the said Negro in his evil actions." The sheriff was immediately ordered to take the slave into custody and give him "thirty one Lashes on ye bare back well laid on." Dorothy was sternly ordered to "forthwith take such effectuall care that no more compl[ain]ts of this nature may be brought before ye Court."[38]

There was no excuse for Dorothy's actions, but she probably did have a motive. She stood to benefit if her servant Margery became pregnant. Unmarried women servants who gave birth could be forced to extend their terms of service by as much as two and a half years, and the punishment for unwed servants with mulatto babies was doubled.[39]

Truly his parents' son, young John Watts had not only mistreated Margery, but he had devised an innovative way of doing so. Margery complained "that John Watts Son of the Said Dorothy Watts had shot her in ye body with a Pistoll charged with Powder & Indian Corne and wounded her therewth." The assault was confirmed by witnesses and by John himself, who acknowledged the incident. It is possible that John, in his confession, expressed sincere regret for his actions. Apparently the justices thought so; his punishment, posting a bond for good behavior and the payment of court charges, amounted to a slap on the wrist.[40]

Because Jennet had initially refused to testify against her brother, she was charged with contempt. The justices ordered that she be taken into the sheriff's custody, where she was to remain until she agreed to swear an oath and give evidence. After a night in jail, Jennet returned to court a different girl. She humbly petitioned the magistrates and acknowledged her error, claiming she committed it out of ignorance.[41]

There was really no longer a reason for Jennet to maintain her silence. By this time, her brother had confessed to shooting Margery with corn, and her mother had already been reprimanded for pushing her slave into criminal activities. Jennet submitted herself to the court, which ordered her to pay court costs and then discharged her.

Severely punished for offences contrived by his mistress, Black Will undoubtedly felt betrayed. After receiving his thirty-one lashes, he endured life on the Watts plantation for about four months, and then, with the pain in his back diminished but not forgotten, Will slipped the bonds of slavery and felt the joy of freedom for the space of ten miles. Then he was recaptured by a young man whose father obtained a certificate for apprehending the runaway.[42] Undoubtedly restored to his life of misery on the Watts plantation, Black Will subsequently vanished from the court records.

Only one month after Black Will's ill-fated escape, Dorothy contracted for another worker who had the temerity to fight back when wronged. Perhaps John Dean was especially desperate for work, or maybe he was unaware of how Widow Watts treated those around her. In March of 1687/88, Dean agreed to stay on Dorothy's plantation and "make a Crop of Corne and Tobacco." Nine weeks later, Dorothy "did force ye Said Dean from her house" and demanded a payment of twenty-five pounds of tobacco. Dean, who sued Dorothy and summoned her old enemy Woodman Stockley as a witness, prevailed in court and was awarded a total of 175 pounds of tobacco. The passage of time had not mellowed Dorothy, who defiantly filed a countersuit. The court, however, dismissed it because she had not legally entered her petition.[43]

In December of 1690, Dorothy, who by now was in her mid fifties, started to feel the effects of age. Since her husband's death she had done her utmost to maintain control of the children and the considerable estate, but now it was getting to be too much. She came to court and petitioned that she had been "appointed sole Executrix of ye s^d Last will as also Guardian to her Children untill they did severally attaine ye age of Sixteen years which they long since attained to and that she being well Stricken in years was not able to take that care y^t she had formerly done." She asked that the estate be divided with the children receiving their shares.[44]

Dorothy and her son John, who had not seen his mother's petition, each chose a suitable representative to oversee the division; Jennet, who was not in court that day, was assigned someone to look out for her interests. Urgent business called the representatives away, however, and almost nine months elapsed before the chosen gentlemen met to begin dividing the earthly possessions of John Watts between his heirs.[45]

It was only when the men met to make the division that John and Jennet became aware of their father's intentions. According to their subsequent petition, they had been "ignorant of what [was] left them by their fathers last Will and Testament untill ye time of their meeting" when the appointed men were "discourseing ye matter." John and Jennet, now probably well into their twenties, were startled to learn that their mother was supposed to relinquish guardianship and give them their inheritances upon their sixteenth birthdays.[46]

In spite of all they knew about their mother, they had trusted her, "not doubting or distrusting but their Said mother intended to act but for their advantage." Now, however, they "had cause to Suspect ye contrary."

John and Jennet went on to complain of "Severall goods being conveyed away by her and Creatures out of the Stock, converting ye produce of all She

Sould [sold] to her own use calling it her own." And that was not all. While the representatives worked to divide the estate, Dorothy, outspoken and self-serving as ever, was "useing threatning words and protestations thereby obstructing ye proceedings."

John and Jennet requested the court to prevent their mother from removing or selling the remaining cattle, hogs, beds and Negroes until the division was complete. After examining their petition and the request of the men actually making the division, the court came to the opinion that Dorothy Watts, who had been entrusted as the "sole Executrix overseer & Guardian" of the will, "had wholly neglected & omitted to p[er]forme the trust reposed in her by ye Testator." Not only had she failed to divide the estate when the children reached sixteen, she had also neglected to have the estate inventoried.

The court ordered the representatives to divide the estate before the next court and "in ye meantime ye s^d Estate [was] not to be removed or disposed of by ye s^d Dorothy or any of them, and it is further ordered that ye sheriff of ye County see to ye due execucon of this order."[47]

On that bitter note, Dorothy disappeared from the records. During her lifetime she had alienated her neighbors, her servants, her slaves, the authorities, and finally her children.

Perhaps John and Jennet took a long hard look at what their mother had become and shuddered at what they saw. Maybe they deliberately tried to become less like her. Though it had seemed that Dorothy's son and daughter were following in their mother's footsteps, something caused them to turn from that path. Jennet apparently gave up stealing household goods and defying courts; no more official reprimands were issued in her direction. And John stopped shooting servants with corn.

In fact, John went from breaking the law to enforcing it. He married the daughter of his magistrate neighbor,[48] became a justice of the court himself in 1699,[49] and two years later was appointed sheriff of Accomack County.[50]

In short, John became a respected gentleman. But John deviated from one tradition typically observed by other gentlemen of the county. Unlike his peers, when it came to christening his daughters, John Watts spurned his mother's given name.[51]

Chapter Thirteen

Alice Boucher

A widow with a secret

Around midnight Alice Boucher was jolted into wakefulness. A forty-year-old widow with at least five children,[1] Alice knew exactly what was happening. She just had not expected the baby to make its appearance so soon and at such an awkward time.

After carefully hiding her condition for months, Alice certainly did not wish to give birth with a talkative field hand in the house. Though her baby may have been coming early, it wasn't coming early enough to prevent a scandal. Alice had been a widow too long to pass the baby off as the legitimate child of her dead husband. If word of the birth reached the authorities, Alice would face the penalty for fornication and bastardy, a fine of 500 pounds of tobacco or twenty-five lashes on her bare back.[2] And Alice was no stranger to the harsh punishments imposed by the court. She had been in trouble before.

Also pregnant eight years earlier when she had her first dealings with the magistrates, Alice was then married to William Boucher, who at fifty-six, was twenty-four years older than his wife.[3] They and their children lived in a little house at the edge of a swamp not far from the Chesapeake Bay. Though some of their nearest neighbors were Dr. Hack and Captain Parker,[4] both influential men of the county, the Bouchers were not wealthy. There is no record that they even owned the land they lived on, and land was relatively cheap in those days. Shortly before he died, however, William had managed to raise enough tobacco to attract the attention of the court; they noticed when he shipped his crop without a certificate.[5]

Isolated as they were, the Bouchers still kept in touch with other colonists and their wandering livestock. The family regularly noted the free-ranging hogs that frequented the swamp, and, like typical Virginians of the time, they could identify their neighbors' hogs by size and color, even when the identifying earmarks had been shredded by dogs.

We know of two instances when folks dropped by the Boucher residence, and both occasions involved the disputed ownership of local hogs. A servant named Phillip Quinton happened along one day just in time to see Dr. Hack's slave woman carrying fire from the Boucher house. Suspicious, Quinton demanded to know where she was going with it. When she said it was to singe a hog, Quinton reported that he "went wth her into yᵉ swamp, where I found Docter Hacks butcher by A sow of my Masters, wch they had killed, and I demanded wherefore they killed my Masters Sow, and So bigg wth pigg." Quinton went on to complain that Hack's servants used "ill language, calling me lying Rogue and said it was their masters Mark." Quinton argued with them, but it was only after he threatened to go call his master that Hack's servants relented and put the dead sow on the mare that Quinton had with him.⁶

The Christmas day hunt of 1663, was a community affair with the neighbors killing all the hogs they could find, regardless of ownership. They planned to sort things out later. When one of the hunters stopped by the Boucher house, William inquired after his luck. The hunt had been successful, but determining who owned the pork required the wisdom of the county magistrates and statements by several witnesses. Two of the depositions were given by Boucher, who had been acquainted with the hogs in question.⁷

It might have been better for Alice if she, too, had confined herself to exchanging pleasantries with hog-hunters instead of jumping to the defense of Elizabeth Leverit, a feisty indentured servant who had just received thirty lashes on her naked shoulders for openly defying her master and a fellow servant.⁸

Like almost everyone else in the county, the Bouchers laid aside the drudgery of plantation work and usually went to church on Sundays. Not only was it against the law to stay away, few folks were willing to miss out on a chance to see friends and catch up on local news. A certain amount of excitement must have attended the parishioners as they gathered at the meeting house and fraternized after church. At least it turned out that way one Sunday in the summer of 1663.

Elizabeth Leverit's shoulders were still scarred with fresh welts when she unburdened herself to a sympathetic Alice. Fortified with righteous indignation and the confidence that comes with outnumbering the foe, they brashly confronted Elizabeth's master. All three then proceeded to defile the Sabbath and scandalize onlookers by engaging in a shouting match that quickly deteriorated into a physical fight. But more shocking than the broken Sabbath or the shattered peace was the fact that Robert Brace proved himself unable to control his female servant and had actually lowered himself to her level by squabbling with her in public.

At the next court the magistrates called Elizabeth Leverit an incorrigible and impudent servant, and noted that she, Alice Boucher and Robert Brace had "lawlessly scolded, fought and misdemeaned themselves on ye Saboth day."⁹ In possession of a newly constructed ducking stool,¹⁰ the justices sentenced the two women to be ducked, a punishment considered especially suitable for female offenders. Citing Brace's failure to control his maidservant as proof that he had degenerated from the state of manhood, the court chose to spotlight Brace's weakness and ordered that he be ducked along with the women.[11]

Later that same day, a humiliated Robert Brace reappeared before the court and pleaded with the justices to remit his punishment. The magistrates finally relented and fined him 100 pounds of tobacco instead.[12] Brace's connection with the ducking stool, however, must have lingered in the memory of the court. A year later when he displayed contempt for a warrant, the justices ordered Brace to stand on the pillory for an hour with his crime written on his hat and then pay for repairs to the ducking stool.[13]

Unlike their male counterpart, Elizabeth and Alice received no leniency and were ducked as ordered. One can only imagine the trauma of being bound to a stool and then forced under water. Almost thirty years earlier, in 1634, a visitor witnessed such a punishment carried out ten miles or so from where Alice lived. The letter he wrote from Hungar's Parish sheds light on what Elizabeth and Alice endured:

> The day afore yesterday at two of ye clock in ye afternoon I saw this punishment given to one Betsey wife of John Tucker, who by ye violence of her tongue had made his house and ye neighborhood uncomfortable. She was taken to ye pond where I am sojourning by ye officer who was joyned by ye magistrate and ye Minister Mr. Cotton, who had frequently admonished her and a large number of people. They had a machine for ye purpose yt belongs to ye Parish, and which I was told had been so used three times this Summer. It is a platform with 4 small rollers or wheels and two upright posts between which works a Lever by a Rope fastened to its shorter or heavier end. At the end of ye longer arm is fixed a stool upon which sd Betsey was fastened by cords, her gown tied fast around her feete. The Machine was then moved up to ye edge of ye pond, ye Rope was slackened by ye officer and ye woman was allowed to go down under ye water for ye space of half a minute. Betsey had a stout stomach, and would not yield until she had allowed herself to be ducked 5 severall times. At length she cried piteously Let me go Let Me go, by Gods help I'll sin no more. Then they drew back ye machine, untied ye Ropes and let her walk home in her wetted clothes a hopefully penitent woman.[14]

Elizabeth survived the punishment, but refused to learn her lesson. She went on to commit fornication and bastardy, for which she was sentenced to another thirty lashes and two additional years of servitude under her detested master.[15]

Alice escaped with her life, but she must have come close to drowning. Her unborn child did not survive the trauma. Understandably angry, Alice later criticized the court and especially her neighbor, Captain Parker, the justice she held responsible for her punishment and loss. Someone heard Alice's remarks and registered a complaint about her "scandallous words spoken ag[ains]t yᵉ Court."[16]

Before deciding Alice's case, the November court heard the deposition of fifty-year-old Joane Brookes. Both she and Alice had been visiting a neighbor the previous Monday. During the course of their conversation, Alice told Joane that "she was wth Child, wth a Child as bigg as her fist, when Capt. Parker caused her to be duckt, and on it she miscarried and yᵗ she would be revenged on him, wthin this twelve month."

When Joane answered that "she should doe it presently, and not keepe it in her breast so long," Alice referred to a previous clash with Justice Parker and accused him of using his position to seek personal revenge.

"Hee kept malice in his breast three yeares for wch I was duckt," asserted Alice, who went on to say that she would have the matter tried in some other place.

Captain Parker, because he was involved in the case, had to excuse himself from the court when Alice was called. So it was before the remaining justices that Alice confessed to making the comments in question and promised better behavior in the future. The magistrates considered Alice's promises and then acquitted her. It may be that they felt a measure of responsibility and secretly regretted the role they had played in handing down a punishment severe enough to snuff out an innocent life.[17]

Alice maintained a low profile for several years after that. Her husband, who appeared in court occasionally for offenses like skipping church and trying to avoid taxes,[18] probably died in 1669, leaving Alice to raise the children and whatever else she could grow on the land around their little house by the swamp.

The Bouchers had planted grain in the spring of 1671. By the beginning of July the crop was ready, but Alice, who was concealing a fairly advanced pregnancy, and whose oldest children were daughters, needed help to reap it.

On Monday, the third of July, help arrived in the form of John Browne, who was twenty-five years old, curious and prone to filing reports with the authorities. John, who just happened by the Boucher place, stayed to help at Alice's request. He later testified that by the time they had finished reaping and had threshed a little, it was so late that "I was enforced to stay all night."[19]

Accommodations were meager in the Boucher home, which was humble even by the standards of the time.[20] With one main-floor room and a crude loft, the house could have been constructed of clapboards, but the walls were more likely wattle and daub, woven sticks plastered with clay. John bedded down in the main room, while Alice, her teenaged daughters and probably the younger children retreated to the loft.

Maybe the exertion of reaping and threshing hastened the onset of Alice's labor. At any rate, she had been in bed only a short time when her unborn child made its intentions painfully clear. With a potential witness sleeping a few feet beneath her, Alice was about to give birth to an illegitimate child. Desperate to avoid the heavy fines or whipping the court would impose, she tried to think of a way to get John out of the house.

Three days later, when he told the story to the authorities, John recalled the events that followed: "About midnight Alice Bouchier called to [me] and told mee that she had dreamed that some of her Neyghbours had raised a scandall of her, saying that shee and [I] had layen together and therefore desired [me] to depart the house immediatly." Unwilling to sleep outdoors or spend night hours traveling to other shelter, John paid no attention to Alice's strange dream and flatly refused to go.

This was not good news for Alice, who now could only hope that her unwelcome visitor would drift back into a sound sleep. John, however, had become fully alert. Curious, he lay back, faked sleep and slyly watched events unfold. He later reported that Alice's "two daughters took light wood fired and went into the Loft where they kept a great light all the night." The lights that fourteen-year-old Dorothy and thirteen-year-old Francis lit and took to the loft underscored the poverty of the fatherless family. Their light came not from candles, but from resinous sticks of wood.

A modern observer would be appalled at the health risks surrounding the impending birth—illuminated by burning sticks, attended by inexperienced teenagers and occurring in a primitive loft. A colonial onlooker would have been disturbed because Alice was breaking the law.

The regulation prohibiting "private" births was not meant to protect the health of the mother. It was intended to deter infanticide and protect the wealth of the parish. Attending midwives were duty-bound to question an unwed mother about the identity of the father as the pain intensified. This was more than idle curiosity; the father would be forced to support the child and thus keep charity cases to a minimum, an overriding goal of the parish. The presence of disinterested attendants also helped ensure punishment for the fornicators and survival for the infants, whose mothers, in the face of severe penalties for bastardy, might do desperate things.[21]

The furtive actions of Alice and her daughters made it clear that something was afoot, and they obviously hoped to keep John in a state of ignorance. He could hear whispering in the loft above him, and twice when Alice sent a daughter to see if John were awake, he deceived her by "lying still as though he were asleep."

Especially remarkable is what John did not hear. It is hard to imagine a woman completely stifling her moans and giving birth in silence, but John, who managed to hear the whispers, did not report a single groan.

Finally about an hour before dawn, the wakeful guest

heard them fetch sizers, whereas looking up through a place of the Loft where the boards lay farr asunder [I] Saw her twoe daughters holding of her, one before and the other behind, and there fell att least a quart of blood from that place of the loft downe on a Chest, and [I] alsoe saw the said Alice Bouchiers leggs that they were all bloodye and a thing hanging downe from her bodye between her legges, and then immediatly sending down again to see whether [I] was asleep, wch [I] fained [my]selfe to be, her Two daughters went out one with a shovell & a howe [hoe] and the other with somewhat wrapped up in her lapp and when they were gone [I] att a distance followed and saw them bury what the hindmost carryed within the corner of the cornefield fence.

After watching the girls bury the dead baby, John sneaked back into the house and observed that it was about daybreak when the girls returned and immediately went up to their mother. No longer feigning sleep, John watched as "Alice Bouchier came downe and [I] saw her leggs to be bloodye and wherever shee stood shee immediatly bloudied the place."

With the harrowing night behind her, Alice now fell into conversation with her guest and attempted something of a coverup. According to John, she was "several times complayning of pain in the bellye, and [asked] whether I knew any thing [that] was good for the Plague of the Gutts or if I thought Tobias Selvey[22] could doe her any good."

Two mornings after he left the Boucher house, John Browne appeared before a justice named Southy Littleton to tell the story of Widow Boucher's secret delivery. Unable to write his name, John signed his examination with an X.

On the 19th of July, Justice Littleton issued a warrant. Because Widow Alice Boucher "had one Child borne of her body the which she conceald, privately buried, and denied," a constable was commanded to bring her to the house of Mr. Thomas Fowlkes, where she was to be delivered into the hands of the sheriff.

The constable did not waste any time, and that same day Alice was questioned by Littleton and the jury. She admitted that about an hour before dawn on the 4th of July, she "was delivered of a Man Child, yor declarant not Knowing whether the said child were living or dead when borne–having noe bodye with mee but my twoe daughters."

She went on to say that she was responsible for "Cutting of the said childs Navell string myselfe and tying of itt; some time after as Soon as conveniently I could, taking of the Child for to dress itt, I found it to be dead." Alice then ordered her two daughters to bury the lifeless baby. When further questioned by the jury, Alice declared that she was certain "the child was living immediatly before itt was borne."

Young Dorothy Boucher and her sister Francis were also questioned. They declared that their "Mother was delivered of a man child being still borne to the best of [our] knowledge." Their mother told them to bury the child, which they did about eight or nine o'clock that same morning.

After examining the evidence, a jury absolved Alice of purposely harming her infant, declaring that the "Child was lost for want of helpe." The court then ordered the sheriff to take Alice, Dorothy and Francis into custody until they posted a bond for their good behavior.

While Alice must have been relieved at the outcome, she still had to face charges of fornication and bastardy. It wasn't until December that the grand jury presented her on those charges. In January she appeared before the court and was ordered to pay a fine of 500 pounds of tobacco or receive corporal punishment. In a surprising twist, it was her old enemy Robert Brace [or Bracy] who agreed to pay her fine.[23] We should not read too much into this apparent act of generosity. It was common for condemned women to negotiate a loan from individuals who would then appear in court to guarantee payment of the fine.

A little more than a year later, Alice may have been considering remarriage. At least she was making provision for the future security of her offspring, which was something widows often did to keep their children's inheritance out of the hands of prospective stepfathers. After dividing eleven cattle between Dorothy, Francis, Robert, Anne and Martha, she granted them legal ownership of the livestock.[24] The name of Alice Boucher then disappeared from the records.

It is possible, though, that she made one final appearance under another name. In the fall of 1674, an Alice Ruff came to court as the guardian of a child named Mathew Bowcher and petitioned for Thomas Smalley to return Mathew's cattle.[25] The court agreed and ordered the animals to be delivered to Alice's house at Pungoteague, a village only a few miles from the little one-room house at the edge of the swamp by Chesapeake Bay.

Chapter Fourteen

Elizabeth Stockley Bowen Towles

First Lady of Chincoteague

Like most 17th century women, Elizabeth Stockley Bowen didn't receive much attention in the record books. But the scant information entered there highlights the courage possessed by an otherwise ordinary colonial widow. With her bare hands Elizabeth fought off a man brandishing a sword and a knife, and, against all odds, lived to testify against her assailant, to marry again and to help tame Chincoteague Island. But the memory and the scars of that vicious attack must have lingered. A single glance down at her hands would have triggered flashbacks of a manservant bursting into her room wielding her dead husband's weapon and, in a twist that must have made the assault especially traumatic, wearing her dead husband's clothes.[1]

Elizabeth Stockley was about twelve years old in 1664,[2] when her father, John Stockley, transported several individuals to Virginia. Stockley had been abroad himself and had handpicked the servants he intended for his own plantation. Among these was a nineteen-year-old named John Bowen.[3] While servants were often considered part of their master's "family" for taxation purposes, they seldom actually became part of the family as Bowen did. His marriage to Elizabeth Stockley probably occurred during the summer of 1670.[4]

By that time Bowen would have been 25 years old, free for a year, and ready to begin a life of his own.[5] Elizabeth, too, was ready for the adult world, having received her portion of her father's estate in February of that year.[6]

When Elizabeth's father died three years later, he left a vulnerable 40-year-old widow with several children still at home, servants, livestock and 2700 acres of land.[7] A man named John Stratton saw opportunity in Mrs. Stockley's loss, and even before the dead husband's will had been presented to the court on 19 August 1673, Stratton had begun to wheedle his way into the widow's life.

In fact, it seems he seldom left her alone. On 7 August, Mrs. Stockley acquired a new servant; Stratton was there to witness the transaction.[8] In September when she was offered a cow, he was there, and bought the cow himself when she refused it. In November, when an argument erupted over the cow, he was at the widow's house.[9] In January, when she sold 100 acres, he was there to witness the deed.[10] That same month he prevailed upon her and two of her sons to testify about his disputed cow.[11]

Aside from his over eager presence at the Stockley place, other aspects of Stratton's behavior should have alarmed Mrs. Stockley. In April 1674, John Stratton was arrested for assaulting a man in the sheriff's custody. What provoked the attack is unknown, but Stratton violently struck the defenseless prisoner and pulled his hair. For this outburst, Stratton was taken into the sheriff's custody himself and ordered to post a bond for his good behavior.[12]

Shortly after this, Widow Stockley, who had held out longer than most women in her position, finally succumbed to the pressure and married John Stratton. This was an unfortunate decision from which the new wife could not escape. The new step-children, however, made every effort to get away.

Elizabeth's brother William went to live with Elizabeth and her husband.[13] Elizabeth's sister Inez remained at home for a while but asked for her inheritance a few months later. By April 1675, it was clear that Stratton was ignoring her request, so Inez went to court. When the magistrates ordered him to pay his stepdaughter, and appointed two men to see that he complied, Stratton's temper flared. Inez had barely left the court when she returned with another complaint against her stepfather, this time for beating and abusing her.[14] Stratton, who was also in trouble for receiving stolen corn and beating an Indian the sheriff sent with a summons, was fined, sent to prison, and ordered to post bonds for his good behavior and for keeping the peace.[15] That September found Stratton making plans to leave the county, but when the magistrates learned that he intended to take the Stockley wealth with him, they ordered Stratton to give his stepchildren their rightful inheritance, or have it seized by the court.[16] With his motive for moving gone, Stratton stuck around to butcher local cattle for the Governor's forces during Bacon's Rebellion, defame a neighbor and carry out a vendetta against his stepson.[17]

The court dismissed Stratton's first action against young John Stockley, but Stratton didn't give up. On a Sunday in 1678, he finally found an accusation that might stick. He piously informed the next court that Stockley was "talking and making a noise when the minister was in divine service." Stratton said he admonished his stepson, who retorted that he "came here to do business"–a comment that cost young Stockley 50 pounds of tobacco.[18] No wonder the Stockley children tried to pretend their mother had never remarried; they pointedly referred to the Stratton home as "my mother's house."[19]

Though it probably was not as substantial, Elizabeth Bowen's house must have been a happier place than her mother's. During these years, the Bowen family grew with the addition of both servants and children. By 1675, four taxable individuals lived in the Bowen household, and that would not have included Elizabeth and the babies.[20] Though he was illiterate and apparently owned no land,[21] John Bowen became a respected citizen and began appearing in court, giving depositions,[22] and serving on the coroner's jury.[23] In 1678, the future looked bright. Even the Bowens' son John, small as he was, owned the makings of a herd of cattle, a gift from his Uncle John Stockley.[24]

But just a few months later, disaster struck. In February 1678/79, John Bowen, though still in his early thirties, became desperately ill. As his life ebbed away, he called in some neighbors to witness his will.

After expressing his hope "at the last day to be raised again & Inherit the kingdome of Heaven," John Bowen turned his attention to the goods he was leaving in this world. Besides giving the corn mill to both of his sons and dispersing his livestock among all four of his children, Bowen gave a gun to son John; "my Rapier and my Pistol" were to go to son Richard. The Bowen daughters, Elizabeth and Ellinor, were to divide the household goods with their mother, who was also bequeathed cattle, horses, hogs and a servant named Thomas Jones.

Probably recalling his own days of servitude, John Bowen treated this servant with uncommon kindness. As one of his last acts, Bowen gave Thomas Jones a hog and "all my wareing cloth[e]s both wollen & Linen."[25]

Bowen's generosity, however, seemed only to encourage the dark ambitions that lurked within his servant. Even as Thomas Jones doffed his servant garb in favor of his master's apparel, he was scheming to shed his servant status as well. Jones aimed to possess everything that had been his master's.

Either Jones hinted at his goal, or Elizabeth was more intuitive than her late husband had been. Whatever the cause, she clearly distrusted Jones, and two months into her widowhood she became so uneasy that she enlisted the help of her husband's old friend, William Waight, asking him to go to her mother's house and get another master for Jones. Elizabeth probably had one of her brothers in mind.

Somehow word of his imminent transfer reached Jones. He could wear his dead master's clothes and even lay hands on his rapier, but his master's position—and young widow—were slipping from his grasp. Frustrated in his attempt to take John Bowen's place, Jones lashed out.[26]

It was a Sunday evening, 18 May 1679, when he burst into Elizabeth's room and "wth a naked Rapier in his hand did tell her he would Kill her." Saying that he knew Elizabeth had sent for a new master for him, Jones sneered that instead "hee would be [Elizabeth's] master."

According to Elizabeth's court testimony, Jones then said "that he would not Kill her if shee would let him ly wth her all night & bade her goe to bed."

Boldly answering that she would not, Elizabeth rushed at Jones, deflected the rapier with her hands, and made for the door.

Thrown off guard by her quick move, Jones shouted that he would "cutt her throat but shee getting the dore did run out of dores & he after her." He caught her in the yard where he tried to make good on his threat. Elizabeth fought furiously, however, repeatedly using her hands to protect her throat from the knife that Jones wielded.

Unable to slash Elizabeth's throat while she was on her feet and fighting for her life, Jones finally flung her to the ground, where he continued his assault "& did there allso indeavour to cutt her throat but she prvented it by defending her throat wth her hands & bending [deflecting] the Knife."

Still unsuccessful in his murderous attack on Elizabeth's throat, Jones "took her Coats [skirt and petticoat] & threw [them] over her head & gave two or three blows in ye face wth his fist."

What happened next was not fully explained in the records and remains somewhat puzzling. According to Elizabeth, her assailant "bade her get her gun." Since the assault subsequently came to a sudden stop, it seems likely that Elizabeth actually did reach a gun. Her distrust of Jones may have led her to keep her late husband's pistol in her pocket, which in those days would have been a pouch dangling from her waist and reached through slits in her outer garments. As Elizabeth groped for her pocket, Jones probably taunted her with his sarcastic challenge. He undoubtedly thought that Elizabeth, reeling from blows to the face and bleeding from deep gashes in her hands, would be unable to handle her gun even if she managed to retrieve it. Certainly her injuries were severe: "wth the Knife [Jones did] Scurrify her throat & brest & cut her right hand wth six or seven Cutts very much & that she wth bending ye Rapier & Knife cut her hands & fingers very much."

Jones had clearly underestimated Elizabeth's resolve, but exactly how she gained the upper hand when she was all but overpowered perplexed even the gentlemen of the court in 1679. Alluding to Providence, but crediting Elizabeth with saving herself, the justices noted that "Thomas Jones her servant in a most barbarous & villanous nature sett upon & most desparatly attempted to murder the sd Bowin wth a naked Rapier and a Knife to cut her throat w^ch [would have] been perpatrated & comitted had it not bee[n] Providentially and strangly prevented by the said Bowins resistance recieveing severall wounds in her endeavours to prevent the sam[e]."

Not only was the murder prevented, but the attacker was taken into custody. Eight days later he was hauled before the court, where he had no choice but to admit to his crime. The justices, after considering Elizabeth's testimony and Jones' confession, pronounced judgment.

For his "horrid offence & Crime," Jones was placed in the custody of the sheriff, who was ordered to punish Jones immediately with "thirty nine lashes on the bare back well laid on." Jones was also "to have his haire cutt off and an Iron Coller.–forthw[th] put about his neck" where it would remain till it pleased the court to remove it.

Varying numbers of lashes, which caused pain that could linger for months[27] and scars that could last a lifetime, were considered adequate punishment for most offences. The seriousness of Jones' misdeeds, however, required extreme measures. By shaving Jones' head, the court effectively humiliated the prisoner and marked him as a criminal. Of course, the iron collar would do that too, only it had the additional advantage of inflicting discomfort along with the shame. We have no way of knowing what Jones' new collar looked like, but it certainly would have chafed his neck and shoulders, and, if it were equipped with projecting spikes, as some of them were, it could have made lying down very difficult.

After pronouncing the corporal punishment, the court proceeded to make sure that Jones would not be running free any time soon. He was ordered to finish serving his original term as a servant, and then to serve an additional three years, one year "for laying violent hands" on his mistress and two years for wounding her. After that, he was to reimburse Elizabeth for the court charges that she had incurred during his prosecution. When the lash-man, the barber and the blacksmith had done their work, the sheriff was to deliver Jones into the custody of Elizabeth Bowen, or someone appointed by her.

The fate of Thomas Jones is a mystery. One can rest assured that the sheriff followed through with the punishment ordered by the court, but we do not know if Jones survived his years of servitude. Thomas Jones was a common name, and there may have been as many as six men in the county that answered to it. Even though the name appears in records both before and after 1679, there is no way of knowing the true identity of the men thus mentioned. Before Jones burst into Elizabeth's room–and the court records–his servant status probably kept him out of most proceedings except John Bowen's will. If he survived his term of punishment, Jones' criminal record probably spurred him to move on to a place where he was less well known.

Earlier on the very same day that Elizabeth Bowen appeared in court to testify against her servant, the magistrates had been ordered to collect the names of the taxable individuals in their precincts. Elizabeth dutifully submitted her name and stated that she had two taxable persons in her household; one of them would have been Thomas Jones. Two months later, when the clerk compiled and recorded the list of the householders in the county, the name of Elizabeth Bowen appeared in the court records for the last time, one of only three widows listed among 272 men.[28]

Given the primitive medical treatment of the time, there was a good chance that infection would set in and finish the job that Thomas Jones had so viciously begun. Elizabeth's name did vanish from the records, but it wasn't because she succumbed to her wounds. Elizabeth Bowen married again. In fact, her story continued for nearly fifty more years, and in spite of Thomas Jones, ended more happily than most.

Probably within a year of the assault, Elizabeth married 29-year-old Henry Towles.[29] In 1680, when her name disappeared from the tax list, Henry appeared and was taxed on three tithables.[30]

Elizabeth, with her own abusive stepfather, had made a more prudent selection for her own children. Henry Towles, who generally appeared in court only to serve on juries, rarely ran afoul of the law. Once, in 1686, he failed to appear for jury duty, but his fine was suspended when he cited the "indisposition" of his family.[31] Many years later, he was accused of helping drive steers on the Sabbath day, but if he suffered any punishment, the court never mentioned it.[32] His other brush with the law, however, was much more serious. According to the complaint of Thomas Welburne, Henry Towles participated in an armed invasion of Chincoteague Island.

Beginning in 1671, a series of hopeful island owners had claimed Chincoteague. But the remoteness of the island and a general unwillingness to live there sabotaged their efforts, and they repeatedly failed to establish the required settlement there. By "deserting" the island, they opened the way for the next land hungry settler to usurp the earlier claims.[33]

During the early part of 1680, Welburne had attempted to "seat" Chincoteague by building a 12 by 15-foot house on a post foundation at an old Indian site. The workers, who cleared an acre, fenced it with brush and planted tobacco, corn and apple trees, later told how they were "very hard put to it and how that the wolves had run away with the porridge pot." Though servants were occasionally sent back to work on the place, no one ever really made the little house their home.[34]

That September a fisherman sailing about halfway down the western side of Chincoteague Island, went ashore and found several Indians staying in the house. The fisherman, who knew the Indians hunted cockles in the area, observed that they were now busy picking and roasting the corn growing there. That night the fisherman stayed in the house which, according to the Indians, belonged to Col. Welburne.[35]

As time wore on, Welburne became absorbed with more pressing duties elsewhere and completely neglected his venture on Chincoteague. The servant who built the house returned to the island in the early part of 1686, and found the place so overgrown with saplings and grapevines that he wouldn't have known it but for the house that was still standing there.[36]

It did not remain standing long, however. That summer Peter Walker, who was fishing in the area, remembered the house and went looking for it. He found it completely burned except for a piece of a post that was left standing.[37] This, of course, was very convenient for Welburne's rivals, who six months later made their move to claim the deserted island for themselves.

Anxious to be known as the owners of Chincoteague Island, the conspirators made no effort to hide their intentions. In early December 1686, Elizabeth's brother John found himself in the company of Welburne, who warned John he would shoot him if he came to the island. Retorting that his gun was as long as Welburne's, John "left him, the said Welburne, damnably madd."[38] Early the next month, when three of John's cohorts were shopping in Onancock, one of them announced that they were going to build a house on Chincoteague Island, and another, when asked to fire his pistol, refused saying he must keep "their Powder for their enemies."[39]

A day or so later Elizabeth's husband and her brother Francis Stockley gathered their guns[40] and joined about a dozen others as they sailed to Chincoteague Island, determined to build a house and claim the island in the name of William Kendall. While the records do not reveal exactly where they planned to build, it would have been logical for Kendall and his crew to take advantage of Welburne's favorable location with its once cleared acre.[41]

That evening back on the mainland, Woodman Stockley, another of Elizabeth's brothers, listened as Welburne angrily complained to the local magistrate about the "forceable Entry" made on his island. Welburne's pleas for the removal of the armed party received a cool reception, however, and he "seemed to be angrey about those seating the Iland and said it was not the building a house should deprive him of his Right and Spake severall thretning words. One of the Company said it was pitty that any of them should loose their lives about an Island, whereupon Mr. Welburne Replyed that if he did kill any of them the Law would beare him out and that he designed [to go] over tomorrow." At that point, Woodman quietly hurried off to report the threat to his brother John and a John Robins, both of whom were also leaving for Chincoteague in the morning.

Calmer than his hotheaded foe, Robins responded that if Welburne came peaceably, he was welcome, but if he hindered construction on the house, he would be tied and removed from the island. Robins wryly noted that Welburne would be a good witness for proving "that wee built a house thare." Robins even excused Welburne's rash words by kindly adding "that it would trouble any of us to loose our Right, for [Welburne] had bin at great Charges about it, and that [Welburne] had as leive loose his life as what he had."

John Robins and John Stockley arrived on Chincoteague Island the next day; a gun was in the boat, but a witness swore that Stockley never used it. Apparently no one else used their guns either, at least not in a malicious way. Welburne wisely decided against launching a singlehanded attack, and the interlopers quickly built, or more accurately, dug a house. According to one

member of the party, "a small house was then built about tenn foot long like
a roofe of a house upon ye ground."

A similar house dating from the 1620's, has been excavated at Martin's
Hundred near Jamestown. Cellar houses, with the floor below ground level
and the roof extending out over the surrounding earth, were more typical of
New England, however. They were generally used by early settlers who
would live in them for a few years while they established more permanent
homes.[42]

When Henry Towles returned home, he and his friends were placed under
arrest till they posted security for their attendance at the next court.[43]
Welburne had concluded that he stood a better chance with the justices in
court than with the usurpers on Chincoteague. Henry and the others dutifully
appeared, but the county magistrates decided that the case was too
complicated and referred it to the General Court in Jamestown, where the
matter dragged on for some time. It wasn't till 1691, that the court finally
granted William Kendall and John Robins a patent for Chincoteague Island.[44]

Why Henry Towles was so involved in the Chincoteague affair is unclear,
but it seems he had some special link to William Kendall. Besides readily
taking up arms to advance Kendall's interests, Henry and Elizabeth named
one of their sons Kendall.[45] In addition, Henry eventually received 500 acres
of Kendall's half of Chincoteague Island.[46]

About this time, the children of Elizabeth's first marriage became involved in
a dispute over a young mare that had joined their roving livestock. Though
Uncle Woodman Stockley defended their claim in court and their stepfather
Henry Towles branded the animal for them, it really was not theirs, a fact that
Elizabeth discovered when she went to a neighbor to learn the truth. The
depositions associated with this incident provide a few updates on the Bowen
children: Elizabeth, who may have been the oldest, had married a man named
Johnson; John, apparently still under guardianship, must not have turned
eighteen yet, though he was probably getting close; Ellinor was still unmarried;
and Richard, who was not mentioned at all, probably had died young.[47]

Four years later, when the three surviving Bowen children had entered
adulthood and their five half-brothers were either in their teens or headed
there, Henry and Elizabeth abandoned the comparatively civilized mainland
and settled on the island that Henry had helped secure for his friend more
than eight years earlier. By 1695, William Kendall mentioned that Henry was
established there on a plantation with housing and fencing,[48] though he did
not yet own the land. A year later, Henry formally purchased 500 acres on
the northern half of Chincoteague Island from Kendall, who died before
giving a deed for the property.[49] Elizabeth, who had bravely faced an armed
attacker seventeen years earlier, now had to summon her courage to face
isolation, hard work and pot-stealing wolves. One can only hope that she did

not have to face living in the ten-foot cellar house that her husband and his friends had thrown together so many years before.

Why they chose to relocate to a remote island inhabited only by livestock, a few hired herders[50] and wild animals is anyone's guess. But by doing so, they gained one distinction that they probably never appreciated. They were the first settlers to actually live on their own land on an island now frequented by thousands of vacationers who can only dream of doing the same. The Towles were among the first families of Chincoteague.

By colonial standards, Henry and Elizabeth, in their mid-forties, were getting on in years.[51] Of course, they had the energy of five youthful sons at their disposal, but even so, the work must have been strenuous and the hours long. So much so, that the Towles family rarely left the island. In fact, Henry Towles' name all but disappeared from the court records. In the fourteen years prior to his island sojourn, Henry was mentioned twenty times; during the twelve years the family lived on Chincoteague Island, Henry was mentioned only once, and that was when he was seen driving steers on a Sabbath day in 1698.[52]

Chincoteague's pristine forests and waters may have been beautiful, and its newly cleared fields productive, but neither natural beauty nor abundant harvest could compensate for the loneliness. The maturing Towle sons must have craved a social life, and a dozen years of separation from family and friends likely wore heavily on Elizabeth; her brother Francis died in 1698, two years after they moved to the island, and her mother died in 1707.[53] Elizabeth and the boys probably encouraged Henry's negotiations with John Custis, who, in December 1709, agreed to give 10,000 nails and 500 acres on the mainland in exchange for the 500 acres on Chincoteague Island that Henry identified as the ones "I now live on."[54]

Once they were back on the mainland, Henry started to appear in the court records once more. During the next seven years, he was mentioned twelve times, usually as a member of the jury, a task that in 1715, he quietly stopped doing. That same year he sold off 293 acres of his plantation.[55] In his mid-sixties, he may have been slowing down, but he was not finished yet. He wrote his will six years later, in January 1720/21, and died less than six months after that. [56]

Henry, who bequeathed what was left of the plantation to son Kendall, specified that his wife should have the use of it for the rest of her life. Elizabeth would have been almost seventy then, and she probably spent her sunset years on the home plantation.

The aging Elizabeth Stockley Bowen Towles just quietly slipped from view. Like most of the women of early Virginia, she had reared children, battled isolation and helped her husband tame a wilderness, but Elizabeth's courage set her apart. She had accomplished it all with scars on her hands.

Appendix I

The Bonwell Orphans

Several couplings contributed children to the list of orphans left by James Bonwell. They included John and Sarah Dorman, whose son John Dorman was born in the late 1640's. James Bonwell, who married Dorman's widow Sarah in the 1650's, had children by her before she died about 1662; her children probably included Hickman (a daughter born in the mid 1650's), and Ann (who married Phillip Quinton). Elizabeth, Mary (Wise) and Sarah (Wise) also most likely belonged to Sarah as did one of two boys named James. Bonwell's next wife, Mary Watson, was the mother of John Bonwell (named in the will of Mary's father) and the second James, who identified Mary as his mother in his own will when he died in 1721. (This will also named Elizabeth, Mary, Sarah and the other James.) Susannah (Mychel) was almost certainly the daughter of Mary, whose own mother was also named Susannah. Thomas, who was born in the mid 1660's, also would have been Mary Bonwell's child as was a younger daughter named Tabitha, whose last name does not appear; she may have been a Bonwell or a daughter of Roger Mikell, whom Mary married in 1668. George Hope was part of Mary's family when she married Roger Mikell (George was called Mikell's stepson), and while Mary is not specifically called his mother, it seems clear that George was Mary's son from a marriage that predated her union with Bonwell. George enjoyed a close and continuous relationship with Mary as well as with Mary's father, but there is a problem with the reputed ages of the people involved. In depositions he gave, Mary's father, Robert Watson, claimed a birth date of about 1623; George Hope (who had good reasons for rushing into adulthood) claimed a birth date of about 1654–which would have made him just 31 years younger than his grandfather. It is true that marriage came early for some of the higher class colonists in those days; examples include Col. Edmund Scarburgh's daughter Tabitha (barely 14), her son Edmund Browne (age 17), and two local girls Elizabeth Charleton and Sarah Douglas (both married at age 12). Both Robert Watson and his daughter Mary could have married very young, and at least in Mary's case, very likely did. Perhaps Watson, who was in his fifties when he recorded his age, was off by a few years. However, it is more likely that grandson George Hope (possibly with his mother's complicity) added a few years to his age to get early access to his inheritance and to provide a refuge for his abused mother and siblings. A possible clue to his age lurks beneath the surface of his request for a new guardian, an action orphans were allowed to take upon reaching age 14; it was on 18 April 1672, that George dumped his stepfather as guardian and selected his grandfather. Assuming he was the normal age for such actions, he was actually four years younger than the age he later claimed. Nottingham, *Wills and Administrations*, 33, 65; *Accomack Order, 1671-1673*, 83. Age of marriage: Whitelaw, *Virginia's Eastern Shore*, 657, 968, 430.

Appendix II

The children of John and Elizabeth Stockley

There are a number of clues to Elizabeth Stockley's age. Her mother, (also named Elizabeth) was born in 1633/34, making her only about fifteen years old when her son William was born in 1649. Six more sons and five daughters were living when their father wrote his will on 3 February 1670/71; they were to receive their portions at age 18 (unless their mother remained a widow). Daughter Elizabeth was not included with her sisters in the will because her portion had already been set apart; this implies that she had already reached her 18th birthday and/or was soon to be married. A younger daughter Inez (or Ince) was probably a little past the age of 18 when she sued her stepfather for her inheritance in 1675, giving her a likely birth date of 1656. The distribution of the family land, while giving no dates, does help with the birth order of most of the Stockley sons; in his will, the father ordered the land be distributed from north to south starting with the oldest. Thomas, who was to receive the home place, was apparently excluded from this formula. A lawsuit implies he was still underage in 1677, probably born after 1659 (*Accomack Orders, 1676-1678*, 76). Except for Thomas on the home plantation, the pieces of land from north to south went to: William, Woodman, John, Joseph, Charles and Francis. The known birth dates of the Stockley children were: William (1649), Woodman (1654), Inez (probably 1656), John (1657) and Thomas (after 1659). It seems most likely that Elizabeth was born about 1651 - 1652, in the gap between William and Woodman, a date that also agrees with the implication in her father's will. If this is correct, Elizabeth would have been about 12 years old in 1664, when John Bowen arrived in Virginia, about 18 or 19 years old when she married after her father wrote his will in 1670, and around 27 years old when she fought off Thomas Jones in 1679. Ages of the mother, William and Woodman–*Accomack Orders, 1673-1676*, 39, 40; Stockley will–*Accomack Orders, 1671-1673*, 231-233; William–*Accomack Orders, 1678-1682*, 199, 228; John–*Accomack Orders, 1676-1678*, 242; Woodman–*Accomack Orders, 1678-1682*, 250, 251; *Accomack Orders, 1682-1697*, 112; Ince–*Accomack Orders, 1673-1676*, 262; Whitelaw, *Virginia's Eastern Shore*, 1225-1233.

Appendix III

Evidence for the marriage of Elizabeth Stockley and John Bowen

No known document states that Elizabeth, daughter of John and Elizabeth Stockley, married John Bowin, but a chain of inter-related evidence suggests that this was the case:

a] John and Elizabeth Stockley had a daughter named Elizabeth. *Accomack Orders 1671-1673*, 231-233.

b] John Bowen, former servant to the Stockleys, married an Elizabeth. *Accomack Wills and Deeds 1676-1690*, 141-144.

c] Elizabeth, the mother of John Bowen's orphans, later became the wife of Henry Towles. *Accomack Orders 1690-1697*, 52a-53a.

d] Henry and Elizabeth Towles had five sons, one of whom was named Stockley. *Accomack Deeds and Wills 1692-1715*, 422.

e] Stockley Towles and his brothers Henry, Thomas and Job were remembered in the will (probated 6 August 1707) of Elizabeth Stockley Stratton, the presumed mother of Elizabeth Bowen Towles. *Accomack Deeds and Wills 1692-1715*, 422.

f] Robert L. Mears, author of the "Mears Collection," has also concluded that Elizabeth, the wife of Henry Towles, was the daughter of John and Elizabeth Stockley. Item #1117, Mears Collection, *Eastern Shore Public Library*, http://www.espl.org

Other clues point to the same conclusion:

a] From the mid 1660's through the 1670's, John Bowen was closely associated with the Stockleys, who both transported and teamed up with Bowen. *Accomack Orders 1663-1666*, 69a; *Accomack Orders 1673-1676*, 194-196.

b] On 17 October 1678, the younger John Stockley, gave Bowen's son John a gift of animals, a generous act in keeping with the assumption that young Bowen was Stockley's nephew. *Accomack Wills and Deeds 1676-1690*, 116.

c] In his will, Bowen appointed John and Woodman Stockley to divide the estate between his wife and children. He appointed John Stockley guardian to his children, John, Richard, Elizabeth and Ellinor Bowen. *Accomack Wills and Deeds 1676-1690*, 141-144.

d] There is no record of Bowen owning land, but it is clear that he lived near the Stockley family; he was taxed in the same district as the Stockleys. *Accomack Orders, 1673-1676*, 194-196, 325-27; *Accomack Orders 1676-1678*, 32-34, 56-58. He was involved in legal matters in the same area. *Accomack Orders 1676-1678*, 114; *Accomack Wills and Deeds 1676-1690*, 60, 84. He had Stockley neighbors witness his will. *Accomack Wills and Deeds 1676-1690*, 141-144.

e] In 1679, it is noted that Elizabeth Bowen sent a messenger to "her Mothers." Attributing home ownership to her mother is what one would expect of Elizabeth Bowen if her father were John Stockley, who had died six years earlier in 1673. *Accomack Orders 1678-1682*, 61; *Nottingham Wills and Administrations*, 5.

f] The widow of the elder John Stockley later married John Stratton, who died in 1697; in his will he mentions Alexander and Eliner Massie. According to the "Miles Files," Elizabeth Bowen's daughter Ellinor married Alexander Massey and lived in Somerset County, MD. *Accomack Wills and Deeds 1676-1690*, 121; *Nottingham Wills and Administrations*, 29; Barry W. Miles and Moody K. Miles, "The Miles Files 4.0," Person Page 357, http://www.espl.org/milesfiles2/p357.htm#i27842.

g] Woodman Stockley was still defending the rights of the Bowen children in 1691, a dozen years after their father's death. *Accomack Orders, 1690-1697*, 45a, 52a-53a.

Notes

The handwritten court records generally used the page/folio system with one number serving for two facing pages. In most of the record books a later hand clarified matters by placing the letter "a" after the number on the right-hand page; these notes follow the latter system.

In citing works in the notes, abbreviated titles have been used for the following court records:

Accomack Orders 1663-1666	*Accomack County, Virginia, Deeds & Wills [& Orders], 1663-1666*, (Library of Virginia microfilm reel 1)
Accomack Orders 1666-1670	*Accomack County, Virginia, Orders 1666-1670*, (Library of Virginia microfilm reel 78)
Accomack Orders 1671-1673	*Accomack County, Virginia, [Deeds], Orders, Wills [of Upper Northampton], 1671-1673*, (Library of Virginia microfilm reel 2)
Accomack Orders 1673-1676	*Accomack County, Virginia, [Deeds], Wills, [Orders], Etc., 1673-1676*, (Library of Virginia microfilm reel 2)
Accomack Orders 1676-1678	*Accomack County, Virginia, Orders, 1676-1678*, (Library of Virginia microfilm reel 79)
Accomack Orders 1678-1682	*Accomack County, Virginia, Wills, Deeds, & Orders, 1678-1682*, (Library of Virginia microfilm reel 4)
Accomack Orders 1682-1697	*Accomack County, Virginia, [Deeds], Wills, Etc., Orders, 1682-1697*, (Library of Virginia microfilm reel 4) [note: The court orders ended with the court held September 1690; deeds and wills and tax lists were added through 1697.]
Accomack Orders 1690-1697	*Accomack County, Virginia, Orders, 1690-1697*, (Library of Virginia microfilm reel 79)
Accomack Orders 1697-1703	*Accomack County, Virginia, Orders, 1697-1703*, (Library of Virginia microfilm reel 79)
Accomack Orders 1703-1709	*Accomack County, Virginia, Orders, 1703-1709*, (Library of Virginia microfilm reel 79)
Accomack Orders 1710-1714	*Accomack County, Virginia, Orders, 1710-1714*, (Library of Virginia microfilm reel 80)
Accomack Orders 1714-1717	*Accomack County, Virginia, Orders, 1714-1717*, (Library of Virginia microfilm reel 80)
Accomack Orders 1717-1719	*Accomack County, Virginia, Orders, 1717-1719*, (Library of Virginia microfilm reel 80)
Accomack Orders 1719-1724	*Accomack County, Virginia, Orders, 1719-1724*, (Library of Virginia microfilm reel 80)
Accomack Wills and Deeds 1676-1690	*Accomack County, Virginia, Wills and Deeds, 1676-1690*, (Library of Virginia microfilm reel 3)

Accomack Deeds and Wills 1692-1715	*Accomack County, Virginia, [Deeds], Wills, Etc., 1692-1715,* (Library of Virginia microfilm reel 5)
Council of Maryland 1681-1685/6	*Proceedings of the Council of Maryland, 1681- 85/86,* vol. 17, Archives of Maryland Online, http://www.mdarchives.state.md.us /megafile/msa/speccol/sc2900/sc2908/html /volumes.html
Council of Maryland 1687/8-1693	*Proceedings of the Council of Maryland, 1687/8-1693,* Archives of Maryland Online, http://www.mdarchives.state.md.us/megafil e/msa/speccol/sc2900/sc2908/html/volumes .html
Maryland General Assembly 1700-1704	*Proceedings and Acts of the General Assembly, April 26, 1700-May 3, 1704,* vol. 24 , Archives of Maryland Online, http://www .mdarchives.state.md.us/megafile/msa /speccol/sc2900/s c2908/html/volumes.html
Northampton Orders 1657-1664	*Northampton County, Virginia, Order Book, 1657-1664,* (Library of Virginia microfilm reel 46)
Northampton Orders 1664-1674	*Northampton County, Virginia, Order Book No. 9, 1664-1674,* (Library of Virginia microfilm reel 26)
Northampton Orders 1678-1683	*Northampton County, Virginia, Order Book No. 11, 1678-1683,* (Library of Virginia microfilm reel 27)
Northampton Orders 1683-1689	*Northampton County, Virginia, Order Book & Wills, No. 12, 1683-1689,* (Library of Virginia microfilm reel 27)
Somerset Proceedings 1665-1668	*Proceedings of the County Courts of Kent (1648-1676), Talbot (1662-1674, and Somerset (1665-1668),* vol. 54, Archives of Maryland Online, http://www.mdarchives .state.md.us/megafile/msa/speccol/sc2900 /sc2908/html/volumes.html
Somerset Judicial Records 1670-1671	*Somerset County Court (Judicial Record) September 1, 1670-October 20, 1671,* vol. 86, Archives of Maryland Online, http://www. mdarchives.state.md.us/megafile/msa /speccol/sc2900/sc2908/html/volumes.html
Somerset Judicial Records 1671-1675	*Somerset County Court (Judicial Record) October 25, 1671-October 20, 1675,* vol. 87, Archives of Maryland Online, http://www. mdarchives.state.md.us/megafile/msa /speccol/sc2900/sc2908/html/volumes.html
Somerset Judicial Records 1683-1683/4	*Somerset County Court (Judicial Record) November 13, 1683 - March 11, 1683[84],* vol. 90, Archives of Maryland Online, http://www.mdarchives.state.md.us/megafile

Somerset Judicial Records 1687-1689   /msa/speccol/sc2900/sc2908/html /volumes.html *Somerset County Court (Judicial Record) September 30, 1687 - June 12, 1689*, vol. 91, Archives of Maryland Online, http://www.mdarchives.state.md.us/megafile /msa/speccol/sc2900/sc2908/html /volumes.html

Somerset Judicial Records 1689-1690   *Somerset County Court (Judicial Record) September 24, 1689 - November 12, 1690*, vol. 106, Archives of Maryland Online, http://www.mdarchives.state.md.us /megafile/msa/speccol/sc2900/sc2908 /html/volumes.html

Somerset Judicial Records 1690-1691   *Somerset County Court (Judicial Record), November 14, 1690 - October 3, 1691*, vol. 191, Archives of Maryland Online, http://www.mdarchives.state.md.us/megafile /msa/speccol/sc2900/sc2908/html /volumes.html

Somerset Judicial Records 1692-1693   *Somerset County Judicial Records, 1692-1693,* Volume 406, Archives of Maryland Online, http://www.mdarchives .state.md.us/megafile/msa/speccol /sc2900/sc2908/html/volumes.html

Somerset Judicial Records 1692-1696   *Somerset Judicial Records 1692-96, Abstracts with Selected Transcriptions,* vol. 535, Archives of Maryland Online, http://www.mdarchives.state.md.us /megafile/msa/speccol/sc2900/sc2908 /html/volumes.html

Preface

1. *Accomack Orders 1671-1673*, 159, 164, 173, 174.

2. *Accomack Orders 1666-1670*, 18, 18a, 26, 26a; *Accomack Orders 1671-1673*, 163,224; *Accomack Orders 1673-1676*, 77, 112.

3. *Accomack Orders 1666-1670*, 3, 8, 9a, 14, 25, 25a, 43a, 86; *Accomack Wills and Deeds 1676-1690*, 423, 423a.

4. *Accomack Orders 1703-1710*, 77a, 81, 90a; *Accomack Orders 1710-1714*, 3, 61, 10, 10a, 25, 53a, 54, 57a, 64, 78a, 81, 82; *Accomack Orders 1714-1717*, 6a.

5. *Northampton Orders 1657-1664*, 62a-64a, 65a, 81a.

6. *Accomack Orders 1663-1666*, 50.

7. *Accomack Orders 1666-1670*, 21, 58a, 60, 62a, 141, 150, 151.

Chapter 1
Mary Burton

1. Describing the family relationships in the Carter case, the court noted that Mary was "the natural daughter of Sarah the wife of him the said Paul." *Accomack Orders 1678-1682,* 172. While one meaning of the term "natural" is illegitimate, there is another quite opposite definition: actually begotten by one (as opposed to adopted), especially in wedlock. Nielson, *Webster's New International Dictionary,* 1630. Sarah may have been married at the time of Mary's birth; the records make no mention of her committing fornication.

2. The following young children and infants belonging to indentured mothers were bound out as servants till attaining the ages of 21 or 24 years: Jean, child of Miles Gray, 1668. *Accomack Orders 1666-1670,* 58a; Elizabeth Lang's infant, 1671/72. *Accomack Orders 1671-1673,* 52; Quinton, Cicely Birke's infant, 1672, *Accomack Orders 1671-1673,* 118, 119, 121; Elizabeth, Mary Ballard's infant, 1673. *Accomack Orders 1671-1673,* 202.

3. *Accomack Orders 1678-1682,* 196.

4. *Northampton Orders 1664-1674,* 198.

5. *Accomack Orders 1671-1673,* 84.

6. *Accomack Orders 1671-1673,* 101, 116.

7. *Accomack Orders 1673-1676,* 195, 260, 266, 326; *Accomack Orders 1676-1678,* 33, 56.

8. *Accomack Orders 1676-1678,* 60.

9. Paul Carter's servant, John Hancock, was brought to court by James Tuck, who must have been an associate of Carter's. *Accomack Orders 1676-1678,* 100.

10. *Accomack Orders 1678-1682,* 132, 133.

11. *Accomack Orders 1678-1682,* 132, 133.

12. *Accomack Orders 1678-1682,* 159, 160.

13. *Accomack Orders 1678-1682,* 160.

14. Midwives were expected to interrogate unwed mothers during childbirth: Berkin and Horowitz, *Women's Voices, Women's Lives,* 51; Spruill, *Women's Life and Work,* 273. Delivering a child "privately" was against the law: *Accomack Orders 1676-1678,* 39; *Accomack Orders 1678-1682,* 218, 235, 236.

14. *Accomack Orders 1678-1682,* 159, 160.

15. *Accomack Orders 1678-1682,* 160.

16. *Accomack Orders 1678-1682,* 160.

17. *Accomack Orders 1678-1682,* 160, 161.

18. *Accomack Orders 1678-1682,* 163.

19. *Accomack Orders 1678-1682,* 161-166.

20. *Accomack Orders 1678-1682,* 162. In 1681, women were also summoned to inspect the body of Margret Pickering to determine if she had given birth. *Accomack Orders 1678-1682,* 233-235.

21. The 24th Act of Assembly stipulated that a grand jury should be impaneled to investigate the presentment, hear the evidence, and deliberate on the matter. If they found the suspects "so farr criminall" that they could not be further tried in the county court, the suspects were to be sent to the General Court in "James Citty" for trial. The local court did not follow the law to the letter, however. They noted that "it hath been the usuall & allowable practice of this County in regard of ye remoteness thereof & great charge thereby arriveing not to follow prcisely y[e] form p[re]scribed in y[e] 24[th] Act of Assem[bly]." They appointed only six jurors to send to Jamestown for the full trial. *Accomack Orders 1678-1682,* 167.

22. *Accomack Orders 1678-1682,* 162.

23. *Accomack Orders 1678-1682,* 163.

24. *Accomack Orders 1678-1682*, 165.

25. *Accomack Orders 1678-1682*, 166, 167.

26. *Accomack Orders 1678-1682*, 172.

27. In December 1680, Mary Burton gave a deposition describing her stay with Bridget Savage, which lasted from the middle of May till the last day of July. *Accomack Orders 1678-1682*, 196, 197.

28. The court of 4 August 1680, ordered that Mary Burton be placed in the care of Capt. William Custis. *Accomack Orders 1678-1682*, 181. This date is four days after Mary said she left the Savages; it should be remembered, however, that Mary, who could not read and write, was recalling this in December. *Accomack Orders 1678-1682*, 196, 197.

29. *Accomack Orders 1678-1682*, 183.

30. The first prison in Accomack County was built at Pungoteague in 1674, but after the courthouse was moved a few years later, the sheriff was responsible for taking care of the prisoners himself. Paul Carter must have escaped from the custody of Daniel Jenifer, who was sheriff during the years 1679 and 1680. Whitelaw, *Virginia's Eastern Shore*, 715, 716. 1034. 1035; *Accomack Orders 1678-1682*, 87, 170.

31. Mary Burton was presented for fornication on 16 December 1680, and appeared in court to answer the charges against her on 18 January 1680/81. *Accomack Orders 1678-1682*, 191, 202.

32. The number of lashes administered for fornication varied though the years, apparently according to the mood of the court. In the summer of 1679, less than a year before Mary Burton's offense, Jane Diton and Rebecca Knight were sentenced to receive 19 lashes for fornication. *Accomack Orders 1678-1682*, 94.

Chapter 2
Mary, Rachel and Elinor

1. In 1672, John Wallop patented the island which later bore his name; originally it was called Kekotank Island or Accocomson Island. The island was taken over by the government during World War II for a Naval Ordnance Station, which was later absorbed by NASA. This facility also encompasses the likely site of John Wallop's mainland home. Whitelaw, *Virginia's Eastern Shore*, 908, 1211, 1242, 1243, 1282, 1304, 1330, 1333, 1338, 1339, 1369; One of the oldest launch sites in the world, Wallops Flight Facility launched its first rocket on 4 July 1945. NASA, *Wallops Flight Facility*, "Wallops History." http://www.wff.nasa.gov/about/history.php.

2. *Accomack Orders 1678-1682*, 176, 177.

3. *Accomack Orders 1678-1682*, 193-196.

4. *Accomack Orders 1678-1682*, 191, 201, 279, 280.

5. *Accomack Orders 1666-1670*, 126, 134.

6. *Accomack Orders 1678-1682*, 176, 177, 195, 196.

7. *Accomack Orders 1678-1682*, 195.

8. *Accomack Orders 1678-1682*, 196.

9. At the court held 17 December 1680. *Accomack Orders 1678-1682*, 193.

10. Mary Storey witnessed both Dorothy Watts' gossip and her subsequent contempt of a warrant. Since Mary's master John Wallop, a justice, issued the warrant at Woodman Stockley's request, it is likely that Mary deliberately positioned herself at the scene of the action. *Accomack Orders 1678-1682*, 244, 250, 251.

11. *Accomack Orders 1678-1682*, 251.

12. 18 November 1681. *Accomack Orders 1678-1682*, 270.

13. On 2 January 1683/84, it was noted that Thomas Welburne's servant named Ann Fish had given birth to an illegitimate child for whose care 1200 pounds of tobacco (the typical cost of a year's support) had yet to be paid. Ann, who had died in childbirth, could not testify, but the court was convinced that another of Welburne's servants named John Dyer was the father of her child. This implies that Dyer had become Welburne's servant almost two years earlier. A year of child support and nine months for the pregnancy would place Dyer on the Welbourne plantation in March or April 1682; Mary Storey was arrested for murder on 17 June 1682. *Accomack Orders 1682-1697*, 30; *Accomack Orders 1678-1682*, 307.

14. Mary Storey was discharged 18 August 1682. *Accomack Orders 1678-1682*, 307, 317.

15. *Accomack Orders 1678-1682*, 195.

16. *Accomack Orders 1678-1682*, 230.

17. *Accomack Orders 1682-1697*, 2a.

18. On 15 June 1683, the court noted that John Wallop "is now gone for England." *Accomack Orders 1682-1697*, 11a.

19. *Accomack Orders 1682-1697*, 2a.

20. Sometime before 2 January 1683/84, the parish had paid 1200 pounds of tobacco to John Wallop, at whose plantation Rachel Hasted's infant had been "put to nurse" for a year. The same amount was to be paid to John Melson, whose wife had been entrusted with the child of Ann Fish. *Accomack Orders 1682-1697*, 30.

21. *Accomack Orders 1682-1697*, 30.

22. *Accomack Orders 1682-1697*, 30.

23. *Accomack Orders 1682-1697*, 30.

24. *Accomack Orders 1682-1697*, 50, 50a, 52, 54.

25. On 5 October 1697, John Dyer, unhappy about being summoned for the grand jury, persisted in using "opprobrious and scurrilous words" to the court. Ordered placed in the stocks, Dyer fled before the sheriff could carry out the punishment. After his arrest, Dyer apologized to the court, promised better behavior and was discharged on 8 December 1697. *Accomack Orders 1690-1697*, 141, 252; *Accomack Orders 1697-1703*, 2a.

26. *Accomack Orders 1719-1724*, 28a; Nottingham, *Wills and Administrations*, 68.

27. Whitelaw, *Virginia's Eastern Shore*, 1327.

28. On 2 August 1680, the court judged William Dixson to be 16 years old and ordered him to serve John Wallop accordingly. William was either large for his age or deliberately misled the court in order to attain an earlier release; when he gave a deposition six years later, William reported his age to be only nineteen years. *Accomack Orders 1678-1682*, 175; *Accomack Orders 1682-1697*, 90. According to the 7th Act of the Assembly, made in 1671, English born minors would remain in servitude till age 24; those born in Virginia, would be free upon turning 21. *Accomack Orders 1682-1697*, 56a, 85a.

29. The story of Elinor Hew's death was told in testimony given by Wallop's sons Samuel and John Jr. as well as Thomas Worsley and William Dixson. *Accomack Orders 1682-1697*, 93a-94a, 96a.

30. Afflicted with an annual breathing problem, Elinor had apparently enjoyed her mother's attention during her previous sick spell in England. *Accomack Orders 1682-1697*, 93a.

31. In July 1674, a servant named Thomas Clifton signed a note saying that he had left England of his own free will and had not been spirited away or enticed to leave. Others, of course, were not so fortunate. *Accomack Orders 1673-1676*, 158.

32. John Wallop was not at home when Elinor died, but he probably was not far away. Ellinor Hew died on 18 June 1686; John Wallop attended court as a justice on both 12 May and 6 July 1686. *Accomack Orders 1682-1697*, 87a, 90, 94.

33. The deposition of Thomas Worsley was taken 9 July 1686. *Accomack Orders 1682-1697*, 94-94a.

34. Even Henry Smith's servant Old John, who died beaten and abused among the hogs in an old tobacco house, was washed and wrapped in an old sail before he was buried. *Accomack Orders 1666-1670*, 136, 137.

35. *Accomack Orders 1682-1697*, 94a.

36. *Accomack Orders 1682-1697*, 91a.

37. *Accomack Orders 1682-1697*, 94a.

38. *Accomack Orders 1682-1697*, 94a.

39. *Accomack Orders 1682-1697*, 96a.

40. *Accomack Orders 1682-1697*, 97.

41. *Accomack Deeds and Wills 1692-1715*, 19.

42. William Dixson paid taxes, 17 November 1691; lived at Widow Holliday's, 16 February 1691/92; and defended his wife Ann, 7 November 1699. *Accomack Orders 1682-1697*, 259, 259a; *Accomack Orders 1690-1697*, 57; *Accomack Orders 1697-1703*, 75a.

43. *Accomack Orders 1682-1697*, 117, 127.

44. John Butt named his abusive master, Henry Smith, as his cause of death. *Accomack Orders 1666-1670*, 102-109. A servant named Mary Lee, injured by one of her fellow servants, said if she died her attacker was the death of her. *Accomack Orders 1671-1673*, 8. Shortly before he died in 1658, a servant named Francis Burkam said he "would lay his death to his masters Charge." But when a doctor "opened ye body" and found "y^t his heart was very defective and much wasted his Lungs beeinge Imperfect black and putrefied," the master was cleared. *Northampton Orders 1657-1664*, 22a-25a. Before Ellinor Cowell died in February 1659/60, she bitterly attributed her looming death to her mistress, Katherine Pannwell. *Northampton Orders 1657-1664*, 62a-64a, 65, 81.

45. Ivan Zbaraschuk, M.D., graciously agreed to read copies of the depositions and express an opinion on the death of Elinor Hew.

46. *Accomack Orders 1678-1682*, 17, 18, 99-101. *Accomack Wills and Deeds 1676-1690*, 211-213.

47. William Wallop's accident occurred on Christmas Day, and he probably died shortly thereafter; the coroner's jury met on 3 January 1677/78. While neither William Wallop's parents nor his age are given in the coroner's report, it is clear that he died on or near the John Wallop plantation. All the landowners on the coroner's jury (who viewed the body) lived within a few miles of John Wallop's home. *Accomack Wills and Deeds 1676-1690*, 211-213. Whitelaw, *Virginia's Eastern Shore*, 1230, 1235, 1235, 1285, 1286, 1329, 1330, 1331, 1369.

48. Sarah Wallop married neighbor John Watts. Whitelaw, *Virginia's Eastern Shore*, 1242, 1328, 1336.

49. John Wallop signed his will on 4 April 1693; it was probated on 19 September 1693. *Accomack Deeds and Wills 1692-1715*, 18-20.

50. Whitelaw, *Virginia's Eastern Shore*, 1336.

Chapter 3
Margaret Teackle

1. Margaret Teackle's party, which began on 2 February 1694/95, entered the court records only after her father brought suit against Elizabeth Parker and her husband Philip on 19 June 1695. *Accomack Orders 1690-1697*, 156a. This narrative is compiled from the partygoers' accounts, which provided a multitude of details. Jane Hall was interrogated by Mr. Teackle, but the others gave one or more depositions. The attendees and secondary witnesses: John Addison, *Accomack Orders 1690-1697*, 160, 160a,161; Jane Hall, *Accomack Orders 1690-1697*, 161, 161a, 162; Mary Major, *Accomack Orders 1690-1697*, 162a;

Agnus/Agnes Milbey, *Accomack Orders 1690-1697*, 162a, 163, 164a, 165; Elizabeth Ballard, *Accomack Orders 1690-1697*, 163, 163a; Mary Doe, *Accomack Orders 1690-1697*, 163a, 164, 164a; Samuel Doe, *Accomack Orders 1690-1697*, 164a.

2. Although Elizabeth Ballard was called "Betty" only by the Does, that name is used here to distinguish the servant from Elizabeth Parker. Presented in court the day before Mr. Teackle sued the Parkers (18 June 1695), Elizabeth "Betty" Ballard had been "lately brought to bed of a bastard child borne of her body." It is reasonable to assume that Betty was four to six months pregnant in February when the party occurred. *Accomack Orders 1690-1697*, 152.

3. The Teackle home was located on Craddock Creek. Passed down through the male line, the home in which Margaret hosted her party is thought to be the one destroyed during the American Revolution. Frustrated in their attempts to capture Col. Thomas Teackle (great grandson of the minister), the British put Mrs. Teackle and her new baby in an outbuilding and set fire to the main house. Whitelaw, *Virginia's Eastern Shore*, 643-645.

4. Whitelaw, *Virginia's Eastern Shore*, 619, 620, 623, 624.

5. Colonial Virginians were able to move from plantation to plantation with ease. According to Bruce, "One single sailing vessel, calling at house after house along the banks of a river, was able to carry a large party of merry pleasure-seekers to an entertainment given in some planter's home standing twenty or even forty miles away from the point where the vessel started on its voyage." Bruce, *Social Life of Virginia*, 171.

6. Though it was never directly stated, it seems likely that Mary Jones was the daughter of Mary Doe by a previous marriage. The Does are consistently listed either with their "daughter" or with Mary Jones, never both. In a deposition, Mary Jones refers to her mother who obtained goods at Teackle's house; Mary Doe was the only mother in attendance. *Accomack Orders 1690-1697*, 160a-162, 163.

7. Whitelaw, *Virginia's Eastern Shore*, 624-635, 639, 640.

8. Whitelaw, *Virginia's Eastern Shore*, 619, 672, 846; Nottingham, *Wills and Administrations*, 46, 47.

9. Whitelaw, *Virginia's Eastern Shore*, 635, 636.

10. Though he was in his mid-sixties, Thomas Teackle was father of a young family, undoubtedly all the children of his second wife, Margaret Nelson, who died some time before 1695. Except for Margaret, the Teackle children (John, Catherine and Elizabeth) were all underage when Teackle made his will in January 1695/96. Whitelaw, *Virginia's Eastern Shore*, 641, 643, 644; *Accomack Deeds and Wills 1692-1715*, 98-99.

11. Indentured servant women found guilty of fornication were not only forced to indemnify their masters for work they were unable to do during pregnancy and childbirth, they also had to work off their fines with additional service. Spruill, *Women's Life and Work*, 317.

12. Ribbon was more than a feminine trifle in the seventeenth century; ribbon loops, bows and rosettes often decorated the clothing of well-dressed gentlemen. Yarwood, *Encyclopedia of World Costume*, 334.

13. The literature suggests that children's interests were rarely considered by Colonial widowers contemplating second marriages. Spruill, *Women's Life and Work*, 62, 63.

14. Accused of adultery and attempted assault by Col. Edmund Scarburgh in 1656, Thomas Teackle was suspended from his pulpit. Thirty-five of his parishioners, who successfully petitioned to have him reinstated, noted the integrity of his former life and his conversation. The court in granting their request mentioned Teackle's civil and honest behavior. Whitelaw, *Virginia's Eastern Shore*, 640, 641.

15. Mr. Teackle's callous attitude becomes apparent in his treatment of Elizabeth "Betty" Ballard, who seems to have been the minister's source of information; details mentioned in Betty's testimony also appeared in the questions Teackle posed to Jane Hall.

Though Betty may have hoped to gain Teackle's favor, it is likely that he separated Betty from her infant even as he was preparing the dance/party lawsuit. On 18 June 1695, shortly after the unmarried Betty had given birth, Teackle took steps "to put the sd Child on ye p[ar]ish," thus indicating his unwillingness to support the infant in any way. In bastardy cases where the mother's master refused to keep the child, the mother would continue in servitude while the baby would be placed with a married woman willing to nurse it for pay. The cost would be borne by the parish if the father was unknown or unable to pay, but since Betty Ballard named Provost Nellson as the father, he was ordered to give security for the child's support. Elizabeth Ballard herself posted security of 2000 pounds of tobacco in lieu of the penalty inflicted by law, usually 15 to 30 lashes on the bare back. *Accomack Orders 1690-1697*, 124a, 152, 152, 159, 198.

16. William Major, who died in 1684, left a widow named Mary living on land not far from Teackles' home. Nottingham, *Wills and Administrations*, 12; Whitelaw, *Virginia's Eastern Shore*, 648.

17. *Accomack Orders 1690-97*, 159a, 160, 160a.

18. With a shilling worth 20 pounds of tobacco (as it was in 1698), one pound sterling would buy 400 pounds of tobacco. Since a day's work was valued at 18 pounds of tobacco (1702), a laborer toiling six days per week for a year might earn 5634 pounds of tobacco, or just over 14 pounds sterling. *Accomack Orders 1697-1703*, 38a, 131.

19. Nottingham, *Wills and Administrations*, 25.

20. Whitelaw, *Virginia's Eastern Shore*, 593, 639, 644.

21. Catherine Teackle, in August 1703, succeeded in convincing the court that her guardian, William Willet, had failed to provide her with necessary clothing for two years. She asked the court for permission to live with Littleton Robins and for Willet to give her "a decent maintenance out of her own estate." With a court order hanging over his head, Willet finally agreed to allow Catherine the clothing she wanted. *Accomack Orders 1703-1709*, 6a. Fourteen years old in 1703, Catherine would have been about eleven years younger than Margaret and six years old when the party occurred in 1695. Catherine married John Robins, the brother of Margaret's husband Littleton Robins. Whitelaw, *Virginia's Eastern Shore*, 181, 643, 698.

22. *Accomack Orders 1703-1709*, 116.

Chapter 4
Mary Calvert Supple

1. Mackey and Groves, *Northampton Record Book*, 1645-1651, 351. Walcyzk, *Northampton, Orders, Deeds, & Wills 1651-1654*, 73, 161.

2. *Accomack Orders 1678-1682*, 257.

3. Whitelaw, *Virginia's Eastern Shore*, 903.

4. Calvert was most likely born between 1615 and 1617. *Accomack Orders 1663-1666*, 47a; *Accomack Orders 1666-1670*, 34.

5. Charles Calvert, son of Christopher, was listed among the tithables in February 1676/77. If he was 21 that year, he would have been only a year or so older than Mary. *Accomack Orders 1676-1678*, 32-34. The records also mention a Christopher Calvert, Jr.; Whitelaw indicates that Christopher Jr. and Charles may have been the same individual. In 1657, Christopher Calvert gave his children Christopher and Mary 400 acres apiece. In later deeds, the male owner is referred to as Charles, though a Christopher Jr. still occasionally appeared in other records. Whitelaw, *Virginia's Eastern Shore*, 903.

6. Although freeborn girls typically married early, this was especially true of young heiresses. Spruill, *Women's Life and Work*, 139-141.

7. *Accomack Orders 1663-1666*, 53; *Accomack Orders 1671-1673*, 27, 49, 108.

8. *Northampton Orders 1657-1664*, 106-107.

9. *Northampton Orders 1657-1664*, 107.

10. During Whitsun Week of 1661 (50 days after Easter), Geo. Parker asked Mrs. Calvert how Mary was doing after her "blooding." At that time Mary was visiting Mrs. Clark, whom Parker identified as the present Mrs. Waters. *Northampton Orders 1657-1664*, 107.

11. By 4 September 1661, Mary had been dead long enough for her lamb to come into dispute between her master and her benefactor, Anto. Hodgkins. *Northampton Orders 1657-1664*, 106-107.

12. George Parker, who was anxious to acquire a woman servant, struck a bargain with John Clifton, mate of the "London Ship" for the purchase of Elizabeth Mitchell, sealing the deal with a drink: "Mate wee will not make a bargaine wth dry lipps." Mr. Ginge, captain of the ship, dallied, however, and eventually refused to honor the bargain. On 3 March 1672/73, Parker took them to court, where Clifton was ordered to deliver the servant with her belongings to Parker. *Accomack Orders 1671-1673*, 179, 180.

13. *Accomack Orders 1671-1673*, 229.

14. *Accomack Orders 1673-1676*, 184, 185.

15. At two different times (18 November 1671, and 20 January 1671/72). Ambrose White declared that Garret Supple, who was indentured to Capt. Pitts for four years, had arrived on the *Dove* on 23 April 1667. On 6 March 1671/72, Vincent Oliver confirmed White's statement and swore that Owen Murphy also had a four-year indenture and had arrived at the same time. Adam Robinson, at one time entrusted with keeping Murphy's indenture, supported Oliver's statement. *Accomack Orders 1671-1673*, 27, 33, 67, 68.

16. *Accomack Orders 1671-1673*, 33.

17. *Accomack Orders 1671-1673*, 67.

18. Anne Toft brought four servants to court to have their ages judged at the court held 27 May 1667: Patrick Easton, 13; Owin Murphy, 15; Garret Supple, 17 and John Murfee, 15. Almost a year later, (16 March 1668/69) she listed their names among 124 individuals whose transportation she had paid, thereby obtaining certificates for 6200 acres of land. *Accomack Orders 1666-1670*, 21a,118, 119. There must have been some misunderstanding, if not deception, involved in the sale of Garret Supple and his friends. Either Capt. Pitt failed to reveal the indentures to purchaser Anne Toft (which seems most likely), or Toft deliberately hid their existence from the justices. In either case, the ignorance of the new servants made the misunderstanding/deception possible.

19. *Accomack Orders 1671-1673*, 33.

20. On 18 November 1671, the administrators of Edmund Scarburgh were ordered to pay Garret Seple (sic) 200 lbs tobacco, taxes for 1671, corn, clothes and court costs. *Accomack Orders 1671-1673*, 27.

21. Anne Toft, who purchased Garret Supple and the Murphy boys, owned vast tracts of land in conjunction with Col. Edmund Scarburgh, and is commonly assumed to have been his mistress. After Scarburgh's death in 1671, his administrators unsuccessfully sued Garret Supple. Whitelaw, *Virginia's Eastern Shore*, 1149-1152; *Accomack Orders 1671-1673*, 54. No doubt bolstered by Garret's success, Owen Murphy obtained his own freedom on 8 March 1671/72, when he gathered witnesses (Vincent Oliver and Adam Robinson) who had seen his four-year indenture. *Accomack Orders 1671-1673*, 68.

22. The incident occurred 19 February 1673/74. The other colonist, Edward Hamond, merely "beinge something overcome in drinke" was fined only 50 pounds of tobacco. *Accomack Orders 1673-1676*, 79.

23. *Accomack Orders 1673-1676*, 146.

24. The youngest Parker child was born in February or March 1672/73; a "sick and weak" George Parker wrote his will in January 1673/74. He was still alive on 19 March 1673/74, when he and his wife sold land, but he appointed Robert Watson Sr. as his attorney to handle the transaction, an indication Parker was too ill to come to court. In his

will, which was proved on 10 September 1674, Parker mentioned six minor children (George, John, Phillippe, Charles, Abigail and one unnamed). In the tax list recorded 4 November 1674, George Parker's widow paid taxes for seven individuals, including an Indian servant named George. This number of servants placed Florence Parker among the largest servant holders in the county; only nine householders out of 286 had seven or more tithables. *Accomack Orders 1671-1673,* 174, 179, 180; *Accomack Orders 1673-1676,* 150, 151; 177, 184, 185, 194-196.

25. Bruce, *Social Life of Virginia,* 232. In 1678, James Matts was ordered to pay 200 pounds of tobacco, the sum due "for his marriage, as being married with a license." *Accomack Orders 1676-1678,* 144.

26. A 12-year-old heiress named Elizabeth Charlton was abducted from school in August 1661, and delivered to John Gething, who ignored pleas for her return while he tried to obtain a marriage license from the Governor's substitute. Failing that, he took Elizabeth across the Bay; by deceiving Col. Yeo, he illegally obtained a license and there married the child. By September 29, the newlyweds had returned home, and Gething initiated proceedings to obtain control of his wife's large estate, though her father's will stipulated she was not entitled to it till age fourteen. The following summer Elizabeth died several months short of her 14th birthday. After a court battle in which Gething's fortune-grabbing marriage was lambasted by Edmund Scarburgh, the dead girl's estate was ultimately divided between her mother and sister. *Northampton Orders 1657-1664,* 156-159. Edmund Scarburgh's argument against John Gething is reprinted in full in Whitelaw, *Virginia's Eastern Shore,* 427-430.

27. According to Bruce, who discusses the regulations sought by the Virginia Assembly, "Runaway matches occurred very frequently throughout this period." Bruce, *Social Life of Virginia,* 233.

28. Mariner, *Off 13,* 136. Between 1896 and 1905, Griffin Callahan photographed landmarks on the Eastern Shore; among his photos is the "Marriage Oak" on the Maryland/Virginia line. Griffin Callahan, "The Callahan Photo Collection," *Eastern Shore Public Library,* http://www.espl.org/mearscol/callagif/callahan.HTM.

29. *Accomack Orders 1678-1682,* 199, 220.

30. Ames discusses this case and the Act of Assembly that would require Mary to serve an extra year beyond her indenture; in this passage, however, Florence Parker is called Florence Upshur. Ames, *Studies of the Virginia Eastern Shore,* 81.

31. *Accomack Orders 1673-1676,* 232.

32. *Accomack Orders 1673-1676,* 256, 257; Whitelaw, *Virginia's Eastern Shore,* 932.

33. Whitelaw, *Virginia's Eastern Shore,* 904.

34. 17 March 1674/75. *Accomack Orders 1673-1676,* 248.

35. On 24 October 1667, this restriction was placed on Nicholas Millichopp and Mary Barton, a servant couple who claimed they had been married in England, but entered the colony as more valuable single servants. *Accomack Orders 1666-1670,* 38a, 39.

36. On 17 March 1674/75. *Accomack Orders 1673-1676,* 248. Underscoring the gravity of Supple's outburst is the severe punishment he received. Between 1663 and 1682, few individuals received so many lashes on one day. Two who did were Thomas Jones, who attacked his mistress with a sword and knife in 1679, and Robert Hudson, who stole several tools and a bag of meal in 1680. *Accomack Orders 1678-1682,* 88, 89, 167. Others received more lashes, but the punishment was spread out over the course of several months or a year. For refusing to clear the highways as ordered, William Silverthorne received 25 lashes at each of two courts in 1667. *Accomack Orders 1666-1670,* 37a. For having three illegitimate children, Elizabeth Furnis received an initial 20 lashes followed by 10 lashes per week for a year in 1668. *Accomack Orders 1666-1670,* 52. Two servant couples (John Hancock/Anne Gray and Adam

Robinson/Penelope Stanford) with two illegitimate children apiece received 20 lashes every month for a year in 1669. *Accomack Orders 1666-1670*,150, 151.

37. *Accomack Orders 1673-1676,* 107.

38. *Accomack Orders 1673-1676,* 265, 298, 318.

39. *Accomack Wills and Deeds 1676-1690,* 25, 26.

40. *Accomack Orders 1676-1678,* 95, 100,117,129.

41. On 16 May 1679/80, Garret and Mary Supple made their marks on the deed selling Mary's last 100 acres to Robert Hutson. *Accomack Wills and Deeds 1676-1690,* 199.

42. Some secondary sources claim Garret Supple was a "lawyer" not a "sawyer." A careful look at the word in the original deed and a cursory glance at how Garret signed his name make it clear that Mr. Supple was cutting boards and not reading law books for his clients.

43. A hopeful resident of the newly laid out town of Onancock paid 100 pounds of tobacco for a lot, but was required to build a 20 foot house before he would be issued a deed. Several lot owners failed to meet the four-month deadline; their property was then sold to someone else. Whitelaw, *Virginia's Eastern Shore,* 906.

44. Garret Supple was appointed to the grand jury on 16 April 1678. *Accomack Orders 1676-1678,* 128. His wife and mother-in-law served on 1 March 1679/80, when twelve women viewed the body of Mary Burton's dead infant. *Accomack Orders 1678-1682,* 159-168.

45. *Accomack Orders 1676-1678,* 257.

46. Norton, *Founding Mothers & Fathers,* 222, 223; Berkin & Horowitz, *Woman's Voices, Women's Lives,* 12; Berkin, *First Generations,* 150.

47. *Accomack Orders 1678-1682,* 114-116, 233-236, 245, 254-257.

48. 14 July 1681. *Accomack Orders 1678-1682,* 247, 249.

49. Garret Supple had James Ewell and his wife arrested for assault and battery on 4 April 1682; they returned the favor and had Garret arrested the same day. *Accomack Orders 1678-1682,* 294.

50. *Accomack Orders 1682-1697,* 43a, 140, 143a. *Accomack Orders 1690-1697,* 12, 25, 25a, 35a, 41, 58, 63a, 117a, 207a..

51. 17 June 1682, *Accomack Wills and Deeds 1676-1690,* 309.

52. *Somerset Judicial Records 1687-1689,* 71, 78, 79, 98, 100, 104, 105; *Somerset Judicial Records 1689-1690,* 133; *Somerset Judicial Records 1692-1693,* 96; *Somerset Judicial Records 1692-1696,* 16.

53. Scharf, *History of Delaware, 1609-1688,* vol. 2, "South Murderkill Hundred," 1147-1171, Accessible Archives, http://www.accessible.com/amcnty/DE/Delaware /delaware62.htm; McKain, "Motherkill Friends Cemetery (Murderkill Cemetery) Magnolia, Kent County, Delaware," *Interment.net Cemetery Transcription Library,* http://www.interment.net/data/us/de/kent/motherkill.htm.

54. In the process of giving depositions, Christopher Calvert gave his age three times. On 16 December 1663, he claimed a birth year of 1615, on 16 August 1667, he claimed a birth year of 1617, and on 18 May 1681, he claimed to be 81 years old, making his birth year 1600. The first deposition is probably the most accurate. *Accomack Orders 1663-1666,* 47a; *Accomack Orders 1666-1670,* 34; *Accomack Orders 1678-1682,* 229.

55. Waitman Supple's obituary states he died on 7 May 1772, "aged 99 Years, wanting 5 Days." However, a birth date of 12 May 1673, does not fit neatly into the known chronology of his parents. If this birth date were correct, Waitman would have been 18 months old when his parents' clandestine marriage came to light. It is unlikely that the pair had been secretly married for more than two years and were parenting a toddler when Mrs. Parker took them to court. And it is unlikely that Waitman was born before his parents' marriage. Garret and Mary were not accused of fornication, and Florence Parker, who stood to gain at least an extra year of service, certainly would have reported such activities had there been any evidence, i.e., a baby. Even if an advancing pregnancy forced the Supples

to announce their secret marriage, the new baby would probably have arrived in late 1674, at the earliest. Waitman could certainly have been in his late nineties when he died, but he may not have been quite as old as was claimed. Obituary of Waitman Sipple, *Pennsylvania Gazette*, May 21, 1772, number 2265.

Chapter 5
Susan Johnson

1. John, Susan and Tony were three of 42 individuals for whom John Stringer received a certificate to claim 2100 acres. The persons named could have arrived months or years earlier than the date of submission, which was 29 October 1661. *Northampton Orders 1657 - 1664*, 107a. Anthony and John Johnson, who had been land owners in the county for nearly ten years, were clearly not arriving for the first time. It was common practice to claim a headright every time a person entered the county.

2. Breen and Innes, *Myne Owne Ground*, 9, 10.

3. Breen and Innes, *Myne Owne Ground*, 10.

4. The marriage of an average Chesapeake couple would be dissolved by death within nine to twelve years. Berkin, *First Generations*, 8.

5. Walczyk, *Northampton County VA Orders Deeds, & Wills 1651-1654*, 110.

6. Breen and Innes, *Myne Owne Ground*, 10, 11.

7. The agreement was made on 10 July 1645. Ames, *County Court Records of Accomack-Northampton, Virginia, 1640-1645*, 457.

8. Walczyk, *Northampton Orders Deeds, & Wills 1651-1654*, 102.

9. Mackey and Groves, *Northampton County Records, 1645-1651*, 453.

10. Breen and Innes, *Myne Owne Ground*, 10-12.

11. Whitelaw, *Virginia's Eastern Shore*, 671.

12. Whitelaw, *Virginia's Eastern Shore*, 669.

13. Breen and Innes, *Myne Owne Ground*, 92, 93.

14. In 1672, John Johnson signed his name to a deed; Susan made her mark. *Accomack Orders 1671-1673*, 122.

15. Mackey and Groves, *Northampton County Records, 1654-1655*, 109.

16. *Northampton Orders 1657-1664*, 107a.

17. *Accomack Orders 1663-1666*, 90a.

18. *Accomack Orders 1663-1666*, 92a.

19. *Accomack Orders 1663-1666*, 94.

20. *Accomack Orders 1663-1666*, 97, 110a.

21. *Accomack Orders 1666-1670*, 62, 169,184, 190. On 30 July 1671, after the death of Col. Edmund Scarburgh, Hannah Leach petitioned for freedom, but the court decreed that beginning on 16 July 1671, she still had three years and five months to serve. *Accomack Orders 1671-1673*, 11.

22. The father of Hannah Leach's third child was a servant named William Davis. *Accomack Orders 1671-1673*, 158, 178, 203.

23. *Accomack Orders 1671-1673*, 122.

24. Breen and Innes, *Myne Owne Ground*, 16.

25. *Somerset Proceedings 1665-1668*, 610, 621, 622, 642, 643, 650, 656, 658, 659, 671, 686, 691.

26. *Somerset Proceedings 1665-1668*, 650, 658, 707, 712.

27. John Johnson claimed an age of 37 years when he gave his deposition in August 1670. *Somerset Judicial Records 1670-1671*, 10.

28. *Somerset Judicial Records 1671-1675*, 159-162.

29. *Somerset Proceedings 1665-1668*, Vol 54, 760.

30. Mary Johnson purchased the mare on 7 July 1676, and on 30 July, she assigned it to John whose last name was Corsale–probably a variation of Casor/Cazara. *Somerset County Judicial Records, 1675-1677*, 77.

31. Breen and Innes, *Myne Owne Ground*, 17.

32. Horle, *Records of the Courts of Sussex County, Delaware*, p 229.

33. John Johnson appeared in court to answer his mother's complaint on 8 March 1694. Horle, *Records of the Courts of Sussex County, Delaware*, 919, 920.

Chapter 6
Mary Beadle Cole

1. In 1673, John Cole opened an ordinary at Pungoteague where the court was then held, and in 1677, he pointed out that he allowed the court to meet in his house free of charge. During the early 1680's the court was held at Onancock, but by 1685, was moved to Cole's land at Matompkin, where he had built a house for the court's use. By the end of 1692, that courthouse had deteriorated, but in spite of attempts to move the courthouse to another site, it has remained at Cole's location ever since. First called Matomkin, the area became Drummond, Drummondtown and finally Accomac. Ames, *Studies of the Virginia Eastern Shore*, 200-203; Whitelaw, *Virginia's Eastern Shore*, 994.

2. *Accomack Orders 1673-1676*, 244, 245.

3. Mary Cole was born in 1649. *Northampton Orders 1664-1674*, 70; *Accomack Orders 1673-1676*, 134, 135.

4. *Northampton Orders 1664-1674*, 66.

5. *Northampton Orders 1657-1664*, 152, 163, 166, 179, 186, 189; Anne Beadle, who was forced into servitude by 1666, had a bastard that same year with John Rickord. *Accomack Orders 1663-1666, 113; Accomack Orders 1666-1670*, 8, 10, 15, 17, 19.

6. The dispute over John Cole's gift to Mary Beadle occurred before 31 October 1663. *Northampton Orders 1657-1664*,179, 183a, 184.

7. Mary Cole's deed of gift to her daughter Frances was made 4 December 1674, with her husband's consent. Mary, who was literate, signed the document. *Accomack Orders 1673-1676*, 226. Mary Cole's deed of gift to her son John was made 16 March 1674/75. *Accomack Orders 1673-1676*, 258.

8. *Accomack Orders 1671-1673*, 221.

9. On 18 February 1665/66, John Cole became administrator of the estate of a Mr. Gilbert, who had left at least two orphans; Sarah Gilbert was probably one of them. *Northampton Orders 1664-1674*, 21a.

10. Mary Cole, aged 20 years, gave a deposition to the Northampton Court regarding the Wiltshire incident. After chasing Sarah Gilbert into the woods, John Wiltshire "come in shewing a Tussock of hare betweene his fingers to us & shee came in after cryinge and Squeellinge." The court determined that "John Wiltshire most inhumanely on the 23[d] of this instant [August 1669] not only shewed his members unto Sarah Gilbert but rune after her into the Woods & there tooke up her coates, & in a most barbarous manner plucked of[f] a Tussock of her hare presupposed of her privityes as by the Testimonyes of John & Mary Coales appears." *Northampton Orders 1664-1674*, 70.

11. Joseph Warren, Alexander Mills and Thomas Sheppard Jr. drank and fought at John Cole's on Sunday, 19 November 1671. *Northampton Orders 1664-1674*, 119a, 121.

12. *Accomack Orders 1673-1676*, 28, 42, 43.

13. *Accomack Orders 1673-1676*, 29, 30.

14. *Accomack Orders 1673-1676*, 30.

15. On 20 April 1674, Mary Coale, aged "24 years & upwrds," gave a deposition detailing John Stratton's attack on prisoner William Onaughton (Norton). *Accomack Orders 1673-1676*, 130,132, 134, 135.

16. On 19 May 1674. *Accomack Orders 1673-1676*, 145-147.

17. On 17 July 1674. *Accomack Orders 1673-1676*, 157, 158.

18. On 17 July 1674, the Coles accused Adam Robinson of stealing clothes from their house, but they lacked proof. *Accomack Orders 1673-1676*, 155.

19. *Accomack Orders 1673-1676*, 286.

20. On 16 April 1678. *Accomack Orders 1676-1678*, 127.

21. Presented on 26 May 1679, and sentenced on 16 July 1679, Ann Harrison swore that Henry Hubanck was the father of her child. She recruited a total of six individuals to help pay her fine. *Accomack Orders 1678-1682*, 78, 95.

22. On 19 November 1675, Alexander Dun bound himself to serve Cole for four years. *Accomack Orders 1673-1676*, 340; *Accomack Orders 1678-1682*, 97. Henry Hansome, who was called a "hired servant" of John Cole on 6 February 1683/84, was actually bound to three years of service. His payment was 1000 pounds of tobacco per year, out of which his clothing was to be deducted "at reasonable" prices. *Accomack Orders 1682-1697*, 36a. John and Elizabeth Terry were working for Cole to pay off a debt. *Accomack Orders 1673-1676*, 233.

23. *Accomack Orders 1678-1682*, 108.

24. John PettiJohn and his older siblings (James, William and Issabell) were orphaned in 1666, when their father James PettiJohn died. John, about four years old at the time, was placed with the Coles. *Northampton Orders 1664-1674*, 5, 37a; *Northampton Orders 1678-1683*, 87.

25. *Accomack Orders 1678-1682*, 207, 214.

26. Whitelaw, *Virginia's Eastern Shore*, 1027.

27. In the case of hog theft, the culprit was required to pay 1000 pounds of tobacco each to the victim and the informer. John PettiJohn was found guilty of stealing Christopher Thompson's hog on 19 May 1681. *Accomack Orders 1678-1682*, 229.

28. William Thorton (Thorroton), aged 36 years, went before Justice William Custis and gave his deposition detailing the death of Christopher Thompson's hog on 26 April 1681. *Accomack Orders 1678-1682*, 232. William Yeo, aged 29 years, focused on the conspiracy and the events at home. His deposition was given in open court on 19 May 1681. *Accomack Orders 1678-1682*, 232, 233. John Terry (Terrey) affirmed what Yeo said in open court, and with his wife Elizabeth swore to the words Mary Cole used while trying to bribe them into denying the truth. *Accomack Orders 1678-1682*, 233.

29. Something of a regular at Coles, William Stevens helped explain Cole's account book to a customer on 16 July 1679, and happened to be with Cole when he negotiated for a quantity of cider a month later. *Accomack Orders 1678-1682*, 93, 94, 119.

30. *Accomack Orders 1678-1682*, 248.

31. *Accomack Orders 1678-1682*, 246.

32. *Accomack Orders 1678-1682*, 265, 271, 287-289.

33. Elizabeth Terry gave her deposition on 17 December 1681, and signed it with her mark. *Accomack Orders 1678-1682*, 288.

34. Richard Johnson Jr. gave his deposition 18 February 1681/82, and signed with his initials. *Accomack Orders 1678-1682*, 289.

35. Henry Hansome registered his complaint on 6 February 1683/84. The second order to provide for Hansome (13 January 1684/85) gives the servant's first name as John, but both entries clearly involve the same servant. *Accomack Orders 1682-1697*, 36a, 57.

36. *Accomack Orders 1682-1697*, 52a.

37. On 14 December 1685, John Cole, who had failed to pay his 38,000 pound tobacco debt, was forced to bind his entire estate to John West. *Accomack Orders 1676-1690*, 414.

38. Lancelot Jacques' debts to John Cole included 400 pounds tobacco (6 February 1683) and 3284 pounds tobacco (8 July 1685). *Accomack Orders 1682-1697*, 59a, 68.

39. *Accomack Orders 1682-1697*, 81. Frances Cole made a mark for a signature in her testimony about Jacques in 1685, but on 22 November 1688, when she was 17 years old "or upward" and giving a deposition regarding horses in William Yeo's corn field, she was able to sign her name. *Accomack Orders 1682-1697*, 145a.

40. On 4 November 1684, Micah Warder agreed to pay the fine of Isabel Pitts (servant of John West) who was presented for fornication and bastardy. *Accomack Orders 1682-1697*, 50.

41. Michael (Mica or Micah) Warder (also Wardel) was bound over to court upon Richard Cutler's complaint on 18 September 1688. *Accomack Orders 1682-1697*, 137a.

42. *Accomack Orders 1678-1682*, 230.

43. On 18 September 1688, the sheriff was ordered to punish Michael Warder "forthwith." It could be that the sheriff either dallied or spread the punishment out over a number of days. At any rate, it seems that Warder's ear was nailed to the pillory on 20 September 1688. *Accomack Orders 1682-1697*, 141.

44. On 20 September 1688, William Parker and John Lewis Jr. saw Mary Cole remove the nail from Warder's ear. *Accomack Orders 1682-1697*, 141.

45. *Accomack Orders 1682-1697*, 141.

46. On 6 March 1688/89, John Cole made his sons Robert and William trustees of his gift to Frances. *Accomack Orders 1682-1697*, 199a. Though the document giving items to Frances did not specify that she work in return, she was in the tavern, apparently working, the night of 16 November 1689, when she witnessed Thomas Simpson cutting up Robert Edge's saddle. By this time, Frances was 20 years old and had married John Doe. On 1 November 1690, John Cole gave Frances possession of 100 acres of land. *Accomack Orders 1682-1697*, 189, 189a; 206a, 207.

47. *Accomack Orders 1682-1697*, 195a. John Cole allotted portions of The Folly to sons William, Robert, John and Richard, all under 21; he also made provision for an unborn child, if male, and gave several personal items to his wife. *Accomack Orders 1682-1697*, 196, 196a.

48. Documents that John and Mary Cole signed as husband and wife after she moved to the plantation include a deed signed 16 December 1691, and the agreement with Gervas Baggale signed 1 September 1693. *Accomack Orders 1682-1697*, 230, 230a; *Accomack Orders 1692-1715*, 32, 32a.

49. *Accomack Orders 1682-1697*, 196a.

50. The John Cole Jr. who testified about the assault of his mother on 17 December 1685, apparently died some time before his father disbursed the 500 acres in February 1690/91, when the younger John is mentioned with his twin brother Richard; on 12 September 1693, John Cole Sr. mentioned the burial place of John Cole in the orchard. *Accomack Orders 1692-1715*, 32. On 20 September 1691, William Yeo, the Coles' long-time servant and associate, deeded a cow and calf to Richard and John Cole, the twin sons of John Cole; if the twins died, the cattle would go to their brother William Cole, their mother, and their sister Angellica, who must have been the unborn child mentioned seven months earlier. *Accomack Orders 1682-1697*, 216a.

51. *Accomack Deeds, Wills, Etc., 1692-1715*, 32-34a.

52. Whitelaw discusses the Accomack County Courthouse, Cole's Tavern and the property once owned by the Coles. Whitelaw, *Virginia's Eastern Shore*, 892-903, 993-1039.

Chapter 7
Mary Watson Hope Bonwell Mikell Hubancks

1. James Bonwell gave a deposition on 17 January 1666/67, in which he is listed as about 46 years old, giving him an approximate birth year of 1620. *Accomack Orders 1666-1670*, 13, 13a.

2. *Accomack Orders 1666-1670*, 29.

3. For a list of couplings and the children they produced, see Appendix I.

4. On 16 December 1667, William Silverthorne swore that he bought an ell and a half (67.5 inches) of linen from Mary, who had also sold an ell to Rebecca Benston. *Accomack Orders 1666-1670*, 41a.

5. Rebecca Benston gave a deposition on 16 December 1667, in which she revealed Mary Bonwell's trickery. *Accomack Orders 1666-1670*, 41a.

6. *Accomack Orders 1666-1670*, 41a.

7. On 8 April 1668, it was noted that Roger Mikell had married the widow of James Bonwell. *Accomack Orders 1666-1670*, 54.

8. Though usually spelled Mikell or Mikeel, Roger's last name had a multitude of variations, many of which seem to indicate that the second syllable was pronounced with a long **e** sound. The variations are listed in order of frequency: Mikell, Mikeel, Mikeell, Mackeell, Michell, Mackeel, Michael, Mickell, Mekell, Mikaell, Mikells; (the following forms appeared only rarely:) Macheell, Mackaell, Makeell, Makeele, Micell, Michaell, Michaels, Micheel, Micheele, Micheell, Michel, Mickeel, Mickeell, Mickell, Mikeele, Mikel, Mikkell, Mockell. He signed his name as Roger Mikell (9 January 1673/74) and Rodger Mikell (19 November 1675, 17 April 1676, 6 July 1680, 19 October 1680), *Accomack Orders 1673-1676*, 43; *Accomack Wills and Deeds 1676-1690*, 2a, 228, 421. Although Mikell may have preferred the spelling "Rodger," the court clerks overwhelmingly voted for "Roger."

9. On 20 November 1672, Robert Watson claimed he transported 21 individuals in addition to himself. *Accomack Orders 1671-1673*, 83, 146.

10. *Accomack Orders 1663-1666*, 87a; *Accomack Orders 1666-1670*, 35, 37.

11. *Accomack Orders 1663-1666*, 92a; *Accomack Orders 1666-1670*, 9, 12, 28, 41, 43, 158; *Accomack Orders 1671-1673, 23, 68, 142, 147, 206.*

12. Mary Watson's signatures: *Accomack Wills and Deeds 1676-1690*, 2, 229,269; Susannah Watson's mark: *Accomack Orders 1671-1673*, 135.

13. On 22 May 1663. *Accomack Orders 1663-1666, 4.*

14. Summer of 1665. *Accomack Orders 1666-1670*, 1, 2, 5, 7.

15. On 16 March 1666/67, Elizabeth Gilman (the servant of James Jolly) swore that Roger Mikell was the father of her bastard child. Roger was taken into custody to receive corporal punishment, but his lashing was remitted two days later when he paid a fine of 500 pounds tobacco. Jolly paid Elizabeth's fine for having Roger's child as well as her fine for a previous indiscretion on the other side of the Bay. On 28 May 1667, Jolly brought suit against Roger, but the case was dropped because Jolly failed to file his complaint. *Accomack Orders 1666-1670*, 17, 18a, 23a.

16. Mary Bonwell was granted administration on 16 July 1667; she was still called Mrs. Bonwell on 16 December 1667, but on 8 April 1668, the court ordered Roger Mikell, who had married the widow of James Bonwell, to pay a debt associated with the estate. *Accomack Orders 1666-1670*, 54.

17. In a deposition given on 9 January 1673/74, Roger Micheel claimed to be about 30 years old, giving him a birth date of about 1643. *Accomack Orders 1673-1676, 42, 43.*

18. *Accomack Orders 1666-1670*, 89.

19. *Accomack Orders 1666-1670*, 148, 153.

20. On 17 March 1668/69. *Accomack Orders 1666-1670*, 127.

21. On 26 January 1669/70, Roger Mikell failed to appear to answer a debt of 1551 pounds tobacco due to John West. At the same court session it was noted that Edward Chapman, a runaway servant delivered by West's servants had escaped from Mikell's custody. On 17 March 1669/70, Mikell was ordered to pay West 621 lbs tobacco, with another 200 lbs alleged due. At the same court Mikell's violent threats and abuse of his wife came to light. *Accomack Orders 1666-1670*, 171, 174, 185, 186.

22. The court ordered George Parker and John Wise to question witnesses about Mikell's abuse of his wife. *Accomack Orders 1666-1670*, 185, 186.

23. *Accomack Orders 1671-1673*, 10.

24. *Accomack Orders 1671-1673*, 11, 24.

25. *Accomack Orders 1673-1676*, 319.

26. *Accomack Orders 1671-1673*, 105, 319.

27. *Accomack Orders 1671-1673*, 53, 68, 82.

28. *Accomack Orders 1671-1673*, 83. In 1670 Mikell branded a mare with an H for George Hope. *Accomack Orders 1671-1673*, 120, 121.

29. *Accomack Orders 1671-1673*, 84.

30. *Accomack Orders 1671-1673*, 205; *Accomack Orders 1673-1676*, 313.

31. Mikell was elected vestryman on 8 February 1672/73, and as such would have helped administer the affairs of the local Church of England. Some secondary sources claim that Mikell was a Quaker, apparently basing their assumption on his refusal to swear in court (2 February 1676/77). It is true that Quakers would not swear, but it seems clear that Mikell's unwillingness had more to do with selfish reasons than with Quaker convictions. *Accomack Orders 1671-1673*, 165, 193; *Accomack Orders 1676-1678*, 30.

32. *Accomack Orders 1671-1673*, 2, 18, 37, 49, 104; *Accomack Orders 1673-1676*, 4, 22, 47, 52, 53, 64, 77, 78; *Accomack Orders 1676-1678*, 6.

33. *Accomack Orders 1671-1673*, 208, 209; *Accomack Orders 1673-1676*, 376, 377; *Accomack Orders 1676-1678*, 72.

34. Roger Mikell, who was drinking at John Cole's tavern the night John Stockley's horse was shot, gave a deposition on 9 January 1673/74. The following year Mikell, arrested for disturbing the peace, admitted he was drunk. He was fined 50 lbs tobacco on 17 March 1674/75. *Accomack Orders 1673-1676*, 42, 43, 249.

35. In 1669, Roger Mikell purchased 600 acres on the north fork of Onancock Creek; in 1670, he bought an additional 800 acres. In 1673, he took out a patent on 1500 acres. He probably began construction on his brick house a few years after his first purchase. In 1722, the will of Joseph Robinson, who died in England, mentioned Mikell's brick house as a landmark. Though the presence of a nearby graveyard implies that the subsequent owners lived there for a number of generations, the fate of Mikell's house is not known. *Whitelaw, Virginia's Eastern Shore*, 935, 938.

36. By the spring of 1681, the Mikells still had not moved into the brick house; the slave girl Betty ran away from the Mikell home and spent the night alone in the brick house. Betty was questioned on 20 May 1681. *Accomack Orders 1678-1682*, 224, 225.

37. Though John Parker wrote the verses in January 1674/75, Mikell did not confront him until September. Mikell's lawsuit was dismissed 19 November 1675. *Accomack Orders 1673-1676*, 336, 337. Another "libelous" poem actually was copied in the court records of Northampton County in 1646. John Henman accused Richard Buckland and John Culpepper of writing verses defaming Ann Smith, who was Henman's stepdaughter. Mackey and Groves, *Northampton County Virginia Record Book 1645-1651*, 129-133.

38. When some of Mikell's items were found in Phillip Quinton's trunk in Mikell's house, the court determined the goods were not stolen. Although Mikell also claimed stockings, drawers and a bundle were taken from his house by his wife's order and were

carried by Quinton to George Hope's house, a jury found no cause for action and the suit was dismissed on 17 September 1675. *Accomack Orders 1673-1676,* 310, 311.

39. On 18 December 1675, Mikell was ordered to deliver the estate to Ann Bonwell, who had married Quinton before August 1671, when Mary sought refuge with them. *Accomack Orders 1673-1676,* 350; *Accomack Orders 1671-1673,* 105.

40. Roger and Mary Mikell sold 200 acres of their 1500 acre "Ramagstieck" plantation to Phillip Quintaine on 17 April 1676. *Accomack Wills and Deeds 1676-1690,* 2a.

41. Between March 1674/75 and April 1676, Roger Mikell was involved in 18 different legal actions.

42. On 5 February 1676/77. *Accomack Orders 1676-1678,* 30.

43. On 18 June 1677. *Accomack Orders 1676-1678,* 47.

44. *Accomack Orders 1676-1678,* 72.

45. *Accomack Orders 1676-1678,* 94.

46. By 16 December 1678, Roger Mikell had left the country and was expected home in June of 1679; he did not return till August of that year. *Accomack Orders 1678-1682,* 40, 50, 102, 103.

47. *Accomack Orders 1678-1682,* 50, 70, 78, 98.

48. On 18 December, 1678. *Accomack Orders 1678-1682,* 51.

49. On 16 December 1678, Thomas Bonwell petitioned to have George Hope as his guardian and to be removed from the care of Roger Mikell. *Accomack Orders 1678-1682,* 40.

50. Before Justice John Wallop on 2 September 1679, Mary swore that she feared for her life at the hands of her husband. *Accomack Orders 1678-1682,* 102, 103.

51. *Accomack Orders 1678-1682,* 116, 117.

52. On 6 November 1679, Elizabeth Letherbury (age 19) and Ann Ewell (age 34) gave depositions describing Roger Mikell's attack on his wife in the Ewell home on the previous Monday. *Accomack Orders 1678-1682,* 116.

53. Mary had begun accumulating evidence regarding Roger's bigamy soon after her husband's return in late August or early September. On 7 November 1679, she produced Benjamin Matson's letter to John West (contents not recorded), the names of Mikell's fellow passengers (Ralph Sedwick, Thomas Adams and Adams' wife), and the depositions regarding most of the incidents on Barbados and during the trip home. *Accomack Orders 1678-1682,* 114-116.

54. On 28 April 1679, Margret Anderson was granted a ticket as a passenger on the ketch *Unity,* which was departing Barbados for Virginia. *English-America: The Voyages, Vessels, People, & Places,* "The Unity, 1679," http://www.english-america.com/spls /679va010.html#Unity.

55. The information regarding the financial status of Margret Pickering's father was provided in the testimony of James Renny (the captain of the ketch *Unity),* who brought suit for the passage of Margret Pickering and her slave. It is also possible that Roger Mikell was late in paying for his own passage. For a time, Renny succeeded in taking possession of Margret's slave girl in lieu of the debt, but as the girl was ultimately returned to Margret, Renny must have received some payment, though his suits against Mikell continued for several months. *Accomack Orders 1678-1682,* 112, 117, 155, 157, 179.

56. Given on 16 October and confirmed on 6 November 1679, the deposition of James Ogelby quoted James Gey, who saw the marriage license of Roger and Margret and who predicted trouble with the wife who was living in Virginia. Ogleby also told of Roger and Margret's sexual conduct, the argument and violence aboard ship and the report at Point Comfort. *Accomack Orders 1678-1682,* 115.

57. Also given on 16 October and confirmed on 6 November 1679, the deposition of John Remney told of the incident on the pathway to the Governor of Barbados, the intimate behavior of Roger and Margret on board ship and the conversation aboard ship while docked at Jamaica. *Accomack Orders 1678-1682,* 115.

58. *Accomack Orders 1678-1682*, 115.

59. *Accomack Orders 1678-1682*, 115.

60. In mid-April 1683, a pirate named John Cook sought refuge in Accomack County, where he and his cohorts refitted one of the vessels they had stolen. They also recruited extra hands from among the crew of Captain Wright's pirate company that had landed in Accomack a year earlier. Shomette, *Pirates of the Chesaspeake*, 66, 67, 80, 81.

61. *Accomack Orders 1678-1682*, 114-117.

62. *Accomack Orders 1678-1682*, 117, 137. On 17 May 1682, food and shelter for Nathaniel Bradford's two sons was valued at 90 pounds of tobacco per month for each son. Food, shelter and clothing for a wife of a prominent individual would be considerably more. *Accomack Orders 1678-1682*, 298, 299.

63. *Accomack Orders 1678-1682*, 142.

64. By January 1679/80, Mikell's debts included: due to Thomas Gooding, 315 lbs tobacco; due to John Parker, 560 lbs tobacco; clothing for servant William Kemp, 250 lbs; due to James Renny, captain of the *Unity*, probably 625 lbs for himself and 1250 lbs for Margret and her slave; penalty for the bond for good behavior, 40,000 lbs; penalty for the administration bond, 500 pounds sterling or 104,166 lbs tobacco; due to George Hope for supporting Mary three months, about 600 lbs; plus an unknown amount for court costs and lawyer's fees. *Accomack Orders 1678-1682*, 141, 142, 155, 157, 179; On 18 May 1681, 12 pounds sterling was valued at 2500 pounds of tobacco, making 1 pound sterling equivalent to 208 lbs tobacco. *Accomack Orders 1678-1682*, 221.

65. In May 1682, a days' work was valued at 20 pounds of tobacco; a yearly wage (six days a week) would be 6240 lbs tobacco. *Accomack Orders 1678-1682*, 298, 299.

66. The will was signed 6 July 1680. *Accomack Wills and Deeds 1676-1690*, 421, 421a. Mikell was gone by 4 August 1680, when he failed to appear in court. *Accomack Orders 1678-1682*, 179.

67. *Accomack Wills and Deeds 1676-1690*, 228, 229.

68. *Accomack Orders 1678-1682*, 218, 233.

69. *Accomack Orders 1678-1682*, 218.

70. *Accomack Orders 1678-1682*, 233, 234.

71. On 17 and 18 May 1681. *Accomack Orders 1678-1682*, 234, 235.

72. On 19 May 1681. *Accomack Orders 1678-1682*, 234, 235.

73. The matrons sworn to examine Margret Pickering on 19 May 1681, were Florance Matts, Penelope Jenkins, Mary Anderson, Amy Parker, Barbary Robins and Ledia Price. *Accomack Orders 1678-1682*, 235.

74. The jury of inquest reached their verdict on 19 May 1681. The bonds were posted by John West (100 pounds sterling) and Edward Brotherton (40 pounds sterling). *Accomack Orders 1678-1682*, 235, 236.

75. Roger assigned the deed to John West on 13 June 1681; Mary signed her permission for the land sale on 13 July 1681. Mikell was "paid" 60 pounds sterling and 5000 pounds tobacco for the 1000 acres. The total would equal about 84 pounds sterling or 17,480 pounds of tobacco. *Accomack Wills and Deeds 1676-1690*, 269. In 1684, John West sold the eastern 400 acres (on which the house stood) to Joseph Robinson, who mentioned Roger Mikell's brick house in his will in 1722. The house must have burned sometime before 1805, when a detailed survey was made of the property; it mentioned a mill, shipyard and small tenant house, but no mansion. Whitelaw, *Virginia's Eastern Shore*, 936, 938.

76. *Accomack Orders 1678-1682*, 255-257.

77. *Accomack Orders 1666-1670*, 97-98, 102-109; *Accomack Orders 1671-1673*, 130; *Accomack Orders 1673-1676*, 181, 193.

78. See Chapter 9; Edward Brotherton's character is more fully revealed in his relationship with Bridget Savage.

79. As punishment for attacking his lame overseer in an orchard during the summer of 1680, Anthony Delapar was ordered to remain a servant for an additional year. At the end of his deposition, it was noted that Delapar was born in Spain, and was a Roman Catholic. *Accomack Orders 1678-1682*, 210, 211, 220.

80. *Accomack Orders 1678-1682*, 254, 255.

81. According to John Tankred's statement, he attended court on Tuesday, 17 May 1681, went home with Roger Mikell on Thursday, when he heard the interview of Betty, and then wrote his description of the incident on Friday, 20 May 1681. *Accomack Orders 1678-1682*, 254, 255.

82. *Accomack Orders 1678-1682*, 255.

83. *Accomack Orders 1678-1682*, 255.

84. Deposition given 18 August 1681. *Accomack Orders 1678-1682*, 255, 256.

85. John Alford heard Sarah's cries in the woods and urged others to join him in the rescue; Teage Andross went to investigate and saw Patrick's bloody shirt. Both depositions were given on 18 August 1681. *Accomack Orders 1678-1682*, 256, 257.

86. Deposition given 18 August 1681. *Accomack Orders 1678-1682*, 257.

87. On 19 October 1681. *Accomack Orders 1678-1682*, 263.

88. Mikell appeared in court on 20 October 1681, when Thomas Bonwell was pressing for the remainder of his estate, but he did not appear for the other court actions on 17 & 18 November 1681, 8 February 1683/84 and 5 August 1684. *Accomack Orders 1678-1682*, 265, 269, 271; *Accomack Orders 1682-1697*, 38, 46a.

89. *Council of Maryland 1681-1685/6*, 351.

90. On 18 January 1680/81, Edward Brotherton, in a dispute over cattle, mentioned going to Watts Island to live. *Accomack Orders 1678-1682*, 204.

91. *Council of Maryland 1681-1685/6*, 350-352.

92. *Council of Maryland 1681-1685/6*, 350, 351.

93. *Council of Maryland 1681-1685/6*, 351.

94. Shomette, *Pirates of the Chesapeake*, 72.

95. Shomette, *Pirates of the Chesapeake*, 73.

96. *Accomack Wills and Deeds 1676-1690*, 421, 421a.

97. Shomette, *Pirates of the Chesapeake*, 73.

98. Pirates John Houghling, Cornelius Frank and Francois Delaunee were hanged on gibbets in three separate locations along the Chesapeake in May 1700. Sixty-three of their companions were sent to England, where they too were hung. Shomette, *Pirates of the Chesapeake*, 149-151.

99. *Northampton Orders 1683-1689*, 127.

100. Although Mathew Scarbrow received a certificate for transporting Henry Hubanck in 7 April 1685, Hubanck had probably arrived in Virginia about seven years earlier; in May 1679 he was accused of fathering Ann Harrison's illegitimate child. *Accomack Orders 1682-1697*, 61a; *Accomack Orders 1678-1682*, 78, 95.

101. *Accomack Orders 1682-1697*, 190a-192, 227a-228a; *Accomack Orders 1690-1697*, 47, 59; *Accomack Orders 1697-1703*, 132, 136; *Accomack Orders 1703-1709*, 3, 3a, 20, 28a, 35a, 50a, 76a, 78a, 79a.

102. *Accomack Orders 1697-1703*, 132.

103. Henry Hubanck may have died before 7 March 1720/21, when Mary, as executrix of James Bonwell, presented her son's will to the court. Hubanck was certainly deceased before 1723, when Mary was called a widow. *Accomack Orders 1719-1724*, 27a, 60.

104. On 4 June 1723, Mary Hughbanks sued John Bonwell. Delayed because Mary's attorney was ill, the case was tried 4 September 1723. *Accomack Orders 1719-1724*, 60, 65.

105. On 5 July 1732, John Wise swore that Mary Hughbanck had died without making a will and was granted administration of her estate. *Accomack Orders 1731-1736*, 34.

106. Aside from her husbands, Mary also outlived her sons Thomas Bonwell (d. 1718), James Bonwell (d. 1721), George Hope (d. 1722) and John Bonwell (d. 1729) and grandsons George Hope Jr. (d. 1714), William Hope (d. 1718) and George Bonwell (d. 1721). Nottingham, *Wills and Administrations*, 53, 59, 65, 66, 70, 87.

Chapter 8
Joanna Matrum Smith

1. *Accomack Orders 1666-1670*, 176.
2. Cowie, *Plague and Fire*, 56.
3. *Accomack Orders 1666-1670*, 108.
4. The Great Fire of London began the night of September 1, 1666, and reached its furthest extent on September 4, 1666. Hanson, *The Great Fire of London*, 1, 59, 107.
5. *Accomack Orders 1666-1670*, 45a, 75.
6. While Joanna's sister is never specifically named, existing evidence, suggests that the sister was Bridget Mikell Savage. First, Joanna's maiden name was Michell (as mentioned by her servant in a deposition); Bridget, who had a close relationship with Roger Mikell, is also generally believed to be a Mikell/Michell. Second, in an undeniably sister-like act, Joanna, when she was suffering abuse at the hands of her husband, summoned Bridget, showed her the scars and bruises and then entrusted her abused daughter to Bridget and her husband Griffith Savage, who readily agreed to take the child without hope of payment. Bridget, who by this time already had a rather unsavory reputation, would not have been a likely choice to care for young Sarah Matrum, unless, of course, the child was her niece. It is also interesting to note that Henry Smith's favorite epithet for Joanna's sister was "whore"–a term that, in Bridget's case, proved to be rather near the truth. *Accomack Orders 1666-1670*, 45a, 74, 75, 80, 81, 88, 131, 177. The date that Bridget Mikell Savage arrived in Virginia is unknown, but she may have come with Roger Mikell, who was in the county as early as 22 May 1663. *Accomack Orders 1663-1666*, 4.
7. Bridget's husband Griffith Savage, who had been transported by Devorax Browne before 17 August 1663, was called Browne's servant by November of that year. Years later they still lived in the same area; Savage caught Browne's servants in the act of drinking their master's brandy in March 1668/69. They later disagreed about a business transaction. *Accomack Orders 1666-1670*, 121, 122, 187.
8. Harben, "Bishopsgate Street," *A Dictionary of London, British History Online,* http://www.british-history.ac.uk/report.asp?compid+2424.
9. *Accomack Orders 1666-1670*, 45a.
10. Capt. Robert Pitt reported Devorax Browne's remarks regarding Joanna's possessions on 16 December 1667. He said their conversation occurred in 1666, which according to the Julian calendar would have ended on the previous March 24. Pitt returned to Virginia in April, 1667, and Browne likely arrived about the same time; he reappeared in court in May of that year after a nine month hiatus. It therefore seems logical to assume that Joanna loaded her goods in February or March 1666/67, and crossed the Atlantic shortly thereafter. *Accomack Orders 1666-1670*, 21a, 22, 35a, 45a.
11. During the early decades of settlement in the Chesapeake area, men outnumbered women by six to one; the ratio had improved to three to one by the 1680's. Berkin, *First Generations*, 6, 7.
12. On 24 May 1662, Mary Jones signed an indenture in Bristol, England, agreeing to serve Henry Smith for five years in Virginia. "Bristol Register of Servants Sent to

Foreign Plantations, 1654-1686," *Virginia Center for Digital History: Virtual Jamestown*, www.virtualjamestown.org/indentures/advsearch_bristol.html

13. Mary Jones was able to inform the court of the crimes Henry Smith had committed against her only after she was called to testify about another matter. She had been marooned on Smith's Island for 14 months after her indenture had expired. *Accomack Orders 1666-1670*, 96, 99, 100, 103, 104,123, 124, 130, 137.

14. It is difficult to identify Henry's first wife, who is never specifically named. It seems most likely that she arrived in Virginia between the summer of 1662 and the fall of 1665, and that her name was Margery. Eliza Carter, a servant whose indenture began 2 June 1662, was already in Virginia when Smith brought his first wife there, and the wife was still living there for some time after Elizabeth Nock began her service on 6 October 1665. Though it seems that she came to Virginia before her relatives arrived, it is possible that "Margery," arrived with them in the fall of 1665, (see the following note). Smith applied for land certificates for transporting the relatives and the servants on 16 August 1667; on the same list were a John Smith, Margery Smith and Henry Smith. It seems quite likely that Smith was obtaining land for transporting his wife and himself, and that this Margery was Henry's wife. However, Henry could have been getting the land for transporting his two children, who bore the same names. In March 1668/69, Smith's two children were called Henry and Margery; at that time they were old enough to converse with the servants who were dressing them, but their ages are unknown. If the children were born in Virginia, which seems likely, then the Margery in the land list would be their mother. The John Smith in the list is a mystery. *Accomack Orders 1666-1670*, 36a, 70, 101, 130; "Bristol Register of Servants Sent to Foreign Plantations, 1654-1686," *Virginia Center for Digital History: Virtual Jamestown*, www.virtualjamestown.org/indentures /advsearch_bristol.html

15. *Accomack Orders 1666-1670*, 68, 70, 101, 104, 107, 177.

16. Henry Smith received a certificate for transporting several servants (including Richard Webb, William Nock, Eliza. Nock, Roger Milles, Richard Chambers and Jane Powell) as well as Joan and Samuel Holbrooke and his wife's niece (Rachel Moody) on 16 August 1667; the in-laws and servants almost certainly sailed together from Bristol to Virginia in the fall of 1665, after the indentures were signed. One of Rachel Moody's depositions shows that she was present in Bristol with Smith when he enlisted Richard Chambers and William Nock, the blacksmiths, on 3 October 1665. Rachel's grandmother lived in Bristol. *Accomack Orders 1666-1670*, 101, 128; "Bristol Register of Servants Sent to Foreign Plantations, 1654-1686," *Virginia Center for Digital History: Virtual Jamestown*, www.virtualjamestown.org/indentures/advsearch_bristol.html

17. *Accomack Orders 1666-1670*, 97, 101.

18. *Accomack Orders 1666-1670*, 70, 94.

19. Joan Holbrooke's jealous fit must have occurred sometime between the winter of 1665/66 and the spring of 1667. By May 1667, both Henry's wife and her sister were apparently deceased, and Henry Smith was in possession of their clothing and linen. Joan's husband Samuel Holbrooke probably died soon after his arrival in Virginia; he certainly pre-deceased Joan. Otherwise, Henry would not have been in possession of Joan's estate. *Accomack Orders 1666-1670*, 25, 70, 94, 104.

20. Whitelaw, *Virginia's Eastern Shore*, 527, 540, 818, 1313, 1319, 1388.

21. In February or March 1665/66, at his Oak Hall plantation, Henry Smith ordered a servant to kill a boar that belonged to John Wallop. *Accomack Orders 1666-1670*, 3-5, 6a.

22. The trip to Capt. Bowman's occurred about October 1666. Smith took with him servants Richard Chambers, William Nock, Elizabeth Nock, Old John and Mary Jones. Smith treated blacksmiths William Nock (brother to Elizabeth) and Chambers slightly more kindly that the others. *Accomack Orders 1666-1670*, 132, 133.

23. *Accomack Orders 1666-1670,* 114, 126, 137.

24. *Accomack Orders 1666-1670,* 133.

25. Beaten by Henry Smith were his wife's niece Rachel Moody and servants Jean Powell, Elizabeth Nock and Mary Jones. *Accomack Orders 1666-1670,* 96, 97, 100.

26. The charity of Elizabeth, the widow of Charles Rackliffe, was credited with keeping Smith's servants alive. *Accomack Orders 1666-1670,* 86. The Rackliffe property adjoined that of Smith's Occohannock plantation. Whitlaw, *Virginia's Eastern Shore,* 540, 541.

27. *Accomack Orders 1666-1670,* 133, 134.

28. Mary Jones, as a 17-year-old, signed an indenture with Smith on 24 May 1662, in Bristol, England. Shortly before her indenture expired five years later, Smith imprisoned her on his island, where she was forced to work for him an additional 14 months."Bristol Register of Servants Sent to Foreign Plantations, 1654-1686," *Virginia Center for Digital History: Virtual Jamestown,* www.virtualjamestown.org/indentures/advsearch_bristol.html; *Accomack Orders 1666-1670,* 94, 96, 99, 100, 103-106, 110, 112, 123, 130, 133, 134.

29. Different entries indicate that Elizabeth Nock was athletic and probably taller than the other women servants: She could reach and enter a trap door that others could not; she was quick enough to catch Old John before he fell into the fire and strong enough to fight off Henry Smith. After her term of service had expired, Elizabeth married a Parker. *Accomack Orders 1666-1670,* 25, 73, 84, 85, 87, 105, 124, 125,130, 134. Elizabeth Nock was about 19 years old when she signed her indenture in Bristol on 6 October 1665, three days after her brother William signed up. "Bristol Register of Servants Sent to Foreign Plantations, 1654-1686," *Virginia Center for Digital History: Virtual Jamestown,* www.virtualjamestown.org/indentures/advsearch_bristol.html

30. Jean Powell was beaten like the other servants, but stands alone as the only servant that did not accuse Smith of trying to rape her. *Accomack Orders 1666-1670,* 60, 73, 82, 83, 134.

31. Rachel Moody, who was not a servant, was beaten like the rest, though there is no indication that Smith tried to rape her. She was probably 18 years old when she came to Virginia about 1665. *Accomack Orders 1666-1670,* 96, 97, 100.

32. *Accomack Orders 1666-1670,* 106.

33. *Accomack Orders 1666-1670,* 106, 112, 113, 124-127, 129, 132-137. Old John, whose real name was John Butt, came to Virginia from Bristol, England. (This reference provides no date for John's indenture, but other servants on the same page signed their indentures in September 1660.) Bristol Record Office, *Servants to Foreign Plantations,* Book 1, p. 381, *English-America: the Voyages, Vessels, People & Places,* http://www.english-america.com/places/br-v1-b3.html#Passsengers. Another website referring to the same Bristol passenger lists erroneously transcribes Old John's name as John Bult. Here the date of his four-year indenture is listed as 10 September 1660; his "occupation" was yeoman. "Bristol Register of Servants Sent to Foreign Plantations, 1654-1686," *Virginia Center for Digital History: Virtual Jamestown,* www.virtualjamestown.org/indentures/advsearch_bristol.html. Since his final beating occurred on Smith's plantation on the south side of Occohannock Creek (which in spite of its name is a very wide body of water), Old John's partially filled grave would have been located there. The property lies in Northampton County, a mile or so west of Morley's Warf, from which it may be easily seen. Whitelaw, *Virginia's Eastern Shore,* 540; Mariner, *Off 13,* 163.

34. *Accomack Orders 1666-1670,* 137.

35. *Accomack Orders 1666-1670,* 45a.

36. On 18 February 1667/68. *Accomack Orders 1666-1670,* 53.

37. Henry Smith had bragged that the Governor would clear him; it was not a hollow boast. Governor Berkeley did indeed favor Henry Smith. *Accomack Orders 1666-1670*, 3, 4a, 5, 6a, 156, 157.

38. As part of the investigation conducted by the court held 4 February 1668/69, the justices "inquired of ye Country" if anyone had heard reports of Smith raping Mary Jones. Different individuals admitted hearing talk, but when nothing happened, they forgot about it. *Accomack Orders 1666-1670*, 104.

39. John Cross, a hot-headed weaver, purchased Ann Cooper from Henry Smith but had trouble paying for her, and both of them wound up serving Henry Smith for a time. In May 1667, Cross, in an attempt to escape from the sheriff, used a razor to slash Richard Chambers (one of Smith's blacksmiths), who was trying to recapture him. The court ordered three parts to Cross's punishment: the sheriff was to "whipe him as longe as hee is able to beare it," he was to serve Henry Smith for six months, and he was to be imprisoned "for a yeare & a day to whipe & worke." Cross, who freed Ann Cooper before he served his sentence, did not survive his punishment; by December 1668, Ann petitioned that Cross's estate and his time serving Smith be calculated so his debts could be paid. *Accomack Orders 1666-1670*, 22a, 23, 24a, 25a, 49a, 72.

40. Ann Cooper talked Rachel Moody, Jean Powell, and Elizabeth Nock into giving her items from Smith's Occohannock plantation. Her case was heard at the court held 28 May 1667. *Accomack Orders 1666-1670*, 25, 25.

41. Ann Cooper was presented for fornication 8 April 1668; she formally accused Smith of fathering her child on 26 October 1668. Smith was found guilty on 7 December 1668. There was some doubt about Ann's accusation; the timing of the birth was slightly off, her reputation was not good (this was her second bastard) and she had been known to "accompany" John Cross. Clearly, there would have been no advantage to attributing the child to Cross, who was probably in prison in October and dead in December. *Accomack Orders 1666-1670*, 54a, 64, 65, 71, 72.

42. *Accomack Orders 1666-1670*, 69, 95, 83, 84, 88, 96, 99, 105, 113.

43. By her own admission, Eliza Carter became Henry Smith's "prostitute" soon after her arrival in Virginia. She had signed a four year indenture on 2 June 1662, in Bristol, England. *Accomack Orders 1666-1670*, 70; "Bristol Register of Servants Sent to Foreign Plantations, 1654-1686," *Virginia Center for Digital History: Virtual Jamestown*, www.virtualjamestown.org/indentures/advsearch_bristol.html.

44. *Accomack Orders 1666-1670*, 87.

45. By law weddings were to be conducted in a church between 8:00 am and noon, but the law was not strictly observed. No matter where they were held, weddings (as well as funerals) were followed by festivities. Bruce, *Social Life of Virginia*, 234-236.

46. *Accomack Orders 1666-1670*, 73.

47. Elizabeth Nock had gone without shoes or socks from the middle of April through the last of November 1668. Henry Smith presumably cared more about ruined cloth than a servant's painful feet. *Accomack Orders 1666-1670*, 87.

48. On 16 June 1668. *Accomack Orders 1666-1670*, 60a.

49. *Accomack Orders 1666-1670*, 90.

50. *Accomack Orders 1666-1670*, 85.

51. Jane Powell's deposition detailing Smith's mistreatment of Sarah Matrum was given 2 December 1668. *Accomack Orders 1666-1670*, 88.

52. *Accomack Orders 1666-1670*, 88.

53. Griffith Savage (aged 29) and his wife Bridget (aged 23) came to Oak Hall during September 1668. They gave depositions regarding the incident on 3 December 1688. *Accomack Orders 1666-1670*, 88.

54. On 27 October 1668, Jean Hill gave a deposition and reported the conversation between Henry Smith and Eliza Carter that occurred at her house about the first of September. *Accomack Orders 1666-1670*, 85.

55. According to Elizabeth Taylor, the birth occurred "about the beginning of September." *Accomack Orders 1666-1670*, 64.

56. Elizabeth Taylor gave her deposition 26 October 1668. *Accomack Orders 1666-1670*, 64.

57. Ruth Bunduck gave her deposition 26 October 1668. *Accomack Orders 1666-1670*, 64.

58. *Accomack Orders 1666-1670*, 63.

59. *Accomack Orders 1666-1670*, 65, 65a.

60. *Accomack Orders 1666-1670*, 65a.

61. *Accomack Orders 1666-1670*, 65a.

62. *Accomack Orders 1666-1670*, 65a.

63. At the court held 7 December 1668, Jean Hill recounted Smith's criticism of the court. *Accomack Orders 1666-1670*, 82.

64. It seems that Marrian Fruin and Ruth Bunduck were alone at the Bunduck house when Henry and Joanna visited there during November. Marrian gave her deposition to Col. Edmund Scarburgh on 4 December 1668; Ruth gave hers in open court three days later. *Accomack Orders 1666-1670*, 80-82.

65. The last name of the "Mrs. Ann," who had physic (powerful laxatives) at her disposal is never mentioned, but it could have been Mrs. Ann Toft. As other court entries show, she had befriended Joanna. *Accomack Orders 1666-1670*, 94.

66. Though Col. Scarburgh was powerful enough to keep the details of his relationship with Ann Toft out of the court, historians and genealogists now commonly agree that Edmund Scarburgh was the father of Ann's three daughters, a conclusion hinted at by Ralph T. Whitelaw in 1951. Whitelaw, *Virginia's Eastern Shore*, 1149-1153.

67. The beating of Joanna at Oak Hall is told from the viewpoint of Smith's servant Jean Powell, and the servant Joanna brought with her from England, Mary Hues. *Accomack Orders 1666-1670*, 82-84, 111.

68. The children that were in bed in the great house when Joanna was beaten were Henry's by his first marriage and possibly Joanna's daughter Mary Matrum. Joanna's daughter Sarah had been given to the Savages a couple of months earlier. *Accomack Orders 1666-1670*, 84.

69. *Accomack Orders 1666-1670*, 84.

70. On 2 December 1668. *Accomack Orders 1666-1670*, 88.

71. *Accomack Orders 1666-1670*, 88.

72. More than 18 individuals gave evidence against Smith in the court that met 7-9 December 1668. In addition to complaints and petitions, there were a total of 24 depositions. *Accomack Orders 1666-1670*, 67-76, 80-90.

73. *Accomack Orders 1666-1670*, 74.

74. Whitelaw, *Virginia's Eastern Shore*, 625-635.

75. *Accomack Orders 1666-1670*, 67.

76. *Accomack Orders 1666-1670*, 67.

77. Neither Mrs. Browne's first name nor that of her husband was recorded, an indication she was so prominent that further identification was not necessary. Most likely she was the wife of Devorax Browne, the man who brought Joanna to Virginia. Browne's wife was Tabitha, the eldest child of Edmund Scarburgh. It is unclear why Henry Smith attempted to obtain favorable testimony from his enemy's daughter. *Accomack Orders 1666-1670*, 68; Whitelaw, *Virginia's Eastern Shore*, 968-971.

78. *Accomack Orders 1666-1670*, 68.

79. Joanna's petition, the agreement she signed with her husband and the testimony of some of the witnesses she called were recorded under a court heading dated December 7, 8 and 9, 1668. *Accomack Orders 1666-1670*, 67-70, 80-88.

80. *Accomack Orders 1666-1670*, 68.

81. *Accomack Orders 1666-1670*, 68.

82. *Accomack Orders 1666-1670*, 68, 76.

83. *Accomack Orders 1666-1670*, 176.

84. *Accomack Orders 1666-1670*, 69.

85. Elizabeth Nock's indenture was to expire on 6 October 1669; Mary Hues, whose passage was paid by Joanna, had an indenture, but Henry insisted that she had none and said she would have to serve the "Custome of the Country," which was five years. *Accomack Orders 1666-1670*, 44a, 45,130.

86. The second attack on Elizabeth Nock occurred shortly after Smith had burned Joanna's clothes, which was probably in October or November 1668. Henry left his wife in the Great House and went out to the servant's quarters where he accosted Elizabeth while she was washing the dishes. Henry "laid hold on her & hal'd her from ye fire into ye other roome & threw her on ye bed & strove to get up her coats to lye wth this Depon^t: wch Continued wth his strife & her Resisting neere a Quarter of an hower, Then this Depon^t said she heard her Mistris coming so he lett her goe & she went to milking & came no more privately in his way." *Accomack Orders 1666-1670*, 25, 131.

87. *Accomack Orders 1666-1670*, 69, 70.

88. *Accomack Orders 1666-1670*, 69, 70.

89. *Accomack Orders 1666-1670*, 70, 71.

90. *Accomack Orders 1666-1670*, 70, 71.

91. The women of the jury seemingly overlooked Jean Hill's testimony that Eliza Carter *often* took physic (not just twice) and deliberately bruised her belly to destroy the child. Instead, the jury attributed the death to an accidental fall. The jurors were: Ann (A) Fookes, Mary Hill, Joan (I) Custis, Eliz^a (U) Bowman, Dorothy (D) Jordan, Hannah Wise, Mary Mikele, Sara (S) Kellam, Elinor (X) Johnson, Ann (A) Addison, Micall (W) Hewit, and Joan (I) Nutwell. *Accomack Orders 1666-1670*, 65a, 71, 89.

92. For some reason, Eliza Carter did not receive her thirty lashes at the next court. A full year later, on 17 December 1669, it was noted that she had gone unpunished. At that time it was ordered that she receive her thirty lashes at the next court, which would have been 25 January 1669/70. *Accomack Orders 1666-1670*, 166.

93. Jean Hill's option of becoming the common whipper was an unusual punishment; naturally, she preferred inflicting a whipping to receiving one. On 16 July 1669, she was given the order to administer twenty lashes each month to John Hancock, Anne Gray, Adam Robinson and Penellope Standford, all servants of Ann Toft. Both couples had produced two illegitimate children. These were not Jean's only customers; she also had to perform the service at other locations. *Accomack Orders 1666-1670*, 75, 76, 150, 151.

94. *Accomack Orders 1666-1670*, 71, 72.

95. *Accomack Orders 1666-1670*, 25, 25a, 49a, 71, 72.

96. Servants Mary Hues, Jean Powell, Eliza Nock, Richard Chambers, William Nock and Roger Mylles detailed Smith's cruelty. *Accomack Orders 1666-1670*, 72-74.

97. *Accomack Orders 1666-1670*, 76, 74.

98. *Accomack Orders 1666-1670*, 74, 75.

99. *Accomack Orders 1666-1670*, 74, 75.

100. *Accomack Orders 1666-1670*, 74.

101. Whitelaw, *Virginia's Eastern Shore*, 149-154.

102. *Accomack Orders 1666-1670*, 94.

103. Mary gave the court a detailed description of the rape on 4 February 1668/69, and 17 March 1668/69. The only other servant on the plantation at the time was Roger Mylles, who was sleeping in a distant house. *Accomack Orders 1666-1670,* 110-112, 123, 124, 130.

104. *Accomack Orders 1666-1670,* 93-101.

105. *Accomack Orders 1666-1670,* 94, 100.

106. *Accomack Orders 1666-1670,* 95, 96.

107. The fire at Oak Hall may have been intentionally set by Smith himself. Had one of the servants been responsible, Smith surely would have demanded reparations as he did with Mary Jones; he accused her of willfully or carelessly burning an old tobacco house, but offered no proof. *Accomack Orders 1666-1670,* 96, 104.

108. *Accomack Orders 1666-1670,* 96.

109. *Accomack Orders 1666-1670,* 94.

110. *Accomack Orders 1666-1670,* 96.

111. The letter from Rachel Moody's grandmother was cited at the court held 17 March 1668/69. *Accomack Orders 1666-1670,* 96, 97, 125. Rachel moved to Maryland and married John Freeman on 7 July 1671; their children were Elizabeth, Esther and John. Lankford, *They Lived in Somerset,* 134.

112. *Accomack Orders 1666-1670,* 97, 98, 112,125.

113. *Accomack Orders 1666-1670,* 96.

114. *Accomack Orders 1666-1670,* 108.

115. After the January 1668/69 court, Henry voluntarily sat in jail because he refused to post bail; after the February court he did not have a choice. *Accomack Orders 1666-1670,* 104, 106, 108.

116. Presented on 4 February 1668/69. *Accomack Orders 1666-1670,* 107.

117. The court's remark about Smith contracting his own ruin probably was referring to the trouble his continued defiance of the court was causing. They also concluded that his various losses proved he was suffering from the judgment of God; since the court put the destruction of Oak Hall in this category, they probably did not consider Henry to be the arson–though there is no indication that they ever investigated the matter. *Accomack Orders 1666-1670,* 104, 107.

118. The men who examined the Occohannock plantation were: Edm: Scarburgh, Richard Hill, Geo. Watson, Osmond Dering, Robt. Johnson, William Nock, Roger Myles and Richard Chambers, the last three being Smith's servants, who would have known their way around the place. Their report was signed on 6 February 1668/69, but the inspection probably occurred a number of days earlier. The Occohannock house and its chimney were of wattle and daub construction. *Accomack Orders 1666-1670,* 113, 114.

119. *Accomack Orders 1666-1670,* 107.

120. *Accomack Orders 1666-1670,* 108.

121. We can be thankful that the record of the court proceedings was being prepared for the Governor's eyes. Many details, like Joanna's losses during the plague in London and the erratic behavior of Smith's attorney would probably otherwise have been omitted. *Accomack Orders 1666-1670,* 108, 109.

122. *Accomack Orders 1666-1670,* 104.

123. The court found the rude behavior and witness tampering of John Tankard, Smith's attorney, to be especially offensive. The leading judge who threatened the arrogant John Tankard could only have been Col. Scarburgh, whose name appears first in the list of the commissioners present. On 17 March 1668/69, the court debarred Tankard from practicing law. *Accomack Orders 1666-1670,* 101, 108, 109, 128.

124. *Accomack Orders 1666-1670,* 119.

125. *Accomack Orders 1666-1670,* 120.

126. *Accomack Orders 1666-1670,* 120.

127. *Accomack Orders 1666-1670*, 120, 121.

128. *Accomack Orders 1666-1670*, 120, 121.

129. On 17 March 1668/69. *Accomack Orders 1666-1670*, 125.

130. *Accomack Orders 1666-1670*, 125, 126.

131. The witnesses slated to make the trip to Jamestown with Henry Smith on 16 April 1669, were William Nock, Rich Chambers, Roger Miles, Mary Jones, Mary Hues, Jane Powell and Eliz[a] Nock Parker. In addition to transporting the prisoner and witnesses, the sheriff was to take inventory of Smith's estate, which would be forfeited to the government if he were found guilty. *Accomack Orders 1666-1670*, 124.

132. *Accomack Orders 1666-1670*, 156.

133. Though there is no date given for the Governor's visit, it must have occurred during the summer of 1669. The court discussion of Smith's bond occurred on 26 August 1669. *Accomack Orders 1666-1670*, 155, 156.

134. Smith went to jail when he refused to post security at the court held 5 January 1668/69; he remained there until about 26 August 1669. *Accomack Orders 1666-1670*, 104, 106, 108, 155, 156.

135. *Accomack Orders 1666-1670*, 177, 180.

136. *Accomack Orders 1666-1670*, 100, 113, 177.

137. Although there is no record of exactly when she left, Joanna's departure for England occurred after April 1669 (when the sheriff searched Henry's estate for her possessions), and almost certainly before Henry's release in August 1669. *Accomack Orders 1666-1670*, 177.

138. On 3 February 1669/70, the court mentioned that Joanna's children had been left to charity. *Accomack Orders 1666-1670*, 177.

139. *Accomack Orders 1666-1670*, 68.

140. *Accomack Orders 1666-1670*, 70.

141. McIlwaine, *Minutes of the Council and General Court*, 212, 217.

142. The Accomack County Court's defense of it's actions implies that the Governor frowned on accepting evidence provided by servants testifying against their masters. *Accomack Orders 1666-1670*, 176.

143. Smith settled on the south side of the Manokin River near Jones Creek on a plantation he called "Smith's Recovery." His house was called the "White House." Torence, *Old Somerset*, 422, 424, 425.

144. On 13 September 1670. *Somerset Judicial Records 1670-1671*, 1.

145. Some of Smith's Maryland activities included: rape, deceptive dealing, servant trouble, boundary dispute, "false clamor," swindling and servant abuse. *Somerset Judicial Records 1671-1675*, 71, 302; *Somerset Judicial Records 1687-1689*, 6, 70, 71, 135; *Somerset Judicial Records 1689-1690*, 48; *Somerset Judicial Records 1692-96*, Vol. 535, 64.

146. On 1 April 1671, a certificate was granted for the transportation of Jonah Smith, the wife of Henry Smith. This was the second time he had obtained land for transporting her–the first time as Joan Smith to Virginia on 18 February 1667/8, shortly after they were married. Lankford, *They Lived in Somerset*, 178; *Accomack Orders 1666-1670*, 53.

147. In the fall of 1671, Randall Revell, while engaged in a property dispute with Smith, referred to Smith's troubles in Accomack, and in colorful language expressed his opinion of Henry Smith as a judge. *Somerset Judicial Records 1671-1675*, 11-13.

148. As Henry Smith's life after 1670, had little to do with Joanna, who is the focus of this narrative, Henry's subsequent wife and children were not thoroughly researched. However, it appears that he next married Ann Charlton, who, as the niece of Col. Scarburgh's wife, should have known better. Ann had at least three children by Henry: William (b. 20 January 1676/[77]), John (b. 4 November 1680) and Tamesen (b. 1 September 1682). Lankford, *They Lived in Somerset*, 178, 179.

149. Henry's children by his first wife were Henry Jr. and Margery both born before 1666. His illegitimate children included the child of Ann Cooper (b. 1668), the child of Elizabeth Carter (b. 1668), and Hanna, the child of Dennis Holland (b. 9 October 1673). *Somerset Judicial Records 1671-1675,* 302, 368. Thomas Jones, whom Henry Smith called "my trusty and well beloved sonn" when he granted him power of attorney on 18 January 1695/96, may have been Smith's son-in-law, though Mrs. Jones' first name was Martha, which was not the name of any of Henry's known daughters. *Somerset Judicial Records 1692-1696,* 149; Lankford, *They Lived in Somerset,* 108, 109.

150. Dennis Holland, a maid servant hired out to Henry Smith in January 1672/73, kept an accurate record of the six times that Henry raped her and later graphically described the attacks and Smith's attempts to make her say the child belonged to her master, William Coleborne. She returned home in February, and when her pregnancy became known, her boyfriend–a fellow servant also named Henry–dropped her because the child was not his. Little Hanna, born on 9 October 1673, was placed in servitude to John Kirke on 11 August 1674; in exchange for maintaining her, Kirke was to have Hanna's service till she came of age. *Somerset Judicial Records 1671-1675,* 302, 368.

151. Henry Smith, who claimed an age of 58 years on 24 December 1692, would have had a birth date of 1634. He died some time before 28 October 1703, when two men (one of whom was Richard Chambers) petitioned for the sale of the land belonging to Capt. Henry Smith of Somerset County, deceased. *Council of Maryland, 1687/8-1693,* 504; *Maryland General Assembly ,1700-1704,* 318.

152. With both father and son named Henry Smith, it is sometimes unclear which individual is meant, though during this period, the father's name was generally preceded by the title Captain. It was almost certainly Junior who stole Richard Kembell's horse; on 13 May 1688, he was found guilty and given five strokes on the bare back. In November of that year both he and his father were involved in stealing and re-branding a black stallion belonging to William Brereton. *Somerset Judicial Records 1687-1689,* 44, 45, 70, 71. Henry Smith Jr. was not the only one with the elder Henry Smith's traits. Thomas Jones, whom Henry identified as his son (though he may have been a son-in-law) in 1695/96, was noted for his "beligerent nature and violent, uncontrolable temper." Torence, *Old Somerset,* 425; *Somerset Judicial Records 1692-1696,* 149. On 13 October 1699, James, an illegitimate child was born to a woman named Christian Duncan and Henry Smith. As the elder Smith was about 65 years old at the time, this child was likely fathered by Henry Smith Jr. Lankford, *They Lived in Somerset,* 178. The younger Smith must also have been the Henry Smith who bound out his illegitimate son (named John Arington) as a servant in March 1701/02. *Accomack Deeds and Wills 1692-1715,* 349a. Though both Henry Smiths, father and son, were partners in horse theft, they had their disagreements. *Somerset Judicial Records 1689-1690,* 13, 170.

Chapter 9
Bridget Savage

1. Griffith Savage was listed as a headright of Devorax Browne on 17 August 1663, and was called Browne's servant on 10 November 1663. *Accomack Orders 1663-1666,* 22a, 36.

2. The Savage land, which was located on Muddy Creek (now called Guilford Creek) near the Chesapeake Bay, was purchased in 1668, by Griffith Savage. Whitelaw, *Virginia's Eastern Shore,* 1188.

3. Whitelaw, *Virginia's Eastern Shore,* 1110, 1112, 1115, 1117, 1118, 1188.

4. *Accomack Orders 1666-1670,* 191-193.

5. When Griffith Savage complained to the court about Martin Moore's wife on 26 January 1669/70, the court deemed it dangerous for her to go at large, and she remained in custody till posting a bond. On 17 March 1669/70, Elizabeth, the wife of Laurance Robinson swore that her life was in danger because of the threats of Bridget Savage. *Accomack Orders 1666-1670,* 171, 186.

6. Accomack Orders 1666-1670, 60.

7. Hugh Bowin and John Murffee, who witnessed the altercation, gave sworn statements to Col. Edmund Scarburgh on 15 June 1668. Their testimony and the participants in the fight appeared in court 16 June 1668. *Accomack Orders 1666-1670,* 59-61.

8. Sebastian Delastatius (whose name was a spelling nightmare for colonial record keepers) was appointed constable in 1697, but lost that position because he was a Frenchman. *Accomack Orders 1690-1697,* 243a.

9. *Accomack Orders 1666-1670,* 59, 60.

10. A wife could not be convicted of a crime committed with her husband because she was assumed to be acting under his direction. Norton, *Founding Mothers & Fathers,* 73.

11. On 17 March 1669/70. *Accomack Orders 1666-1670,* 186.

12. On 3 September 1668. *Accomack Orders 1666-1670,* 88.

13. *Accomack Orders 1666-1670,* 88.

14. *Accomack Orders 1666-1670,* 74.

15. *Accomack Orders 1666-1670,* 177.

16. Activities of Griffith Savage between 1670 and 1675: *Accomack Orders 1666-1670,* 193; 195; *Accomack Orders 1673-1676,* 20, 24, 75, 85, 179, 194-196, 200, 307, 325-327, 336, 337, 348.

17. *Accomack Orders 1671-1673,* 193; *Accomack Orders 1673-1676,* 349, 377; *Accomack Orders 1676-1678,* 16, 17. 31, 96. Griffith Savage continued as church warden until at least December 1677. *Accomack Orders 1676-1678,* 31, 96.

18. *Accomack Orders 1678-1682,* 196, 197.

19. On 17 February 1675/76. *Accomack Orders 1673-1676,* 373, 374.

20. *Accomack Orders 1678-1682,* 2, 3, 12, 39.

21. Whitelaw, *Virginia's Eastern Shore,* 1189.

22. *Accomack Orders 1678-1682,* 153, 154, 157, 176, 180, 183.

23. It was not common for a healthy person to make a will; of the more than twenty individuals who had wills probated between March 1684/85 and March 1688/89, only Griffith Savage claimed perfect health. One other did not mention his health; all the others had health ranging from imperfect to very sick and weak. *Accomack Wills and Deeds 1676-1690,* 423, 425, 429, 433a, 434, 448, 453, 458a, 459-462, 468a-470, 479a, 480a, 482a, 484, 493a, 497, 502.

24. The will of Griffith Savage was written 6 July 1680 and probated on 11 March 1685/86. *Accomack Wills and Deeds 1676-1690,* 421, 421a.

25. Mary Burton was removed from the home of her stepfather on 27 April 1680. *Accomack Orders 1678-1682,* 172.

26. On 17 December 1680, Mary Burton gave a deposition describing her stay with Bridget Savage, which lasted from the middle of the previous May till the last day of July. *Accomack Orders 1678-1682,* 196, 197.

27. Griffith Savage, though mentioned as absent from home during part of Mary Burton's stay, must not have been gone for more than a few weeks. He was at home 6 July 1680, when he made his will and had apparently returned in time for the court held 4 August 1680. *Accomack Orders 1678-1682,* 176, 180.

28. *Accomack Orders 1678-1682,* 35, 36.

29. *Accomack Orders 1678-1682,* 196, 197.

30. *Northampton Orders 1683-1689,* 127.

31. *Accomack Wills and Deeds 1676-1690*, 421, 421a.

32. When he gave a deposition on 9 January 1673/74, Roger Micheel was "about" 30 years old, giving him a birth year of 1643. Bridget, who was about 23 in 1668, was born in 1645. *Accomack Orders 1673-1676*, 43; *Accomack Orders 1666-1670*, 88.

33. *Accomack Orders 1678-1682*, 196, 197.

34. On 4 August 1680, the same day that Mary Burton was ordered removed from the Savage home, Griffith Savage unsuccessfully brought action against two individuals, Francis Wharton and John Bessant; both suits were dismissed. These setbacks may have intensified Bridget's frustration, but since she was directly concerned with Mary Burton, it seems more likely that the order for Mary's removal provoked Bridget's anger and contemptuous behavior. *Accomack Orders 1678-1682*, 179, 180, 181,

35. *Accomack Orders 1678-1682*, 183, 184.

36. *Accomack Orders 1682-1697*, 62.

37. *Accomack Orders 1678-1682*, 228.

38. On 13 July 1681. *Accomack Orders 1678-1682*, 243, 244.

39. *Accomack Wills and Deeds 1676-1690*, 421, 421a.

40. *Accomack Orders 1678-1682*, 184, 270; *Accomack Orders 1682-1697*, 26.

41. Moveable property owned by a woman became the property of her husband at their marriage; her real estate became his to manage. As a "feme covert" a married woman had few legal rights; she could not sue, be sued, or write a will. Norton, *Founding Mothers & Fathers*, 72, 73, 83, 84. A single woman or widow, as a "feme sole" was allowed a legal status more typical of that enjoyed by men. Berkin, *First Generations*, 14, 15.

42. *Accomack Orders 1678-1682*, 330, 331.

43. It is possible that Edward Brotherton was already married; when he died he had a wife and daughter, both named Mary. Nottingham, *Wills and Administrations*, 69.

44. On 13 January 1684/85, it was noted that Bridget, the widow of Griffith Savage, was married to Mr. Jearvis Bagale. *Accomack Orders 1682-1697*, 56a. When he gave a deposition on 19 June 1695, Jarvis Baggale claimed a birth year of 1658; Bridget Savage was born in 1645. *Accomack Orders 1690-1697*, 156. *Accomack Orders 1666-1670*, 88.

45. On 12 May 1685, Abraham Dorton and John Baggwell gave depositions detailing Edward Brotherton's role in the marital troubles of Bridget and Jarvis Baggale. *Accomack Orders 1682-1697*, 65, 65a.

46. Jarvis Baggale registered his complaint against Bridget and Edward Brotherton on 6 November 1684. *Accomack Orders 1682-1697*, 52.

47. *Accomack Orders 1682-1697*, 65.

48. Proceedings regarding the estate of Griffith Savage were halted by the Governor in the early part of 1685. *Accomack Orders 1682-1697*, 65.

49. *Accomack Orders 1682-1697*, 65a.

50. *Accomack Wills and Deeds 1676-1690*, 421, 421a.

51. Many men allowed their widows the use of their estate only so long as they did not remarry. Berkin, *First Generations*, 18, 19. In Accomack County, between the spring of 1686, and early 1689, over half of the wills mentioning wives penalized the widows if they were to remarry. *Accomack Wills and Deeds 1676-1690*, 433a, 459-462, 480a, 502.

52. *Accomack Wills and Deeds 1676-1690*, 421a.

53. While the possibility exists that Bridget and Brotherton tampered with the will, things probably turned out much the way that Griffith Savage Sr. would have wanted. His son received most of the estate, though not without a struggle. Court orders regarding the inventory of the Savage estate: *Accomack Orders 1682-1697*, 65, 72.

54. *Accomack Orders 1697-1703*, 50a.

55. *Accomack Orders 1682-1697*, 65, 65a.

56. *Accomack Orders 1682-1697*, 65a.

57. *Accomack Orders 1682-1697*, 72.

58. *Accomack Orders 1682-1697*, 78.

59. *Accomack Orders 1682-1697*, 92a.

60. *Accomack Orders 1682-1697*, 112.

61. *Accomack Orders 1682-1697*, 117a, 121, 138, 145.

62. Since the colonies still used the Julian calendar, the attack likely occurred on 25 March 1691. *Accomack Orders 1690-1697*, 64, 64a.

63. *Accomack Orders 1697-1703*, 50a.

64. *Accomack Orders 1703-1710*, 8a, 11a, 13a, 151a.

65. Edward Brotherton's will was written on 3 September 1721, and probated 3 October 1721. Nottingham, *Wills and Administrations*, 69.

66. On 3 October 1721. *Accomack Orders 1719-1724*, 35a.

67. The child of Edward Brotherton and Bridget Savage may have died young. It is estimated that 40% to 55% of all white children born in the Chesapeake area in the later 1600's died before their twentieth birthday. Berkin, *First Generations*, 7.

68. *Accomack Orders 1682-1697*, 65, 65a; Whitelaw, *Virginia's Eastern Shore*, 1029.

69. Gervas Baggale [Baggaly] obtained a license for operating taverns in Onancock, Virginia, and near the courthouse, November 1696, December 1697, June 1699, and June 1704. *Accomack Orders 1690-1697*, 200a; *Accomack Orders 1697-1703*, 8a. *Accomack Orders 1703-1709*, 28. A meeting of the justices was held at Gervas Baggale's house at Onancock in June 1699. *Accomack Orders 1697-1703*, 65a. On 2 February 1702/03, Gervas Baggale was granted a year's renewal of his license for keeping a tavern at the courthouse, "where he now lives." *Accomack Orders 1697-1703*, 135. Gervas Baggale was sworn in as the jailer on 1 August 1699. *Accomack Orders 1697-1703*, 66. By June 1703, however, Baggale was calling himself a gunsmith. *Accomack Deeds and Wills 1692-1715*, 309, 309a.

70. *Accomack Orders 1690-1697*, 172a, 173, 177.

71. *Accomack Orders 1703-1709*, 30, 30a, 47.

72. Between March and June 1705, Elizabeth Baggale, widow of Gervas, "embezzled" the estate, deliberately tried to avoid paying her husband's debts, abused her servant (Margrett Carvill) and was cited for contempt. *Accomack Orders 1703-1709*, 41-42, 43a, 44, 46, 47.

73. *Accomack Orders 1690-1697*, 41, 96.

74. In December 1698. *Accomack Orders 1697-1703*, 50a.

75. *Accomack Orders 1697-1703*, 76a; *Accomack Orders 1703-1709*, 52a, 57-58.

76. *Accomack Orders 1703-1709*, 8a, 11a, 13a, 151a.

77. *Accomack Orders 1697-1703*, 67, 67a.

78. Whitelaw, *Virginia's Eastern Shore*, 1190, 1191.

79. The first wife of Griffith Savage was Ann Bagwell; in June 1704, Ann, along with Griffith Savage, agreed to a sale of land. Since Ann is not mentioned in Griffith's previous transactions, it is possible that they were married between 1701 and 1704. *Accomack Orders 1703-1709*, 29a. Whitelaw, *Virginia's Eastern Shore*, 1118.

80. Griffith Savage's second wife was Patience the daughter of George Hope, who In his will, (probated 7 August 1722) remembered his granddaughters Mary and Patience Savage, the daughters of Griffith Savage. Nottingham, *Wills and Administrations*, 70, 140.

81. In his will (written 5 February 1638/39 and probated 7 June 1639) Griffith Savage mentioned the following children: Griffith, George, William, Elizabeth (Riley), Patience, Sarah, Scarburgh [daughter] and Bridget (Dix). He did not mention his daughter Mary, but he did name his son-in-law William White, who left a widow named Mary. Nottingham, *Wills and Administrations*, 120, 230.

Chapter 10
Tabitha Scarburgh Smart Browne Custis Hill

1. Whitelaw, *Virginia's Eastern Shore*, 968.
2. Whitelaw, *Virginia's Eastern Shore*, 629.
3. Walcyzk, *Northampton Orders, Deeds & Wills 1651-1654*, 129.
4. Whitelaw, *Virginia's Eastern Shore*, 320.
5. In November 1663, Devorax Browne claimed an age of 25 years. By this time he was a county commissioner. *Accomack Orders 1663-1666*, 1, 50.
6. *Accomack Orders 1663-1666*, 72a.
7. *Accomack Orders 1671-1673*, 93-97.
8. *Accomack Orders 1663-1666*, 26a, 27, 62.
9. *Accomack Orders 1666-1670*, 121-123.
10. *Accomack Orders 1666-1670*, 21a, 22, 160.
11. *Accomack Orders 1666-1670*, 40a.
12. Devorax Browne was absent from the court records during the year following 16 February 1664/65, and again between 16 April 1666 and 27 May 1667, when depositions show he was in England. *Accomack Orders 1666-1670*, 45a, 121.
13. *Accomack Orders 1666-1670*, 121.
14. The escape, which was planned for around Christmas time in 1670, grew to include the following servants: Alexander Swan, Lawrence Gary, Reyney Sadler, John Bayly, Isack Medcalfe, John Carter, John Franklin, William Warren, Thomas Watts, Rowland Binen, James (servant to Capt. Hill), Francis (a woman servant to John West; her surname was probably Chambers), Robin (a man servant), a servant to Mr. Hutchinson, and Black James, who was to act as the pilot. Six of these servants gave depositions regarding the attempted escapes. *Accomack Orders 1671-1673*, 93-97.
15. *Accomack Orders 1666-1670*, 44a.
16. *Accomack Orders 1671-1673*, 28.
17. *Accomack Orders 1666-1670*, 189; *Accomack Orders 1671-1673*, 112.
18. On 18 April 1672. *Accomack Orders 1671-1673*, 83.
19. On the evening of 8 May 1670, Martin Moore attacked Col. Edmund Scarburgh on Ann Toft's plantation. *Accomack Orders 1666-1670*, 191-193.
20. Whitelaw, *Virginia's Eastern Shore*, 633.
21. Whitelaw, *Virginia's Eastern Shore*, 626, 632, 633.
22. Whitelaw, *Virginia's Eastern Shore*, 633.
23. Whitelaw, *Virginia's Eastern Shore*, 629, 631, 633.
24. *Accomack Orders 1666-1670*, 68.
25. McIlwaine, *Minutes of the Council and General Court*, 238.
26. *Accomack Orders 1671-1673*, 74.
27. Whitelaw, *Virginia's Eastern Shore*, 634.
28. *Accomack Orders 1671-1673*, 126, 127.
29. *Accomack Orders 1671-1673*, 187-193.
30. *Accomack Orders 1671-1673*, 25, 148, 149.
31. Mary Carter's deposition was given 18 November 1672. *Accomack Orders 1671-1673*, 149. This Mary Carter, who was entrusted with the keys, was the same servant who had provided food and linen for the 1670 escape attempt. Mary Warrener, at age 31, had recently married John Carter, but because their child had arrived too early, they were convicted of fornication and were forced to pay a fine of 1000 pounds of tobacco. *Accomack Orders 1671-1673*, 158, 178, 203.
32. *Accomack Orders* 1671-1673, 131.
33. *Accomack Orders 1671-1673*, 140.

34. *Accomack Orders 1671-1673*, 161, 176.

35. On 7 January 1673/74. *Accomack Orders 1673-1676, 23.*

36. The original suit was on 9 April 1674; Edward Grindley (Greenley) was ordered to pay Tabitha Browne on 1 October 1674. McIlwaine, *Minutes of the Council and General Court*, 374, 383.

37. *Accomack Orders 1671-1673*, 151, 152.

38. *Accomack Orders 1671-1673*, 204.

39. *Accomack Orders 1673-1676*, 117.

40. *Accomack Orders 1673-1676*, 179-181.

41. Whitelaw, *Virginia's Eastern Shore*, 968.

42. *Accomack Orders 1678-1682*, 174.

43. *Accomack Deeds and Wills 1692-1715*, 440.

44. Luccketti, "Archaeology at Arlington," 8-10.

45. Luccketti, "Archaeology at Arlington," 3, 10,15, 20.

46. Anne the Wife of Edward Smith was called to court for defaming John Custis on 28 October 1664; she was ordered to acknowledge her offense in open court and to pay all costs and charges in the suit. *Northampton Orders 1657-1664*, 199a.

47. Susie M. Ames, *Studies of the Virginia Eastern Shore*, 11, 12.

48. *Northampton Orders 1683-1689*, 378, 379.

49. *Accomack Orders 1678-1682*, 76, 79, 156, 250.

50. *Accomack Orders 1678-1682*, 174.

51. Martha Davis Browne obtained the parish marriage record on 21 August 1679; the document was certified in London on 13 October 1679. *Accomack Orders 1678-1682*, 174.

52. *Accomack Orders 1678-1682*, 177.

53. *Accomack Wills and Deeds 1676-1690*, 400, 400a.

54. John Custis obtained a patent for Edmund Browne's deserted land in 1682; ten years later he obtained a new patent for the property, only this time it contained 4600 acres. Whitelaw, *Virginia's Eastern Shore*, 1288.

55. Martha Browne submitted the inventory on 5 March 1684/85. *Accomack Wills and Deeds 1676-1690*, 400a.

56. In 1699, when she sold the plantation, Martha Davis Browne was married to Matthew Trim, a mariner of Middlesex, England. Whitelaw, *Virginia's Eastern Shore*, 657.

57. Straube, "Selected Artifacts," in Luccketti, "Archaeology at Arlington," 31.

58. Straube, "Selected Artifacts," in Luccketti, "Archaeology at Arlington," 32.

59. Straube, "Selected Artifacts," in Luccketti, "Archaeology at Arlington," 31.

60. *Northampton Orders 1678-1683*, 126.

61. *Northampton Orders 1683-1689*, 74.

62. *Accomack Wills and Deeds 1676-1690*, 400, 400a.

63. *Accomack Wills and Deeds 1676-1690*, 387.

64. Lynch, *Custis Chronicles*, vol. 1, *The Years of Migration*, 178, 179.

65. Mary Scarburgh's will was signed 14 June 1691, the appendix in which she castigated her son Charles was signed 18 October 1691; the will was probated 15 December 1691. *Accomack Orders 1682-1697*, 228a, 229.

66. Col. John Custis's petition was filed at "James Citty" some time before 16 April 1692, when the petition was copied into the Accomack County records. *Accomack Deeds and Wills 1692-1715*, 3. It is interesting to note that Col. Custis's great-granddaughter Patsy Custis (who is better known as George Washington's step-daughter) was also subject to violent fits, one of which caused her death on 19 June 1773, when she was in her mid-teens. Lynch, *The Custis Chronicles*, vol. 2, *The Virginia Generations*, 133-135.

67. William Whittington, the husband of Tabitha II, went on to marry four more times. Before his wife Tabitha Smart Whittington died, she had a son Smart Whittington and a daughter Tabitha Whittington. Whitelaw, *Virginia's Eastern Shore*, 320.

68. Whitelaw, *Virginia's Eastern Shore*, 971.

69. Whitelaw, *Virginia's Eastern Shore*, 116.

70. Walczyk, *Northampton County Orders & Wills, 1689-1698*, vol. 2, 60-63.

71. Whitelaw, *Virginia's Eastern Shore*, 968, 969.

72. Barry W. Miles and Moody K. Miles, "The Miles Files 4.0," Person Page, 236, http://www.espl.org/milesfiles2/p236.htm#i20108.

73. *Shirley Plantation*, "Introduction to Shirley Plantation Archaeology," http://www.shirleyplantation.com/archaeology.html.

74. Ames, *Studies of the Virginia Eastern Shore*, 36.

75. Barry W. Miles and Moody K. Miles, "The Miles Files 4.0," Person Page, 236, http://www.espl.org/milesfiles2/p236.htm#i20108.

76. The will of Edmund Custis was written 12 August 1700; it was probated 14 February 1700/01. Nottingham, *Wills and Administrations*, 31. His wife Tabitha Scarburgh Whittington Custis (Tabitha III) had died some time after 1696, when she received property at the death of her brother Smart Whittington. Whitelaw, *Virginia's Eastern Shore*, 966.

77. *Accomack Deeds and Wills 1692-1715*, 279; Whitelaw, *Virginia's Eastern Shore*, 115, 116.

78. *Accomack Deeds and Wills 1692-1715*, 262, 262a; *Accomack Orders 1697-1703*, 117, 118.

79. *Accomack Orders 1697-1703*, 118.

80. *Accomack Orders 1697-1703*, 121a. Francis Makemie, who claimed his inventory of the Custis estate had been completed in December 1701, submitted it to the court on 7 April 1702, the same day as Tabitha Hill, who had apparently finished hers on 26 March 1702. *Accomack Deeds and Wills 1692-1715*, 287a-290.

81. *Accomack Orders 1697-1703*, 127, 127a, 128.

82. *Accomack Orders 1697-1703*, 129.

83. *Accomack Deeds and Wills 1692-1715*, 357a; *Accomack Orders 1703-1710*, 37.

84. *Accomack Orders 1703-1710*, 60a, 61.

85. *Accomack Orders 1703-1710*, 61.

86. *Accomack Orders 1703-1710*, 164a.

87. *Accomack Orders 1703-1710*, 45, 70, 95, 116a.

88. *Accomack Orders 1682-1690*, 51.

89. *Accomack Orders 1703-1710*, 58a, 73a.

90. Whitelaw, *Virginia's Eastern Shore*, 1287.

91. *Accomack Orders 1703-1710*, 118a.

92. *Accomack Deeds and Wills 1692-1715*, 440.

93. *Accomack Deeds and Wills 1692-1715*, 440.

94. Nottingham, *Wills and Administrations*, 38.

95. *Accomack Orders 1703-1710*, 164a.

96. *Accomack Orders 1703-1710*, 168.

97. *Accomack Orders 1697-1703*, 140; *Accomack Orders 1703-1710*, 25a, 60, 111; Whitelaw, *Virginia's Eastern Shore*, 853, 854.

98. *Accomack Orders 1703-1710*, 153a, 154.

99. Nottingham, *Wills and Administrations*, 55.

100. *Accomack Orders 1710-1714*, 114.

101. Whitelaw, *Virginia's Eastern Shore*, 971.

102. *Accomack Deeds and Wills, 1715-1729*, 37a..

103. Among other things, Tabitha Hill's inventory included the typical array of kitchen utensils, a large chest and two trunks, some half worn clothes, a feather bed, blankets and sheets, towels and linen, a parcel of several spices, ten glass bottles, thimbles, needles, thread, cloth, scissors, a box of medicines, two new pewter spoons, two ivory combs and one of horn, four candlesticks (two pewter, one brass and one tin), three Indian bowls, eight head of cattle, 193 pounds 5 shillings sterling, and, strangely, two claw hammers. *Accomack Deeds and Wills, 1715-1729*, 81a.

104. *Accomack Orders 1717-1719*, 7a.

Chapter 11
Rhodea Fawsett Franklin

1. Rhode Fawsett was 30 years old when she gave a deposition on 11 September 1674. *Accomack Orders 1673-1676*, 181.

2. The marriage of John Fawsett and Rhoda Lamberton was recorded in the records of Hungar's Parish, Northampton County, Virginia. Marshall, *Abstracts of the Wills and Administrations*, 68. Both the last name of the groom and the first name of the bride were subject to multiple spelling variations throughout the years.

3. On 19 Aug 1673, John Fawsett gave his age as 43 years. *Accomack Orders 1671-1673*, 226.

4. The fact that the younger John Fawsett entered an action against Rhodea on 17 May 1678, and then on 20 August of the same year was put in possession of the home plantation, indicates that before May of that year he had reached his 18th birthday–the age he was to receive his inheritance as specified in his father's will. *Accomack Orders 1673-1676*, 7-1; *Accomack Orders 1678-1682*, 5, 26. A year later on 26 May 1679, John Fauset accused Samuel Serjent of taking advantage of Fauset's youth by convincing him to live on Serjent's plantation at Occohannock in "inconsiderable and unconscionable conditions." Because Fawsett's attorney could not prove his client of age, it seems clear that Fawsett had not yet turned 21 years old. John's birth would therefore have occurred after June 1658 and before May 1660, and most likely closer to the later date. *Accomack Orders 1678-1682*, 78, 79. In a deposition given 21 November 1677, John's younger brother William Fauset claimed he was 16 years old, giving him a birth date of 1661. *Accomack Orders 1676-1678*, 91.

5. On 23 March 1662/63. *Northampton Orders 1657-1664*, 166.

6. *Accomack Orders 1663-1666*, 80.

7. *Accomack Orders 1663-1666*, 99.

8. The actors were Cornellius Watkinson, Phillip Howard and William Darby; the informant was Edward Martin. *Accomack Orders 1663-1666*, 102a, 110, 110a.

9. On 16 August 1667. *Accomack Orders 1666-1670*, 35a.

10. *Accomack Orders 1663-1666*, 98.

11. On 16 July 1669, two of the orphans of John Coulston received new masters. Elizabeth stayed with Richard Buckland (who had not properly reprimanded her and her sister), Anne was moved from Buckland to William Chase, and Sara was moved from Chase to John Fawsett. *Accomack Orders 1666-1670*, 151.

12. *Accomack Orders 1671-1673*, 135.

13. *Accomack Orders 1671-1673*, 135.

14. *Accomack Orders 1671-1673*, 135.

15. *Accomack Orders 1671-1673*, 130, 131.

16. *Accomack Orders 1671-1673*, 143.

17. *Accomack Orders 1671-1673*, 198.

18. On 17 June 1673. *Accomack Orders 1671-1673*, 218-220.

19. *Accomack Orders 1671-1673*, 226.

20. John Fawsett's will was written 15 August 1673, and probated 16 October 1673. *Accomack Orders 1671-1673*, 7-11.

21. John Fawsett, along with several others, had heard Benjamin Salisbury accuse Southy Littleton (one of the justices) and his wife of keeping a bawdy house where Mrs. Littleton would shake her belly with her hands as an invitation. Salisbury's own words suggest his motive. Apparently attracted to but ignored by Mrs. Littleton, he grumbled that "Every dirty fellow is better respected by her than [me]." Salisbury's punishment consisted of paying Littleton 10,000 pounds of tobacco, and at the next three courts apologizing on his knees as well as standing at the court door with his crime, in capital letters, attached to his hat. *Accomack Orders 1671-1673*, 223, 226-228.

22. *Accomack Orders 1673-1676*, 25.

23. *Accomack Orders 1673-1676*, 180, 182, 199, 203, 204.

24. *Accomack Orders 1673-1676*, 199.

25. *Accomack Orders 1673-1676*, 250.

26. *Accomack Orders 1673-1676*, 263.

27. *Accomack Orders 1673-1676*, 269.

28. The date would have been 4 March 1686/87. "John Cropper," *Maryland Prerogative Court (Testamentary Proceedings)* Book 13, 458-461, 485, *Ocean City Life-Saving Station Museum*, http://www.ocmuseum.org/genealogy.

29. *Accomack Orders 1673-1676*, 269.

30. *Accomack Orders 1673-1676*, 299, 332, 351, 370.

31. *Accomack Orders 1673-1676*, 371.

32. Jone Bud was lashed according to law, and while the number of her lashes is not specified, the typical punishment for fornication at this time was 25 lashes for those who could not pay the 500 pound tobacco fine. *Accomack Orders 1673-1676*, 80, 286.

33. *Accomack Orders 1676-1678*, 5.

34. *Accomack Orders 1676-1678*, 121.

35. William and Charles Fossit along with servants Ann Fox and a young man called Joseph were working in Cropper's corn field when Richard Price approached them. *Accomack Orders 1676-1678*, 92.

36. Ann Fox (aged 22), who was originally Cropper's servant, testified against Cropper after she was traded to Thomas Hall for the runaway Richard Price. *Accomack Orders 1676-1678*, 92-94.

37. *Accomack Orders 1676-1678*, 93.

38. *Accomack Orders 1676-1678*, 94.

39. "John Cropper," *Maryland Prerogative Court*, Book 13, 458-461, *Ocean City Life-Saving Museum*, http://www.ocmuseum.org/genealogy.

40. William Fawsett prosecuted his complaint on 14 September 1677. *Accomack Orders 1676-1678*, 60, 64, 80, 91, 92.

41. *Accomack Wills and Deeds 1676-1690*, 68.

42. *Accomack Orders 1676-1678*, 94.

43. *Accomack Wills and Deeds 1676-1690*, 114, 115.

44. On 19 February 1677/78, and 21 February 1677/78. *Accomack Orders 1676-1678*, 115, 121.

45. *Accomack Orders 1676-1678*, 148.

46. *Accomack Orders 1678-1682*, 5, 26.

47. On 26 May 1679. *Accomack Orders 1678-1682*, 78, 79.

48. On 25 October 1679. *Accomack Wills and Deeds 1676-1690*, 167.

49."John Cropper," *Ocean City Life-Saving Museum*, http://www.ocmuseum .org/genealogy.

50. *Accomack Wills and Deeds 1676-1690*, 181, 198, 199.

51. *Accomack Orders 1678-1682*, 158.

52. On 17 August 1663, John Cropper testified in support of Thomas Osbourne. *Accomack Orders 1663-1666*, 27-28a. In December 1667, there was a controversy over a house built by John Cropper; Thomas Osburne had collected the bill. *Accomack Orders 1666-1670*, 46a, 49. John Cropper named his "brother" Thomas Osburne in the margin of his will written 5 September 1686. *Maryland Prerogative Court (Wills)*, Book 6, 1688-1700, 33.

53. *Early Settlers of Maryland*, 7, 116.

54. On 4 August 1680. *Accomack Orders 1678-1682*, 179, 184.

55. On 10 June 1681. *Somerset Proceedings, 1665-1668*, 780.

56. *Somerset Judicial Records 1683-1683/4*, 21, 22.

57. On 13 November 1683, John Cropper's servant identified only as Jane was accused of bearing a bastard about the previous June. This is almost certainly the same woman who was called Joan Garrett in February 1682/83, and Jane Garrett in March 1683/84. *Somerset Judicial Records 1683-1683/4*, 1, 16, 27.

58. According to depositions she had given 20 years earlier, Guslin Venettson's wife Bridget had just celebrated her 40th birthday when she took on the responsibility of nursing Rhodea's infant. As a teenaged newlywed, Bridget had had her own brush with the law when her first child arrived only seven months after her marriage. Her midwife, however, swore that the baby had come before its time, and Bridget was cleared of charges of fornication. *Accomack Orders 1663-1666*, 20, 24a, 36, 49, 49a, 51.

59. On 8 February1683/84. *Accomack Orders 1682-1697*, 38.

60. In 1659, William Taylor gave a heifer to John Cropper, his 14-year-old "son-in-law," which in those days was another term for step-son. It is logical to assume that William Taylor Jr. was either a step-brother or half brother to John Cropper. Whitelaw, *Virginia's Eastern Shore*, 1040.

61. *Accomack Orders 1682-1697*, 38.

62. *Accomack Orders 1682-1697*, 43.

63. *Somerset Judicial Records 1689-1690*, 39, 201.

64. The will of John Cropper was signed 25 September 1686, and was probated 14 December 1688. *Maryland Prerogative Court (Wills), 1688-1700*, Book 6, 33-35; John Fawsett later swore that John Cole of Virginia (one of the witnesses), had written the will. *Somerset Judicial Records 1692-1696*, 31.

65. On 17 August 1663, John Cropper gave his age as 18 years, giving him a birth year of 1645. Though he claimed an age of 35 in February 1682/83, the earlier document is probably the more accurate. *Accomack Orders 1663-1666*, 28; *Somerset Judicial Records 1683-1683/4*, 22.

66. Cropper was careful to specify the acreage contained in each of several pieces of property. The acreage of one, Hog Quarter, was obscured by an ink blot in the will, but other sources show that it contained 200 acres, thus giving Cropper a total of 3800 acres. *Somerset Judicial Records 1689-1690*, 162.

67. Though John Cropper called one of Rhodea's sons John Cropper in the will, this boy was later known as Jn° ffossett. On 14 June 1693, when he was still under 18 years of age, he petitioned that John Cole (the "ancient man" who wrote his father's will) be allowed to swear to his identity—that "Jn°.ffossett is the same Jn°: Cropper mentioned in the Will of John:Cropper deceased." *Maryland Prerogative Court (Wills), 1688-1700*, Book 6, 33-35; *Somerset Judicial Records, 1692-1696*, 31.

68. Gertrude's father, Edmund Bowman, whose will was written 26 February 1691, gave his daughter Gertrude Cropper the home plantation and named grandsons Sebastian,

Edmund and Nathaniel Cropper. Of the three, only Sebastian was not named in John Cropper's will. Nottingham, *Wills and Administrations*, 20, 21.

69. *Maryland Prerogative Court (Wills), 1688-1700,* Book 6, 34.

70. "John Cropper," *Maryland Prerogative Court,* Book 13, 458-461, 485, Ocean City Life-Saving Museum, http://www.ocmuseum.org/genealogy.

71. Gertrude Cropper's attorney was William Whittington, the same man who initiated an action against Cropper in March 1683/84. Whether it was on the behalf of Gertrude is unknown. *Somerset Judicial Records 1683-1683/4,* 27.

72. *Maryland Prerogative Court (Testamentary Proceedings),* Book 14, 121-122, *Ocean City Life-Saving Museum,* http://www.ocmuseum.org/genealogy.

73. *Maryland Prerogative Court (Wills), 1688-1700,* Book 6, 33-35.

74. *Somerset Judicial Records 1687-1689,* 133.

75. By 16 January 1689/90, Rhodea Fawsett had married John Franklin. *Somerset Judicial Records 1689-1690,* 39.

76. *Maryland General Assembly 1700-1704,* 129.

77. The Cropper inventory was taken 14 December 1688. In addition to the grindstone and debts due, it included one slave, 3 servants, 28 cattle, 10 horses, 13 sheep, various household goods and carpenter tools. *Somerset Judicial Records 1690-1691,* 7.

78. On 15 March 1692/93. *Somerset Judicial Records 1692-1696,* 191.

79. On 14 June 1693, and 9 August 1693. *Somerset Judicial Records 1692-1696,* 64, 136.

80. "John Cropper," *Maryland Prerogative Court Book 15a,* 22 August 1693, *Ocean City Life-Saving Museum,* http://www.ocmuseum.org/genealogy.

81. *Somerset Judicial Records 1692-1696,* 136.

82. *Somerset Judicial Records 1683-1683/4,* p. 21, 27.

83. "John Cropper," *Maryland Prerogative Court (Testamentary Proceedings),* Book 14, 121, 122, *Ocean City Life-Saving Museum,* http://www .ocmuseum.org/genealogy.

Chapter 12
Dorothy Watts

1. Dorothy [Williams] Watts was born about 1635; in a deposition given in August 1663, she claimed an age of 28 years. *Accomack Orders 1663-1666,* 30a.

2. Walter Williams was established in Northampton County by 1642. Ames, *County Court Records of Accomack-Northampton, Virginia, 1640-1645,* 214. He and his wife Ann had a daughter named Seaborne, who was given a calf in June 1654. Walcyzk, *Northampton Co., VA, Orders, Deeds & Wills 1651-1654,* 159.

3. *Northampton Orders 1657-1664,* 38a.

4. The Northampton County Court met at Williams' ordinary, as well as other locations on a rotating basis, and with occasional interruptions from 1649 through 1658. Whitelaw, *Virginia's Eastern Shore,* 407, 408.

5. Dorothy Watts signed documents with a mark: *Northampton Orders 1657-1664,* 95a; *Accomack Orders 1663-1666,* 30a; *Accomack Orders 1671-1673,* 63; *Accomack Orders 1678-1682,* 227. Dorothy revised her signature throughout the years; no two of them are alike.

6. Funerals in early Virginia were often extravagant affairs at which guests were entertained with copious amounts of food and strong drink. Bruce, *Social Life of Virginia,* 218-222; Spruill, *Women's Life and Work,* 87.

7. *Northampton Orders 1657-1664,* 46a, 67.

8. *Northampton Orders 1657-1664,* 38a.

9. *Northampton Orders 1657-1664*, 40.

10. *Northampton Orders 1657-1664*, 46a.

11. In 1661 John Watts signed a deposition with his mark–a pair of open scissors. *Northampton Orders 1657-1664*, 95. In the tax list of 1665, John Watts was called a tailor. *Accomack Orders 1663-1666*, 102. On a deed signed in 1671/72, and in an indenture made in 1673, John Watts, who was called a planter, again used a drawing of a pair of scissors as his mark. *Accomack Orders 1671-1673*, 63, 233, 234.

12. *Northampton Orders 1657-1664*, 93a, 95, 95a.

13. Ellinor Cowell, whose mistress struck her in the face with a skewer which broke off and became infected, named her mistress as her killer, February 1659/60. *Northampton Orders., 1657-1664*, 63. The evening before he died, John Butt said that the blows given by his master would be his death, November 1666. *Accomack Orders 1666-1670*, 136.

14. *Northampton Orders 1657-1664*, 95, 95a.

15. *Northampton Orders 1657-1664*, 94.

16. *Accomack Orders 1663-1666*, 5, 5a.

17. *Accomack Orders 1663-1666*, 30a.

18. In February 1667/68. *Accomack Orders 1666-1670*, 52, 52a.

19. *Accomack Orders 1663-1666*, 35, 40a, 72, 91, 103a, 110a, 112a, 116a, 118 a, 125; *Accomack Orders 1666-1670*, 18, 18a, 21, 26, 26a.

20. *Accomack Orders 1663-1666*, 103.

21. *Accomack Orders 1663-1666*, 20, 25 100a, 103, 103a, 104, 104a, 106.

22. *Accomack Orders 1663-1666*, 25, 62, 106.

23. *Accomack Orders 1666-1670*, 46a, 47, 50a, 53, 53a, 56a-57a.

24. The Watts purchased 450 acres from Southy and Sarah Littleton in 1668. Whitelaw, *Virginia's Eastern Shore*, 1328.

25. In January 1671/72: *Accomack Orders 1671-1673*, 63; Whitelaw, *Virginia's Eastern Shore*, 831.

26. *Accomack Orders 1676-1678*, 72.

27. Early court records contain many references to livestock with marked ears–or missing ears. Animals bereft of identifying marks were the subject of a rare example of colonial humor. In 1663, James Atkinson (as quoted by Joseph Pitman) offered his assessment of Robert Huitt [Hewitt] by saying that "Robt Huitt did kill a hogg of Richard Hills, and cutt of[f] y^c head of y^c hogg and Run away wth it, and y^t he killed but two beeves, and carried foure hides to Col. Scarburgh and y^t hee y^c s^d Huitt killed Racoones as much as two men could lift." Atkinson was implying, of course, that these hefty dead raccoons had recently been living hogs that belonged to neighbors. *Accomack Orders 1663-1666*, 34.

28. *Accomack Orders 1678-1682*, 223-228.

29. *Accomack Orders 1678-1682*, 244.

30. Whitelaw, *Virginia's Eastern Shore*, 1328, 1331, 1333, 1334, 1336.

31. In August 1681. *Accomack Orders 1678-1682*, 250, 251.

32. *Accomack Orders 1682-1697*, 15, 18, 23, 25a, 26, 120a, 139a.

33. *Accomack Orders 1676-1678*, 149.

34. When the will of John Watts was written in April 1680, three of his children (Margery, Jannett and John) were under 16 years of age and one (Tabitha) was already married to a man named John Tarr. Margery may have died young. According to the will, Watts owned 450 acres in northern Accomack County, Virginia, and another 850 acres in Maryland. The will was probated in June 1684. *Accomack Wills and Deeds 1676-1690*, 381, 381a. John Tarr, who was accused of fathering Elizabeth Mings' illegitimate child in August 1678, apparently did not get along with his father-in-law; Tarr and John Watts were on opposite sides in a lawsuit in July 1679. *Accomack Orders 1678-1682*, 3, 96.

35. *Accomack Orders 1682-1697,* 59a, 63, 72a, 84a, 91a, 96, 98, 111a, 120a, 126a.

36. *Accomack Orders 1682-1697,* 86a.

37. *Accomack Orders 1671-1673,* 159, 164, 173, 174.

38. *Accomack Orders 1682-1697,* 119.

39. Spruill, *Women's Life and Work,* 317; *Accomack Orders 1673-76,* 156; Accomack Orders 1682-1697, 119a; *Accomack Orders 1690-1697,* 73a, 74, 83a, 84.

40. *Accomack Orders 1682-1697,* 121a.

41. *Accomack Orders 1682-1697,* 118a, 121a, 122.

42. In February 1687/88. *Accomack Orders 1682-1697,* 119, 129.

43. *Accomack Orders 1682-1697,* 139, 139a, 141.

44. *Accomack Orders 1690-1697,* 12a, 13.

45. The controversy over the Watts estate extended from December 1690 to September 1691. *Accomack Orders 1690-1697,* 26a, 32a, 38a, 39.

46. *Accomack Orders 1690-1697,* 38a, 39.

47. *Accomack Orders 1690-1697,* 38a, 39.

48. By March 1694/95. *Accomack Orders 1690-1697,* 151.

49. *Accomack Orders 1697-1703,* 66.

50. *Accomack Orders 1697-1703,* 114; *Accomack Deeds and Wills 1692-1715,* 272.

51. As listed in his will (written January 1724/25, probated April 1726), the children of John Watts were John, William, Easter, Sarah, Mary, Jannat and Elizabeth. *Accomack Deeds and Wills, 1715-1729,* 246. 246a.

Chapter 13
Alice Boucher

1. Alice Boucher was "40 years or thereabouts" on 2 August 1671. Her children were Dorothy (the eldest), Francis, Robert, Anne and Martha Boucher. *Accomack Orders 1671-1673,* 8, 112.

2. *Accomack Orders 1671-1673,* 203.

3. William Boucher was "56 years or thereabouts" on 22 May 1663. He was still about 56 years of age on 11 November 1663. *Accomack Orders 1663-1666,* 9, 49.

4. The ownership of the local hogs makes it clear that the Bouchers lived near George Nicholas Hack and Capt. George Parker, both of whom resided on the Bay Side. Whitelaw, *Virginia's Eastern Shore,* 671, 684-690, 695.

5. In 1668. *Accomack Orders 1666-1670,* 77.

6. In May 1663. *Accomack Orders 1663-1666,* 8.

7. *Accomack Orders 1663-1666,* 9, 48a, 48, 49a.

8. In July 1663. *Accomack Orders 1663-1666,* 17a, 18.

9. In August 1663. *Accomack Orders 1663-1666,* 26.

10. At the July court in 1663, George Crump agreed to construct a ducking stool; in exchange, his servant Issabella Wall was remitted from her court-ordered whipping. The device was mentioned four other times. *Accomack Orders 1663-1666,* 17a, 26, 27, 38, 73, 73a.

11. *Accomack Orders 1663-1666,* 26.

12. *Accomack Orders 1663-1666,* 27.

13. In October 1664. *Accomack Orders 1663-1666,* 73, 73a.

14. Thomas Hartley is believed to have been the author of the letter written from Hungar's Parish, Virginia in 1634. Spruill, *Women's Life and Work,* 331, 332.

15. *Accomack Orders 1663-1666,* 87, 91, 97, 98; *Accomack Orders 1666-1670,* 39a, 46.

16. In November 1663. *Accomack Orders 1663-1666,* 38.

17. *Accomack Orders 1663-1666,* 38.

18. *Accomack Orders 1663-1666*, 51a; *Accomack Orders 1666-1670*, 52a, 77.

19. John Browne was examined about the birth of Alice Boucher's child on 6 July 1671. The trial and examination of Alice Boucher and her daughters occurred 19 July 1671. *Accomack Orders 1671-1673*, 8-10.

20. For a discussion of house construction in 17th century Virginia see Hume, *Martin's Hundred*, 248, 249, and Whitelaw, *Virginia's Eastern Shore*, 14. Even the better quality homes during this period were small. Pear Valley, a house still standing in Northampton County, Virginia, features one room, 20 ft. 8 in, by 16 ft. 3 in., with a large fireplace on the main floor; the second floor has two tiny rooms beneath the steeply sloped roof. Though Whitelaw cites a chimney brick dated 1672, recent dendrochronology indicates the little house was built about 1740. Whitelaw, *Virginia's Eastern Shore*, 329-331; *Association for the Preservation of Virginia Antiquities*, "Pear Valley," http://www.apva.org/apva /pear_valley.php.

21. Berkin and Horowitz, *Women's Voices, Women's Lives*, 51; Spruill, *Women's Life and Work*, 273; *Accomack Orders 1676-1678*, 39; *Accomack Orders 1678-1682*, 218, 235, 236.

22. Tobias Sellvey was called a "chirurgion" or surgeon in 1675. Whitelaw, *Virginia's Eastern Shore*, 660. Court records show that he collected fees for his services. *Accomack Orders 1673-1676*, 77, 152.

23. *Accomack Orders 1671-1673*, 39, 40, 56.

24. On 12 May 1672: *Accomack Orders 1671-1673*, 112.

25. *Accomack Orders 1673-1676*, 199.

Chapter 14
Elizabeth Stockley Bowen Towles

1. In his will (signed 8 February 1678/79, probated 18 March 1678/79) John Bowen bequeathed his clothing to his servant. *Accomack Wills and Deeds 1676-1690*, 141-144.

2. For a discussion of the age of Elizabeth Stockley and her siblings, see Appendix II.

3. On 19 July 1664, John Stockley was granted a certificate for 400 acres for transporting eight individuals including himself and an Eliza Stockley and John Bowin. *Accomack Orders 1666-1670*, 69a.

4. The preponderance of evidence indicates that Elizabeth Stockley married John Bowin. For a discussion of the evidence, see Appendix III.

5. John Bowin was born about 1645; he claimed to be about 33 years old when he gave a deposition on 19 February 1677/78. If his term of servitude was typical, Bowen's indenture would have expired on his 24th birthday in 1669. *Accomack Orders 1676-1678*, 114.

6. *Accomack Orders 1671-1673*, 231-233.

7. The elder John Stockley first wrote his will 3 February 1670, and signed it again on 9 April 1673. It was proved by the oaths of Wm. Custis and Thomas Bagwell on 18 August 1673. Three days earlier, the widow, who was not well at the time, had written the court requesting the court to "swear witness" to the will, which was done 19 August 1673. In the document Stockley names his wife Elizabeth, sons William, Woodman, John and Thomas, and daughters Jane, Hanna, Ann and Elizabeth. *Accomack Orders 1671-1673*, 231-233.

8. *Accomack Orders 1671-1673*, 233, 234.

9. *Accomack Orders 1673-1676*, 39, 40.

10. *Accomack Orders 1673-1676*, 60, 61.

11. *Accomack Orders 1673-1676*, 39, 40.

12. *Accomack Orders 1673-1676,* 132, 133, 134, 135.

13. In 1674, John Bowen and William Stockley were taxed together, though a Will. Stockley also appears elsewhere in the list of tithables. *Accomack Orders 1673-1676,* 194-196.

14. *Accomack Orders 1673-1676,* 262, 263.

15. On 16 April 1675. *Accomack Orders 1673-1676,* 263.

16. *Accomack Orders 1673-1676,* 325, 329, 366.

17. *Accomack Orders 1676-1678,* 61, 64, 67, 76, 81.

18. *Accomack Orders 1678-1682,* 12.

19. *Accomack Orders 1678-1682,* 88, 199.

20. *Accomack Orders 1673-1676,* 325-27, 194-196. Tithable individuals were free men, servants and slaves.

21. *Accomack Wills and Deeds 1676-1690,* 141-144.

22. *Accomack Orders 1676-1678,* 114.

23. *Accomack Wills and Deeds 1676-1690,* 60, 84.

24. *Accomack Wills and Deeds 1676-1690,* 116.

25. The will of John Bowen was written 8 February 1678/79, and proved 18 March 1768/79. *Accomack Wills and Deeds 1676-1690,* 141-144.

26. Thomas Jones attacked Elizabeth Bowen, his master's widow exactly two months after John Bowen's will was proved in court. Eight days later, on 26 May, 1679, Elizabeth appeared in open court and was questioned about the attack; she signed the examination with an X. She was most likely illiterate, but it is possible that her injuries were such that she could do little more than make a mark. Immediately after Elizabeth's testimony, the judges passed judgment on Thomas Jones. *Accomack Orders 1678-1682,* 88, 89.

27. The pain from Joan Odawly's (or Dawley) court-ordered whipping lingered for at least three months. *Accomack Orders 1710-1714,* 78a, 81, 82.

28. *Accomack Orders 1678-1682,* 1678-1682, 86, 99-101.

29. In a deposition he gave on 19 November 1691, Henry Towles was listed as about 40 years. *Accomack Orders 1690-1697,* 52a, 53.

30. *Accomack Wills and Deeds 1676-1690,* 213.

31. *Accomack Orders 1682-1697,* 88, 90.

32. On 4 October 1698. *Accomack Orders 1697-1703,* 43.

33. In 1671, both Daniel Jenifer and William Whittington received competing patents for the island, which they called Gingoteage and Jengoteag, respectively. Claiming Whittington had deserted the Island, Jenifer got a new patent for it in 1677. Thomas Welburne, whose wife Arcadia was Jenifer's step-daughter, had a few crops planted and a small house built on the island in the early months of 1680, but no one lived there. So, in 1684, claiming the island had been deserted by Jenifer, Thomas Clayton received a patent for Chincoteague Island and then assigned it to William Kendall. The trouble between Welburne and Kendall occurred when Kendall and John Robins led an armed group of men onto the island to "seat" it in 1687. The local court sent the matter to the General Court in James City, where (according to a deed written by Kendall's son in 1691) the 1671 claim of Jenifer was condemned and granted to Kendall. Whitelaw, *Virginia's Eastern Shore,* 1278, 1377; *Accomack Orders 1682-1697,* 106a, 107, 109a, 112-113a, 142, 142a, 167a, 168, 208, 208a.

34. *Accomack Orders 1682-1697,* 113, 142, 142a.

35. Edward Hamond of Somerset County, Maryland, visited Chincoteague Island on a fishing trip. *Accomack Orders 1682-1697,* 167, 168.

36. *Accomack Orders 1682-1697,* 113.

37. *Accomack Orders 1682-1697,* 142a.

38. *Accomack Orders 1682-1697,* 112a.

39. *Accomack Orders 1682-1697*, 113.

40. *Accomack Orders 1682-1697*, 113.

41. The men who helped to seat Chincoteague Island were: John Robins, William Kendall, Dr. Eyres, John Stockley, Henry Toles, John Jackson, Francis Stockley, Thomas Worsley, John Robins' son, Walter Mannington, John Bonner, John Morris, and an unnamed shoemaker. *Accomack Orders 1682-1697*, 106, 109a, 112, 113. The main party of island claimers arrived on Chincoteague on "twelfth day," or 6 January 1686/87. *Accomack Orders 1682-1697*, 112 -113a.

42. The Martin's Hundred cellar house, at 18 feet by 16 ½ feet, was much larger than the house constructed on Chincoteague Island. Hume's book includes three photos and a sketched cross section of the Martin's Hundred house, along with a description of the excavation and literary research. Hume, *Martin's Hundred*, 53-59.

43. *Accomack Orders 1682-1697*, 106a, 107, 112, 112a.

44. Whitelaw, *Virginia's Eastern Shore*, 1377.

45. The names of Henry and Elizabeth Towles's sons were Henry, Stockle[y], Kendall, Job and Thomas. Nottingham, *Wills and Administrations*, 68.

46. Whitelaw, *Virginia's Eastern Shore*, 1377, 1379.

47. *Accomack Orders 1690-1697*, 45a, 52a., 53. The deposition of Nathaniel Racklife, given on 17 November 1691, specifically identifies the wife of Henry Towles as the mother of the Bowen orphans. *Accomack Orders 1690-1697*, 53.

48. *Accomack Deeds and Wills 1692-1715*, 95.

49. Whitelaw, *Virginia's Eastern Shore*, 1379.

50. A few herders and tenants had lived on Chincoteague Island, but no land owner was known to reside on the island before 1696, when the Towles purchased land there. One herder and his wife, George and Hannah Blake, may have been living on the island when Henry and Elizabeth arrived; it is not known when they were sent to the island. Placed on Chincoteague to look after cattle, they eventually came into possession of 100 acres that they left to a son John in 1726. Whitelaw, *Virginia's Eastern Shore*, 1380; *Accomack Wills and Deeds 1676-1690*, 460.

51. Henry Towles would have been 45 years old and Elizabeth 44 years old when they moved to Chincoteague Island in 1696.

52. *Accomack Orders 1697-1703*, 43.

53. *Accomack Deeds and Wills 1692-1715*, 422.

54. Whitelaw, *Virginia's Eastern Shore*, 1379; *Accomack Orders 1703-1709*, 223, *Accomack Orders 1710-1714*, 10; *Accomack Deeds and Wills 1692-1715*, 513, 524a, 570a, 571.

55. *Accomack Deeds and Wills 1692-1715*, 647.

56. Nottingham, *Wills and Administrations*, 68.

Bibliography

Accomack County, Virginia, Deeds & Wills [& Orders], 1663-1666. Library of Virginia microfilm reel 1.

Accomack County, Virginia, Orders 1666-1670. Library of Virginia microfilm reel 78.

Accomack County, Virginia, [Deeds], Orders, Wills [of Upper Northampton], 1671-1673. Library of Virginia microfilm reel 2.

Accomack County, Virginia, [Deeds], Wills, [Orders], Etc., 1673-1676. Library of Virginia microfilm reel 2.

Accomack County, Virginia, Orders, 1676-1678. Library of Virginia microfilm reel 79.

Accomack County, Virginia, Wills, Deeds, & Orders, 1678-1682. Library of Virginia microfilm reel 4.

Accomack County, Virginia, [Deeds], Wills, Etc., Orders, 1682-1697. Library of Virginia microfilm reel 4.

Accomack County, Virginia, Orders, 1690-1697. Library of Virginia microfilm reel 79.

Accomack County, Virginia, Orders, 1697-1703. Library of Virginia microfilm reel 79.

Accomack County, Virginia, Orders, 1703-1709. Library of Virginia microfilm reel 79.

Accomack County, Virginia, Orders, 1710-1714. Library of Virginia microfilm reel 80.

Accomack County, Virginia, Orders, 1714-1717. Library of Virginia microfilm reel 80.

Accomack County, Virginia, Orders, 1717-1719. Library of Virginia microfilm reel 80.

Accomack County, Virginia, Orders, 1719-1724. Library of Virginia microfilm reel 80.

Accomack County, Virginia, Wills and Deeds, 1676-1690. Library of Virginia microfilm reel 3.

Accomack County, Virginia, [Deeds], Wills, Etc., 1692-1715. Library of Virginia microfilm reel 5.

Accomack County, Virginia, Deeds, Wills, Etc., 1715-1729. Library of Virginia microfilm reel 8.

Ames, Susie M. *County Court Records of Accomack-Northampton, Virginia, 1640-1645.* Charlottesville, Virginia: University Press of Virginia, 1973.

------. *Studies of the Virginia Eastern Shore in the Seventeenth Century.* Richmond, VA: Dietz Press, 1940.

Berkin, Carol. *First Generations: Women in Colonial America.* New York: Hill and Wang, 1996.

------ and Leslie Horowitz, eds., *Women's Voices, Women's Lives: Documents in Early American History.* Boston: Northeastern University Press, 1998.

Breen, T. H. and Stephen Innes, *"Myne Owne Ground": Race & Freedom on Virginia's Eastern Shore 1640-1676.* New York: Oxford University Press, 1980.

Bristol Record Office. *Servants to Foreign Plantations,* Book 1. *English-America: the Voyages, Vessels, People & Places.* http://www.english-america.com /places/br-v1-b3.html#Passsengers

"Bristol Register of Servants Sent to Foreign Plantations, 1654-1686." *Virginia Center for Digital History: Virtual Jamestown.* www.virtualjamestown.org /indentures/advsearch_bristol.html

Bruce, Philip Alexander. *Social Life of Virginia in the Seventeenth Century.* Bowie, MD: Heritage Books, 1995.

Callahan, Griffin. "The Callahan Photo Collection," *Eastern Shore Public Library,* http://www.espl.org/mearscol/callagif/callahan.HTM

Cotton, Jane Baldwin, and Roberta Bolling Henry, eds. The *Maryland Calendar of Wills,* 1726-1732. Vol. 6. Baltimore: Kohn & Pollock, 1920.

Cowie, Leonard. *Plague and Fire, London 1665-6.* London: Wayland Publishers, 1970.

Miles, Barry W. and Moody K. Miles. "The Miles Files 4.0". *Eastern Shore Public Library*. www.espl.org.

Hanson, Neil. *The Great Fire of London: In That Apocalyptic Year, 1666.* New York: John Wiley & Sons, 2002.

Harben, Henry A. "Bishopsgate Street," *A Dictionary of London.* London. H. Jenkins Ltd., 1918. *British History Online.* www.british-history.ac.uk.

Horle, Craig W. *Records of the Courts of Sussex County Delaware, 1677-1710.* Philadelphia: University of PA Press, 1991.

Hume, Ivor Noel. *Martin's Hundred: The Discovery of a Lost Colonial Virginia Settlement.* New York: Delta, 1983.

"John Cropper," *Maryland Prerogative Court (Testamentary Proceedings).* Book 13. *Ocean City Life-Saving Station Museum.* http://www.ocmuseum.org /genealogy.

"John Cropper," *Maryland Prerogative Court (Testamentary Proceedings).* Book 14. *Ocean City Life-Saving Station Museum.* http://www.ocmuseum.org /genealogy.

"John Cropper," *Maryland Prerogative Court.* Book 15a. *Ocean City Life-Saving Station Museum,* http://www.ocmuseum.org/genealogy

Lankford, Wilmer O. *They Lived in Somerset: 17th Century Marylanders.* Princess Anne, MD: Manokin Press, 1990.

Luccketti, Nicholas M. "Archaeology at Arlington: Excavations at the Ancestral Custis Plantation, Northampton County, Virginia," with contributions by Edward A. Chappell and Beverly A. Straube. Virginia Company Foundation and The Association for the Preservation of Virginia Antiquities, 1999. *Association for the Preservation of Virginia Antiquities.* www.apva.org /resource/other/arlington.pdf.

Lynch, James B., Jr. *The Custis Chronicles.* Vol. 1, *The Years of Migration.* Camden, Maine: Picton Press, 1992.

------. *The Custis Chronicles.* Vol. 2, *The Virginia Generations.* Camden, Maine: Picton Press, 1997.

Mackey, Howard and Marlene Alma Hinkley Groves. *Northampton County Virginia Record Book: Orders, Deeds, Wills &c., 1645-1651.* Vol. 3. Rockport Maine: Picton Press, 2000.

Mariner, Kirk. *Off 13: The Eastern Shore of Virginia Guidebook.* New Church, VA: Miona Publications, 2000.

Marshall, James Handley. *Abstracts of the Wills and Administrations of Northampton County, Virginia 1632-1802.* Camden, Maine: Picton Press, 1994.

Maryland Prerogative Court (Wills), 1688-1700. Book 6.

McIlwaine, H. R., ed. *Minutes of the Council and General Court of Colonial Virginia, 1622-1632, 1670-1676, with Notes and Excerpts from Original Council and General Court Records, into 1683, Now Lost.* Richmond, VA, 1924.

McKain, Keith A. "Motherkill Friends Cemetery (Murderkill Cemetery) Magnolia, Kent County, Delaware," *Interment.net Cemetery Transcription Library,* http://www.interment.net/data/us/de/kent/motherkill.htm

Mears, Robert L. *Mears Collection.* Winter 2003/2004 update. *Eastern Shore Public Library.* www.espl.org.

Miles, Barry W. and Moody K. Miles III. *Miles Files, 100's of Families from the Eastern Shore of Virginia,*Version 4.0. *Eastern Shore Public Library.* http://www.espl.org.

NASA. "Wallops History." *Wallops Flight Facility.* http://www.wff.nasa.gov /about/history.php.

Neilson, William Allan, Thomas A. Knott and Paul W. Carhart, eds. *Webster's New International Dictionary of the English Language.* 2nd edition, unabridged. Springfield, MA: G. & C. Merriam Co., 1961.

Norton, Mary Beth. *Founding Mothers & Fathers: Gendered Power and the Forming of American Society.* New York: Vintage Books, 1996.

Northampton County, Virginia, Order Book, 1657-1664. Library of Virginia microfilm reel 46.

Northampton County, Virginia, Order Book No. 9, 1664-1674. Library of Virginia microfilm reel 26.

Northampton County, Virginia, Order Book No. 11, 1678-1683. Library of Virginia microfilm reel 27.

Northampton County, Virginia, Order Book & Wills, No. 12, 1683-1689. Library of Virginia microfilm reel 27.

Nottingham, Stratton. *Wills and Administrations of Accomack County, Virginia 1663-1800*. Bowie, MD: Heritage Books, 1990.

Proceedings and Acts of the General Assembly, April 26, 1700-May 3, 1704. Vol. 24. *Archives of Maryland Online*. http://www.mdarchives.state.md.us /megafile/msa/speccol/sc2900/sc2908/html/volumes.html.

Proceedings of the Council of Maryland, 1681- 1685/86. Vol. 17. *Archives of Maryland Online*. http://www.mdarchives.state.md.us/megafile/msa/speccol /sc2900/sc2908/html/volumes.html.

Proceedings of the Council of Maryland, 1687/8-1693. Vol. 8. *Archives of Maryland Online*. http://www.mdarchives.state.md.us/megafile/msa/speccol /sc2900/sc2908/html/volumes.html.

Proceedings of the County Courts of Kent (1648-1676), Talbot (1662-1674, and Somerset (1665-1668). Vol. 54. *Archives of Maryland Online*. http://www. mdarchives.state.md.us/megafile/msa/speccol/sc2900/sc2908 /html/volumes.html.

Scharf, Thomas J. *History of Delaware, 1609-1888*. Vol. 2. *Accessible Archives*, http://www.accessible.com/amcnty/DE/Delaware/delaware62.htm

Shirley Plantation. http://shirleyplantation.com/archaeology.html.

Shomette, Donald. *Pirates of the Chesaspeake: being a true history of pirates, picaroons, and raiders on Chesapeake Bay, 1610-1807*. Centreville, MD: Tidewater Publishers, 1985.

Skordas, Gust. *Early Settlers of Maryland*. Baltimore: Genealogical Pub. Co., 1968.

Somerset County Court (Judicial Record) September 1, 1670-October 20, 1671. Vol. 86. *Archives of Maryland Online*, http://www.mdarchives.state.md .us/megafile/msa/speccol/sc2900/sc2908/html/volumes.html.

Somerset County Court (Judicial Record) October 25, 1671-October 20, 1675. Vol. 87. *Archives of Maryland Online*, http://www.mdarchives.state.md.us /megafile/msa/speccol/sc2900/sc2908/html/volumes.html.

Somerset County Court (Judicial Record) November 13, 1683 - March 11, 1683[84]. Vol. 90. *Archives of Maryland Online*, http://www.mdarchives .state.md.us/megafile/msa/speccol/sc2900/sc2908/html/volumes.html.

Somerset County Court (Judicial Record) September 30, 1687 - June 12, 1689. Vol. 91. *Archives of Maryland Online*, http://www.mdarchives.state.md.us /megafile/msa/speccol/sc2900/sc2908/html/volumes.html.

Somerset County Court (Judicial Record) September 24, 1689 - November 12, 1690. Vol. 106. *Archives of Maryland Online,* http://www.mdarchives.state .md.us/megafile/msa/speccol/sc2900/sc2908/html/volumes.html.

Somerset County Court (Judicial Record), November 14, 1690 - October 3, 1691. Vol. 191. *Archives of Maryland Online,* http://www.mdarchives.state.md.us /megafile/msa/speccol/sc2900/sc2908/html/volumes.html.

Somerset Judicial Records 1692-96, Abstracts with Selected Transcriptions. Vol. 535. *Archives of Maryland Online,* http://www.mdarchives.state.md.us /megafile/msa/speccol/sc2900/sc2908/html/volumes.html.

Spruill, Julia Cherry. *Women's Life and Work in the Southern Colonies.* New York: W.W. Norton & Company, 1972.

Torence, Clayton. *Old Somerset on the Eastern Shore of Maryland: A Study in Foundations and Founders.* Richmond, VA: Whittet & Shepperson, 1935.

Walcyzk, Frank V. *Northampton County, Virginia, Orders, Deeds & Wills 1651-1654.* Book 4. Coram, NY: Peter's Row, 1998.

------. *Northampton County Virginia, Orders & Wills, 1689-1698, 1694-1698.* Vol. 2. Coram NY: Peter's Row, 2000.

Whitelaw, Ralph T. *Virginia's Eastern Shore: A History of Northampton and Accomack Counties.* 2 vols. Gloucester, MA, 1968.

Yarwood, Doreen. *The Encyclopedia of World Costume.* New York: Bonanza Books, 1986.

Index

Other books by JoAnn Riley McKey:

Accomack County, Virginia Court Order Abstracts, Volume 1: 1663-1666

Accomack County, Virginia Court Order Abstracts, Volume 2: 1666-1670

Accomack County, Virginia Court Order Abstracts, Volume 3: 1671-1673

Accomack County, Virginia Court Order Abstracts, Volume 4: 1673-1676

Accomack County, Virginia Court Order Abstracts, Volume 5: 1676-1678

Accomack County, Virginia Court Order Abstracts, Volume 6: 1678-1682

Accomack County, Virginia Court Order Abstracts, Volume 7: 1682-1690

Accomack County, Virginia Court Order Abstracts, Volume 8: 1690-1697

Accomack County, Virginia Court Order Abstracts, Volume 9: 1697-1703

Accomack County, Virginia Court Order Abstracts, Volume 10: 1703-1710

Accomack County, Virginia Court Order Abstracts, Volume 11: 1710-1714

Accomack County, Virginia Court Order Abstracts, Volumes 12 and 13: 1714-1719

Accomack County, Virginia Court Order Abstracts, Volume 14: 1729-1724

Accomack County, Virginia Court Order Abstracts, Volume 15: 1724-1731

Accomack County, Virginia Court Order Abstracts, Volume 16: 1731-1736

CD: *Accomack County, Virginia Court Order Abstracts, Volumes 1-10: 1663-1710*

*Baptismal Records of the Dutch Reformed Churches in the
City of Groningen, Netherlands, Volume 1: 1640-1649*

*Baptismal Records of the Dutch Reformed Churches in the
City of Groningen, Netherlands, Volume 2: 1650-1659*

CD: *Baptismal Records of the Dutch Reformed Churches in the
City of Groningen, Netherlands*

Wenches, Wives and Widows: Sixteen Women of Early Virginia

CPSIA information can be obtained at www.ICGtesting.com
Printed in the USA
LVOW05s1220051014

407331LV00014B/325/P